Lecture Notes in Artificial Intelligence   9861

Subseries of Lecture Notes in Computer Science

More information about this series at http://www.springer.com/series/1244

Jiřina Vejnarová · Václav Kratochvíl (Eds.)

Belief Functions:
Theory and Applications

4th International Conference, BELIEF 2016
Prague, Czech Republic, September 21–23, 2016
Proceedings

 Springer

Editors
Jiřina Vejnarová
Institute of Information Theory and
 Automation
Czech Academy of Sciences
Prague
Czech Republic

Václav Kratochvíl
Institute of Information Theory and
 Automation
Czech Academy of Sciences
Prague
Czech Republic

ISSN 0302-9743   ISSN 1611-3349 (electronic)
Lecture Notes in Artificial Intelligence
ISBN 978-3-319-45558-7   ISBN 978-3-319-45559-4   (eBook)
DOI 10.1007/978-3-319-45559-4

Library of Congress Control Number: 2016949600

LNCS Sublibrary: SL7 – Artificial Intelligence

Printed on acid-free paper

This Springer imprint is published by Springer Nature
The registered company is Springer International Publishing AG Switzerland

Preface

The theory of belief functions, also referred to as evidence theory or Dempster-Shafer theory, is a well-established general framework for reasoning with uncertainty. It has well-understood connections to other frameworks, such as probability, possibility, and imprecise probability theories. First introduced by Arthur P. Dempster in the context of statistical inference, the theory was later developed by Glenn Shafer into a general framework for modeling epistemic uncertainty. These early contributions have provided the starting points for many important developments, including the Transferable Belief Model and the Theory of Hints.

The biennial BELIEF conferences (organized by the Belief Functions and Applications Society) are dedicated to the exchange of ideas, reporting of recent achievements, and presenting the wide range of applications of this theory. This conference series was started in Brest, France, in 2010; the second event was held in Compiègne, France, in May 2012; and the third in Oxford, UK, in September 2014.

The present volume contains the proceedings of the 4th International Conference on Belief Functions, which took place in Prague, Czech Republic, on September 21–23, 2016. The book contains 25 peer-reviewed papers (out of a total number of 33 submissions) describing recent developments concerning both theoretical issues (including combination rules, conflict management, and generalized information theory) and applications in various areas (such as image processing, material sciences, and navigation).

The editors would like to thank all those who contributed to this volume as well as those who helped with organizing the conference. We would especially like to thank Thierry Denœux and Arnaud Martin, members of the Steering Committee, whose experience with conference organization was invaluable, and the members of the Program Committee and external reviewers for carefully reviewing all the submissions. We would also like to thank the administration of the Institute of Information Theory and Automation of the Czech Academy of Sciences, where the conference took place.

July 2016

Jiřina Vejnarová
Václav Kratochvíl

Organization

Steering Committee

Fabio Cuzzolin   Oxford Brookes University, UK
Thierry Denœux   Université de Technologie de Compiègne, France
Arnaud Martin   Université de Rennes1/IRISA, France

Program Committee

Alessandro Antonucci   IDSIA, Switzerland
Giulianella Coletti   Università degli Studi di Perugia, Italy
Olivier Colot   Université Lille 1, France
Frank Coolen   Durham University, UK
Inés Couso   University of Oviedo, Spain
Fabio Cuzzolin   Oxford Brookes University, UK
Milan Daniel   Jan Becher - Karlovarská Becherovka, a.s., Czech Republic
Thierry Denœux   Université de Technologie de Compiègne, France
Sébastien Destercke   CNRS, UMR Heudiasyc, France
Jean Dezert   Onera, France
Zied Elouedi   Institut Supérieur de Gestion de Tunis, Tunisia
Thomas Fetz   University of Innsbruck, Austria
Michel Grabisch   Université Paris 1, France
Radim Jiroušek   University of Economics, Czech Republic
Anne-Laure Jousselme   NATO CMRE, Italy
Tomáš Kroupa   Czech Academy of Sciences, Czech Republic
Éric Lefèvre   LGI2A Université d'Artois, France
Weiru Liu   Queen's University Belfast, UK
Liping Liu   The University of Akron, USA
Arnaud Martin   Université de Rennes1/IRISA, France
David Mercier   Université d'Artois, France
Enrique Miranda   University of Oviedo, Spain
Serafín Moral   University of Granada, Spain
Michael Oberguggenberger   University of Innsbruck, Austria
Michele Rombaut   Gipsa-lab, France
Prakash P. Shenoy   University of Kansas School of Business, USA
Johan Schubert   Swedish Defence Research Agency, Sweden
Barbara Vantaggi   Università "La Sapienza", Italy
Jiřina Vejnarová   Czech Academy of Sciences, Czech Republic

Paolo Vicig   University of Trieste, Italy
Ronald Yager   Machine Intelligence Institute - Iona College, USA

BELIEF 2016 was organized by the Institute of Information Theory and Automation,
Czech Academy of Sciences on behalf of BFAS - Belief Functions and Applications
Society.

Local Organizing Committee

Jiřina Vejnarová (Chair)   Czech Academy of Sciences, Czech Republic
Milan Daniel   Jan Becher - Karlovarská Becherovka, a.s.,
                                         Czech Republic
Radim Jiroušek   University of Economics, Czech Republic
Václav Kratochvíl   Czech Academy of Sciences, Czech Republic

Support

The conference was supported by:
Belief Functions and Applications Society
Institute of Information Theory and Automation, Czech Academy of Sciences

Contents

Theoretical Issues

Entropy of Belief Functions in the Dempster-Shafer Theory: A New Perspective

Radim Jiroušek[1,3] and Prakash P. Shenoy[2(✉)]

[1] Faculty of Management, University of Economics,
Jindřichův Hradec, Czech Republic
[2] School of Business, University of Kansas, Lawrence, KS, USA
pshenoy@ku.edu
[3] Institute of Information Theory and Automation, Academy of Sciences,
Prague, Czech Republic
radim@utia.cas.cz

Abstract. We propose a new definition of entropy of basic probability assignments (BPA) in the Dempster-Shafer (D-S) theory of belief functions, which is interpreted as a measure of total uncertainty in the BPA. We state a list of five desired properties of entropy for D-S belief functions theory that are motivated by Shannon's definition of entropy of probability functions, together with the implicit requirement that any definition should be consistent with semantics of D-S belief functions theory. Three of our five desired properties are different from the five properties described by Klir and Wierman. We demonstrate that our definition satisfies all five properties in our list, and is consistent with semantics of D-S theory, whereas none of the existing definitions do. Our definition does not satisfy the sub-additivity property. Whether there exists a definition that satisfies our five properties plus sub-additivity, and that is consistent with semantics for the D-S theory, remains an open question.

1 Introduction

The main goal of this paper is to provide a new definition of entropy of belief functions in the D-S theory that is consistent with semantics of the D-S theory. By entropy, we mean a real-valued measure of uncertainty in the tradition of Hartley [12] and Shannon [30]. Also, while there are several theories of belief functions (see, e.g., [10,36]), our goal is to define entropy for the D-S theory that uses Dempster's product-intersection rule [6] as the combination rule.

Hartley's Entropy. Suppose X is a discrete random variable with a finite state space Ω_X, whose elements are assumed to be mutually exclusive and exhaustive. Suppose this is all we know about X, i.e., we do not know the probability mass function (PMF) of X. What is a measure of uncertainty? Hartley [12] defines entropy of Ω_X as follows:

$$U(\Omega_X) = \log_2(|\Omega_X|), \qquad (1)$$

© Springer International Publishing Switzerland 2016
J. Vejnarová and V. Kratochvíl (Eds.): BELIEF 2016, LNAI 9861, pp. 3–13, 2016.
DOI: 10.1007/978-3-319-45559-4_1

where $U(\Omega_X)$ denotes a real-valued measure of uncertainty of Ω_X, with units of *bits*. First, notice that $U(\Omega_X)$ does not depend on the labels attached to the states in Ω_X, only on the number of states in Ω_X. Second, Rényi [26] shows that Hartley's definition in Eq. (1) is characterized by the following three properties.

1. (*Additivity*) Suppose X and Y are random variables with finite state spaces Ω_X and Ω_Y, respectively. The joint state space of (X, Y) is $\Omega_X \times \Omega_Y$. Then, $U(\Omega_X \times \Omega_Y) = U(\Omega_X) + U(\Omega_Y)$.
2. (*Monotonicity*) If $|\Omega_{X_1}| > |\Omega_{X_2}|$, then $U(\Omega_{X_1}) > U(\Omega_{X_2})$.
3. (*Units*) If $|\Omega_X| = 2$, then $U(\Omega_X) = 1$ bit.

Shannon's Entropy. Now suppose we learn of a probability mass function P_X of X. What is the information content of P_X? Or alternatively, we can ask: What is the uncertainty in P_X? Shannon [30] provides an answer to the second question as follows:

$$H_s(P_X) = \sum_{x \in \Omega_X} P_X(x) \log_2 \left(\frac{1}{P_X(x)} \right), \tag{2}$$

where $H_s(P_X)$ is called Shannon's measure of entropy (uncertainty) in PMF P_X. Shannon's entropy is characterized (up to a constant) by the following two properties [30].

1. (*Monotonicity*) If P_X is an equally likely PMF, then $H_s(P_X)$ is a monotonically increasing function of $|\Omega_X|$.
2. (*Compound distributions*) If a PMF $P_{X,Y}$ is factored into two PMFs $P_{X,Y}(x, y) = P_X(x) P_{Y|x}(y)$, then $H_s(P_{X,Y}) = H_s(P_X) + \sum_{x \in \Omega_X} P_X(x) H_s(P_{Y|x})$.

The uncertainty prior to learning P_X was $U(\Omega_X)$. After learning P_X, it is now $H_s(P_X)$. Thus, if $I(P_X)$ denotes information content of P_X, then we have the equality

$$I(P_X) + H_s(P_X) = U(\Omega_X). \tag{3}$$

The maximum value of $H_s(P_X)$ (over the space of all PMFs for X) is $\log_2(|\Omega_X|)$, which is attained by the uniform PMF for X, $P_X(x) = 1/|\Omega_X|$ for all $x \in \Omega_X$. Thus, $I(P_X) \geq 0$, with equality if and only if P_X is the uniform PMF. At the other extreme, $H_s(P_X) \geq 0$, with equality if and only if there exists $x \in \Omega_X$ such that $P_X(x) = 1$. Such a PMF has no uncertainty, and therefore, it must have maximum information. Thus $I(P_X) \leq U(\Omega_X)$, with equality if and only if there exists $x \in \Omega_X$ such that $P_X(x) = 1$.

Entropy for the D-S Theory. In the case of D-S theory of belief functions, if m is a basic probability assignment (BPA) for X, let $H(m)$ denote the entropy of BPA m. First, the D-S theory is a generalization of probability theory. The equiprobable PMF is represented by a Bayesian uniform basic probability assignment (BPA) m_u for X such that $m_u(\{x\}) = 1/|\Omega_X|$ for all $x \in \Omega_X$. So to be consistent with probability theory, we should have $H(m_u) = \log_2(|\Omega_X|)$. However, such a BPA, m_u for X, does not have the maximum uncertainty. The vacuous BPA ι_X for X such that $\iota_X(\Omega_X) = 1$ has more uncertainty than the equiprobable Bayesian m_u. As we cannot imagine a BPA for X that has more uncertainty than ι_X, we assume that $H(\iota_X)$ has the maximum uncertainty. Klir [16] and others argue that a measure of uncertainty can capture a measure of conflict as well as a measure of non-specificity. Assuming that each of these two measures is scaled so that they are each measured on a scale $[0, \log_2(|\Omega_X|)]$, then, $H(\iota_X) = 2\log_2(|\Omega_X|)$. Like in probability theory, we can define a measure of information content of BPA m for X so that the following holds:

$$I(m) + H(m) = 2\log_2(|\Omega_X|), \tag{4}$$

where $I(m)$ denotes the information content of BPA m for X. Thus, for the vacuous BPA ι_X for X, we have $I(\iota_X) = 0$, whereas for the Bayesian uniform BPA m_u for X, we have $I(m_u) = \log_2(|\Omega_X|)$.

In this paper, we are interested in defining a measure of entropy (uncertainty) of BPAs m for X in the D-S theory of belief functions on the scale $0 \leq H(m) \leq 2\log_2(|\Omega_X|)$, so that $H(m) \leq 2\log_2(|\Omega_X|)$ with equality if and only if $m = \iota_X$, and $H(m) \geq 0$, with equality if and only if m is such that $m(\{x\}) = 1$ for some $x \in \Omega_X$. Also, we require a monotonicity property, a probability consistency property, an additivity property, and a requirement that any definition should be based on semantics consistent with D-S theory. These are discussed in detail in Sect. 2.

Literature Review. There is a rich literature on information theoretic measures for the D-S theory of belief functions. Some, e.g., [13,23,32,38], define the information content of BPA m so that $I(\iota_X) = 0$. Some define entropy on the scale $[0, \log_2(|\Omega_X|)]$ so that they define entropy only as a measure of conflict (e.g., [35]), or only as a measure of non-specificity [8]. Some, e.g., [11,15,17,18,21,24,25,37] define entropy as a measure of conflict and non-specificity, but on a scale $[0, \log_2(|\Omega_X|)]$, so that $H(m_u) = H(\iota_X) = \log_2(|\Omega_X|)$. Some, e.g., [1,3,22] define entropy as a measure of conflict and non-specificity on the scale $[0, 2\log_2(|\Omega_X|)]$, but they do so using semantics of belief functions (credal sets of PMFs) that are inconsistent with Dempster's rule of combination [10,29]. Our definition is the only one that defines entropy as a measure of conflict and non-specificity, on the scale $[0, 2\log_2(|\Omega_X|)]$, using semantics of belief functions that are consistent with Dempster's combination rule.

2 Desired Properties of Entropy of BPAs in the D-S Theory

First, we explain our informal requirement that any definition of entropy for D-S theory should be consistent with the semantics of this theory. Next, we propose five formal properties that a definition of entropy of BPAs in the D-S theory should satisfy, Finally, we compare these properties with those proposed by Klir and Wierman [19] for the same purposes.

Consistency with D-S Theory Semantics Requirement. First, let us stress once more that we are concerned in this paper only with the D-S belief functions theory that includes Dempster's combination rule as the operation for aggregating knowledge. There are theories of belief functions that use other combination rules. Let 2^{Ω_X} denote the set of all *non-empty* subsets of Ω_X. A BPA m for X can be considered as an encoding of a collection of PMFs $\mathcal{P}_m$ for X such that for all $\mathsf{a} \in 2^{\Omega_X}$ we have:

$$Bel_m(\mathsf{a}) = \sum_{\mathsf{b} \in 2^{\Omega_X}: \mathsf{b} \subseteq \mathsf{a}} m(\mathsf{b}) = \min_{P \in \mathcal{P}_m} \sum_{x \in \mathsf{a}} P(x). \tag{5}$$

$\mathcal{P}_m$ is referred to as a *credal* set corresponding to m in the imprecise probability literature (see, e.g., [36]). For such a theory of belief functions, Fagin and Halpern [9] propose a combination rule that is different from Dempster's combination rule. Thus, a BPA m in the D-S theory cannot be interpreted as a collection of PMFs satisfying Eq. (5) [10,28]. There are, of course, semantics that are consistent with D-S theory, such as multivalued mappings [6], random codes [28], transferable beliefs [34], and hints [20].

Example 1. Consider a BPA m_1 for X with state space $\Omega_X = \{x_1, x_2, x_3\}$ as follows: $m_1(\{x_1\}) = 0.5$, $m_1(\Omega_X) = 0.5$. With the credal set semantics of a BPA function, m_1 corresponds to a set of PMFs $\mathcal{P}_{m_1} = \{P \in \mathcal{P} : P(x_1) \geq 0.5\}$, where $\mathcal{P}$ denotes the set of all PMFs for X. Now suppose we get a distinct piece of evidence m_2 for X such that $m_2(\{x_2\}) = 0.5$, $m_2(\Omega_X) = 0.5$. m_2 corresponds to $\mathcal{P}_{m_2} = \{P \in \mathcal{P} : P(x_2) \geq 0.5\}$. The only PMF that is in both $\mathcal{P}_{m_1}$ and $\mathcal{P}_{m_2}$ is $P \in \mathcal{P}$ such that $P(x_1) = P(x_2) = 0.5$, and $P(x_3) = 0$. Notice that if we use Dempster's rule to combine m_1 and m_2, we have: $(m_1 \oplus m_2)(\{x_1\}) = \frac{1}{3}$, $(m_1 \oplus m_2)(\{x_2\}) = \frac{1}{3}$, and $(m_1 \oplus m_2)(\Omega_X) = \frac{1}{3}$. The set of PMFs $\mathcal{P}_{m_1 \oplus m_2} = \{P \in \mathcal{P} : P(x_1) \geq \frac{1}{3}, P(x_2) \geq \frac{1}{3}\}$ is not the same as $\mathcal{P}_{m_1} \cap \mathcal{P}_{m_2}$. Thus, credal set semantics of belief functions are not compatible with Dempster's rule of combination.

Second, given a BPA m for X in the D-S theory, there are many ways to transform m to a corresponding PMF P_m for X [5]. However, only one of these ways, called the *plausibility transform* [4], is consistent with m in the D-S theory in the sense that $P_{m_1} \otimes P_{m_2} = P_{m_1 \oplus m_2}$, where $\otimes$ is the combination rule in probability theory [31], and $\oplus$ is Dempster's combination rule in D-S theory [4]. [7,15,25] define entropy of m as the Shannon's entropy of the pignistic transform of m. The pignistic transform of m is not compatible with Dempster's combination rule [4], and therefore, this definition is not consistent with D-S theory semantics. Thus, as per our consistency with D-S theory semantics requirement, any method for defining entropy of m in the D-S theory by first transforming m to a corresponding PMF should use the plausibility transform method. Notice that we are not claiming that a definition of entropy for D-S theory must use the plausibility transform method, only that if one takes the path of first transforming a BPA m to an equivalent PMF and then using Shannon's entropy of the PMF as the definition of entropy of m, then to be compatible with D-S theory semantics, the transformation method used must be the plausibility transform method.

Example 2. Consider a situation where we have vacuous prior knowledge of X with $\Omega_X = \{x_1, \ldots, x_{70}\}$ and we receive evidence represented as BPA m for X as follows: $m(\{x_1\}) = 0.30$, $m(\{x_2\}) = 0.01$, and $m(\{x_2, \ldots, x_{70}\}) = 0.69$. The pignistic transform of m [33], denoted by $BetP_m$, is as follows: $BetP_m(x_1) = 0.30$, $BetP_m(x_2) = 0.02$, and $BetP_m(x_3) = \ldots = BetP_m(x_{70}) = 0.01$. Thus, as per the pignistic transform, BPA m is interpreted as evidence where x_1 is 15 times more likely than x_2. Now suppose we receive another distinct piece of evidence that is also represented by m. As per the D-S theory, our total evidence is now $m \oplus m$. If on the basis of m (or $BetP_m$), x_1 was 15 times more likely than x_2, then now that we have evidence $m \oplus m$, x_1 should be $15^2 = 225$ times more likely than x_2. But $BetP_{m \oplus m}(x_1) \approx 0.156$ and $BetP_{m \oplus m}(x_2) \approx 0.036$. So according to $BetP_{m \oplus m}$, x_1 is only 4.33 more likely than x_2. Thus, $BetP_m$ is *not* consistent with Dempster's combination rule.

Thus, one requirement we implicitly assume is that any definition of entropy of m should be based on semantics for m that are consistent with the basis tenets of D-S theory. Also, we implicitly assume existence and continuity—given a BPA m, $H(m)$ should always exist, and $H(m)$ should be a continuous function of m. We do not list these three requirements explicitly.

Desired Properties of Entropy for the D-S Theory. The following list of desired properties of entropy $H(m_X)$, where m_X is a BPA for X, is motivated by the properties of Shannon's entropy of PMFs [30].

Let X and Y denote random variables with state spaces Ω_X and Ω_Y, respectively. Let m_X and m_Y denote distinct BPAs for X and Y, respectively. Let ι_X and ι_Y denote the vacuous BPAs for X and Y, respectively.

1. (*Non-negativity*) $H(m_X) \geq 0$, with equality if and only if there is a $x \in \Omega_X$ such that $m_X(\{x\}) = 1$. This is similar to the probabilistic case.
2. (*Maximum entropy*) $H(m_X) \leq H(\iota_X)$, with equality if and only if $m_X = \iota_X$. This makes sense as the vacuous BPA ι_X for X has the most uncertainty among all BPAs for X. Such a property is advocated in [3].
3. (*Monotonicity*) If $|\Omega_X| < |\Omega_Y|$, then $H(\iota_X) < H(\iota_Y)$. A similar property is used by Shannon to characterize his definition of entropy of PMFs.
4. (*Probability consistency*) If m_X is a Bayesian BPA for X, then $H(m_X) = H_s(P_X)$, where P_X is the PMF of X corresponding to m_X.
5. (*Additivity*) $H(m_X \oplus m_Y) = H(m_X) + H(m_Y)$. This is a weaker form of the compound property of Shannon's entropy of a PMF.

Klir and Wierman [19] also describe a set of properties that they believe should be satisfied by any meaningful measure of uncertainty based on intuitive grounds. Two of the properties that they suggest, probability consistency and additivity, are also included in the above list. Our maximum entropy property is not in their list. Two of the properties that they require do not make intuitive sense to us.

First, Klir and Wierman require a property they call "set consistency" as follows: $H(m) = \log_2(|a|)$ whenever m is deterministic (i.e., it has only one focal element) with focal set a. This property would require that $H(\iota_X) = \log_2(|\Omega_X|)$. The probability consistency property requires that for the Bayesian uniform BPA m_u, $H(m_u) = \log_2(|\Omega_X|)$. Thus, these two requirements entail that $H(\iota_X) = H(m_u) = \log_2(|\Omega_X|)$. We disagree, as there is greater uncertainty in ι_X than in m_u.

Second, Klir and Wierman require a property they call "range" as follows: For any BPA m_X for X, $0 \le H(m_X) \le \log_2(|\Omega_X|)$. The probability consistency property requires that $H(m_u) = \log_2(|\Omega_X|)$. Also including the range property prevents from having $H(\iota_X) > H(m_u)$. So we do not include it in our list.

Finally, Klir and Wierman require a sub-additivity property defined as follows. Suppose m is a BPA for $\{X, Y\}$, with marginal BPAs $m^{\downarrow X}$ for X, and $m^{\downarrow Y}$ for Y. Then,

$$H(m) \le H(m^{\downarrow X}) + H(m^{\downarrow Y}) \tag{6}$$

We agree that this property is important, and the only reason we do not include it in our list is because we are unable to meet this requirement in addition to the five requirements that we do include, and our implicit requirement that any definition be consistent with the semantics of D-S theory of belief functions.

The most important property that characterizes Shannon's definition of entropy is the compound property $H_s(P_{X,Y}) = H_s(P_X \otimes P_{Y|X}) = H_s(P_X) + H_s(P_{Y|X})$, where $H_s(P_{Y|X}) = \sum_{x \in \Omega_X} P_X(x) H_s(P_{Y|x})$. This translated to the D-S theory of belief function would require factorizing a BPA m for $\{X, Y\}$ into BPA $m^{\downarrow X}$ for X, and BPA $m_{Y|X}$ for $\{X, Y\}$ such that $m = m^{\downarrow X} \oplus m_{Y|X}$. This cannot be done for all BPA m for $\{X, Y\}$ [31]. But, we could construct m for $\{X, Y\}$ such that $m = m_X \oplus m_{Y|X}$, where m_X is a BPA for X, and $m_{Y|X}$ is a BPA for $\{X, Y\}$ such that $m_{Y|X}^{\downarrow X} = \iota_X$, and m_X and $m_{Y|X}$ are non-conflicting, i.e., the normalization constant in Dempster's combination rule is 1. Notice that such a constructive BPA m would have the property $m^{\downarrow X} = (m_X \oplus m_{Y|X})^{\downarrow X} = m_X$. For such constructive BPAs m, we could require a *compound* property as follows:

$$H(m_X \oplus m_{Y|X}) = H(m_X) + H(m_{Y|X}). \tag{7}$$

However, we are unable to formulate a definition of $H(m)$ to satisfy such a compound property. So like the sub-additivity property, we do not include a compound property in our list of properties. The additivity property included in Klir-Wierman's and our list is so weak that it is satisfied by any definition on a log scale. All definitions of entropy of belief functions in the literature are defined on a log scale, and, thus, they all satisfy the additivity property.

3   A New Definition of Entropy of BPAs in the D-S Theory

In this section, we propose a new definition of entropy of BPAs in the D-S theory. The new definition of entropy is based on the plausibility transform of a belief function to an equivalent probability function. Therefore, we start this section by describing the plausibility transform introduced originally in [4].

Plausibility Transform of a BPA to a PMF. Suppose m is a BPA for X. What is the PMF of X that best represents m in the D-S theory? An answer to this question is given by Cobb and Shenoy [4], who propose the plausibility transform of m as follows. First consider the plausibility function Pl_m corresponding to m. Next, construct a PMF for X, denoted by P_{Pl_m}, by the values of Pl_m for singleton subsets suitably normalized, i.e.,

$$P_{Pl_m}(x) = K^{-1} \cdot Pl_m(\{x\}) = K^{-1} \cdot Q_m(\{x\}) \tag{8}$$

for all $x \in \Omega_X$, where K is a normalization constant that ensures P_{Pl_m} is a PMF, i.e., $K = \sum_{x \in \Omega_X} Pl_m(\{x\}) = \sum_{x \in \Omega_X} Q_m(\{x\})$.

[4] argues that of the many methods for transforming belief functions to PMFs, the plausibility transform is one that is consistent with Dempster's rule of combination in the sense that if we have BPAs $m_1, \ldots, m_k$ for X, then $P_{Pl_{m_1 \oplus \ldots \oplus m_k}} = P_{Pl_{m_1}} \otimes \ldots \otimes P_{Pl_{m_k}}$, where $\otimes$ denotes pointwise multiplication followed by normalization (i.e., Bayesian combination [31]). It can be shown that the plausibility transform is the *only* method that has this property, which follows from the fact that Dempster's rule of combination is pointwise multiplication of commonality functions followed by normalization [27].

Example 3. Consider a BPA m for X as described in Example 2. Then, Pl_m for singleton subsets is as follows: $Pl_m(\{x_1\}) = 0.30$, $Pl_m(\{x_2\}) = 0.70$, $Pl_m(\{x_3\}) = \cdots = Pl_m(\{x_{70}\}) = 0.69$. The plausibility transform of m is as follows: $P_{Pl_m}(x_1) = 0.3/49.72 \approx 0.0063$, and $P_{Pl_m}(x_2) = 0.7/49.72 \approx 0.0.0146$, and $P_{Pl_m}(x_3) = \cdots = P_{Pl_m}(x_{70}) \approx 0.0144$. Notice that P_{Pl_m} is quite different from $BetP_m$. In $BetP_m$, x_1 is 15 times more likely than x_2. In P_{Pl_m}, x_2 is 2.33 times more likely than x_1. Now consider the scenario where we get a distinct piece of evidence that is identical to m, so that our total evidence is $m \oplus m$. If we compute $m \oplus m$ and $P_{Pl_{m \oplus m}}$, then as per $P_{Pl_{m \oplus m}}$, x_2 is 2.33^2 more likely than x_1. This is a direct consequence of the consistency of the plausibility transform with Dempster's combination rule.

A New Definition of Entropy of a BPA. Suppose m is a BPA for X. The entropy of m is defined as follows:

$$H(m) = \sum_{x \in \Omega_X} P_{Pl_m}(x) \log_2 \left(\frac{1}{P_{Pl_m}(x)} \right) + \sum_{a \in 2^{\Omega_X}} m(a) \log_2(|a|). \tag{9}$$

The first component is Shannon's entropy of P_{Pl_m}, and the second component is generalized Hartley's entropy of m [8]. Like some of the definitions in the literature, the first component in Eq. (9) is designed to measure conflict in m, and the second component is designed to measure non-specificity in m. Both components are on the scale $[0, \log_2(|\Omega_X|)]$, and therefore, $H(m)$ is on the scale $[0, 2\log_2(|\Omega_X|)]$.

Theorem 1. *The entropy $H(m)$ of BPA m for X defined in Eq. (9) satisfies the non-negativity, maximum entropy, monotonicity, probability consistency, and additivity properties. It is also consistent with semantics of the D-S theory.*

A proof of this theorem can be found in [14] (that can be downloaded from ⟨http://pshenoy.faculty.ku.edu/Papers/WP330.pdf⟩). Finally, we provide an example that shows our definition does not satisfy the sub-additivity property.

Example 4. Consider a BPA m for binary-valued variables $\{X, Y\}$: $m(\{(x, y)\}) = m(\{(x, \bar{y})\}) = 0.1$, $m(\{(\bar{x}, y)\}) = m(\{(\bar{x}, \bar{y})\}) = 0.3$, $m(\Omega_{\{X,Y\}}) = 0.2$. It is easy to verify that $H(m) \doteq 2.35$. The marginal BPA $m^{\downarrow X}$ is as follows: $m^{\downarrow X}(\{x\}) = 0.2$, $m^{\downarrow X}(\{\bar{x}\}) = 0.6$, and $m^{\downarrow X}(\Omega_X) = 0.2$. It is easy to verify that $H(m^{\downarrow X}) \doteq 1.12$. Similarly, the marginal BPA $m^{\downarrow Y}$ is as follows: $m^{\downarrow Y}(\{y\}) = 0.4$, $m^{\downarrow Y}(\{\bar{y}\}) = 0.4$, and $m^{\downarrow Y}(\Omega_Y) = 0.2$. It is easy to verify that $H(m^{\downarrow Y}) \doteq 1.20$. Thus, $H(m) \doteq 2.35 > H(m^{\downarrow X}) + H(m^{\downarrow Y}) \doteq 1.12 + 1.20 = 2.32$.

The only definition that satisfies the five properties we state plus the sub-additivity property is that due to Maeda and Ichihashi [22], but this definition is based on credal set semantics of a belief function that is inconsistent with Dempster's combination rule. Whether there exists a definition that satisfies our five properties plus sub-additivity, and that is based on semantics consistent with the basic tenets of D-S theory, remains an open question.

4   Summary and Conclusions

Interpreting Shannon's entropy of a PMF of a discrete random variable as the amount of uncertainty in the PMF [30], we propose five desirable properties of entropy of a basic probability assignment in the D-S theory of belief functions. These five properties are motivated by the analogous properties of Shannon's entropy of PMFs, and they are based on our intuition that a vacuous belief function has more uncertainty than an equiprobable Bayesian belief function. Also, besides the five properties, we also require that any definition should be based on semantics consistent with the D-S theory of belief functions (with Dempster's rule as the combination rule), $H(m)$ should always exist, and $H(m)$ should be a continuous function of m. Thus, a monotonicity-like property suggested by Abellán-Masegosa [2], based on credal set semantics of belief functions that are not compatible with Dempster's rule, is not included in our set of requirements.

It would be ideal if we can state the consistency with D-S theory semantics as a formal requirement, but we are unable to do so. In our opinion, the additivity property for the case of two distinct BPAs for disjoint sets of variables does not fully capture consistency with D-S theory semantics. In any case, the definitions of entropy based on credal sets of probability distributions and pignistic transforms are not consistent with Dempster's combination rule, and therefore, in our perspective, not appropriate for the D-S theory of evidence.

As first suggested by Lamata and Moral [21], we propose a new definition of entropy of BPA as a combination of Shannon's entropy of an equivalent PMF that captures the conflict measure of entropy, and Dubois-Prade's entropy of a BPA that captures the non-specificity (or generalized Hartley) measure of entropy. The equivalent PMF is that obtained by using the plausibility transform [4]. This new definition satisfies all five properties we propose. More importantly, our definition is consistent with the semantics for the D-S theory of belief functions.

An open question is whether there exists a definition of entropy of BPA m in the D-S theory that satisfies the five properties we list in Sect. 2, the sub-additivity property, and most importantly, that is consistent with semantics for the D-S theory. Our definition satisfies the five properties and is consistent with semantics for the D-S theory, but it does not satisfy the sub-additivity property.

Acknowledgements. This article is a short version of [14], which has been supported in part by funds from grant GAČR 15-00215S to the first author, and from the Ronald G. Harper Distinguished Professorship at the University of Kansas to the second author. We are extremely grateful to Thierry Denoeux, Marc Pouly, Anne-Laure Jousselme, Joaquín Abellán, and Mark Wierman for their comments on earlier drafts of [14]. We are grateful to two anonymous reviewers of Belief-2016 conference for their comments. We are also grateful to Suzanna Emelio for a careful proof-reading of the text.

References

1. Abellán, J.: Combining nonspecificity measures in Dempster-Shafer theory of evidence. Int. J. Gen. Syst. **40**(6), 611–622 (2011)
2. Abellán, J., Masegosa, A.: Requirements for total uncertainty measures in Dempster-Shafer theory of evidence. Int. J. Gen. Syst. **37**(6), 733–747 (2008)
3. Abellán, J., Moral, S.: Completing a total uncertainty measure in Dempster-Shafer theory. Int. J. Gen. Syst. **28**(4–5), 299–314 (1999)
4. Cobb, B.R., Shenoy, P.P.: On the plausibility transformation method for translating belief function models to probability models. Int. J. Approx. Reason. **41**(3), 314–340 (2006)
5. Daniel, M.: On transformations of belief functions to probabilities. Int. J. Intell. Syst. **21**(3), 261–282 (2006)
6. Dempster, A.P.: Upper and lower probabilities induced by a multivalued mapping. Ann. Math. Stat. **38**(2), 325–339 (1967)
7. Dezert, J., Smarandache, F., Tchamova, A.: On the Blackman's association problem. In: Proceedings of the 6th Annual Conference on Information Fusion, Cairns, Queensland, Australia, pp. 1349–1356. International Society for Information Fusion (2003)
8. Dubois, D., Prade, H.: Properties of measures of information in evidence and possibility theories. Fuzzy Sets Syst. **24**(2), 161–182 (1987)
9. Fagin, R., Halpern, J.Y.: A new approach to updating beliefs. In: Bonissone, P., Henrion, M., Kanal, L., Lemmer, J. (eds.) Uncertainty in Artificial Intelligence, vol. 6, pp. 347–374. North-Holland (1991)
10. Halpern, J.Y., Fagin, R.: Two views of belief: belief as generalized probability and belief as evidence. Artif. Intell. **54**(3), 275–317 (1992)

11. Harmanec, D., Klir, G.J.: Measuring total uncertainty in Dempster-Shafer theory: a novel approach. Int. J. Gen. Syst. **22**(4), 405–419 (1994)
12. Hartley, R.V.L.: Transmission of information. Bell Syst. Tech. J. **7**(3), 535–563 (1928)
13. Höhle, U.: Entropy with respect to plausibility measures. In: Proceedings of the 12th IEEE Symposium on Multiple-Valued Logic, pp. 167–169 (1982)
14. Jiroušek, R., Shenoy, P.P.: A new definition of entropy of belief functions in the Dempster-Shafer theory. Working Paper 330, University of Kansas School of Business, Lawrence, KS (2016)
15. Jousselme, A.-L., Liu, C., Grenier, D., Bossé, E.: Measuring ambiguity in the evidence theory. IEEE Trans. Syst. Man Cybern. Part A: Syst. Hum. **36**(5), 890–903 (2006)
16. Klir, G.J.: Where do we stand on measures of uncertainty, ambiguity, fuzziness, and the like? Fuzzy Sets Syst. **24**(2), 141–160 (1987)
17. Klir, G.J., Parviz, B.: A note on the measure of discord. In: Dubois, D., Wellman, M.P., D'Ambrosio, B., Smets, P. (eds.) Uncertainty in Artificial Intelligence: Proceedings of the Eighth Conference, pp. 138–141. Morgan Kaufmann (1992)
18. Klir, G.J., Ramer, A.: Uncertainty in the Dempster-Shafer theory: a critical re-examination. Int. J. Gen. Syst. **18**(2), 155–166 (1990)
19. Klir, G.J., Wierman, M.J.: Uncertainity Elements of Generalized Information Theory, 2nd edn. Springer, Berlin (1999)
20. Kohlas, J., Monney, P.-A.: A Mathematical Theory of Hints: An Approach to the Dempster-Shafer Theory of Evidence. Springer, Berlin (1995)
21. Lamata, M.T., Moral, S.: Measures of entropy in the theory of evidence. Int. J. Gen. Syst. **14**(4), 297–305 (1988)
22. Maeda, Y., Ichihashi, H.: An uncertainty measure under the random set inclusion. Int. J. Gen. Syst. **21**(4), 379–392 (1993)
23. Nguyen, H.T.: On entropy of random sets and possibility distributions. In: Bezdek, J.C. (ed.) The Analysis of Fuzzy Information, pp. 145–156. CRC Press, Boca Raton (1985)
24. Pal, N.R., Bezdek, J.C., Hemasinha, R.: Uncertainty measures for evidential reasoning II: a new measure of total uncertainty. Int. J. Approx. Reason. **8**(1), 1–16 (1993)
25. Pouly, M., Kohlas, J., Ryan, P.Y.A.: Generalized information theory for hints. Int. J. Approx. Reason. **54**(1), 228–251 (2013)
26. Rényi, A.: On measures of information and entropy. In: Proceedings of the 4th Berkeley Symposium on Mathematics, Statistics and Probability, pp. 547–561 (1960)
27. Shafer, G.: A Mathematical Theory of Evidence. Princeton University Press, Princeton (1976)
28. Shafer, G.: Constructive probability. Synthese **48**(1), 1–60 (1981)
29. Shafer, G.: Perspectives on the theory and practice of belief functions. Int. J. Approx. Reason. **4**(5–6), 323–362 (1990)
30. Shannon, C.E.: A mathematical theory of communication. Bell Syst. Tech. J. **27**(379–423), 623–656 (1948)
31. Shenoy, P.P.: Conditional independence in valuation-based systems. Int. J. Approx. Reason. **10**(3), 203–234 (1994)
32. Smets, P.: Information content of an evidence. Int. J. Man Mach. Stud. **19**, 33–43 (1983)

33. Smets, P.: Constructing the pignistic probability function in a context of uncertainty. In: Henrion, M., Shachter, R., Kanal, L.N., Lemmer, J.F. (eds.) Uncertainty in Artificial Intelligence, vol. 5. pp, pp. 29–40. North-Holland, Amsterdam (1990)
34. Smets, P., Kennes, R.: The transferable belief model. Artif. Intell. **66**(2), 191–234 (1994)
35. Vejnarová, J., Klir, G.J.: Measure of strife in Dempster-Shafer theory. Int. J. Gen. Syst. **22**(1), 25–42 (1993)
36. Walley, P.: Statistical Reasoning with Imprecise Probabilities. Chapman & Hall, London (1991)
37. Wierman, M.J.: Measuring granularity in evidence theory. Int. J. Gen. Syst. **30**(6), 649–660 (2001)
38. Yager, R.: Entropy and specificity in a mathematical theory of evidence. Int. J. Gen. Syst. **9**(4), 249–260 (1983)

A New Matrix Addition Rule for Combining Linear Belief Functions

Liping Liu[(✉)]

The University of Akron, Akron, USA
liu@acm.org

Abstract. Linear models, obtained from independent sources, may be combined via Dempster's rule as linear belief functions. When they are represented as matrices, the combination is reduced to the addition of the matrices in fully swept forms. This paper improves this combination rule by further reducing unnecessary sweeping operations.

Keywords: Linear belief functions · Matrix sweepings · Dempster's rule

1 Introduction

Linear models, including observations with or without missing values, linear regressions, linear equations, and ignorance, as well as marginal and conditional multivariate normal distributions of linear combinations of variables, are all manifestations of the concept of linear belief functions [3] in a unified matrix representation [4]. To combine linear belief functions, Dempster proposed summing their matrix representations in fully swept forms [1], i.e., the combination of two linear belief functions corresponds to the addition of their matrix representations if both matrices have been fully swept.

This paper shows that two linear belief functions can still be combined by summing their matrix representations if the matrices are partially swept from their common variables. It also proves that, if a matrix happens to be swept from an uncommon variable due to the nature of its representation, it does not have to be reversed in order to be combined. Thus, two matrices can be directly added regardless whether they are swept or not from any uncommon variables. This new matrix addition rule avoids unnecessary sweeping operations, and renders more efficient the computation for combining linear models.

2 Linear Belief Functions

The essence of the concept of belief functions is limited divisibility of beliefs [7]: a belief function is made of indivisible atomic subsets, called *focal elements*, and indivisible *probability mass numbers*. A linear model is a belief function. In the simple case of linear equations, e.g., $3X + 5Y = 4$, the truth is on the hyperplane s determined by the equation, but the equation alone provides no further information on the whereabouts of the truth. Thus, s is the only focal

© Springer International Publishing Switzerland 2016
J. Vejnarová and V. Kratochvíl (Eds.): BELIEF 2016, LNAI 9861, pp. 14–24, 2016.
DOI: 10.1007/978-3-319-45559-4_2

element, and $m(s) = 1$. In general, a linear belief function is a normal distribution over a partition of parallel hyperplanes [3], e.g., $3X + 5Y \sim N(2, 10)$, where the frame of discernment is $\mathbb{R}^2$, focal elements are parallel hyperplanes, and the mass number for each hyperplane $s(w) = \{(x, y) \mid 3x + 5y = w\}$ is density value $f(w)$ for $N(2, 10)$; this belief function contains knowledge about both X and Y, and yet the mass number $f(w)$ cannot be reallocated to any subset of points in $s(w)$.

Instead of focal elements and mass values, a linear belief function on $X = (X_1, X_2, ..., X_n)$ can be more conveniently expressed as a $(n + 1) \times n$ matrix:

$$M(X_1, ..., \overrightarrow{X_i}, ..., X_n) = \begin{array}{c} \\ X_1 \\ \vdots \\ \overrightarrow{X_i} \\ \vdots \\ X_n \end{array} \begin{array}{c} X_1 \cdots \overrightarrow{X_i} \cdots X_n \\ \begin{bmatrix} v_1 & \cdots & v_i & \cdots & v_n \\ \sigma_{11} & \cdots & \sigma_{1i} & \cdots & \sigma_{1n} \\ \vdots & \vdots & \vdots & \vdots & \vdots \\ \sigma_{i1} & \cdots & \sigma_{ii} & \cdots & \sigma_{in} \\ \vdots & \vdots & \vdots & \vdots & \vdots \\ \sigma_{n1} & \cdots & \sigma_{ni} & \cdots & \sigma_{nn} \end{bmatrix} \end{array} \tag{1}$$

here one or more variables like X_i have been swept, denoted by $\overrightarrow{X_i}$. The key to understanding Eq. 1 are forward and reverse sweeping operations:

Definition 1. *Assume real matrix A is made of submatrices as $A = (A_{ij})$ and assume A_{ij} is a square submatrix. Then a forward (or reverse) sweeping of A from A_{ij} replaces submatrix A_{ij} by its negative inverse $-(A_{ij})^{-1}$, any other submatrix A_{ik} in row i and any submatrix A_{kj} in column j are respectively replaced by $(A_{ij})^{-1}A_{ik}$ (or $-(A_{ij})^{-1}A_{ik}$) and $A_{kj}(A_{ij})^{-1}$ (or $-A_{kj}(A_{ij})^{-1}$), and the remaining submatrix A_{kl} not in the same row or column as A_{ij}, i.e., $k \neq i$ and $j \neq l$, by $A_{kl} - A_{kj}(A_{ij})^{-1}A_{il}$.*

Here forward and reverse sweepings operationally differ only in the sign for the elements in the same column or row as the sweeping point. Yet, they cancel each other in effect. A_{ij} is called *a sweeping point*, which is usually an element or a square submatrix; a sweeping from a positive definite submatrix is equivalent to successive sweepings from each of the leading diagonal elements of the submatrix.

Sweeping points in Eq. 1 are leading diagonal elements, e.g., σ_{ii}, of the lower $n \times n$ submatrix. Since σ_{ii} is the intersection between row X_i and column X_i, we may also call X_i a sweeping point, and the matrix is swept from X_i. If the sweeping point consists of all variables or is the entire lower $n \times n$ submatrix, then we say the $(n + 1) \times n$ matrix is fully swept. For example, if X is Gaussian, its distribution $X \sim N(\mu, \Sigma)$ is expressed as Eq. 1:

$$M(X) = \begin{bmatrix} \mu \\ \Sigma \end{bmatrix}. \tag{2}$$

Sweeping this matrix from all variables produces a fully swept form

$$M(\overrightarrow{X}) = \begin{bmatrix} \mu\Sigma^{-1} \\ -\Sigma^{-1} \end{bmatrix}. \tag{3}$$

For partial sweepings, let us consider the matrix representation of a multi-variate normal distribution on X and Y in the block form:

$$M(X,Y) = \begin{bmatrix} \mu_X & \mu_Y \\ \Sigma_{XX} & \Sigma_{XY} \\ \Sigma_{YX} & \Sigma_{YY} \end{bmatrix},$$

where μ_X and μ_Y are respectively the mean vectors of X and Y, and Σ_{XX}, Σ_{YY}, Σ_{XY} and Σ_{YX} are respectively covariance matrices. Then, applying forward sweepings from X or Σ_{XX} produces the partially swept matrix:

$$M(\overrightarrow{X},Y) = \begin{bmatrix} \mu_X(\Sigma_{XX})^{-1} & \mu_Y - \mu_X(\Sigma_{XX})^{-1}\Sigma_{XY} \\ -(\Sigma_{XX})^{-1} & (\Sigma_{XX})^{-1}\Sigma_{XY} \\ \Sigma_{YX}(\Sigma_{XX})^{-1} & \Sigma_{YY} - \Sigma_{YX}(\Sigma_{XX})^{-1}\Sigma_{XY} \end{bmatrix}.$$

here $\mu_X(\Sigma_{XX})^{-1}$ and $-(\Sigma_{XX})^{-1}$ determine the density function of X in the potential form according to Eq. 3. The remaining blocks of $M(\overrightarrow{X},Y)$ define a conditional normal distribution of Y given $X = x$ as follows: $(\Sigma_{XX})^{-1}\Sigma_{XY} = [\Sigma_{YX}(\Sigma_{XX})^{-1}]^T$ is the coefficient of the multivariate regression line, $\mu_Y - \mu_X(\Sigma_{XX})^{-1}\Sigma_{XY}$ is the Y-intercept of the regression line or the expected value of Y given $X = 0$, and the conditional covariance matrix $\Sigma_{YY} - \Sigma_{YX}(\Sigma_{XX})^{-1}\Sigma_{XY}$ is the covariance matrix of the residual term ϵ when the conditional distribution is expressed as a linear regression $Y = [\mu_Y - \mu_X(\Sigma_{XX})^{-1}\Sigma_{XY}] + x(\Sigma_{XX})^{-1}\Sigma_{XY} + \epsilon$, where ϵ is the white noise $\epsilon \sim N(0, \Sigma_{YY} - \Sigma_{YX}(\Sigma_{XX})^{-1}\Sigma_{XY})$.

The following is how Eq. 1 represents linear belief functions. The basic case is probabilistic knowledge about X modeled as multinormal as in Eq. 2. As its special case, if X takes on value x with certainty, then

$$M(X) = \begin{bmatrix} x \\ 0 \end{bmatrix}, \tag{4}$$

because $\Sigma = 0$ when there is no uncertainty. In an opposite case, we may have complete ignorance on X, we represent the case as a fully swept matrix

$$M(\overrightarrow{X}) = \begin{bmatrix} 0 \\ 0 \end{bmatrix}. \tag{5}$$

As in the case of complete certainty, there is no density function for X in the case of ignorance, and Eq. 5 is simply the definition of ignorance. However, one may make sense of the definition by imaging it to be the limit of the fully swept matrix in Eq. 3 when all the variances approach infinity or the inverse covariance matrix approaches zero.

Between complete certainty and full ignorance, there are intermediate cases involving partial ignorance, where we have ignorance on some variables but probabilistic or deterministic knowledge on others. Without loss of generality, let us assume that we have ignorance on X and probabilistic knowledge on Y as linear regression model $(Y \mid X = x) \sim N(B + xA, \Sigma_{YY})$, where A is the coefficient matrix, B is an intercept vector, and Σ is a conditional covariance matrix. Note that $M(\vec{X}, Y)$ contains a marginal distribution on X and a conditional distribution on Y given X. Here we are ignorant on X, and thus the terms corresponding to the density function of X will be 0. Thus,

$$M(\vec{X}, Y) = \begin{bmatrix} 0 & B \\ 0 & A \\ A^T & \Sigma_{YY} \end{bmatrix}. \tag{6}$$

Equation 6 has two interesting special cases. The first is when $\Sigma_{YY} = 0$, or we have deterministic knowledge on Y given X. Then we have a standard linear equation $Y = B + XA$, which will be represented as

$$M(\vec{X}, Y) = \begin{bmatrix} 0 & B \\ 0 & A \\ A^T & 0 \end{bmatrix}. \tag{7}$$

The second special case is when X and Y are independent, or coefficient matrix $A = 0$. This case corresponds to a proper normal distribution; since Y is independent of X, its conditional becomes its marginal. Thus, we have ignorance on X and a marginal distribution on Y. Assume $Y \sim N(\mu_Y, \Sigma_{YY})$. Then we have a special case of Eq. 6:

$$M(\vec{X}, Y) = \begin{bmatrix} 0 & \mu_Y \\ 0 & 0 \\ 0 & \Sigma_{YY} \end{bmatrix}. \tag{8}$$

If we further assume $\Sigma_{YY} = 0$ in Eq. 8, then we have the case of observations with missing data; we have observed values $Y = y$ but missing values on X. We represent the case as:

$$M(\vec{X}, Y) = \begin{bmatrix} 0 & y \\ 0 & 0 \\ 0 & 0 \end{bmatrix}. \tag{9}$$

The representations so far all involve explicit knowledge, or a lack of it, about a set of variables. A more general form of linear belief functions is a normal distribution over hyperplanes, which carries implicit knowledge on some variables, but the knowledge does not, or at least not readily, specify how each variable is distributed. One approach to represent such a model is to transform it into explicit knowledge such as a conditional distribution or any of the representation that we have discussed so far. For example, the distribution $3X + 5Y \sim N(2, 10)$ can be transformed into the following regression model $Y \sim N(-0.6X + 0.4, 0.4)$. The second approach is a more direct representation; we may introduce auxiliary variables and then represent the model as composed of a few components. For example, $3X + 5Y \sim N(2, 10)$ may be directly represented using two separate models: $W = 3X + 5Y$ and $W \sim N(2, 10)$, or in the matrix format as

$$M(\vec{X}, \vec{Y}, W) = \begin{bmatrix} 0 & 0 & 0 \\ 0 & 0 & 3 \\ 0 & 0 & 5 \\ 3 & 5 & 0 \end{bmatrix}, M(W) = \begin{bmatrix} 2 \\ 10 \end{bmatrix}.$$

In general, for $XA \sim N(\mu, \Sigma)$, we introduce a auxiliary vector Z and represent the distribution into two parts: $Z = XA$ and $Z \sim N(\mu, \Sigma)$, both of which can be readily represented as matrices. Such a direct representation is equivalent to the original distribution because, as we will see later, the combination of the component models is the same as the original distribution over hyperplanes.

3   A New Rule for Combination

The combination of two linear belief functions corresponds to the intersection of the hyperplanes and the multiplication of two normal density functions. In the case of usual normal distributions represented as Eq. 1, we can verify:

Theorem 1. *For two normal distributions on X with positive definite covariance matrices represented respectively by $M_1(X)$ and $M_2(X)$ as in Eq. 1, their combination via Dempster's rule is a normal distribution of X with a matrix representation in fully swept form as $M(\overrightarrow{X}) = M_1(\overrightarrow{X}) + M_2(\overrightarrow{X})$.*

The essence of Theorem 1 appeared in [3]. Note that, when X is a single variable, this theorem basically states that the mean of the combined distribution is a weighted average of component means with the inverse variances as weights. It is interesting to compare it with how Kalman filter [2] estimates the true state from measurements containing noises. As a simple demonstration, assume x_t is a measurement of an unknown true value μ at time t, contaminated by the white noise with standard deviation σ_t. Assume that the observations x_t are independent and normally distributed with the same mean μ. Then the maximum likelihood estimate for the true value μ is $\hat{\mu} = (\sum x_t/\sigma_t^2)/(\sum 1/\sigma_t^2)$. Thus, Kalman filtering is similar to the combination of independent estimates.

Theorem 1 implies a general matrix addition rule, which simplifies Dempster's rule of combination based on set intersections and mass multiplications into one based on matrix sweepings and additions:

Definition 2. *Combination Rule 1: The combination of any two linear belief functions obtained from independent sources is the addition of their matrix representations in fully swept form.*

This rule was proposed by [1] and shown to satisfy Shenoy and Shafer axioms such as commutativity and associativity [4]. It applies not only to normal distributions, but also any linear belief functions, including linear regressions, linear equations, ignorance, or normal distributions over hyperplanes [5,6,10]. Note that, in degenerate cases, variances may be zero or not exist so the weighting mechanism based on inverse variances fails. However, this rule is applicable to all cases including ignorance, which have no finite expressions in probability theory.

Theorem 1 assume two normal distributions bear on the same random vector X. What if they bear on different random vectors? A vacuous extension must be applied to make them bear on the same random vector. If X is vacuous, and $M(\overrightarrow{X}, Y)$ contains the same knowledge as $M(Y)$. Then $M(\overrightarrow{X}, Y)$ is called a *vacuous extension* of $M(Y)$, denoted by $M^{\uparrow X}(Y)$ [9]. In general, for any matrix M, in which variables may have mixed swept status with some but not all variables swept, a vacuous extension to include additional variables X is

$$M^{\uparrow X}(...) = M(\overrightarrow{X},...) = \begin{bmatrix} 0 \, ... \\ 0 \; 0 \\ 0 \, ... \end{bmatrix}. \tag{10}$$

After extension, $M^{\uparrow X}$ keeps the same values as in M for existing variables and assumes full ignorance for X and no correlation between X and the existing variables. Thus, $M^{\uparrow X}$ represents no more and no less information than the original.

Suppose $M_1(X)$ and $M_2(Y)$ are respectively the matrices for two linear belief functions. To combine them, first, both matrices are fully swept into $M_1(\overrightarrow{X})$ and $M_2(\overrightarrow{Y})$. Then, they are vacuously extended so that they bear on the same variables. Finally, the extended matrices are added to obtain the combination:

$$M(\overrightarrow{X} \cup \overrightarrow{Y}) = M_1^{\uparrow Y}(\overrightarrow{X}) + M_2^{\uparrow X}(\overrightarrow{Y}) \tag{11}$$

A question arises regarding whether the combination of two normal distributions on different variables can be so combined via Dempster's rule. A more important question is whether there is an explicit, analytical expression of the combined distribution derived from Dempster's rule. The following answers these questions, and as a by-product, implies a new, improved matrix addition rule. Note that one may be tempted to derive the analytical expression of the combination by multiplying the density functions directly. However, the derivation is overwhelming. Here I approach the problem indirectly. First, I need:

Lemma 1. *Assume X, Y, and Z are three distinct random vectors such that $X \sim N(\mu_X, \Sigma_{XX})$ and the conditional distributions of Y and Z given X:*

$$(Y \mid X = x) \sim N(B_Y + xA_Y, \Sigma_{YY}),$$
$$(Z \mid X = x) \sim N(B_Z + xA_Z, \Sigma_{ZZ}).$$

Then the joint distribution of X, Y, and Z has the following partially swept matrix representation:

$$M(\overrightarrow{X}, Y, Z) = \begin{bmatrix} \mu_X(\Sigma_{XX})^{-1} & B_Y & B_Z \\ -(\Sigma_{XX})^{-1} & A_Y & A_Z \\ (A_Y)^T & \Sigma_{YY} & 0 \\ (A_Z)^T & 0 & \Sigma_{ZZ} \end{bmatrix}.$$

This lemma along with Theorem 1 leads to an analytical expression for the combination of two arbitrary normal distributions via Dempster's rule:

Theorem 2. *The combination of any two normal distributions is also a normal distribution. In addition, assume two vectors of random variables have common subvector X and different subvectors respectively as Y and Z such that their matrix representations are respectively $M_1(X, Y)$ and $M_2(X, Z)$. Let $M(X, Y, Z)$ denote their combination via Dempster's rule. Then*

$$M(\overrightarrow{X}, Y, Z) = M_1^{\uparrow Z}(\overrightarrow{X}, Y) + M_2^{\uparrow Y}(\overrightarrow{X}, Z). \tag{12}$$

A formal proof is not included here, but a sketch is as follows. Assume that two normal distributions are respectively for (X, Y) and (X, Z), where Y and Z are disjoint. I can factor out from the distributions respectively marginals $N(\mu_{1,X}, \Sigma_{1,XX})$ and $N(\mu_{2,X}, \Sigma_{2,XX})$, which can then be combined into a single marginal $N(\mu_X, \Sigma_{XX})$ via Theorem 1. The other factors, i.e., conditionals $(Y \mid X = x)$ and $(Z \mid X = x)$, are then combined with $N(\mu_X, \Sigma_{XX})$ to produce the product of two original distributions. Lemma 1 represents this combination simply as the sum of the matrices.

Theorem 2 represents the combination of two multivariate normal distributions elegantly in an analytical expression, generalizing the result in Theorem 1. It states that the combination of two normal distributions is simply the sum of their matrix representations if both matrices have been swept from each common variable but have not been swept from any uncommon variable.

What if a matrix happens to be swept from an uncommon variable because of the nature of its representation? The following theorem states that such matrices can still be added directly.

Theorem 3. *Assume X is the common set of variables between normal distributions represented by $M_1(\overrightarrow{X}, Y_1, Y_2)$ and $M_2(\overrightarrow{X}, Z_1, Z_2)$. Let $M(\overrightarrow{X}, Y_1, Y_2, Z_1, Z_2)$ be their combination. Then*

$$M(\overrightarrow{X}, \overrightarrow{Y_1}, Y_2, \overrightarrow{Z_1}, Z_2) = M_1^{\uparrow Z_1 \cup Z_2}(\overrightarrow{X}, \overrightarrow{Y_1}, Y_2) + M_2^{\uparrow Y_1 \cup Y_2}(\overrightarrow{X}, \overrightarrow{Z_1}, Z_2).$$

Thus, the combination of two normal distributions corresponds to the addition of their matrix representations as long as they have been swept from all common variables. As far as uncommon variables, they can be either swept or not swept from. Therefore, it improves the result of Theorem 2 one step further by not requiring uncommon variables to be unswept.

Note that vacuous extensions bring in additional vacuous variables as swept ones into the matrices. For example, Eq. 12 becomes

$$M(\overrightarrow{X}, Y, Z) = M_1(\overrightarrow{X}, Y, \overrightarrow{Z}) + M_2(\overrightarrow{X}, \overrightarrow{Y}, Z), \tag{13}$$

which is not true in general because both $M_1(\overrightarrow{X}, Y, \overrightarrow{Z})$ and $M_2(\overrightarrow{X}, \overrightarrow{Y}, Z)$ now have variable X, Y, and Z in common, and according to Theorem 2, both matrices have to be fully swept before they can be added. However, it holds when Z is vacuous in M_1 and Y is vacuous in M_2, and in which case, Eq. 13 is identical to Eq. 12. Summarizing the above results, I can state a more efficient combination rule based on partial matrix sweepings and additions:

Definition 3. *Combination Rule 2: The combination of any two linear belief functions from independent sources is the addition of their matrix representations if the matrices are partially swept from each common variable. Furthermore, if a common variable is vacuous in one of the linear belief functions, then the matrix representation of the other does not have to be swept from the variable.*

It is easy to see the difference between the two combination rules. Assume M_1 and M_2 are two linear models respectively for two sets of variables X and Y.

By Rule 1, the combination asks for fully sweeping both the matrices into $M_1(\overrightarrow{X})$ and $M_2(\overrightarrow{Y})$ and then extending them into $M_1(\overrightarrow{X}, \overrightarrow{Y})$ and $M_2(\overrightarrow{X}, \overrightarrow{Y})$ to be added. By Rule 2, we just need to sweep both matrices from the common variables in the intersection $X \cap Y$ and leave the swept status of other variables in either X or Y as is, and then extend and add the resulting matrices.

There are some special cases the new rule is convenient and efficient. First, if there is no common variable, then no sweeping is necessary according to the new rule. For example, to combine a distribution for variable X in potential form $M(\overrightarrow{X}) = (0.2, -0.1)^T$, and normal distribution $Y \sim N(1, 4)$, a simple addition, after vacuous extensions, gets the combination

$$M(\overrightarrow{X}, Y) = \begin{bmatrix} 0.2 & 1 \\ -0.1 & 0 \\ 0 & 4 \end{bmatrix}. \tag{14}$$

without first sweeping the moment matrix for $Y \sim N(1, 4)$. Second, when a linear model is a linear equation or regression model, it is already in partially swept form, and so sweeping may be unnecessary. For example, assume we have another linear regression model

$$M(\overrightarrow{X}, Z) = \begin{bmatrix} 0 & 4 \\ 0 & 1 \\ 1 & 10 \end{bmatrix}, \tag{15}$$

which is from a source independent of that of $M(\overrightarrow{X}, Y)$ in Eq. 14. Then we may combine $M(\overrightarrow{X}, Y)$ and $M(\overrightarrow{X}, Z)$ without any sweeping:

$$M(\overrightarrow{X}, Y, Z) = \begin{bmatrix} 0.2 & 1 & 4 \\ -0.1 & 0 & 1 \\ 0 & 4 & 0 \\ 1 & 0 & 10 \end{bmatrix}. \tag{16}$$

Third, for a linear equation or a direct observation, sweeping operations will usually involve divisions by zero. Dempster proposes a walk-around by turning a division by zero into a symbolic division by ϵ and let $\epsilon \longrightarrow 0$ when the opportunity arises [1]. However, the computation can easily become intractable. Recently, I propose a notion of imaginary extreme numbers and represent $\frac{1}{0}$ by the imaginary number e. Then, sweeping operations on real matrices essentially become ones on imaginary numbers. In contrast, the new combination rule can avoid such an enigma or reduce its occurrence if linear equations are appropriately represented.

A general linear belief function, or a normal distribution over hyperplanes, is expressed as matrices directly as components. For example, the distributions $3X + 5Y \sim N(2, 10)$ and $X - Y \sim N(-1, 4)$ can be represented respectively as $Z \sim N(2, 10)$ with $Z = 3X + 5Y$ and $W \sim N(-1, 4)$ with $W = X - Y$. Here Z and W are auxiliary variables. The following shows the matrix representation of the four models, where M_1 is for $Z = 3X + 5Y$, M_2 is for $Z \sim N(2, 10)$, M_3 is for $W = X - Y$, and the last is normal distribution $W \sim N(-1, 4)$.

$$M_1(\overrightarrow{X}, \overrightarrow{Y}, Z) = \begin{bmatrix} 0 & 0 & 0 \\ 0 & 0 & 3 \\ 0 & 0 & 5 \\ 3 & 5 & 0 \end{bmatrix}, \quad M_3(\overrightarrow{X}, \overrightarrow{Y}, W) = \begin{bmatrix} 0 & 0 & 0 \\ 0 & 0 & 1 \\ 0 & 0 & -1 \\ 1 & -1 & 0 \end{bmatrix}.$$

The normal distribution $Z \sim N(2, 10)$ is shown as $M_2(Z) = (2, 10)^T$, and $W \sim N(-1, 4)$ as $M_4(W) = (-1, 4)^T$. There are a few different paths for the four models to be combined, but they are all equivalent [4]. By the new combination rule, it makes sense to combine M_1 with M_3 to obtain M_{13} and M_2 with M_4 obtain M_{24} first (see below). Note that M_2 and M_4 have no common variables, and the common variables for M_1 and M_3 are X and Y with both being already swept. Thus, these combinations require no extra sweepings.

$$M_{13}(\overrightarrow{X}, \overrightarrow{Y}, Z, W) = \begin{bmatrix} 0 & 0 & 0 & 0 \\ 0 & 0 & 3 & 1 \\ 0 & 0 & 5 & -1 \\ 3 & 5 & 0 & 0 \\ 1 & -1 & 0 & 0 \end{bmatrix}, \quad M_{24}(Z, W) = \begin{bmatrix} 2 & -1 \\ 10 & 0 \\ 0 & 4 \end{bmatrix}.$$

Then, we can combine the two intermediate matrices M_{13} and M_{24}. To do so, we need to sweep them from both Z and W. This can be easily done for the second matrix. However, to sweep the first matrix from Z or W, we encounter the division-by-zero problem, which is generally handled by sweeping over imaginary extreme numbers [8]. Sweeping the matrix representation of a linear equation from a variable is essentially the same as moving the variable to the right-hand side of the linear equation. Thus, above M_{13} represents the solution to X and Y as $X = 0.125Z + 0.625W$ and $Y = 0.125Z - 0.375W$.

$$M_{24}(\overrightarrow{Z}, \overrightarrow{W}) = \begin{bmatrix} 0.2 & -0.25 \\ -0.1 & 0 \\ 0 & -0.25 \end{bmatrix}, \quad M_{13}(X, Y, \overrightarrow{Z}, \overrightarrow{W}) = \begin{bmatrix} 0 & 0 & 0 & 0 \\ 0 & 0 & 0.125 & 0.625 \\ 0 & 0 & 0.125 & -0.375 \\ 0.125 & 0.125 & 0 & 0 \\ 0.625 & -0.375 & 0 & 0 \end{bmatrix}$$

Now that all common variables have been swept, the new combination rule applies, and the result is shown below as M_{1234}:

$$M_{1234}(X, Y, \overrightarrow{Z}, \overrightarrow{W}) = \begin{bmatrix} 0 & 0 & 0.2 & -0.25 \\ 0 & 0 & 0.125 & 0.625 \\ 0 & 0 & 0.125 & -0.375 \\ 0.125 & 0.125 & -0.1 & 0 \\ 0.625 & -0.375 & 0 & -0.25 \end{bmatrix}$$

Applying reverse sweepings from Z and W, and we obtain the moment matrix of four variables X, Y, Z, and W:

$$M_{1234}(X, Y, Z, W) = \begin{bmatrix} -0.375 & 0.625 & 2 & -1 \\ 1.71875 & -0.78125 & 1.25 & 2.5 \\ -0.78125 & 0.71875 & 1.25 & -1.5 \\ 1.25 & 1.25 & 10 & 0 \\ 2.5 & -1.5 & 0 & 4 \end{bmatrix}$$

Since Z and W are auxiliary variables, we can now get rid of them by marginalizing the moment matrix to the one for X and Y as follows:

$$M(X, Y) = \begin{bmatrix} -0.375 & 0.625 \\ 1.719 & -0.781 \\ -0.781 & 0.719 \end{bmatrix}.$$

4   Conclusion

The combination of linear belief functions corresponds to the addition of their matrix representations if the matrices are fully swept. This paper improves this matrix addition rule by reducing the requirement of full sweeping and states that two belief functions can be combined by summing their matrix representations as long as each matrix is partially swept from the variables common to the both belief functions. As far as those variables distinct to each belief function, the corresponding matrix can be either swept or unswept depending on its natural representation and does not affect the rule.

To arrive at this new rule, I also derived an analytical expression for the combination of two multivariate normal distributions that bear on the different sets of variables. The straightforward application of Dempster's rule to this case is mathematically intractable. However, thanks to the marriage between sweeping operations and conditional distributions, I obtained such an analytical expression in the form of a conditional distribution, which corresponds to the sum of the moment matrices for the two normal distributions when each is partially swept from all the common variables. Besides its consequence to the new matrix addition rule, the analytical expression may find its application in statistics; assuming we have observations from two different but overlapping populations, then the joint likelihood function is the product of the two multivariate normal density functions and thus may allow one to make cross-population inferences.

The new matrix addition rule has some advantages. First, it improves computational efficiency. By avoiding unnecessary sweepings, the new rule reduces computation costs up to $O(n^3)$ divisions, multiplications, and subtractions for combining two linear models in comparison to the original matrix addition rule. Second, it reduces the chances to encounter the division-by-zero enigma. When applying the old matrix addition rule, the issue is sure to occur because fully sweeping the matrix representation of a linear equation will certainly involve divisions by zero. In contrast, with the new rule, the problem may be avoided if a linear equation is represented appropriately.

References

1. Dempster, A.P.: Normal belief functions and the Kalman filter. In: Saleh, A.K.M.E. (ed.) Data Analysis from Statistical Foundations, pp. 65–84. Nova Science Publishers, Hauppauge (2001)
2. Kalman, R.E.: A new approach to linear filtering and prediction problems. J. Basic Eng. **82**, 35–45 (1960)
3. Liu, L.: A theory of Gaussian belief functions. Int. J. Approx. Reason. **14**, 95–126 (1996)
4. Liu, L.: Local computation of Gaussian belief functions. Int. J. Approx. Reason. **22**, 217–248 (1999)
5. Liu, L.: Combining linear equation models via Dempster's rule. In: Denoeux, T., Masson, M.-H. (eds.) Belief Functions: Theory and Applications. AISC, vol. 164, pp. 255–265. Springer, Heidelberg (2012)
6. Liu, L., Shenoy, C., Shenoy, P.P.: Knowledge representation and integration for portfolio evaluation using linear belief functions. IEEE Trans. Syst. Man Cybern. Ser. A **36**(4), 774–785 (2006)
7. Liu, L., Yager, R.: Classic works on the Dempster-Shafer theory of belief function: an introduction. In: Yager, R., Liu, L. (eds.) Classic Works of the Dempster-Shafer Theory of Belief Functions. Studies in Fuzziness and Soft Computing, pp. 1–34. Springer, New York (2008)
8. Liu, L.: Imaginary numbers for combining linear equation models via Dempster's rule. Int. J. Approx. Reason. **55**, 294–310 (2014)
9. Shafer, G.: A Mathematical Theory of Evidence. Princeton University Press, Princeton (1976)
10. Srivastava, R.R., Liu, L.: Applications of belief functions in business decisions: a review. Inf. Syst. Front. **5**(4), 359–378 (2003)

On Internal Conflict as an External Conflict of a Decomposition of Evidence

Alexander Lepskiy[(✉)]

Higher School of Economics, 20 Myasnitskaya Ulitsa, Moscow 101000, Russia
alex.lepskiy@gmail.com

Abstract. Conflictness is an important a priori characteristic of combining rules in the belief functions theory. A new approach to the estimation of internal conflict offered in this article. This approach is based on the idea of decomposition of the initial body of evidence on the set of bodies of evidence by means of some combining rule. Then the (external) conflict of this set of beliefs is estimated. The dependence of change of internal conflict from the choice of the combining rules is analyzed in this study.

Keywords: Internal conflict · Belief functions theory · Combining rules · Imprecision index

1 Introduction

Conflictness is an important a priori characteristic of combining rules in the belief functions theory [5,17]. Usually the conflict of two or more pieces of evidence is evaluated by a functional (measure), taking values in [0,1]. The conflict of pieces of evidence characterizes the information inconsistency given by corresponding bodies of evidence. Historically, the functional associated with Dempster's combining rule is the first conflict measure [5]. Recently the study of a conflict measure in the framework of the belief functions theory was allocated as a separate problem. So, the axiomatic of a conflict measure defined on pairs of bodies of evidence was discussed in [6,15]. An axiomatic of a conflict measure defined on arbitrary subsets of a finite set of bodies of evidence was considered in [3]. There are several approaches to the estimation of conflict of evidence. The metric approach is one of the most popular approaches [9,10,14]. A structural approach was considered in [15]. The degree of inclusion of focal elements of one evidence in the focal elements of other evidence took into account in this approach. The algebraic approach to the estimation of a conflict was discussed in [12]. In this case, the conflict measure was defined as a bilinear form satisfying a certain conditions.

Also, conflictness of single evidence is considered together with the conflict between the bodies of evidence. In the first case we talk about the external conflict, in the second case we talk about the internal conflict. For example, we have the following evidence in which a large internal conflict is observed:

© Springer International Publishing Switzerland 2016
J. Vejnarová and V. Kratochvíl (Eds.): BELIEF 2016, LNAI 9861, pp. 25–34, 2016.
DOI: 10.1007/978-3-319-45559-4_3

the value of the company shares will be tomorrow in the interval [0,10] or [30,35]. The internal conflict considered beginning in the early 1980s. This conflict estimated with the help of different measures: dissonance, confusion, discord, strife etc. [11]. Also the axiomatic of an internal conflict was considered in [1]. In [4] internal conflict was determined in the case of a finite set of alternatives as minimum of the belief function, which is taken over all subsets of alternatives that complement the singletons to the entire set. In [16] internal conflict was defined as a conflict among the so-called generalized simple support functions on which the original evidence decomposes uniquely.

In this paper we will consider and study another approach (but also used the idea of decomposition, as in [16]) to the definition of internal conflict. The following assumption is the basis of this approach. Evidence with a great internal conflict has been obtained as a result of aggregating information from several different sources with the help of some combining rule. Then the (external) conflict of the decomposed set of evidence can be regarded as an internal conflict of the original evidence. It is understood that the decomposition result (and hence the value of the internal conflict) is ambiguous. Therefore we can talk only about the upper and lower estimates of the internal conflict in this case. In addition, it is necessary to introduce some additional restrictions on the set of combinable evidence in order to the result is not trivial or degenerate. These restrictions are related with the character of combining rules, as will be shown below. Thus the optimization problem formulates in this paper to estimation of the internal conflict of evidence. The solution of this problem is studies for Dempster's rule and Dubois and Prade's disjunctive consensus rule. The dependence of change of internal conflict from the choice of the combining rules is analyzed in this study. The decomposition method described above discussed in detail for the case of two alternatives set of evidence.

2   Basic Concepts of the Belief Functions Theory and a Conflict Measure

Let X be a finite set and 2^X be a powerset of X. The mass function is a set function $m : 2^X \rightarrow [0,1]$ that satisfies the conditions $m(\emptyset) = 0$, $\sum_{A \subseteq X} m(A) = 1$. The value $m(A)$ characterizes the relative part of evidence that the actual alternative from X belongs to set $A \in 2^X$.

The subset $A \in 2^X$ is called a focal element, if $m(A) > 0$. Let $\mathcal{A} = A$ be a set of all focal elements of evidence. The pair $F = (\mathcal{A}, m)$ is called a body of evidence. Let $F_A = (A, 1)$ (i.e. $\mathcal{A} = A$ and $m(A) = 1$), $A \in 2^X$ and $\mathcal{F}(X)$ be a set of all bodies of evidence on X.

If we know the body of evidence $F = (\mathcal{A}, m)$ then we can estimate the degree of confidence that the true alternative of X belongs to set B with the help of belief function [17] $g : 2^X \rightarrow [0,1]$, $g(B) = \sum_{A \subseteq B} m(A)$.

The belief function corresponding to body of evidence $F_A = (A, 1)$ is called a categorical belief function and it is denoted as η_A. In particular η_X is called a vacuous belief function because the body of evidence $F_X = (X, 1)$ is totally uninformative.

Let us have two bodies of evidence $F_1 = (\mathcal{A}_1, m_1)$ and $F_2 = (\mathcal{A}_2, m_2)$. For example, these bodies of evidence can be obtained from two information sources. We have a question about a conflict between these bodies of evidence. Historically, the conflict measure $K_0(F_1, F_2)$ associated with Dempster's rule [5,17] is the first among conflict measures:

$$K_0 = K_0(F_1, F_2) = \sum_{\substack{B \cap C = \emptyset, \\ B \in \mathcal{A}_1, C \in \mathcal{A}_2}} m_1(B) m_2(C). \tag{1}$$

The value $K_0(F_1, F_2)$ characterizes the amount of conflict between two sources of information described by the bodies of evidence F_1 and F_2. If $K_0 \neq 1$, then we have the following Dempster's rule for combining of two evidence:

$$m_D(A) = \frac{1}{1 - K_0} \sum_{B \cap C = A} m_1(B) m_2(C), \quad A \neq \emptyset, \quad m_D(\emptyset) = 0.$$

Below in this paper we will consider only the conflict measure (1).

Dubois and Prade's disjunctive consensus rule is a dual rule to Dempster's rule in some sense. This rule is defined by a formula [8]:

$$m_{DP}(A) = \sum_{B \cup C = A} m_1(B) m_2(C), \quad A \in 2^X. \tag{2}$$

3   Decomposition of Evidence

In general case we can assume that some evidence describing with the help of body of evidence $F = (\mathcal{A}, m)$ has a great internal conflict, if its information source is a heterogeneous. For example, information about the prognostic value of shares was obtained with the help of several different techniques. In this case we can consider that the body of evidence $F = (\mathcal{A}, m)$ is a result of combining of several bodies of evidence $F_i = (\mathcal{A}_i, m_i) \in \mathcal{F}(X)$, $i = 1, ..., l$ with the help of some combining rule R: $F = R(F_1, ..., F_l)$. Therefore we can estimate the internal conflict by the formula

$$K_{in}^R(F) = K(F_1, ..., F_l)$$

assuming that

$$F = R(F_1, ..., F_l),$$

where K is some fixed (external) conflict measure, R is a fixed combining rule. Since the equation $F = R(F_1, ..., F_l)$ has many solutions then we can consider the optimization problem of finding the largest $\overline{K}_{in}^R(F)$ and smallest $\underline{K}_{in}^R(F)$ conflicts:

$$\overline{K}_{in}^R(F) = \operatorname*{arg\,max}_{F = R(F_1, ..., F_l)} K(F_1, ..., F_l), \quad \underline{K}_{in}^R(F) = \operatorname*{arg\,min}_{F = R(F_1, ..., F_l)} K(F_1, ..., F_l). \tag{3}$$

Let $S_n = \{(s_i)_{i=1}^n : s_i \geq 0, i = 1, ..., n, \sum_{i=1}^n s_i = 1\}$ be a n-dimensional simplex. Let us consider some special cases of this problem.

Decomposition of Evidence with the Help of Dempster's Rule. Let $R = D$ be Dempster's Rule. Then optimization problems (3) for $l = 2$ have the following formulation. We have to find the bodies of evidence $F_i = (\mathcal{A}_i, m_i) \in \mathcal{F}(X)$, $i = 1, 2$, that satisfy the condition

$$K_0(F_1, F_2) = \sum_{\substack{B \cap C = \emptyset, \\ B \in \mathcal{A}_1, C \in \mathcal{A}_2}} m_1(B)m_2(C) \rightarrow \max \quad (\min) \qquad (4)$$

with constraints

$$(m_1(B))_{B \in \mathcal{A}_1} \in S_{|\mathcal{A}_1|}, \quad (m_2(C))_{C \in \mathcal{A}_2} \in S_{|\mathcal{A}_2|}, \qquad (5)$$

$$(1 - K_0(F_1, F_2)) \, m(A) = \sum_{\substack{B \cap C = A, \\ B \in \mathcal{A}_1, C \in \mathcal{A}_2}} m_1(B)m_2(C), \qquad A \in \mathcal{A}. \qquad (6)$$

This is a problem of quadratic programming with linear (5) and quadratic (6) restrictions. Note, that in the case of the general formulation (4)–(6) $\underline{K}_{in}^D(F) = 0$ and this value is achieved on the pair $F_1 = F$, $F_2 = F_X$. In the same time we have $\overline{K}_{in}^D(F) = 1$ and this value achieved for such $F_i = (\mathcal{A}_i, m_i) \in \mathcal{F}(X)$, $i = 1, 2$, that $B \cap C = \emptyset \; \forall B \in \mathcal{A}_1, \forall C \in \mathcal{A}_2$. The latter being bodies of evidence are not related with the initial body of evidence F. Therefore, in general formulation the problem (4)-(6) to finding $\overline{K}_{in}^D(F)$ and $\underline{K}_{in}^D(F)$ is not meaningful.

At the same time, Dempster's rule is an optimistic rule in the following sense. If one evidence argues that the true alternative belongs to the set A, and the other – to the set B, then after combination of evidence in accordance with Dempster's rule we get that the true alternative belong to the set $A \cap B$ (see [13]). Therefore, we can require from unknown bodies of evidence $F_i = (\mathcal{A}_i, m_i) \in \mathcal{F}(X)$, $i = 1, 2$ that their imprecision would not be less than imprecision of initial evidence F:

$$f(F) \leq f(F_i), \qquad i = 1, 2, \qquad (7)$$

where $f : \mathcal{F}(X) \rightarrow [0, 1]$ is a some imprecision index [2], for example, the generalized Hartley measure [7]:

$$f(F) = \frac{1}{\ln |X|} \sum_{A \in \mathcal{A}} m(A) \ln |A|.$$

It is known that the estimation (7) is always true for any linear imprecision index f and non-conflicting set of evidence (see [13]). Note that the conditions (7) are performed for the bodies of evidence $F_1 = F$ and $F_2 = F_X$ since $f(F_X) = 1$. Therefore we have always $\underline{K}_{in}^D(F) = 0$. Then the problem can be put to find bodies of evidence with the largest conflict (4) and satisfying the conditions (5)–(7).

In addition, the form of initial body of evidence $F = (\mathcal{A}, m) \in \mathcal{F}(X)$ and the combining rule defines a class of evidence in which we should seek solutions.

Example 1. It is necessary to estimate the internal conflict of evidence given by a belief function

$$g = m_0 \eta_X + \sum_{i=1}^{n} m_i \eta_{\{x_i\}}, \quad (m_i)_{i=0}^{n} \in S_{n+1}.$$

In other words, we have the following set of focal elements $\mathcal{A} = \{\{x_1\}, \ldots, \{x_n\}, X\}$ and $m(\{x_i\}) = m_i$ for $i = 1, \ldots, n$, $m(X) = m_0$. Let us assume that Dempster's rule is used to combine of belief functions. In this case combinable belief functions g_1 and g_2 should have a form similar to function g:

$$g_1 = \alpha_0 \eta_X + \sum_{i=1}^{n} \alpha_i \eta_{\{x_i\}}, \quad g_2 = \beta_0 \eta_X + \sum_{i=1}^{n} \beta_i \eta_{\{x_i\}}.$$

Then

$$K_0(g_1, g_2) = \sum_{\substack{B \cap C = \emptyset, \\ B \in \mathcal{A}_1, C \in \mathcal{A}_2}} m_1(B) m_2(C) = \sum_{i=1}^{n} \sum_{j=1, i \neq j}^{n} \alpha_i \beta_j =$$

$$(1 - \alpha_0)(1 - \beta_0) - \sum_{i=1}^{n} \alpha_i \beta_i. \tag{8}$$

The conditions (5)–(6) have the following form

$$(\alpha_i)_{i=0}^{n} \in S_{n+1}, \quad (\beta_i)_{i=0}^{n} \in S_{n+1}, \tag{9}$$

$$\left(1 - (1 - \alpha_0)(1 - \beta_0) + \sum_{i=1}^{n} \alpha_i \beta_i\right) m_i = \alpha_i \beta_i + \alpha_i \beta_0 + \alpha_0 \beta_i, \quad i = 1, \ldots, n, \tag{10}$$

$$\left(1 - (1 - \alpha_0)(1 - \beta_0) + \sum_{i=1}^{n} \alpha_i \beta_i\right) m_0 = \alpha_0 \beta_0.$$

The last equation follows from (9) and (10). The condition (7) for the generalized Hatrley measure (and for any linear imprecision index [2]) has the form

$$m_0 \leq \alpha_0, \quad m_0 \leq \beta_0. \tag{11}$$

Thus, the problem of finding the largest internal conflict $\overline{K}_{in}^{D}$ has a form: it is necessary to find the largest value of the function (8) with constraints (9)–(11).

Decomposition of Evidence with the Help of Dubois and Prade's Disjunctive Consensus Rule. Let $R = DP$ be a Dubois and Prade's disjunctive consensus rule (2). Then the conditions (2) will be used instead of the conditions (6) in the problem of finding the internal conflict. In addition (see [13]), the following estimation holds for Dubois and Prade's disjunctive consensus rule and any linear imprecision index f [2]:

$$f(F) \geq f(F_i), \qquad i = 1, 2, \tag{12}$$

i.e. imprecision of evidence is not reduced after the application of this combining rule. The inequalities (12) reflect the pessimism of Dubois and Prade's disjunctive consensus rule. If the one evidence states that true alternative belongs to the set A and another evidence states that the true alternative belongs to the set B then true alternative should be belong to the set $A \cup B$ after combining of these evidence with the help of Dubois and Prade's disjunctive consensus rule.

Thus, we have a problem of finding of bodies of evidence having the largest (smallest) conflict (4) and satisfying constraints (2), (5), (12).

Note that it is convenient to consider that the empty set can also be a focal element of evidence in the case of using Dubois and Prade's disjunctive consensus rule. This can be interpreted as $x \notin X$ and a value $m(\emptyset)$ characterizes the degree of belief to the fact $x \notin X$. Then the largest value of conflict measure (4) satisfying conditions (2), (5), (12) will be equal $\overline{K}_{in}^{DP}(F) = 1$. This value is achieved for the following decomposition body of evidence F: $F_1 = F$, $F_2 = F_\emptyset$ (in this case we assume by definition that $f(F_\emptyset) = 0$ for any imprecision index f).

4   Estimates of the Internal Conflict in the Case $|X| = 2$

Decomposition with the Help of Dempster's Rule. We solve the problem of finding of measuring internal conflict for body of evidence F with the help of its decomposition by using Dempster's rule, if $X = \{x_1, x_2\}$. In this case the information is described by a belief function $g = m_0 \eta_X + m_1 \eta_{\{x_1\}} + m_2 \eta_{\{x_2\}}$ with $\mathbf{m} = (m_i)_{i=0}^2 \in S_3$. Since $\underline{K}_{in}^D(F) = 0$, then we will find the maximum of the function (8) with constraints (9)–(11) for computing of $\overline{K}_{in}^D(F)$. We have

$$K_0(g_1, g_2) = \alpha_1 \beta_2 + \alpha_2 \beta_1$$

after the exclusion of variables α_0, β_0 and conditions (9)–(11) can be rewritten as

$$(1 - \alpha_i)(1 - \beta_i) = (1 - \alpha_1 \beta_2 - \alpha_2 \beta_1)(1 - m_i), \qquad i = 1, 2, \tag{13}$$

$$\alpha_1 + \alpha_2 \leq m_1 + m_2, \quad \beta_1 + \beta_2 \leq m_1 + m_2, \quad \alpha_i \geq 0, \ \beta_i \geq 0, \quad i = 1, 2. \tag{14}$$

Let $\Omega = \{(\alpha_1, \alpha_2) \in [0, 1]^2 : \alpha_1 + \alpha_2 \leq m_1 + m_2\}$. We solve the system (13) with respect to β_1, β_2. The determinant $\Delta(\alpha_1, \alpha_2)$ of this system is equal

$$\Delta(\alpha_1, \alpha_2) = (1 - \alpha_1)(1 - \alpha_2) - (1 - m_2)\alpha_1(1 - \alpha_1) - (1 - m_1)\alpha_2(1 - \alpha_2)$$

and $\Delta(\alpha_1, \alpha_2) \geq 0$ in Ω. We have $\Delta(\alpha_1, \alpha_2) > 0$, if $m_0 = 1 - m_1 - m_2 > 0$. We consider precisely this case ($m_0 > 0$). Then

$$\beta_i(\alpha_1, \alpha_2) = \frac{1}{\Delta(\alpha_1, \alpha_2)}(m_i - \alpha_i + \alpha_i m_{3-i} - \alpha_{3-i} m_i), \quad i = 1, 2.$$

Conditions (14) define the set

$$\Omega_0 = \{(\alpha_1, \alpha_2) \in [0,1]^2 : (1 - m_{3-i})\alpha_i + m_i\alpha_{3-i} \le m_i, \ i = 1, 2\} \subseteq \Omega.$$

Thus, finding the largest internal conflict $\overline{K}_{in}^D$ reduces to the solution of the problem

$$K_0 = \frac{\alpha_1\beta_2(\alpha_1, \alpha_2) + \alpha_2\beta_1(\alpha_1, \alpha_2)}{\Delta(\alpha_1, \alpha_2)} \to \max, \quad (\alpha_1, \alpha_2) \in \Omega_0.$$

The unique stationary point $\alpha_i^0 = 1 - \dfrac{\sqrt{1-m_i}}{\sqrt{1-m_1}+\sqrt{1-m_2}-\sqrt{1-m_1-m_2}}, i = 1, 2$, of this function is a saddle point. The solution of problem is achieved on the border $\partial \Omega_0$ and

$$\overline{K}_{in}^D = K_0(0, \tfrac{m_2}{1-m_1}) = K_0(\tfrac{m_1}{1-m_2}, 0) = \frac{m_1 m_2}{(1-m_1)(1-m_2)} = \frac{m_1 m_2}{(m_0+m_1)(m_0+m_2)}.$$

The set Ω_0 and level lines of K_0 for $m_1 = 0.4$, $m_2 = 0.3$ are shown on Fig. 1.

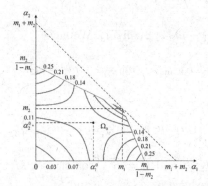

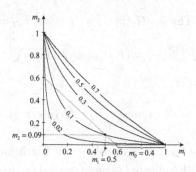

Fig. 1. The set Ω_0 and level lines of K_0 for $m_1 = 0.4$, $m_2 = 0.3$.

Fig. 2. Level lines of $\overline{K}_{in}^D$.

We have $\overline{K}_{in}^D \approx 1$ if $m_0 \ll \min\{m_1, m_2\}$ (see Fig. 2). In particular, the last condition is fulfilled when $m_0 \approx 0$ and $\min\{m_1, m_2\} \gg 0$, i.e. the belief function is close to probability measure but not a Dirac measure. Since $\underline{K}_{in}^D(F) = 0$, then the uncertainty of internal conflict will be maximum in this case. At that the value $\overline{K}_{in}^D$ is more when the distance $|m_1 - m_2|$ is less for one and the same value of m_0.

Conversely, we have $\overline{K}_{in}^D \approx 0$ (and hence $K_{in}^D \approx 0$), if the belief function is either close to the Dirac measure $m_1 \approx 1 \vee m_2 \approx 1$, or it is closer to the vacuous belief function η_X ($m_0 \approx 1$).

Decomposition with the Help of Dubois and Prade's Disjunctive Consensus Rule. Now we will estimate the internal conflict in the case of $X = \{x_1, x_2\}$ in suggestion that Dubois and Prade's disjunctive consensus rule is used for decomposition of evidence and the external conflict is computed in the formula (1). The conditions (2), (9), (12) can be rewritten as

$$m_1 = \alpha_1 \beta_1, \quad m_2 = \alpha_2 \beta_2, \tag{15}$$

$$\alpha_1 + \alpha_2 \geq m_1 + m_2, \quad \beta_1 + \beta_2 \geq m_1 + m_2, \tag{16}$$

$$(\alpha_i)_{i=0}^2 \in S_3, \quad (\beta_i)_{i=0}^2 \in S_3 \tag{17}$$

correspondingly. We should find the minimum (maximum) of $K_0(g_1, g_2) = \alpha_1 \beta_2 + \alpha_2 \beta_1$ with constraints (15)–(17) for calculation of conflict measure's borders $\underline{K}_{in}^{DP}$ and $\overline{K}_{in}^{DP}$. We solve this problem assuming that $m_1 \neq 0$, $m_2 \neq 0$. Then our problem is reduced to finding minimum (maximum) of the function

$$K_0 = \frac{\alpha_1}{\alpha_2} m_2 + \frac{\alpha_2}{\alpha_1} m_1$$

in the set

$$\Omega_1(m_1, m_2) = \left\{ (\alpha_1, \alpha_2) \in (0, 1]^2 : \alpha_1 + \alpha_2 \leq 1, \frac{m_1}{\alpha_1} + \frac{m_2}{\alpha_2} \leq 1 \right\}.$$

The set $\Omega_1(m_1, m_2) \neq \emptyset \Leftrightarrow m_0 = 1 - m_1 - m_2 \geq 2\sqrt{m_1 m_2}$. We have

$$\underline{K}_{in}^{DP}(F) = (K_0)_{\min} = 2\sqrt{m_1 m_2}, \quad \overline{K}_{in}^{DP} = (K_0)_{\max} = m_0 = 1 - m_1 - m_2.$$

Let

$$M = \left\{ (m_1, m_2) \in \overset{\circ}{S}_2 : \Omega_1(m_1, m_2) \neq \emptyset \right\} = \left\{ (m_1, m_2) \in \overset{\circ}{S}_2 : \sqrt{m_1} + \sqrt{m_2} \leq 1 \right\}.$$

The level lines are shown in Fig. 3 for $\underline{K} = \underline{K}_{in}^{DP}$ and $\overline{K} = \overline{K}_{in}^{DP}$ on the set M, which indicated by grey color. In particular, we have $\underline{K}_{in}^{DP}(F) \approx 0$ and $\overline{K}_{in}^{DP} \approx 1$, if $m_0 \approx 1$ ($m_1 \approx 0 \wedge m_2 \approx 0$). In this case the uncertainty of estimating conflict is maximal.

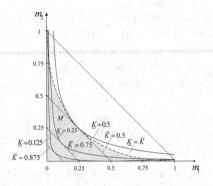

Fig. 3. Level lines of $\underline{K} = \underline{K}_{in}^{DP}$, $\overline{K} = \overline{K}_{in}^{DP}$.

If $m_0 \approx 0$, then the belief function is close to a Dirac measure and $\overline{K}_{in}^{DP} \approx 0$ in this case (and consequently, $K_{in}^{DP} \approx 0$).

The estimation of internal conflict results in a unique $\underline{K}_{in}^{DP} = \overline{K}_{in}^{DP} = 2\sqrt{m_1}\left(1 - \sqrt{m_1}\right)$, $0 < m_1 < 1$, on the curve $\sqrt{m_1} + \sqrt{m_2} = 1$, which noted by dashed line in Fig. 3. In particular, this unique value is maximal and it is equal to 0.5 for belief function $g = \frac{1}{2}\eta_X + \frac{1}{4}\eta_{\{x_1\}} + \frac{1}{4}\eta_{\{x_2\}}$.

We can make the following conclusions comparing decompositions with the help of Dempster's rule and Dubois and Prade's disjunctive consensus rule. The obtained estimations of an internal conflict are different but do not contradict each other. In addition, it is easy to show also, that $\overline{K}_{in}^{D}(m_1, m_2) < \underline{K}_{in}^{DP}(m_1, m_2)$ for all $(m_1, m_2) \in \Omega_1$. This means that the estimation of an internal conflict obtained with the help of optimistic Dempster's rule is always less than the estimation of an internal conflict obtained with the help of pessimistic Dubois and Prade's disjunctive consensus rule.

5   Conclusions

The approach to the estimation of internal conflict of evidence based on the decomposition of the body of evidence on the set of bodies of evidence with the help of some combining rule and later computing of external conflict measure of decomposed set of evidence is considered in this article. This approach is discussed in more detail for decomposition with the help of Dempster's rule and Dubois and Prade's disjunctive consensus rule. The decomposition method discussed in detail for the case of a set of evidence with two alternatives. In particular, it is shown that:

- interval estimations of internal conflict obtained with the help of decomposition by Dempster's rule and Dubois and Prade's disjunctive consensus rule do not intersect;
- in the case of decomposition by Dempster's rule, the greatest uncertainty ($0 \leq K_{in}^{D} \leq 1$) is achieved for the belief function close to a probability measure but not close to a Dirac measure; the value $K_{in}^{D} \approx 0$ is achieved for belief function close to a Dirac measure either it is close to the vacuous belief function;
- in the case of decomposition by Dubois and Prade's disjunctive consensus rule, the greatest uncertainty ($0 \leq K_{in}^{DP} \leq 1$) is achieved for a vacuous belief function $F = \eta_X$; the value $K_{in}^{DP} \approx 0$ is achieved for a Dirac measure.

Acknowledgments. The financial support from the Government of the Russian Federation within the framework of the implementation of the 5-100 Programme Roadmap of the National Research University Higher School of Economics is acknowledged. This work was supported by the grant 14-07-00189 of RFBR (Russian Foundation for Basic Research).

References

1. Bronevich, A., Klir, G.J.: Measures of uncertainty for imprecise probabilities: an axiomatic approach. Int. J. Approx. Reason. **51**, 365–390 (2010)
2. Bronevich, A., Lepskiy, A.: Imprecision indices: axiomatic, properties and applications. Int. J. Gen. Syst. **44**(7–8), 812–832 (2015)
3. Bronevich, A., Lepskiy, A., Penikas, H.: The application of conflict measure to estimating incoherence of analyst's forecasts about the cost of shares of Russian companies. Proc. Comput. Sci. **55**, 1113–1122 (2015)
4. Daniel, M.: Conflict between belief functions: a new measure based on their non-conflicting parts. In: Cuzzolin, F. (ed.) BELIEF 2014. LNCS, vol. 8764, pp. 321–330. Springer, Heidelberg (2014)
5. Dempster, A.P.: Upper and lower probabilities induced by multivalued mapping. Ann. Math. Stat. **38**, 325–339 (1967)
6. Destercke, S., Burger, T.: Toward an axiomatic definition of conflict between belief functions. IEEE Trans. Cybern. **43**(2), 585–596 (2013)
7. Dubois, D., Prade, H.: A note on measures of specificity for fuzzy sets. Int. J. Gen. Syst. **10**, 279–283 (1985)
8. Dubois, D., Prade, H.: On the combination of evidence in various mathematical frameworks. In: Flamm, J., Luisi, T. (eds.) Reliability Data Collection and Analysis, pp. 213–241. Kluwer Acad. Publ., Dordrecht (1992)
9. Jousselme, A.-L., Grenier, D., Bosse, E.: A new distance between two bodies of evidence. Inf. Fusion **2**, 91–101 (2001)
10. Jousselme, A.-L., Maupin, P.: Distances in evidence theory: comprehensive survey and generalizations. Int. J. Approx. Reason. **53**, 118–145 (2012)
11. Klir, G.J.: Uncertainty and Information: Foundations of Generalized Information Theory. Wiley, Hoboken (2006)
12. Lepskiy, A.: About relation between the measure of conflict and decreasing of ignorance in theory of evidence. In: Proceedings of the 8th Conference of the European Society for Fuzzy Logic and Technology, pp. 355–362. Atlantis Press, Amsterdam (2013)
13. Lepskiy, A.: General schemes of combining rules and the quality characteristics of combining. In: Cuzzolin, F. (ed.) BELIEF 2014. LNCS, vol. 8764, pp. 29–38. Springer, Heidelberg (2014)
14. Liu, W.: Analysing the degree of conflict among belief functions. Artif. Intell. **170**, 909–924 (2006)
15. Martin, A.: About conflict in the theory of belief functions. In: Denoeux, T., Masson, M.-H. (eds.) Belief Functions: Theory and Applications. AISC, vol. 164, pp. 161–168. Springer, Heidelberg (2012)
16. Schubert, J.: The internal conflict of a belief function. In: Denoeux, T., Masson, M.-H. (eds.) Belief Functions: Theory and Applications. AISC, vol. 164, pp. 161–168. Springer, Heidelberg (2012)
17. Shafer, G.: A Mathematical Theory of Evidence. Princeton Univ. Press, Princeton (1976)

Decission

Designing an Evidential Assertion Language for Multiple Analysts

David Burke[(✉)]

Galois, Inc., Portland, OR, USA
davidb@galois.com

Abstract. This paper describes our work in designing an expressive evidence-based language for use by analysts as part of a decision support system for managing cyber threats. The underlying design concept for our system is that of *perspective*: there is not necessarily a definitive or objective means of combining all of the potential evidence, and therefore, how evidence is combined reflects a particular analyst's point of view. We describe how our design provides flexibility to analysts in terms of expressing and combining evidence, while supporting rich interactions between analysts, and then illustrate our approach with examples.

Keywords: Epistemic uncertainty · Combination rules · Belief functions · Evidence theory · Dempster-Shafer theory · Transferable Belief Model

1 Introduction

This paper describes our work in designing an expressive evidence-based language for use by analysts as part of a decision support system for managing cyber threats. The most precious resource for analysts is their attention - are they addressing the most salient threats? It is difficult for analysts to answer this question definitively, because they are always dealing with large amounts of threat evidence that is dynamic, incomplete, ambiguous, and contradictory - they are operating in a world of irreducible uncertainty.

The system we have been building is designed to augment analyst capabilities by aggregating both primary-sourced threat evidence and the beliefs of other analysts in order to make effective assessments about the current threat landscape. Early in this effort, it became clear that the type of uncertainty that best characterizes the cyber domain is epistemic, not aleatory. As an example, consider the class of so-called "zero-day" attacks. What makes these attacks so insidious is that by definition, they capitalize on software vulnerabilities that are unknown to the defender. You cannot meaningfully say "There is a 70 percent chance of our site being hit by a zero-day in the next month" because zero-days are not about probabilities; they are about ignorance.

In addressing the challenge of epistemic uncertainty in the cyber domain, we were immediately attracted to a belief function-based approach [11]. Our research has focused on extending aspects of Dempster-Shafer theory [8] and the

© Springer International Publishing Switzerland 2016
J. Vejnarová and V. Kratochvíl (Eds.): BELIEF 2016, LNAI 9861, pp. 37–45, 2016.
DOI: 10.1007/978-3-319-45559-4_4

Transferable Belief Model (TBM) [9,10] in order to create an expressive language of evidence aggregation, and then implementing these capabilities as a software module for use by analysts.

2   Design Dimensions

The underlying design concept for our system is that of "perspective" - there is not necessarily a definitive or objective means of combining all of the potential evidence, and therefore, how evidence is combined reflects a particular analyst's point of view.

Analysts work in teams, so the typical workflow is not one analyst making all of the decisions with respect to evidence availability, relevance, and probative force. Instead, each analyst may see different pieces of evidence in the first place, and their varied experiences, topic specializations, and cognitive biases lead them to weigh that evidence differently in terms of the relevance and the strength of that evidence. This includes not just how they deal with primary sources (sensors, for example), but also how they weigh the assertions of other analysts. At the end of the process, a decision represents a judgement that is dependent on how evidence was aggregated.

To support varied workflows, we aimed for a system architecture that gives analysts flexibility in terms of how to combine evidence, and that also supports rich interactions between analysts. Certain dimensions stood out as being key, and these became the underlying principles of our design:

1. *Multiple Combinators:* Instead of requiring the use of the same conjunctive or disjunctive combinator for all calculations, the analyst gets to select the appropriate one. A complex evidential assertion may contain a mixture of combinators and multiple pieces of evidence.
2. *Evidence Discounting:* Given that evidence is likely to be ambiguous or incomplete, we do not want to be forced to treat all evidence as equally trustworthy, whether that piece of evidence is a primary source, or some other analyst's assessment of evidence. Therefore, we provide an explicit discounting operator.
3. *Evidence Naming:* Evidential assertions can be named, so that other analysts can refer to it, and treat it as a unit. In other words, the result of A's analysis becomes a single, named piece of evidence that other analysts can incorporate into their analyses.
4. *Multiple Assertions:* Not all of the evidence that an analyst is considering needs to be combined in one assertion. Instead, analysts can make a number of evidential assertions, specifying their relative weights, giving them the ability to create complex and nuanced narratives about how evidence should be combined.
5. *Evidential Consistency:* One of our design principles stems (inadvertently) from Zadeh's notorious critique [14] of the Dempster-Shafer approach. It was a contrived example, and Haenni addressed this critique [4] by pointing out that more realistic models of the scenario would lead to reasonable outcomes.

We drew the additional conclusion that it would be very desirable to be able to make explicit assertions about evidential consistency. An analyst should be able to state how important it is to their analysis that two or more pieces of evidence be consistent with each other.

6. *Reduction Modes:* We make explicit whether our calculations are taking place in a 'closed' universe in which we believe that we are considering all of the relevant possible worlds, and the 'open' universe which also contains conclusions corresponding to "none of the above" (that is, the actual state of affairs lives outside the current enumeration of possible worlds). Making this distinction visible to an analyst allows them to assess whether a segment of their current analysis should be redone with a wider set of possible worlds (i.e., a more diverse set of initial assumptions).

In the next two sections, we'll build up the basic machinery and then the overall evaluation strategies for our approach that incorporates these design principles. This will be followed by a couple of illustrative examples, and then our conclusions and thoughts on future work.

3   Basic Machinery

All evaluation of evidence is done with respect to a specific frame of discernment Ω where $\Omega = (W_1, W_2, \ldots W_n)$, a finite set of mutually exclusive possible worlds W_i. Each frame of discernment is typed: Ω^T where the choices for the type T are "open" and "closed". The definitional relationship between an open world $\Omega^{T=\mathcal{O}}$ and its associated closed world $\Omega^{T=\mathcal{C}}$ is simply $\mathcal{P}(\Omega^{T=\mathcal{O}}) - \emptyset \equiv \mathcal{P}(\Omega^{T=\mathcal{C}})$ (where normalization is done in the usual way).

Given a typed frame of discernment Ω^T, we define a basic belief assignment (*bba*) as a mapping m from $\mathcal{P}(\Omega^T)$ to the interval $[0,1]$, under the constraint $\sum_{A \subseteq \Omega^T} m(A) = 1$. In practice, we care only about the so-called focal elements of this mapping - those pairs (s_i, m_i) where $s_i \subset \Omega^T$ and $m_i > 0$. Therefore, we can think of a *bba* as a tuple consisting a list of focal pairs (s_i, m_i) along with the typed frame of discernment Ω^T:

$$\text{bba} = ([(s_1, m_1), (s_2, m_2), \ldots (s_k, m_k)], \ \Omega^T)$$

$$\text{where } \forall i \in [1, k] : s_i \in \mathcal{P}(\Omega^T), m_i \in (0, 1], \sum m_i = 1$$

A *bba* along with its associated frame of discernment is the simplest form of evidence; to construct more complex evidential assertions, we define an assertion as an evidence tree. Every leaf of the evidence tree is a *bba*; the other nodes of the trees are one of the following operators:

1. *Discounting:* Just as in the TBM, the discounting operator $\mathcal{D}$ takes a *bba* and a discount factor f, and applies f to all the focal masses in the *bba*, with the exception of the set Ω, which gets all the "extra" mass so that $\sum m_i = 1$ after discounting.

2. *Named Lookup:* We can assign any evidence tree a unique name, which is stored in an 'evidence base'. This operator takes a name as argument, and returns the corresponding evidence tree from the evidence base. This feature allows for both reuse of evidence trees, and sharing among analysts.

3. *Binary Operators:* We provide conjunctive and disjunctive operators, $\oslash$ and $\oslash$. These work in the usual way [2], involving set intersections and set unions, respectively. These operations are defined for both open and closed frames of discernment (additional details below).

4. *Negation:* Given that we've defined binary operators roughly corresponding to "and" and "or", it seems natural to want to define a "not" operator $\neg$, in analogy with binary expressions [15]. Further justification for this operator is the fact that the domain of cyberspace can involve deception; we may be working with a piece of evidence that we do not simply want to discount completely, but rather take the opposite of it. The $\neg$ operator works on a *bba* as follows: we replace every s_i that appears in a (s_i, m_i) pair of the *bba* with its set complement so that the negated *bba* is the pair $(s_i^{\complement}, m_i)$.

Reduction of an evidence tree results in a bba, but before we can actually carry out that reduction, we need to specify one more thing – a reduction mode. This is necessary because when using a binary operator to evaluate $bba_1 \oslash bba_2$ or $bba_1 \oslash bba_2$, we need to take into account the types of $\Omega_1^{\mathcal{T}}$ and $\Omega_2^{\mathcal{T}}$ when calculating the type of the resultant frame of discernment.

We define two reduction modes, a *conservative* mode, and an *inclusive* mode. The conservative mode favors a closed universe over an open universe, and the inclusive mode favors an open universe over a closed one. The rules are simple: in conservative mode, iff either of the two input frames is closed, then the resultant frame is closed. In inclusive mode, iff either input frame is open, then the resultant frame is open.

The two reduction modes and discernment types are important because they tell us how to proceed when using binary operators on frames of discernment that aren't the same. An example will help to make this clearer. Suppose we have two basic belief assignments, the first one from a closed world {a,b,c}, and the second from the open world {a,b,e}:

$$\text{bba}_1 = ([(\{a\}, .5), (\{a,b\}, .3), (\{a,b,c\}, .2)], \Omega_1^{\mathcal{T}=\mathcal{C}} = \{a,b,c\})$$
$$\text{bba}_2 = ([(\{a,b\}, .6), (\{a,b,e\}, .4)], \Omega_2^{\mathcal{T}=\mathcal{O}} = \{a,b,e\})$$

We wish to combine these two pieces of evidence using the $\oslash$ operator in the conservative mode. First of all, since the first frame of discernment is closed, and we're operating in the conservative mode, we know that the resultant frame of discernment will be closed and be contain only the possible worlds that appear in the first frame of discernment: $\Omega_r^{\mathcal{T}=\mathcal{C}} = \{a,b,c\})$. The second belief assignment is from an open world, however, and therefore must be extended to account for the fact that world c (from the first belief assignment) is a possible world that thus far has been inaccessible to it. This extension operation is done by simply adding world c to all the sets in bba$_2$, leaving the mass values the same:

$$\text{bba}_2 = ([(\{a,b,c\}, .6), (\{a,b,c,e\}, .4)], \Omega_2^{\mathcal{T}=\mathcal{O}} = \{a,b,c,e\})$$

Now the two belief assignments can be combined using the usual Dempster-Shafer combination rule, with the resultant belief assignment as follows:

$$\text{bba}_r = ([(\{a\}, .38), (\{a,b\}, .12), (\{a,c\}, .3), (\{a,b,c\}, .2)], \Omega_r^{\mathcal{T}=\mathcal{C}} = \{a,b,c\})$$

4   Multiple Assertions and Decisions

The previous section has discussed how to reduce a single evidence tree (one assertion); we now discuss how to handle a sequence of assertions. Our approach is consistent with the discussion of the TBM in [10], in which a distinction is made between the "credal" and "pignistic" levels of analysis. The TBM defines the *Pignistic transformation*, $\mathbb{P}$, that takes a bba as argument, and induces a probability distribution over the singleton members (and potentially $\emptyset$ too, if $\Omega^{\mathcal{T}=\mathcal{O}}$) that can inform a subsequent decision:

$$\mathbb{P}(\text{bba}) = [(s_1, m_1), (s_2, m_2), \ldots (s_k, m_k)]$$
$$\text{where } \forall i \in [1, k] : s_i \in \mathcal{P}(\Omega^{\mathcal{T}}), |s_i| = 1 \text{ or } s_i = \emptyset, m_i \in (0, 1], \sum m_i = 1$$

An analyst makes a sequence of assertions, each assertion being an evidence tree, bba_i. Each assertion is assigned a nonnegative weight w_i by the analyst (with arbitrary scaling, since the result will be normalized in the end). These pairs are collected in a "evidence forest" vector. Our strategy is to reduce the vector element by element, giving us the flexibility to choose the relative weights applied to each assertion, instead of aggregating assertions first before reduction, and being forced to choose the semantics of a specific binary operator such as $\oslash$ or $\obslash$ to combine all of the assertions. We start with the evidence forest vector $\mathcal{F}$:

$$\mathcal{F} = [(bba_1, w_1), (bba_2, w_2), \ldots (bba_k, w_k)]$$

Reduction of this vector begins with the piecewise application of $\mathbb{P}$:

$$\mathbb{P}(\mathcal{F}) = [(\mathbb{P}(bba_1), w_1), (\mathbb{P}(bba_2), w_2), \ldots (\mathbb{P}(bba_k), w_k)]$$

We further reduce each vector element $\mathbb{P}(\mathcal{F})$ by scalar multiplication with w_i:

$$\mathbb{P}(\text{bba}_j) \cdot w_j = [(s_{j1}, m_{j1} \cdot w_j), (s_{j2}, m_{j2} \cdot w_j), \ldots (s_{jk}, m_{jk} \cdot w_j)]$$

The final reduction step is to look across all the elements of the vectors, collecting like s-terms, and summing their masses, normalizing the sum to be 1. This gives us the resultant distribution, which we denote as $\mathcal{R}(\mathcal{F})$.

The system also keeps track of two measures pertaining to the quality of the evidence. If not all evidence is assessed in closed universes, then we can track the value of the mass of the empty set $m(\emptyset)$ as our first metric. Recall that the semantics of $\emptyset$ is the measure of how likely the actual state of affairs lives outside the current enumeration of possible worlds. Analysts can set a threshold τ for the size of $m(\emptyset)$; if $m(\emptyset) > \tau$, then the system reports that the analysis ought to be redone under different assumptions. The second metric involves measuring evidential inequality through a measure such as the Gini coefficient [3]. The idea here is to again set a threshold: If the existing evidence is too equally spread out across too many hypotheses, then the analysis might be too inconclusive to be useful.

5   Illustrative Examples

Here are a couple of examples that illustrate the approach we've described in the previous sections, inspired by Zadeh's example [14].

Let t = tumor, f = flu, and m = meningitis. There are two doctors, each of whom is making a diagnosis in the closed universe $\Omega^{T=C} = \{\text{m,t,f}\}^{T=C}$. Doctor 1 is virtually certain that it is a tumor, with a very slight chance of meningitis. Doctor 2 is equally certain that it is a case of flu, with a very slight chance of meningitis. We represent these assertions by bba_1 and bba_2:

$$\text{bba}_1 = ([(\text{t}, .99), (\text{m}, .01)], \Omega^{T=C})$$
$$\text{bba}_2 = ([(\text{f}, .99), (\text{m}, .01)], \Omega^{T=C})$$

Now consider two additional medical personnel also weighing in with a diagnosis:

Analyst 1: The first analyst makes two assertions: first, it is extremely important that the final diagnosis be consistent with the evidence from the two doctors, and secondly, that there is some evidence (say, with a confidence of .7) for a new mystery disease d that the doctors weren't able to run tests against, with new universe $\Omega_1^{T=C} = \{\text{m,t,f,d}\}^{T=C}$. The analyst represents these two assertions as follows:

$$\text{bba}_3 = (\text{bba}_1 \oslash \text{bba}_2)$$
$$\text{bba}_4 = ([(\text{d}, .7), (\{\text{m,t,f,d}\}, .3)], \Omega_1^{T=C})$$

Analyst 1 decides to assign these two assertions relative weights of 95 and 30, respectively (Analyst 1 uses an arbitrary assertion weighting scale from 1 to 100) to generate an evidence forest $\mathcal{F}_1$ for evaluation:

$$\mathcal{F}_1 = [(\text{bba}_3, 95), (\text{bba}_4, 30)]$$

Analyst 1 now calculates $\mathcal{R}(\mathcal{F}_1)$ using the conservative evaluation mode:

$$\mathcal{R}(\mathcal{F}_1) = [(m, .78), (d, .19), (f, .02), (t, .02)]$$

For Analyst 1, meningitis is clearly the most likely candidate, with disease d in solid second place. There is very little support for either flu or tumor.

Analyst 2: The second analyst is somewhat skeptical about doctors and their diagnoses. She believes, in fact, that Doctor 1 is a fool, and you cannot go too far wrong by placing a bet on the opposite of anything he recommends. She has more confidence in Doctor 2, but generally discounts the confidence level in Doctor 2's diagnoses by about 25 percent. Analyst 2 also believes that the real culprit is possibly communicable disease e, or perhaps one of mystery disease d or e, even though an outbreak of either hasn't been observed in the region (this is represented by assertion bba$_7$)), with new universe $\Omega_2^{T=O} = \{m,t,f,d,e\}^{T=O}$. Finally, Analyst 2 makes a final assertion combining bba$_4$ (generated by Analyst 1) with bba$_7$.

$$bba_5 = (\neg(bba\,1))$$
$$bba_6 = (\mathcal{D}(bba_2, .25))$$
$$bba_7 = ([(e, .6), (\{d,e\}, .3), (\{m,t,f,d,e\}, .1)], \Omega_2^{T=O}))$$
$$bba_8 = (bba_4 \otimes bba_7)$$

Analyst 2 decides to assign her four assertions relative weights of .55, .80, and .40, and .70 (Analyst 2 uses a weighting scale in the interval (0,1]) in generating evidence forest $\mathcal{F}_2$ for evaluation:

$$\mathcal{F}_2 = [(bba_5, .55), (bba_6, .80), (bba_7, .40), (bba_8, .70)]$$

Analyst 2 prefers to employ the inclusive evaluation mode when calculating $\mathcal{R}(\mathcal{F}_2)$. The result is the following:

$$\mathcal{R}(\mathcal{F}_2) = [(f, .41), (e, .24), (m, .16), (d, .14), (t, .05)]$$

For Analyst 2, flu is the most likely candidate, although the evidence is spread out more equally among the possibilities than in the previous analysis. A tumor is the least likely possibility, mostly due to *bba$_5$* and its negation of *bba$_1$*.

6   Conclusions and Future Work

This paper has described our approach to designing an evidence-based modeling tool that enables the expression of complex evidential assertions across teams of analysts. Initial reactions from domain experts to our approach have been positive: they have told us that our explicit modeling of epistemic uncertainty through belief functions should be a useful addition to their current suite of tools for reasoning under uncertainty. It is also worth noting that even though this work was done in a cyber threat domain, our approach is not domain-specific and therefore could be applied in other domains where multiple analysts are sharing and assessing evidential assertions.

The capabilities described in this paper have been implemented as a stand-alone software module, but we do not consider the language to be complete. The following are extensions that we intend to pursue:

1. *Binary Operators:* We currently implement two binary operators ⊘ and ⊙, and we're aware that many more have been defined (for example, as described in [2,7,13]). We intend to implement additional binary operators, keeping in mind that there is a trade-off involved: more operators provides additional expressiveness, but at the cost of making the language less intuitive, and therefore potentially less useful as a modeling tool.

2. *Decision Transforms:* We currently use the $\mathbb{P}$ function to transform evidence at the credal level into the decision level. There are other rules that we could have used, such as those in [12], and in the future, we want to offer analysts multiple transform methods.

3. *Correlations:* A key requirement in belief function analysis is that the pieces of evidence are evidentially independent. In practice, though, it is common for two pieces of evidence to be correlated, in the sense that higher confidence in one would cause an analyst to believe the other as more plausible. Lifschitz and colleagues developed a "correlation calculus" in the context of a deductive AI challenge [5]; we intend to develop a "correlation combinator" to express these situations in the context of a belief function analysis.

4. *Fixed Point Analysis:* The current implementation doesn't prevent the undesirable mutual recursion that would result from a situation such as "A's analysis depends on the results of B's analysis, and B's analysis depends the results from A's analysis" - analysts need to manually ensure that this isn't taking place. However, in analogy to how mutual recursion is handled in other programming languages [6], we will implement a mathematically-based "fixed point" solution that automatically resolves the mutual recursions.

During the design process, we were influenced by Box's famous quip that "all models are wrong, but some are useful" [1], and this remains our design objective.

References

1. Box, G.: Science and statistics. J. Am. Stat. Assoc. **71**, 791–799 (1976)
2. Denoeux, T.: Conjunctive and disjunctive combination of belief functions induced by non distinct bodies of evidence. Artif. Intell. **172**, 234–264 (2008)
3. Gini, C.: On the measure of concentration with special reference to income and statistics. Colorado College Publication, General Series No. 208, pp. 73–79 (1936)
4. Haenni, R.: Shedding new light on Zadeh's criticism of Dempter's rule of combination. In: FUSION 2005, 8th International Conference on Information Fusion, vol. 2, pp. 879–884, Philadelphia, USA (2005)
5. Bailey, D., Harrison, A., Lierler, Y., Lifschitz, V., Michael, J.: The Winograd schema challenge and reasoning about correlation. Working Notes of the Symposium on Logical Formalizations of Commonsense Reasoning, AAAI Press (2015)
6. Peyton Jones, S.: The Implementation of Functional Programming. Prentice Hall International, Englewood Cliffs (1987)
7. Sentz, K., Ferson, S.: Combination of evidence in Dempster-Shafer Theory. Technical report, SANDIA National Laboratories (2002)
8. Shafer, G.: A Mathematical Theory of Evidence. Princeton University Press, New Jersey (1976)

9. Smets, P.: The combination of evidence in the transferable belief model. IEEE Pattern Anal. Mach. Intell. **12**, 447–458 (1990)

10. Smets, P., Kennes, R.: The transferable belief model. Artif. Intell. **66**, 191–234 (1994)

11. Srivastava, R.: Decision making under ambiguity: a belief-function perspective. Arch. Control Sci. **6 (XLII)**(1–2), 5–27 (1997)

12. Strat, T.: Decision analysis using belief functions. Int. J. Approx. Reason. **4**(5), 391–417 (1990)

13. Yager, R.: On the Dempster-Shafer framework and new combination rules. Inf. Sci. **41**, 93–137 (1987)

14. Zadeh, L.: Review of Shafer's "A Mathematical Theory of Evidence". AI Mag. **5**, 81–83 (1984)

15. Dubois, D., Prade, H.: A set-theoretic view of belief functions: logical operators and approximations by fuzzy sets. Int. J. Gen Syst **12**, 193–226 (1986)

A New ER-MCDA Mapping
for Decision-Making Based on Imperfect
Information

Simon Carladous[1,2,4]([✉]), Jean-Marc Tacnet[1], Jean Dezert[3],
Guillaume Dupouy[1], and Mireille Batton-Hubert[4]

[1] Université Grenoble Alpes, Irstea, UR ETGR, 2 rue de la Papeterie-BP76,
38402 St-Martin-d'Hères, France
{simon.carladous,jean-marc.tacnet,guillaume.dupouy}@irstea.fr
[2] AgroParisTech, 19 avenue du Maine, 75732 Paris, France
[3] The French Aerospace Lab, 91761 Palaiseau, France
jean.dezert@onera.fr
[4] ENSMSE - DEMO, 29, rue Ponchardier, 42100 Saint-Etienne, France
mbatton@emse.fr

Abstract. The Evidential Reasoning for Multi Criteria Decision Analysis (ER-MCDA) is based on a mapping process transforming a possibility
distribution into a Bayesian basic belief assignment (BBA) related to a
qualitative frame of discernement (FoD). Each element of the FoD is a
fuzzy set. A new improved mapping method is proposed to get a final
potentially non-Bayesian BBA on the FoD. We apply it to assess the
stability of protective check dams against torrential floods given their
imprecise scouring rate.

Keywords: Fuzzy sets · Possibility theory · Belief functions · Mapping ·
ER-MCDA

1 Introduction

Evidential Reasoning for Multi-Criteria Decision-Analysis (ER-MCDA) is a
multi-criteria decision method which is able to take into account both imperfect
evaluation of quantitative and qualitative criteria and multiple more or less reliable sources [1]. The principle is first to represent imperfect evaluation of each
criterion through a possibility distribution. As it uses fusion, those evaluations
must be transformed into a common Frame of Discernment (FoD). Therefore, a
mass of belief is assigned to consonant intervals with a confidence level which
correspond to the possibility distribution. The mapping process establishes the
link between the basic belief assignment BBA $m(\cdot)$ on quantitative intervals
with a BBA in the common FoD. It can be interpreted as a function from the
possibility distribution to a BBA on the common FoD. The initial principle of
mapping is based on a geometrical projection. It induces several issues such as its

© Springer International Publishing Switzerland 2016
J. Vejnarová and V. Kratochvíl (Eds.): BELIEF 2016, LNAI 9861, pp. 46–55, 2016.
DOI: 10.1007/978-3-319-45559-4_5

theoretical justification but also its limited ability to provide positive masses of belief on singletons only. Our approach aims at improving this mapping process.

We consider an application case where ER-MCDA is used to assess the stability (high, medium, low) of check dams against torrential risk in mountains. This evaluation is based on several criteria, such as the scouring rate (expressed in percentage) which is a damageable loss of foundation support[1] [2]. In this application context, the Fig. 1 shows how an expert often provides an imperfect evaluation of check dam stability according to its foundation's scouring rate. Indeed, a precise and direct measure would be somewhere too dangerous.

Upstream view

Scouring

Question: What is the stability level of this check dam between 'high', 'medium', and 'low'?

Lateral view

- **Expert answer - step 1**: It depends on its foundation's scouring rate. If it is between 0% and 30%, it is completely 'high'. If it is between 50% and 60%, it is completely 'medium'. If it is between 70% and 100%, it is completely 'low'.

- **Expert answer - step 2**: It is too dangerous to measure the scouring rate precisely. I am certain it is between 40 and 60 %. I am not sure at all, but I think it is 50%.

Expert

- **Expert answer - step 3**: I think this check dam's stability is 'medium' but it could be 'medium' or 'high'. I am sure it is not 'low'.

Fig. 1. A real example of imperfect evaluation of check dam stability according to its foundation's scouring rate.

In this paper, our scope is not to develop a theoretical proof of the mapping process but to highlight some theoretical issues to propose another method. In Sect. 2, we briefly recall some basics of fuzzy sets, possibility and belief function

---

[1] Scouring is a process due to which the particles of the soil or rock under the check dam's foundation gets eroded and removed over a certain depth called scour depth and over the foundation area called scouring rate. Scouring often occurs in torrent because of the velocity and energy of the flowing in steep slopes.

theories. We introduce the classical transformation and we propose a new method in Sect. 3. In Sect. 4, we compare the two methods on a sample decision context of our application case.

2 Fuzzy Sets, Possibility and Belief Function Theories

In the fuzzy set theory [4], U is the universe of discourse of individual elements u. μ_A is the membership function which associates each $u \in U$ to the class (fuzzy set) A with the grade of membership $\mu_A(u) \in [0,1]$. A fuzzy set A is normal when there is an element $u \in U$ such as $\mu_A(u) = 1$. We use trapezoidal functions defined by the quadruplet $\{a, b, c, d\}$ (Eq. (1), Fig. 2) given their simplicity to approximate fuzzy intervals [5]. Intervals $[a, d]$ and $[b, c]$ are respectively the fuzzy set's support ($supp_A$) and its core (A^c) [5]. We denote $\bar{A}$ the complement of A for $u \in U$, defined by the membership function $\mu_{\bar{A}}$ of the Eq. (2) and shown in the Fig. 2. Given $\mu_B \neq \mu_A$ which represents another fuzzy set B for $u \in U$, the membership function $\mu_{A \cup B}$ of the Eq. (3) represents the union of A and B while $\mu_{A \cap B}$ of the Eq. (4) represents their intersection [4] (see Fig. 2).

$$\mu_{\bar{A}}(u) \triangleq 1 - \mu_A(u), u \in U \tag{2}$$

$$\mu_A(u) \triangleq \begin{cases} 0 & \text{if } u \notin supp_A \\ \frac{u-a}{b-a} & \text{if } u \in [a, b] \\ 1 & \text{if } u \in A^c \\ \frac{u-d}{c-d} & \text{if } u \in [c, d] \end{cases} \tag{1}$$

$$\mu_{A \cup B}(u) \triangleq \max_{u \in U}(\mu_A(u), \mu_B(u)) \tag{3}$$

$$\mu_{A \cap B}(u) \triangleq \min_{u \in U}(\mu_A(u), \mu_B(u)) \tag{4}$$

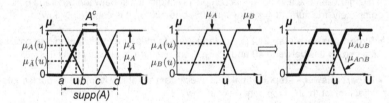

Fig. 2. Given U, trapezoidal fuzzy sets A, $\bar{A}$, $A \cup B$ and $A \cap B$.

In the possibility theory framework [6], F is the fuzzy set of possible values of $u \in U$. The possibility distribution π is given by $\mu_F(u) \triangleq \pi(u) \in [0,1]$ also defined by a quadruplet $\{a, b, c, d\}$ [7]. Given X a subset of U and $\bar{X}$ its complement, the possibility measure is $\Pi(X) \triangleq \sup_{u \in X} \pi(u)$ [6] and the necessity is [8] $N(X) \triangleq 1 - \Pi(\bar{X}), \forall X, \bar{X} \subseteq U$ as shown in the Fig. 3. Considering the fuzzy set μ_A and a possibility distribution μ_F, the Eq. (5) gives the possibility measure of A [6].

Considering F as a nested family of α-cuts $\{F_\alpha | \alpha \in (0,1]\}$, one has $F_\alpha \triangleq \{u | \mu_F(u) \geqslant \alpha\}$ [5]. Viewing F_α as a uniformly distributed random set from $\alpha \in (0,1]$ to $F_\alpha \subseteq U$, one has $\mu_F(u) \triangleq \int_0^1 \mu_{F_\alpha}(u)\mathrm{d}\alpha$. Considering a finite nested family of subsets $\{F_{\alpha_1} = \left]u_{\alpha_1}^-; u_{\alpha_1}^+\right[\subseteq \ldots \subseteq F_{\alpha_l} = \left]u_{\alpha_{l_{\max}}}^-; u_{\alpha_{l_{\max}}}^+\right[\}$, the set $\{\alpha_1 > \ldots > \alpha_l > \ldots > \alpha_{l_{\max}}\}$ and $m_l \triangleq \alpha_l - \alpha_{l+1} \in [0,1]$ with $\alpha_{l+1} = 0$ (Fig. 3), one has the Eq. (6).

$$\Pi(A) \triangleq \sup_{u \in U} \mu_{A \cap F}(u) \qquad (5)$$

$$\pi(u) \triangleq \sum_{u \in F_{\alpha_l}} m_l \qquad (6)$$

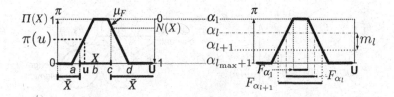

Fig. 3. Possibility distribution, possibility and necessity measures, α-cuts.

In the belief function theory, a basic belief assignment (BBA), or mass of belief $m(\cdot)$, represents the imperfect knowledge of a body of evidence (or source) on a given FoD denoted as $\Theta = \{\theta_1, \theta_2, \ldots, \theta_q\}$. In the classical Shafer's model [9], all elements $\theta_k, k = 1, \ldots, n$ are assumed exhaustive and mutually exclusive. The powerset 2^Θ is the set of all subsets of Θ, empty set $\emptyset$ included. For $X \in 2^\Theta$, we denote $\bar{X} \subseteq \Theta$ its complement. For each source, the mass function $m(\cdot) : 2^\Theta \to [0,1]$ must satisfy $m(\emptyset) = 0$, and $\sum_{X \subseteq \Theta} m(X) = 1, \forall X \neq \emptyset \in 2^\Theta$. Considering the universe of discourse U as the FoD and assuming a normal fuzzy set F, $m(\cdot)$ is extracted considering $F_{\alpha_l} \in 2^U, l = 1, \ldots, l_{\max}$.

Given $m(\cdot)$ on 2^Θ, the belief of the hypothesis $Y \in 2^\Theta$ is defined by $Bel(Y) \triangleq \sum_{X \subseteq Y | X \in 2^\Theta} m(X)$. Its plausibility is defined by $Pl(Y) \triangleq \sum_{X \cap Y \neq \emptyset | X \in 2^\Theta} m(X)$ [10]. Considering that the universe of discourse U is the FoD Θ, the plausibility measure $Pl(X)$ is a possibility measure $\Pi(X), \forall X \subseteq \Theta = U$ [7].

Shafer's assumption of exhaustivity of the FoD means that it is considered as a "closed-world" (*c.w.*). In some practical problems, this assumption is too strict and it is more convenient to consider the original FoD as an "open-world" (*o.w.*). Dealing with it can be done in two manners as shown in the Fig. 4.

1. In Smets' Transferable Belief Model (TBM) [11], $\Theta^{o.w.} \triangleq \{\theta_1, \ldots, \theta_q\}$ and $\emptyset = \bar{\Theta}^{o.w.}$. One has $\sum_{X \in 2^\Theta} m(X) = 1$, and one allows $m(\emptyset) \geqslant 0$.
2. In Yager's approach [12], the open-world is closed by an hedge element θ^c, so that $\Theta^{c.w.} \triangleq \Theta^{o.w.} \cup \{\theta^c\}$. Setting $m^{c.w.}(\theta^c) = 0$ and $m^{c.w.}(\emptyset) = 0$, one has $Bel^{c.w.}(A) = 0$ and $m^{c.w.}(A) = 0$ for each subset $A \subseteq \Theta^{o.w.}$. For each $X \subseteq \Theta^{c.w.}$, one computes $Bel^{c.w.}(X)$ and $m^{c.w.}(X)$ in the Eqs. (7) and (8).

$$Bel^{c.w.}(X) \triangleq \begin{cases} 0 & \text{if } X = A \subseteq \Theta^{o.w.} \subset \Theta^{c.w.} \\ 1 - Pl^{c.w.}(\bar{X}) & \text{if } X = A \cup \theta^c \subseteq \Theta^{c.w.} \end{cases} \quad (7)$$

$$m^{c.w.}(X) \triangleq \begin{cases} 0 & \text{if } X = A \subseteq \Theta^{o.w.} \subset \Theta^{c.w.} \\ 0 & \text{if } X = \theta^c \subset \Theta^{c.w.} \\ \sum_{Y \subseteq A}(-1)^{|A-Y|}Bel^{c.w.}(Y \cup \theta^c) & \text{if } X = A \cup \theta^c \subseteq \Theta^{c.w.} \end{cases} \quad (8)$$

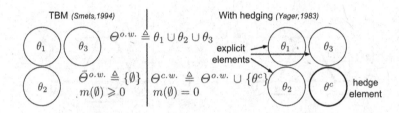

Fig. 4. TBM and hedging models under an "open-world" with exclusivity, for $q = 3$.

3   Transforming Possibility Distributions to BBAs on Θ

The FoD $\Theta = \{\theta_1, \ldots, \theta_q\}$ of decision gathers q qualitative labels. For each criterion, scoring results from an evaluation scale which is the specific universe of discourse U. To take into account its imprecise and uncertain evaluation, a possibility distribution $\pi : U \to [0,1]$ is given by the expert according to Eq. (6). To combine all the possibility distributions provided by several sources for several criteria, each one must be represented by a BBA $m^\Theta(\cdot)$ established on 2^Θ for the common FoD Θ as shown in the Fig. 5.

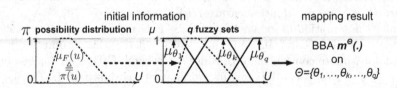

Fig. 5. The general principle and objective of the mapping process.

A mapping model [1] is therefore based on q membership functions $\mu_{\theta_k}: U \to [0,1]$ for $k = 1, \ldots, q$ according to Eq. (1), corresponding to each θ_k of the FoD. The construction of the q fuzzy sets respects the condition $\sum_{k=1}^q \mu_{\theta_k} \leqslant 1$

for mutual exclusivity: if an element $u^\star \in U$ totally belongs to a label θ_k $(\mu_{\theta_k}(u^\star) = 1, k \in [1,q])$, it cannot partially belongs to another label of Θ $(\mu_{\theta_m}(u^\star) = 0, m \neq k \in [1,q])$. By construction, there is at least $u^\star \in U$ for which $\mu_{\Theta=\cup\{\theta_k | k \in [1,q]\}}(u^\star) \leqslant 1$: it corresponds to an "open-world" assumption.

3.1 Classical Transformation

Given the possibility distribution π and the q functions μ_{θ_k} for $k = 1, \ldots, q$, the classical mapping [1] consists of the three following steps (shown in Fig. 6):

1. Given $l_{\max}$ α-cuts with $F_{\alpha_l} \in 2^U, l = 1, \ldots, l_{\max}$, $m^U(\cdot)$ is extracted for the FoD U from π as shown in Fig. 3. Each F_{α_l} is a focal element and its corresponding mass is denoted $m^U(F_{\alpha_l})$. The BBA $m^U(\cdot)$ thus represents the imperfect evaluation of a quantitative or qualitative evaluation of $u \in U$. Each focal element is an interval which represents evaluation imprecision. Each mass of an interval takes into account the confidence level or uncertainty. By definition of $m^U(\cdot)$, one has $\sum_{l=1}^{l_{\max}} m^U(F_{\alpha_l}) = 1$.

2. For each $F_{\alpha_l} =]u_{\alpha_l}^-; u_{\alpha_l}^+[, l = 1, \ldots, l_{\max}$, the area A_{k_l} under each curve μ_{θ_k} is given by $A_{k_l} \triangleq \int_{u_{\alpha_l}^-}^{u_{\alpha_l}^+} \mu_{\theta_k}(u)du$. One has $A_l \triangleq \sum_{k=1}^{q} A_{k_l}$ and computes the mass $m_l^\Theta(\theta_k) \triangleq \frac{A_{k_l}}{A_l}$ for each F_{α_l} and each θ_k. Thus, by definition of A_l, one has $\sum_{k=1}^{q} m_l^\Theta(\theta_k) = 1$.

3. One then builds the Bayesian[2] BBA $m^\Theta(\cdot)$ on 2^Θ for the FoD $\Theta = \{\theta_1, \theta_2, \ldots, \theta_q\}$ with $m^\Theta(\theta_k) \triangleq \sum_{l=1}^{l_{\max}} m^U(F_{\alpha_l}) \times m_l^\Theta(\theta_k), k = 1, \ldots, q$. This equation can be justified as follows.
   From the two previous points, one has $\sum_{k=1}^{q} m_l^\Theta(\theta_k) \times \sum_{l=1}^{l_{\max}} m^U(F_{\alpha_l}) = 1$. Thus $\sum_{k=1}^{q} \sum_{l=1}^{l_{\max}} m_l^\Theta(\theta_k) \times m^U(F_{\alpha_l}) = 1$. By definition, $\sum_{k=1}^{q} m^\Theta(\theta_k) = 1$. As a consequence, $m^\Theta(\theta_k) \triangleq \sum_{l=1}^{l_{\max}} m^U(F_{\alpha_l}) \times m_l^\Theta(\theta_k), k = 1, \ldots, q$.

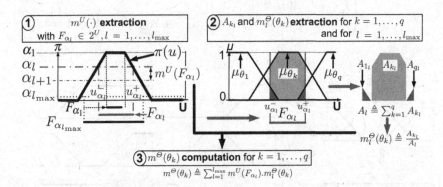

Fig. 6. Steps of the ER-MCDA's classical mapping process: α-cuts choice, BBA $m^U(\cdot)$ calculation, and projection on the mapping model to get a final BBA $m^\Theta(\cdot)$.

---

[2] The focal elements of a Bayesian BBA are only singletons of 2^Θ.

This principle of simple geometric transformation is however not fully satisfying since it only assigns BBAs to singletons and arbitrarily shares a BBA on several elements of the FoD regardless of partial or total ignorance. Moreover, from a practical point of view, this classical method needs an arbitrary setting of the value of l_{max} but also of all the values of α_l. That is why, it was first proposed that experts give their imprecise evaluation through intervals with a confidence level. It corresponds to a possibility distribution after α-cut, each α_l being the confidence level given by the expert [1]. Nevertheless, in practice, we think that it is easier to give only the quadruplet $\{a, b, c, d\}$ of Fig. 3 than several intervals with a confidence level.

3.2 New Transformation

Our new method is based on four steps to get a BBA $m^\Theta(\cdot)$ on all focal elements $X \in 2^\Theta$ and not only on singletons of $\Theta = \{\theta_1, \ldots, \theta_k, \ldots, \theta_q\}$. Given the construction of the q fuzzy sets, it assumes mutual exclusivity without exhaustivity. Thereafter we detail the method using Yager's model with hedging even if a similar approach has been also studied using the TBM. One thus considers $\Theta^{o.w.} = \{\theta_1, \ldots, \theta_k, \ldots, \theta_q\}$ and $\Theta^{c.w.} = \Theta^{o.w.} \cup \{\theta^c\}$. Different steps are:

1. Construction of $2q - 1$ functions $\mu_{A \cup \theta^c}^{c.w.}$ for all $A \neq \emptyset \subseteq \Theta^{o.w.}$ (see Fig. 7): given q functions $\mu_{\theta_k}^{o.w.} : U \to [0, 1]$ for $k = 1, \ldots, q$, the Eq. (3) gives the $2^q - 1$ functions $\mu_A^{o.w.} : U \to [0, 1]$. One uses the Eq. (9) to close the world and get the $2^q - 1$ functions $\mu_{A \cup \theta^c}^{c.w.} : U \to [0, 1]$.

$$
\mu_{A \cup \theta^c}^{c.w.}(u) \triangleq
\begin{cases}
1 & \text{if } \mu_A^{o.w.}(u) = 1 \\
\mu_A^{o.w.}(u) & \text{if } \mu_A^{o.w.}(u) < 1 \\
& \text{and if } \sum_{i=1}^{2^q} \mu_{Y_i}^{o.w.}(u) > 0, Y_i \subseteq \Theta^{o.w.}, Y_i \cap A = \emptyset \\
1 & \text{if } \mu_A^{o.w.}(u) < 1 \\
& \text{and if } \sum_{i=1}^{2^q} \mu_{Y_i}^{o.w.}(u) = 0, Y_i \subseteq \Theta^{o.w.}, Y_i \cap A = \emptyset
\end{cases}
\tag{9}
$$

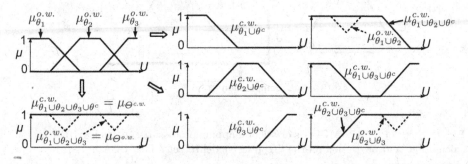

Fig. 7. Step 1 of the new mapping for $q = 3$.

2. The Eq. (2) gives the $2^q - 1$ functions $\mu_{\overline{A \cup \theta^c}}^{c.w.} : U \to [0,1]$. Given π (or μ_F), the Eq. (5) gives the possibility measures $\Pi^{c.w.} \cdot (\overline{A \cup \theta^c}) \triangleq \sup_{u \in U} \mu_{\overline{A \cup \theta^c} \cap F}$, $\forall A \in 2^{\Theta^{o.w.}} - \{\emptyset\}$ corresponding to the plausibility measures $Pl^{c.w.} \cdot (\overline{A \cup \theta^c})$.
3. The Eq. (7) first provides $Bel^{c.w.} \cdot (\cdot)$. The Eq. (8) then gives $m^{c.w.} \cdot (\cdot)$ on $2^{\Theta^{o.w.}}$.

4   Application to the Scouring Rate of a Check Dam

In practice, the check dam stability is assessed through qualitative labels of the FoD $\Theta = \{\theta_1 = \text{High}, \theta_2 = \text{Medium}, \theta_3 = \text{Low}\}$ [13]. The lower is the scouring rate, the higher is check dam structural stability. The FoD cardinality $|\Theta|$ is here $q = 3$. For each check dam, the choice of the stability label notably depends on the scouring rate u of its foundation, with u a continuous value in $U = [0\,\%, 100\,\%]$. μ_{θ_k} is the membership function linking the scouring rate $u \in U$ to each stability label θ_k. Each μ_{θ_k} of the mapping model is represented in the Table 1 through a quadruplet $\{a, b, c, d\}$ according to the Eq. (1). The practical way of defining such a mapping model has been developed in [13]. It is based on a civil engineering analysis of the check dams stability given several hypotheses of scouring rate. They respect the exclusivity and "open-world" conditions given in the third paragraph of the Sect. 3.

In practice, experts imperfectly measure scouring rate as shown in Fig. 1. Therefore, we compare evaluations through possibility distributions provided by six different experts. Each evaluation is represented by a quadruplet $\{a, b, c, d\}$ in the Table 1, from a very imprecise evaluation (expert 1) to very precise ones (experts 5 and 6). The evaluation illustrated in Fig. 1 is given by expert 3.

Table 1. 3 fuzzy sets $\mu_{\theta_k}(u)$ and expert possibility distributions $\pi(u)$, $\forall u \in U$.

μ_{θ_k}	θ_1	θ_2	θ_3		
a,b,c,d	0,0,30,50	30,50,60,70	60,70,100,100		
π	Expert 1	Expert 2	Expert 3	Expert 4	Expert 5	Expert 6
a,b,c,d	20,30,80,90	30,40,60,80	40,50,50,60	30,40,40,50	40,40,40,40	45,45,45,45

To apply the classical transformation on the Table 1, we assume $l_{\max} = 4$ with α-cuts $\alpha_1 = 1$, $\alpha_2 = 0.7$, $\alpha_3 = 0.4$, and $\alpha_4 = 0.1$ to extract the BBAs $m^U(\cdot)$ [10]. One gets the final Bayesian BBAs $m^\Theta(\cdot)$ in columns "1" in the Table 3.

After steps 1 and 2 using Table 1 values, one gets the values of $Pl^{c.w.} \cdot (\overline{A \cup \theta^c})$, $\forall A \in 2^{\Theta^{o.w.}} - \{\emptyset\}$, with $\Theta^{o.w.} = \{\theta_1, \theta_2, \theta_3\}$. Using them in the step 4, one gets the belief functions $Bel^{c.w.} \cdot (\cdot)$ in the Table 2 and the BBAs $m^{c.w.} \cdot (\cdot)$ in columns "2" in the Table 3. The latter gathers only focal elements with a positive mass.

Results given in the Table 3 show that the new method affects a positive mass to total (experts 1 and 2) or partial ignorance with $m^{c.w.} \cdot (\theta_1 \cup \theta_2 \cup \theta^c) > 0$ (experts 3 and 4) according to the imprecision degree of initial evaluations. The less precise is the initial evaluation of the scouring rate, the less informative is the mapped BBA. It improves the classical transformation and it propagates the imperfection of the initial information on $\Theta^{c.w.}$.

Table 2. Intermediary $Bel^{c.w.}(A \cup \theta^c)$ for the new mapping.

$A \cup \theta^c$	Expert 1	Expert 2	Expert 3	Expert 4	Expert 5	Expert 6
$\theta_1 \cup \theta^c$	0	0	0	0.333	0.5	0.25
$\theta_2 \cup \theta^c$	0	0.333	0.667	0.333	0.5	0.75
$\theta_1 \cup \theta_2 \cup \theta^c$	0	0.333	1	1	1	1
$\theta_3 \cup \theta^c$	0	0	0	0	0	0
$\theta_1 \cup \theta_3 \cup \theta^c$	0	0	0	0.333	0.5	0.25
$\theta_2 \cup \theta_3 \cup \theta^c$	0	0.333	0.667	0.333	0.5	0.75
$\theta_1 \cup \theta_2 \cup \theta_3 \cup \theta^c$	1	1	1	1	1	1

Table 3. BBAs using two approaches: $1 = m^\Theta(\cdot)$ for classical, and $2 = m^{c.w.}(\cdot)$ for new.

Focal elements	Expert 1		Expert 2		Expert 3		Expert 4		Expert 5		Expert 6	
	1	2	1	2	1	2	1	2	1	2	1	2
θ_1	0.24	0	0.15	0	0.05	0	0.5	0	0.5	0	0.25	0
θ_2	0.44	0	0.75	0	0.95	0	0.5	0	0.5	0	0.75	0
θ_3	0.32	0	0.10	0	0	0	0	0	0	0	0	0
$\theta_1 \cup \theta^c$	-	0	-	0	-	0	-	$\frac{1}{3}$	-	0.5	-	0.25
$\theta_2 \cup \theta^c$	-	0	-	$\frac{1}{3}$	-	$\frac{2}{3}$	-	$\frac{1}{3}$	-	0.5	-	0.75
$\theta_1 \cup \theta_2 \cup \theta^c$	-	0	-	0	-	$\frac{1}{3}$	-	$\frac{1}{3}$	-	0	-	0
$\theta_1 \cup \theta_2 \cup \theta_3 \cup \theta^c$	-	1	-	$\frac{2}{3}$	-	0	-	0	-	0	-	0

5   Conclusion

This paper proposes a new mapping process in the ER-MCDA methodology. It allows to get a belief mass on non singletons elements of the powerset of the FoD. Unlike the initial approach [1], the possibility distribution is represented by its support and core and setting of values of $l_{\max}$ and α_l are not needed for an α-cut approach. It is based on the conjunction between the possibility distribution and fuzzy sets but also takes into account the relationship between the possibility and the plausibility measures. To relax the hypothesis of exhaustivity of the classical Shafer's model, we have chosen Yager's hedging model instead of Smets' TBM model to prevent from introducing an ambiguity in the interpretation of the empty set. According to application cases, the hypothesis of exclusivity should be relaxed. It will be studied in forthcoming publications.

Acknowledgments. The authors thank the support of both French Ministry for Agriculture, Forest (MAAF) and Environment (MEEM).

References

1. Tacnet, J.-M., Dezert, J., Batton-Hubert, M.: AHP and uncertainty theories for decision making using the ER-MCDA methodology. In: 11th International Symposium on AHP, Sorrento, Italy (2011)
2. Carladous, S., Tacnet, J.-M., Dezert, J., Batton-Hubert, M.: Belief function theory based decision support methods: application to torrent protection work effectiveness and reliability assessment. In: 25th International Conference on ESREL, Zürich, Switzerland (2015)
3. Dezert, J., Tacnet, J.-M.: Evidential reasoning for multi-criteria analysis based on DSmT-AHP. In: 11th International Symposium on AHP, Sorrento, Italy (2011)
4. Zadeh, L.A.: Fuzzy sets. Inf. Control 8(3), 338–353 (1965)
5. Dubois, D., Prade, H.: Fuzzy sets, probability and measurement. Eur. J. Oper. Res. 40, 135–154 (1989)
6. Zadeh, L.A.: Fuzzy sets as a basis for a theory of possibility. Fuzzy Set. Syst. 1, 3–28 (1978)
7. Dubois, D., Prade, H.: Properties of measures of information in evidence and possibility theories. Fuzzy Set. Syst. 24, 161–182 (1987)
8. Dubois, D., Prade, H.: Possibility Theory - An approach to Competurized Processing of Uncertainty. Springer, Heidelberg (1988)
9. Shafer, G.: A Mathematical Theory of Evidence. Princeton University Press, Princeton (1976)
10. Baudrit, C., Guyonnet, D., Dubois, D.: Postprocessing the hybrid method for addressing uncertainty in risk assessments. J. Environ. Eng. 131, 1750–1754 (2005)
11. Smets, P., Kennes, R.: The transferable belief model. Artif. Intell. 66, 191–234 (1994)
12. Yager, R.R.: Hedging in the combination of evidence. J Inf. Sci. 1, 73–81 (1983)
13. Carladous, S., Tacnet, J.-M., Di Ciocco, G., Curt, C., Batton-Hubert, M.: Approche quantitative pour élaborer une échelle d'évaluation floue d'un indicateur de stabilité structurale. Application à l'affouillement d'ouvrages de stabilisation torrentielle. In: 9th Conference on JFMS, Nancy, France (2016)

Applying ER-MCDA and BF-TOPSIS to Decide on Effectiveness of Torrent Protection

Simon Carladous[1,2,5]([✉]), Jean-Marc Tacnet[1], Jean Dezert[3], Deqiang Han[4], and Mireille Batton-Hubert[5]

[1] Université Grenoble Alpes, Irstea, UR ETGR,
2 Rue de la Papeterie-BP76, 38402 St-Martin-d'Hères, France
{simon.carladous,jean-marc.tacnet}@irstea.fr
[2] AgroParisTech, 19 Avenue du Maine, 75732 Paris, France
[3] The French Aerospace Lab, 91761 Palaiseau, France
jean.dezert@onera.fr
[4] CIESR, Xi'an Jiaotong University, Xi'an 710049, China
deqhan@gmail.com
[5] ENSMSE - DEMO, 29, Rue Ponchardier, 42100 Saint-Etienne, France
mbatton@emse.fr

Abstract. Experts take into account several criteria to assess the effectiveness of torrential flood protection systems. In practice, scoring each criterion is imperfect. Each system is assessed choosing a qualitative class of effectiveness among several such classes (high, medium, low, no). Evidential Reasoning for Multi-Criteria Decision-Analysis (ER-MCDA) approach can help formalize this Multi-Criteria Decision-Making (MCDM) problem but only provides a coarse ranking of all systems. The recent Belief Function-based Technique for Order Preference by Similarity to Ideal Solution (BF-TOPSIS) methods give a finer ranking but are limited to perfect scoring of criteria. Our objective is to provide a coarse and a finer ranking of systems according to their effectiveness given the imperfect scoring of criteria. Therefore we propose to couple the two methods using an intermediary decision and a quantification transformation step. Given an actual MCDM problem, we apply the ER-MCDA and its coupling with BF-TOPSIS, showing that the final fine ranking is consistent with a previous coarse ranking in this case.

Keywords: Belief functions · BF-TOPSIS · ER-MCDA · Torrent protection

1 Introduction

In mountainous areas, torrents put people and buildings at risk. Thousands of check dams, clustered in series, have been built to protect them. Risk managers must assess their effectiveness given several criteria such as their structural stability or their hydraulic dimensions. This is a Multi-Criteria Decision-Making (MCDM) problem. In practice, scoring each criterion is difficult and imperfect. Experts affect each check dam series to one of several qualitative evaluation

© Springer International Publishing Switzerland 2016
J. Vejnarová and V. Kratochvíl (Eds.): BELIEF 2016, LNAI 9861, pp. 56–65, 2016.
DOI: 10.1007/978-3-319-45559-4_6

classes of effectiveness (high, medium, low, no) [1]. Evidential Reasoning for Multi Criteria Decision Analysis (ER-MCDA) has been developed on the basis of fuzzy sets, possibility and belief function theories [2,3] to decide on such MCDM problems, taking into account imperfect assessment of criteria provided by several sources.

Given the final qualitative label for each check dam series, a coarse ranking of all of them can be provided, as shown in recent applications [1]. Nevertheless, risk managers need a finer ranking to choose the most effective one. To help it, the recent Belief Function-based Technique for Order Preference by Similarity to Ideal Solution (BF-TOPSIS) methods [4] are more robust to rank reversal problems than other classical decision-aid methods such as the Analytic Hierarchy Process (AHP) [5]. Nevertheless, the BF-TOPSIS methods are limited to MCDM problems with precise quantitative evaluation of criteria.

To help risk managers rank several check dam series according to their effectiveness, the BF-TOPSIS should take into account the initial imperfect assessment of criteria. Therefore, we propose to combine the ER-MCDA and BF-TOPSIS methods. We first detail the ER-MCDA process and apply it to an actual case with a final coarse ranking. We then combine ER-MCDA with BF-TOPSIS. Applying it to the same example, we finally show that the finer ranking result obtained is consistent with the previous coarse ranking result in this case.

2   Some Basics of Belief Function Theory

Shafer proposed belief function theory [6] to represent imperfect knowledge (imprecision, epistemic uncertainty, incompleteness, conflict) through a basic belief assignment (BBA), or belief mass $m(\cdot)$, given the frame of discernment (FoD) Θ. All elements $\theta_k, k = 1, \ldots, q$ of Θ are considered exhaustive and mutually exclusive. The powerset 2^Θ is the set of all subsets (focal elements) of Θ, the empty set included. Each body (or source) of evidence is characterized by a mapping $m(\cdot) : 2^\Theta \to [0,1]$ with $m(\emptyset) = 0$, and $\sum_{X \subseteq \Theta} m(X) = 1, \forall X \neq \emptyset \in 2^\Theta$. For a categorical BBA denoted m_X, it holds that $m_X(X) = 1$ and $m_X(Y) = 0$ if $Y \subseteq \Theta \neq X$.

Given Θ, numerous more or less effective rules allow combining several BBAs. Before their combination, each BBA $m(\cdot)$ can be differently discounted by the source reliability or importance [7]. The comparison of the combination rules is not the main scope of this paper, and hereafter we use the 6th Proportional Conflict Redistribution (PCR6) fusion rule, developed within the framework of Dezert-Smarandache Theory (DSmT) [8] (vol. 3). The latter is a modification of belief function theory, designed to palliate the disadvantages of the classical Dempster fusion rule [9].

Given $m(\cdot)$, choosing a singleton $\hat{\theta} \in \Theta$ or subset $\hat{X} \subseteq \Theta$ is the decision issue. In general, it consists in choosing $\hat{\theta} = \theta_{k^*}, k = 1, \ldots, q$ with $k^* \triangleq \arg\max_k C(\theta_k)$, where $C(\theta_k)$ is a decision-making criterion. Among several $C(\theta_k)$, the most widely used one is the belief $\text{Bel}(\theta_k) \triangleq m(\theta_k)$ corresponding to a pessimistic attitude of the Decision-Maker (DM). On the contrary, the plausibility $Pl(\theta_k) \triangleq \sum_{X \cap \{\theta_k\} \neq \emptyset | X \in 2^\Theta} m(X)$ is used for an optimistic attitude. Between those two extreme attitudes, an attitude of compromise is represented by the decision based on the maximum probability. For this, the BBA $m(\cdot)$ is transformed into a subjective probability measure $P(\cdot)$ through a probabilistic transformation such as the pignistic one [10], the normalized plausibility transformation [11], etc.

In some cases, taking into account non-singletons $X \subseteq \Theta$ is needed to make a decision. As shown in [12], the minimum of any strict distance metric $d(m, m_X)$ between $m(\cdot)$ and the categorical BBA m_X can be used in Eq. (1). If only singletons of 2^Θ are accepted, the decision is defined by Eq. (2).

$$\hat{X} \triangleq \arg\min_{X \in 2^\Theta \setminus \{\emptyset\}} d(m, m_X) \qquad (1)$$

$$\hat{\theta} \triangleq \theta_{k^\star} \triangleq \arg\min_{k=1,\dots,q} d(m, m_{\{\theta_k\}}) \qquad (2)$$

Among the few true distance metrics[1] between two BBAs $m_1(\cdot)$ and $m_2(\cdot)$, the Belief Interval-based Euclidean $d_{BI}(m_1, m_2) \in [0, 1]$ defined by Eq. (3) [13] provides reasonable results. It is based on the Wasserstein distance defined by Eq. (4) [14] with $[a_1, b_1] \triangleq BI_1(X) \triangleq [\text{Bel}_1(X), \text{Pl}_1(X)]$ and $[a_2, b_2] \triangleq BI_2(X) \triangleq [\text{Bel}_2(X), \text{Pl}_2(X)]$ for $X \subseteq \Theta$.

$$d_{BI}(m_1, m_2) \triangleq \sqrt{\frac{1}{2^{|\Theta|-1}} \cdot \sum_{X \in 2^\Theta} d_W^2(BI_1(X), BI_2(X))} \qquad (3)$$

$$d_W([a_1, b_1], [a_2, b_2]) \triangleq \sqrt{\left[\frac{a_1 + b_1}{2} - \frac{a_2 + b_2}{2}\right]^2 + \frac{1}{3}\left[\frac{b_1 - a_1}{2} - \frac{b_2 - a_2}{2}\right]^2} \qquad (4)$$

The quality indicator $q(\hat{X})$ defined by Eq. (5) evaluates how good the decision $\hat{X}$ is with respect to other focal elements: the higher $q(\hat{X})$ is, the more confident in its decision $\hat{X}$ the DM should be. If only singletons of 2^Θ are accepted, $q(\hat{X}) = q(\{\hat{\theta}\})$ is defined by Eq. (6).

$$q(\hat{X}) \triangleq 1 - \frac{d_{BI}(m, m_{\hat{X}})}{\sum_{X \in 2^\Theta \setminus \{\emptyset\}} d_{BI}(m, m_X)} \qquad (5)$$

$$q(\{\hat{\theta}\}) \triangleq 1 - \frac{d_{BI}(m, m_{\{\hat{\theta}\}})}{\sum_{k=1}^q d_{BI}(m, m_{\{\theta_k\}})} \qquad (6)$$

3 From ER-MCDA to Decision-Making

3.1 Multi-Criteria Decision-Making Problems

In a MCDM problem, the DM compares alternatives $A_i \in \mathcal{A} \triangleq \{A_1, A_2, \dots, A_M\}$ through N criteria C_j, scored with different scales. Each C_j has an importance

---

[1] For any BBAs x, y, z defined on 2^Θ, a true distance metric $d(x, y)$ satisfies the properties of non-negativity ($d(x, y) \geq 0$), non-degeneracy ($d(x, y) = 0 \Leftrightarrow x = y$), symmetry ($d(x, y) = d(y, x)$), and triangle inequality ($d(x, y) + d(y, z) \geq d(x, z)$).

weight $w_j \in [0,1]$ assuming $\sum_{j=1}^{N} w_j = 1$. The N-vector $\mathbf{w} = [w_1, \ldots, w_N]$ represents the DM preferences between criteria. The AHP process helps extract it, comparing criteria pairwisely [5]. The DM gives an $M \times N$ score matrix $\mathbf{S} = [S_{ij}]$ in Eq. (7). S_{ij} is a score value of A_i according to the scoring scale of the criterion C_j. In practice, S_{ij} for each alternative A_i is given in hazardous situations, with no sensor and in a limited amount of time. The sources of information can therefore be imprecise, epistemically uncertain, incomplete and possibly conflicting.

Given the matrix $\mathbf{S}$,

$$\mathbf{S} \triangleq \begin{bmatrix} S_{11} & \ldots & S_{1j} & \ldots & S_{1N} \\ & & \vdots & & \\ S_{i1} & \ldots & S_{ij} & \ldots & S_{iN} \\ & & \vdots & & \\ S_{M1} & \ldots & S_{Mj} & \ldots & S_{MN} \end{bmatrix} \tag{7}$$

we consider two different decision-making assessments (DMA1 and DMA2). Given a final FoD $\Theta = \{\theta_1, \ldots, \theta_q\}$, DMA1 involves choosing a singleton $\hat{\theta}(A_i) \in \Theta$ for each alternative A_i, $i = 1, \ldots, M$. Given $\mathbf{S}$, DMA2 consists in totally ranking the M alternatives A_i and choosing the best one A_{i^*}.

3.2   The ER-MCDA for the DMA1 Given Imperfect S_{ij}

- **Step1$_{\text{old}}$ ($\mathbf{M}^\Theta$ construction):** Given the FoD $\Theta = \{\theta_1, \ldots, \theta_q\}$ of qualitative labels, the set $\mathcal{A}$ of M alternatives, the N criteria C_j and w_j, the $M \times N$ BBA matrix $\mathbf{M}^\Theta = [m_{ij}^\Theta(\cdot)]$ is provided in Eq. (8). For each criterion C_j, a possibility distribution π_{ij} [15] is provided by an expert through intervals F_{α_ι}, $\iota = 1, \ldots, \iota_{\max}$ with a confidence level. This represents the imprecise scoring of S_{ij} of each alternative A_i. The mapping [2] of each possibility distribution into q fuzzy sets θ_k, $k = 1, \ldots, q$ [16] provides each BBA $m_{ij}^\Theta(\cdot)$ on 2^Θ for each A_i, $i = 1, \ldots, M$ and C_j, $j = 1, \ldots, N$ in the BBA matrix M^Θ.

$$\mathbf{M}^\Theta \triangleq \begin{bmatrix} m_{11}^\Theta(\cdot) & \ldots & m_{1j}^\Theta(\cdot) & \ldots & m_{1N}^\Theta(\cdot) \\ & & \vdots & & \\ m_{i1}^\Theta(\cdot) & \ldots & m_{ij}^\Theta(\cdot) & \ldots & m_{iN}^\Theta(\cdot) \\ & & \vdots & & \\ m_{M1}^\Theta(\cdot) & \ldots & m_{Mj}^\Theta(\cdot) & \ldots & m_{MN}^\Theta(\cdot) \end{bmatrix} \tag{8}$$

The algorithm of the geometric mapping process is detailed in [2]. A BBA $m_{ij}^{X_j}(\cdot)$ is first extracted from each π_{ij}: the FoD is the scoring scale X_j of the criterion C_j; focal elements are the intervals F_{α_ι}, $\iota = 1, \ldots, \iota_{\max}$. Then each interval F_{α_ι} is mapped into each fuzzy set θ_k to obtain its geometric area $A_{\iota,k}$, with $A_\iota \triangleq \sum_{k=1}^{q} A_{\iota,k}$. A final BBA is then computed for the FoD Θ with $m_{ij}^\Theta(\theta_k) \triangleq \sum_{\iota=1}^{\iota_{\max}} m_{ij}^{X_j}(F_{\alpha_\iota}) \frac{A_{\iota,k}}{A_\iota}$.

- **Step2$_{\text{old}}$** (DMA1): We refer the reader to [3] for details. Each BBA $m_{ij}^{\Theta}(\cdot)$ is discounted by the importance weight w_j of each criterion C_j. For each $A_i \in \mathcal{A}$, the N BBAs $m_{ij}^{\Theta}(\cdot)$ are combined[2] with importance discounting [3] to obtain the BBA $m_i^{\Theta}(\cdot)$ for each ith-row. Given that the FoD $\Theta = \{\theta_1, \ldots, \theta_k, \ldots, \theta_q\}$ and for each A_i, $\hat{\theta}(A_i) = \arg\min_{k=1,\ldots,q} d_{BI}(m_i^{\Theta}, m_{\{\theta_k\}})$ is chosen, where $m_{\{\theta_k\}}$ is the categorical BBA focused on the singleton $\{\theta_k\}$ only, based on the minimum of d_{BI} defined by Eq. (3).

Given a preference ranking of the q elements of Θ, comparing all the $\hat{\theta}(A_i)$ chosen for each A_i helps rank the A_i alternatives. Nevertheless, it is not necessarily a strict ranking since the label $\hat{\theta}(A_i)$ may be the same for several A_i.

3.3   BF-TOPSIS Methods for the DMA2 Given Precise S_{ij}

Four BF-TOPSIS methods were developed to decide on the corresponding $M \times N$ matrix $\mathbf{S} = [S_{ij}]$ (Eq. (7)), with the precise score value S_{ij}. Details are given in [4].

All BF-TOPSIS methods start with the same construction of the $M \times N$ matrix $\mathbf{M}^{\mathcal{A}} = [m_{ij}^{\mathcal{A}}(\cdot)]$ from $\mathbf{S}$ for the FoD $\mathcal{A} \triangleq \{A_1, A_2, \ldots, A_M\}$. In the sequel, $\bar{A}_i$ denotes the complement of A_i in the FoD $\mathcal{A}$. For each A_i and each C_j, the positive support $\text{Sup}_j(A_i) \triangleq \sum_{k \in \{1,\ldots,M\}|S_{kj} \leq S_{ij}} |S_{ij} - S_{kj}|$ measures how much A_i is better than other alternatives according to criterion C_j. The negative support $\text{Inf}_j(A_i) \triangleq -\sum_{k \in \{1,\ldots,M\}|S_{kj} \geq S_{ij}} |S_{ij} - S_{kj}|$ measures how much A_i is worse than other alternatives according to C_j. Given $A_{\max}^j \triangleq \max_i \text{Sup}_j(A_i)$ and $A_{\min}^j \triangleq \min_i \text{Inf}_j(A_i)$, each $m_{ij}^{\mathcal{A}}(\cdot)$ is consistently defined by the triplet $(m_{ij}^{\mathcal{A}}(A_i), m_{ij}^{\mathcal{A}}(\bar{A}_i), m_{ij}^{\mathcal{A}}(A_i \cup \bar{A}_i))$ presented on the FoD $\mathcal{A}$ by:

$$m_{ij}^{\mathcal{A}}(A_i) \triangleq \begin{cases} \frac{\text{Sup}_j(A_i)}{A_{\max}^j} & \text{if } A_{\max}^j \neq 0 \\ 0 & \text{if } A_{\max}^j = 0 \end{cases} \qquad (9)$$

$$m_{ij}^{\mathcal{A}}(\bar{A}_i) \triangleq \begin{cases} \frac{\text{Inf}_j(A_i)}{A_{\min}^j} & \text{if } A_{\min}^j \neq 0 \\ 0 & \text{if } A_{\min}^j = 0 \end{cases} \qquad (10)$$

$$m_{ij}^{\mathcal{A}}(A_i \cup \bar{A}_i) \triangleq m_{ij}^{\mathcal{A}}(\Theta) \triangleq 1 - (\text{Bel}_{ij}^{\mathcal{A}}(\bar{A}_i) + \text{Bel}_{ij}^{\mathcal{A}}(A_i)) \qquad (11)$$

To help rank all alternatives $A_i \in \mathcal{A}$, the main idea of BF-TOPSIS methods is to compare each A_i with the best and worst ideal solutions. It is directly inspired by the technique for order preference by similarity to the ideal solution (TOPSIS) developed in [17]. The four BF-TOPSIS methods differ from each other in how they process the $M \times N$ matrix $\mathbf{M}^{\mathcal{A}}$ with an increasing complexity and robustness to rank reversal problems. In this paper, we focus on BF-TOPSIS3 (the 3rd BF-TOPSIS method using the PCR6 fusion rule) [4].

---

[2] with the PCR6 rule in this paper [8] (Vol. 3).

1. For each A_i, the N BBAs $m_{ij}^A(\cdot)$ are combined to give $m_i^A(\cdot)$ on 2^A, taking into account the importance factor w_j of each criterion C_j [7].

2. For each $A_i \in \mathcal{A}$, the best ideal BBA defined by $m_i^{A,\text{best}}(A_i) \triangleq 1$ and the worst ideal BBA defined by $m_i^{A,\text{worst}}(\bar{A}_i) \triangleq 1$ means that A_i is better, and worse, respectively, than all other alternatives in $\mathcal{A}$. Using Eq. (3), one computes the Belief Interval distance $d^{\text{best}}(A_i) = d_{BI}(m_i^A, m_i^{A,\text{best}})$ between the computed BBA $m_i^A(\cdot)$ and the ideal best BBA $m_i^{A,\text{best}}(\cdot)$. Similarly, one computes the distance $d^{\text{worst}}(A_i) = d_{BI}(m_i^A, m_i^{A,\text{worst}})$ between $m_i^A(\cdot)$ and the ideal worst BBA $m_i^{A,\text{worst}}(\cdot)$.

3. The relative closeness of each alternative A_i with respect to an unreal ideal best solution defined by A^{best} is given by $C(A_i, A^{\text{best}}) \triangleq \frac{d^{\text{worst}}(A_i)}{d^{\text{worst}}(A_i) + d^{\text{best}}(A_i)}$.
   Since $d^{\text{worst}}(A_i) \geq 0$ and $d^{\text{best}}(A_i) \geq 0$, then $C(A_i, A^{\text{best}}) \in [0, 1]$.
   If $d^{\text{best}}(A_i) = 0$, then $C(A_i, A^{\text{best}}) = 1$, meaning that alternative A_i coincides with A^{best}. On the contrary, if $d^{\text{worst}}(A_i) = 0$, then $C(A_i, A^{\text{best}}) = 0$, meaning that alternative A_i coincides with the ideal worst solution A^{worst}.
   Thus, the preference ranking of all alternatives $A_i \in \mathcal{A}$ is made according to the descending order of $C(A_i, A^{\text{best}})$.

3.4 BF-TOPSIS Coupled with ER-MCDA to Deal with Imperfect S_{ij}

To deal with the DMA2 and imperfect information, we propose to couple (mix) BF-TOPSIS with ER-MCDA according to the following steps:

- **Step1$_{\text{new}}$ = Step1$_{\text{old}}$ ($\mathbf{M}^\Theta$ construction)**: We use the same step 1 from ER-MCDA to obtain the matrix $\mathbf{M}^\Theta = [m_{ij}^\Theta(\cdot)]$ defined by Eq. (8) for the FoD $\Theta = \{\theta_1, \ldots, \theta_k, \ldots, \theta_q\}$.

- **Step2$_{\text{new}}$ ($\mathbf{M}^A$ construction)**: ER-MCDA is coupled with BF-TOPSIS in this step. We obtain the BBA matrix $\mathbf{M}^A = [m_{ij}^A(\cdot)]$ related to the FoD $\mathcal{A}$ from the BBA matrix $\mathbf{M}^\Theta$ as follows:

   1. For each $m_{ij}^\Theta(\cdot), i = 1, \ldots, M, j = 1, \ldots, N$, restricting the decision to singletons, one chooses $\hat{\theta}(A_i, C_j)$ applying Eq. (2) with $m = m_{ij}^\Theta$. This gives the $M \times N$ matrix $\mathbf{S}^\Theta = [\hat{\theta}(A_i, C_j)]$ with qualitative scores $\hat{\theta}(A_i, C_j)$. The corresponding quality indicator is computed by $q(\hat{\theta}(A_i, C_j))$ applying Eq. (5) with $m = m_{ij}^\Theta$.

   2. A quantitative transformation of each element θ_k in Θ is made to obtain the $M \times N$ matrix $\mathbf{S} = [S_{ij}]$, S_{ij} being the quantitative transformation of $\hat{\theta}(A_i, C_j)$. Several transformations are possible. We are aware that the choice of one can impact the final results. We introduce it as a general step and propose to analyze the results given different transformations in forthcoming publications.

   3. From the score matrix $\mathbf{S} = [S_{ij}]$, we use the formulas (9)-(11) to obtain the BBA matrix $\mathbf{M}^A = [m_{ij}^A(\cdot)]$ for $\mathcal{A} = \{A_1, A_2, \ldots, A_M\}$.

- **Step3$_{\text{new}}$** (ranking alternatives): We use $q(\hat{\theta}(A_i, C_j))$ as the reliability factor to discount each BBA $m_{ij}^{\mathcal{A}}(\cdot)$ using the Shafer discounting method [6]. For each A_i, we combine them with the PCR6 rule to obtain the BBA $m_i^{\mathcal{A}}(\cdot)$, taking into account the importance factor w_j of each criterion C_j [7]. As explained in points 2 and 3 of subsect. 3.4, the relative closeness factors $C(A_i, A^{\text{best}})$ are calculated, from which the preference ranking of all A_i is deduced.

4 Effectiveness of Torrential Check Dam Series

To reduce potential damage on at-risk housing, each torrential check dam series stabilizes the torrent's longitudinal profile to curtail sediment release from the headwaters. Their effectiveness in achieving this function depends on $N = 7$ technical criteria C_j with their importance weights w_j, as shown in Fig. 1. An expert assesses $M = 4$ check dam series A_i according to their effectiveness given an imperfect evaluation of each C_j and using ER-MCDA step 1. After this common step, ER-MCDA step 2 is used to assess (DMA1) the effectiveness of each A_i expressed by four qualitative labels (levels) in $\Theta = \{\text{high, medium, low, no}\}$ [1]. Then steps 2 and 3 of the method based on BF-TOPSIS3 developed in Sect. 3.4 are used to rank all A_i and to choose the most effective one, A_{i*} (DMA2).

- **Step1$_{\text{new}}$ = Step1$_{\text{old}}$** (M$^{\Theta}$ construction): The expert evaluates each criterion C_j for each A_i through possibility distributions. $N = 7$ fuzzy scales are specified, each one gathering the $q = 4$ fuzzy sets θ_k, $k = 1, \ldots, q$. The BBA matrix $\mathbf{M}^{\Theta} = [m_{ij}^{\Theta}(\cdot)]$ obtained for $\Theta = \{\text{high, medium, low, no}\}$ is given in Table 1.
- **DMA1** (based on Step 2$_{\text{old}}$ described in Sect. 3.2): given $\mathbf{M}^{\Theta}$ in Table 1, the column $d_{BI}^{\min}$ in Table 2 lists the minimal value obtained for $d_{BI}(m_i^{\Theta}, m_{\{\theta_k\}})$ defined by Eq. (3), for each $A_i \in \mathcal{A}$. The best label $\hat{\theta}(A_i)$ is chosen for each A_i. Three check dam series A_1, A_2, and A_4 are declared as medium, and A_3 is declared as low. The DM coarsely has $A_1 \succ A_3$, $A_2 \succ A_3$ and $A_4 \succ A_3$.
- **DMA2** (based on Step 2$_{\text{new}}$ and Step 3$_{\text{new}}$ described in Sect. 3.2): given $\mathbf{M}^{\Theta}$ in Table 1, for each A_i and C_j, one computes $\arg\min_{k=1,\ldots,q} d_{BI}(m_{ij}^{\Theta}, m_{\{\theta_k\}})$ between each $m_{ij}^{\Theta}(\cdot)$ and the categorical BBA $m_{\{\theta_k\}}(\cdot)$, with $\Theta = \{\theta_1 = \text{high}, \theta_2 = \text{medium}, \theta_3 = \text{low}, \theta_4 = \text{no}\}$. The linear quantitative transformation: $\theta_1 = 4, \theta_2 = 3, \theta_3 = 2, \theta_4 = 1$ is assumed to establish the matrix $\mathbf{S} = [S_{ij}]$ in Table 3. For each A_i and C_j, the quality factor $q(\hat{\theta}(A_i, C_j))$ is also computed in Table 3 applying Eq. (5) with $m = m_{ij}^{\Theta}$.

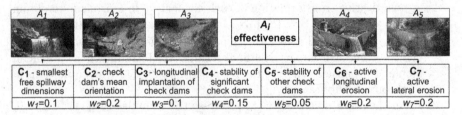

A_1	A_2	A_3	A_i effectiveness		A_4	A_5
C_1 - smallest free spillway dimensions	C_2 - check dam's mean orientation	C_3 - longitudinal implantation of check dams	C_4 - stability of significant check dams	C_5 - stability of other check dams	C_6 - active longitudinal erosion	C_7 - active lateral erosion
w_1=0.1	w_2=0.2	w_3=0.1	w_4=0.15	w_5=0.05	w_6=0.2	w_7=0.2

Fig. 1. Formalization of the actual MCDM problem.

Table 1. $\mathbf{M}^{\Theta}$ provided by Step 1_{new} = Step 1_{old}.

	A_i	Focal element	$m_{ij}^{\Theta}(\cdot)$						
			C_1	C_2	C_3	C_4	C_5	C_6	C_7
$\mathbf{M}^{\Theta}$	A_1	θ_1	0.2963	0.1755	0.0161	0.0000	0.0000	0.0000	0.1378
		θ_2	0.6270	0.7556	0.9107	0.0000	0.0391	0.1748	0.8083
		θ_3	0.0467	0.0389	0.0432	0.0009	0.4099	0.7786	0.0239
		θ_4	0.0000	0.0000	0.0000	0.9691	0.5210	0.0166	0.0000
		Θ	0.0300	0.0300	0.0300	0.0300	0.0300	0.0300	0.0300
	A_2	θ_1	0.8446	0.0052	0.0310	0.9281	0.0693	0.6434	0.0073
		θ_2	0.1254	0.2677	0.9232	0.0419	0.3469	0.3266	0.9250
		θ_3	0.0000	0.6050	0.0158	0.0000	0.2670	0.0000	0.0377
		θ_4	0.0000	0.0921	0.0000	0.0000	0.2868	0.0000	0.0000
		Θ	0.0300	0.0300	0.0300	0.0300	0.0300	0.0300	0.0300
	A_3	θ_1	0.7159	0.0019	0.6463	0.0000	0.0000	0.7154	0.0000
		θ_2	0.2541	0.1464	0.3237	0.0451	0.0338	0.2546	0.3769
		θ_3	0.0000	0.6655	0.0000	0.3786	0.2188	0.0000	0.5578
		θ_4	0.0000	0.1562	0.0000	0.5463	0.7174	0.0000	0.0353
		Θ	0.0300	0.0300	0.0300	0.0300	0.0300	0.0300	0.0300
	A_4	θ_1	0.3372	0.3950	0.3849	0.0000	0.0576	0.0022	0.0000
		θ_2	0.4731	0.5676	0.2460	0.1562	0.3390	0.7030	0.5075
		θ_3	0.1597	0.0074	0.3391	0.7831	0.5147	0.2643	0.4371
		θ_4	0.0000	0.0000	0.0000	0.0307	0.0587	0.0005	0.0254
		Θ	0.0300	0.0300	0.0300	0.0300	0.0300	0.0300	0.0300

Table 2. Final results for **DMA1** based on ER-MCDA step 2_{old} from $\mathbf{M}^{\Theta}$.

A_i	d_{BI}^{min}	$\hat{\theta}(A_i)$	Final class	Ranking
A_1	0.3769	θ_2	Medium	1-3
A_2	0.4837	θ_2	Medium	1-3
A_3	0.5096	θ_3	Low	4
A_4	0.3911	θ_2	Medium	1-3

Table 3. S_{ij} and $q(\hat{\theta}(A_i, C_j))$ ($= q(i,j)$) provided by Step 2_{new} from $\mathbf{M}^{\Theta}$.

C_j, w_j	$C_1, 0.1$		$C_2, 0.2$		$C_3, 0.1$		$C_4, 0.15$		$C_5, 0.05$		$C_6, 0.2$		$C_7, 0.2$	
$A_i \downarrow$	S_{i1}	$q(i,1)$	S_{i2}	$q(i,2)$	S_{i3}	$q(i,3)$	S_{i4}	$q(i,4)$	S_{i5}	$q(i,5)$	S_{i6}	$q(i,6)$	S_{i7}	$q(i,7)$
A_1	3	0.8747	3	0.9226	3	0.9754	1	0.9921	1	0.8332	2	0.9287	4	0.9404
A_2	4	0.9505	2	0.8708	3	0.9794	4	0.9797	3	0.8737	4	0.8754	3	0.9794
A_3	4	0.9029	2	0.8953	4	0.8765	1	0.8435	1	0.9078	4	0.9027	2	0.8469
A_4	3	0.8747	3	0.9226	4	0.9754	2	0.9921	2	0.8332	3	0.9287	3	0.9404

Table 4. Final results for **DMA2** based on step 3_{new} from Table 3.

A_i	$d^{\text{best}}(A_i)$	$d^{\text{worst}}(A_i)$	$C(A_i, A^{\text{best}})$	Ranking
A_1	0.5965	0.3061	0.3391	3
A_2	0.4930	0.4069	0.4521	1
A_3	0.6431	0.2683	0.2944	4
A_4	0.5033	0.4090	0.4483	2

After the reliability discounting of BBAs from Table 1 by the factors $q(\hat{\theta}(A_i, C_j))$ from Table 3, one obtains $\mathbf{M}^{\mathcal{A}} = [m_{ij}^{\mathcal{A}}(\cdot)]$ for $\mathcal{A} = \{A_1, A_2, \ldots, A_M\}$. After applying BF-TOPSIS3, we obtain the relative closeness $C(A_i, A^{best})$ values in Table 4. The ranking of all A_i according to their effectiveness is consistent with the DMA1 results: $A_2 \succ A_4 \succ A_1 \succ A_3$. The most effective check dam series is A_2.

5   Conclusion

The ER-MCDA helps provide a coarse ranking of torrential check dam series according to their effectiveness, taking into account several imperfectly scored criteria. Given the same imperfect MCDM problem, risk managers may need a finer ranking. For this purpose, we suggested coupling the ER-MCDA and BF-TOPSIS methods. We have shown the consistency of coarse and finer ranking results for only one example. Further studies are needed to determine whether such consistency holds in general or for certain classes of examples. Moreover, an intermediary decision step and a quantitative transformation are needed to meet this goal. The sensitivity of results to their definition is under evaluation and will be reported in forthcoming publications.

Acknowledgments. The authors extend their thanks to the French Ministry of Agriculture, Forest (MAAF), and Environment (MEEM), the Grant for State Key Program for Basic Research of China (973) (No. 2013CB329405), the National Natural Science Foundation (No. 61573275), and the Science and technology project of Shaanxi Province (No. 2013KJXX-46) for their support.

References

1. Carladous, S., Tacnet, J.-M., Dezert, J., Batton-Hubert, M.: Belief function theory based decision support methods: application to torrent protection work effectiveness and reliability assessment. In: 25th International Conference on ESREL, Zürich, Switzerland (2015)
2. Tacnet, J.-M., Dezert, J., Batton-Hubert, M.: AHP and uncertainty theories for decision making using the ER-MCDA methodology. In: 11th International Symposium on AHP, Sorrento, Italy (2011)

3. Dezert, J., Tacnet, J.-M.: Evidential reasoning for multi-criteria analysis based on DSmT-AHP. In: 11th International Symposium on AHP, Sorrento, Italy (2011)
4. Dezert, J., Han, D., Yin, H.: A new belief function based approach for multi-criteria decision-making support. In: 19th International Conference on Fusion, Heidelberg, Germany (2016)
5. Saaty, T.: The Analytic Hierarchy Process. McGraw Hill, New York (1980)
6. Shafer, G.: A Mathematical Theory of Evidence. Princeton University Press, Princeton (1976)
7. Smarandache, F., Dezert, J., Tacnet, J.-M.: Fusion of sources of evidence with different importances and reliabilities. In: 13th International Conference on Fusion, Edinburgh, UK (2010)
8. Smarandache, F., Dezert, J.: Advances and applications of DSmT for information fusion, vol. 1–4. ARP (2004–2015). http://www.onera.fr/fr/staff/jean-dezert
9. Dezert, J., Tchamova, A.: On the validity of Dempster's fusion rule and its interpretation as a generalization of Bayesian fusion rule. Int. J. Intell. Syst. **29**(3), 223–252 (2014)
10. Smets, P., Kennes, R.: The transferable belief model. Artif. Intell. **66**, 191–234 (1994)
11. Cobb, B.R., Shenoy, P.P.: On the plausibility transformation method for translating belief function models to probability models. IJAR **41**(3), 314–330 (2006)
12. Dezert, J., Han, D., Tacnet, J.-M., Carladous, S.: Decision-making with belief interval distance. In: 4th International Conference on Belief Functions, Prague, Czech Republic (2016)
13. Han, D., Dezert, J., Yang, Y.: New distance measures of evidence based on belief intervals. In: 3rd International Conference on Belief Functions, Oxford, UK (2014)
14. Irpino, A., Verde, R.: Dynamic clustering of interval data using a Wasserstein-based distance. Pattern Recogn. Lett. **29**, 1648–1658 (2008)
15. Zadeh, L.A.: Fuzzy sets as a basis for a theory of possibility. Fuzzy Sets Syst. **1**, 3–28 (1978)
16. Zadeh, L.A.: Fuzzy sets. Inf. Control **8**(3), 338–353 (1965)
17. Lai, Y.J., Liu, T.Y., Hwang, C.L.: TOPSIS for MODM. Eur. J. Oper. Res. **76**(3), 486–500 (1994)

Decision-Making with Belief Interval Distance

Jean Dezert[1(✉)], Deqiang Han[2], Jean-Marc Tacnet[3], Simon Carladous[3,4,5], and Yi Yang[6]

[1] The French Aerospace Lab, 91761 Palaiseau, France
jean.dezert@onera.fr
[2] CIESR, Xi'an Jiaotong University, Xi'an 710049, China
deqhan@gmail.com
[3] UGA, Irstea, UR ETGR,
2 rue de la Papeterie-BP 76, 38402 St-Martin-d'Hères, France
{jean-marc.tacnet,simon.carladous}@irstea.fr
[4] AgroParisTech, 19 avenue du Maine, 75732 Paris, France
[5] ENSMSE - DEMO, 29, rue Ponchardier, 42100 Saint-Etienne, France
[6] SKLSVMS, School of Aerospace, Xi'an Jiaotong University, Xi'an 710049, China
jiafeiyy@mail.xjtu.edu.cn

Abstract. In this paper we propose a new general method for decision-making under uncertainty based on the belief interval distance. We show through several simple illustrative examples how this method works and its ability to provide reasonable results.

Keywords: Belief functions · Decision-making · Distance between BBAs

1 Introduction

Dempster-Shafer Theory (DST), also known as the Mathematical Theory of Evidence or the Theory of Belief Functions (BF), was introduced by Shafer in 1976 [1] based on Dempster's previous works [2]. This theory offers an elegant theoretical framework for modeling uncertainty, and provides a method for combining distinct bodies of evidence collected from different sources. In the past more than three decades, DST has been used in many applications, in fields including information fusion, pattern recognition, and decision making [3]. Although belief functions are very appealing for modeling epistemic uncertainty, the two main important questions related to them remain still open:

1. How to combine efficiently several independent belief functions?
   This open question is out of the scope of this paper and it has been widely disputed by many experts [4–14]. In this short paper, we focus on the second question below.
2. How to take a final decision from a belief function?
   This second question is also very crucial in many problems involving epistemic uncertainty where the final step (after beliefs elicitation, and beliefs combination) is to make a decision.

© Springer International Publishing Switzerland 2016
J. Vejnarová and V. Kratochvíl (Eds.): BELIEF 2016, LNAI 9861, pp. 66–74, 2016.
DOI: 10.1007/978-3-319-45559-4_7

In the sequel, we assume that the reader is familiar with Demspter-Shafer Theory of belief functions [1] and its notations. Due to space restriction, we will not recall the definitions of basic belief assignment $m(\cdot)$, belief $Bel(\cdot)$ (also called credibility by some authors), and plausibility functions $Pl(\cdot)$ functions defined over a given finite discrete frame of discernment (FoD) Θ. For any focal element X of the powerset of Θ, denoted by 2^Θ, the interval $BI(X) \triangleq [Bel(X), Pl(X)]$ is called the belief interval of X. Its length $Pl(X) - BeI(X)$ characterizes the uncertainty on X (also called ambiguity in [15]). This paper is organized as follows. In Sect. 2, we recall the common decision-making techniques used so far to make a decision from belief functions. In Sect. 3 we recall the new distance measure based on Belief interval, and we present a new general method for decision-making with belief functions. Finally, examples of this new approach are given in Sect. 4, with concluding remarks in Sect. 5.

2   Classical Decision-Making Methods with Belief Functions

We assume a given FoD $\Theta = \{\theta_1, \ldots, \theta_n\}$ and a given BBA $m(\cdot)$ defined on 2^Θ. We want to make a decision from $m(\cdot)$. It consists in choosing a particular element of the FoD that solves the problem under consideration, which is represented by the set of potential solutions (choices) θ_i, $i = 1, \ldots, n$. How to do this in an effective manner is the fundamental question of decision-making under epistemic uncertainty. Many decision-making criteria have been proposed in the literature. Some advanced techniques developed in the 1990s [15–19] have not been widely used so far in the BF community, probably because of their complexity of implementation. In this section, we only present briefly the simplest ones frequently used.

1. Decision based on maximum of credibility:
   This decision-making scheme is the so-called prudent (or pessimistic) scheme. It consists in choosing the element of the FoD Θ that has the maximum of credibility. In other terms, one will decide $\hat{\theta} = \theta_{i^\star}$ with[1]

$$\theta_{i^\star} = \arg\max_i Bel(\theta_i) \tag{1}$$

2. Decision based on maximum of plausibility:
   On the contrary, if we prefer to adopt a more optimistic decision-making (less prudent) attitude, one will choose the element of the FoD Θ that has the maximum of plausibility. In other terms, one will decide $\hat{\theta} = \theta_{i^\star}$ with

$$\theta_{i^\star} = \arg\max_i Pl(\theta_i) \tag{2}$$

---

[1] The notation with hat indicates the decision taken. Here $\hat{\theta}$ specifies that the decision taken is only a singleton of Θ.

3. Decision based on maximum of probability:
   Usually decision-makers prefer to adopt a more balanced decisional attitude making a compromise between the aforementioned pessimistic and optimistic attitudes. For this, the BBA $m(\cdot)$ is transformed into a subjective probability measure $P(\cdot)$ compatible with the belief interval $[Bel(\cdot), Pl(\cdot)]$, and one will choose the element of the FoD Θ that has the maximum of probability. In other terms, one will decide $\hat{\theta} = \theta_{i^*}$ with

$$\theta_{i^*} = \arg\max_i P(\theta_i) \qquad (3)$$

In practice, many probabilistic transformations are available to approximate (or transform) a BBA $m(\cdot)$ in a probability measure $P(\cdot)$. By example, the pignistic transformation [20], the plausibility transformation [21], the DSmP transformation and other ones presented in [22], etc.

Of course, in case of multiple maximum values, no decision can be clearly drawn. Usually if only one decision must be made, a random sample between elements θ_i generating the maximal decision-making criterion value is used to make a unique final decision $\hat{\theta}$. Another more prudent decision scheme is to use the disjunction of all elements generating the maximal decision-making criterion value, to provide a less specific final decision (if it is allowed for the problem under concern).

Our main criticism about using these decision-making schemes is that they do not use the whole information contained in the original BBA, which is in fact expressed by the whole belief interval. The pessimistic attitude uses only the credibility values, whereas the optimistic attitude uses only the plausibility values. The prudent attitude based on the criteria (3) requires a particular choice of probabilistic transformation which is often disputed by users. Making a decision from the $P(.)$ measure is theoretically not satisfactory at all because the transformation is lossy since we cannot retrieve $m(\cdot)$ from $P(\cdot)$ when some focal elements of $m(\cdot)$ are not singletons. In the next section, we propose a better justified decision scheme based on the belief interval distance [23, 24].

3   Decision-Making Method Using Belief Interval Distance

In our previous works [23, 24], we have defined a Euclidean belief interval distance between two BBAs $m_1(\cdot)$ and $m_2(\cdot)$ defined on the powerset of a given FoD $\Theta = \{\theta_1, \ldots, \theta_n\}$ as follows

$$d_{BI}(m_1, m_2) \triangleq \sqrt{N_c \cdot \sum_{X \in 2^\Theta} d_W^2(BI_1(X), BI_2(X))} \qquad (4)$$

where $N_c = 1/2^{n-1}$ is a normalization factor to have $d_{BI}(m_1, m_2) \in [0, 1]$, and $d_W(BI_1(X), BI_2(X))$ is the Wassertein's distance [25] between belief intervals

$BI_1(X) \triangleq [Bel_1(X), Pl_1(X)] = [a_1, b_1]$ and $BI_2(X) \triangleq [Bel_2(X), Pl_2(X)] = [a_2, b_2]$. More specificly,

$$d_W([a_1, b_1], [a_2, b_2]) \triangleq \sqrt{\left[\frac{a_1 + b_1}{2} - \frac{a_2 + b_2}{2}\right]^2 + \frac{1}{3}\left[\frac{b_1 - a_1}{2} - \frac{b_2 - a_2}{2}\right]^2} \quad (5)$$

In [23], we have proved that $d_{BI}(x, y)$ is a true distance metric because it satisfies the properties of non-negativity $(d(x, y) \geq 0)$, non-degeneracy $(d(x, y) = 0 \Leftrightarrow x = y)$, symmetry $(d(x, y) = d(y, x))$, and the triangle inequality $(d(x, y) + d(y, z) \geq d(x, z))$, for any BBAs x, y and z defined on 2^Θ. The choice of Wasserstein's distance in d_{BI} definition is justified by the fact that Wasserstein's distance is a true distance metric and it fits well with our needs because we have to compute a distance between $[Bel_1(X), Pl_1(X)]$ and $[Bel_2(X), Pl_2(X)]$.

For notation convenience, we denote m_X the categorical BBA having only X as focal element, where $X \neq \emptyset$ is an element of the powerset of Θ. More precisely, m_X is the particular (categorical) BBA defined by $m_X(X) = 1$ and $m_X(Y) = 0$ for any $Y \neq X$. Such basic BBA plays an important role in our new decision scheme because its corresponding belief interval reduces to the degenerate interval $[1, 1]$ which represents the certainty on X. The basic principle of the new decision scheme we propose is very simple and intuitively makes sense. It consists in selecting as the final decision (denoted by $\hat{X}$) the element of the powerset for which the belief interval distance between the BBA $m(\cdot)$ and m_X, $X \in 2^\Theta \setminus \{\emptyset\}$ is the smallest one[2]. Therefore, take as the final decision $\hat{X}$ given by

$$\hat{X} = \arg \min_{X \in 2^\Theta \setminus \{\emptyset\}} d_{BI}(m, m_X) \quad (6)$$

where $d_{BI}(m, m_X)$ is computed according to (4). $m(\cdot)$ is the BBA under test and $m_X(.)$ the categorical BBA focused on X defined above.

This decision scheme is very general in the sense that the decision making can be done on any type of element[3] of the power-set 2^Θ, and not necessarily only on the elements (singletons) of the FoD (see examples in the next section). This method not only provides the final decision $\hat{X}$ to make, but also it evaluates how good this decision is with respect to its alternatives if we define the quality indicator $q(\hat{X})$ as follows

$$q(\hat{X}) \triangleq 1 - \frac{d_{BI}(m, m_{\hat{X}})}{\sum_{X \in 2^\Theta \setminus \{\emptyset\}} d_{BI}(m, m_X)} \quad (7)$$

One sees that the quality indicator $q(\hat{X})$ of the decision $\hat{X}$ made will become maximum (equal to one) when the distance between the BBA $m(\cdot)$ and $m_{\hat{X}}$ is zero, which means that the BBA $m(\cdot)$ is focused in fact only on the element $\hat{X}$. The higher $q(\hat{X})$ is, the more confident in the decision $\hat{X}$ we should be.

---

[2] This simple principle has also been proposed by Essaid et al. [26] using Jousselme's distance.

[3] Empty set excluded.

Of course, if a decision must be made with some extra constraint[4] defined by a (or several) condition(s), denoted $c(X)$, then we must take into account $c(X)$ in Eq. (6), that is $\hat{X} = \arg\min_{X \in 2^\Theta \setminus \{\emptyset\}\ s.t.\ c(X)} d_{BI}(m, m_X)$, and also in the derivation of quality indicator by taking $\sum_{X \in 2^\Theta \setminus \{\emptyset\}\ s.t.\ c(X)} d_{BI}(m, m_X)$ as denominator in (7). Theoretically any other strict distance metric, for instance Jousselme's distance [27–29], could be used instead of $d_{BI}(\cdot, \cdot)$. We have chosen d_{BI} distance because of its ability to provide good and reasonable behavior [23] as will be shown. When there exists a tie between multiple decisions $\{\hat{X}_j, j > 1\}$, then the prudent decision corresponding to their disjunction $\hat{X} = \cup_j \hat{X}_j$ should be preferred (if allowed), otherwise the final decision $\hat{X}$ is made by a random selection of elements $\hat{X}_j$.

4 Examples and Comparisons

In this section we present several examples when the cardinality of the FoD $|\Theta|$ is only 2 and 3 because it is easier to see whether the decision-making results make sense or not. We compare and discuss decisions only made with the belief interval distance d_{BI} and Jousselme's distance d_J because the other lossy decision schemes do not exploit both credibility and plausibility values. The examples corresponding to cases where the BBA $m(\cdot)$ is focused on a single element X of 2^Θ are not presented because one trivially gets $\hat{X} = X$ using either d_{BI} or d_J distances. The next tables present several BBAs from which a decision has to be made. By convention, and since we work with normal BBAs satisfying $m(\emptyset) = 0$, the empty set is not included in the tables. The rows for $d_{BI}^{\min}(m_i, m_X)$ and for $d_J^{\min}(m_i, m_X)$ list the minimal values obtained for $d_{BI}(m_i, m_X)$ and $d_J(m_i, m_X)$. The rows for $\hat{X}^{d_{BI}}$ and for $\hat{X}^{d_J}$ list the decision(s) $\hat{X}$ made when using $d_{BI}(m_i, m_X)$ and $d_J(m_i, m_X)$ respectively. The rows for $q(\hat{X}^{d_{BI}})$ and $q(\hat{X}^{d_J})$ list the quality indicators of decision(s) made using $d_{BI}(m_i, m_X)$ and $d_J(m_i, m_X)$ respectively. Depending on the BBA, it is possible to have multiple decisions $\{\hat{X}_j\}$ in case of a tie. If a tie occurs either a random sampling of $\{\hat{X}_j\}$ must be drawn, or (if allowed) the disjunction of decisions $\hat{X}_j$ is preferred. In the next subsections, we present results in free-constraint case (i.e. $c(X) = \emptyset$), as well as when the decisions are restricted to be singletons (i.e. $c(X) \equiv$ "$|X| = 1$").

4.1 Examples with $\Theta = \{A, B\}$

Table 1 shows the decisions made when there is no constraint on the cardinality of the decision $\hat{X}$.

One sees that methods based on min of $d_{BI}(m, m_X)$ and on min of $d_J(m, m_X)$ yield the same reasonable decisions in almost all cases. With m_2, one has multiple decisions $\hat{X}^{d_J} = \{A, B, A \cup B\}$ with quality 0.6667 when using d_J, which is a bit surprising in our opinion because there is a real tie between A and B. Consequently, the decision $A \cup B$ should be preferred when there is no constraint

---

[4] For instance, making a choice only among the singletons of 2^Θ.

Table 1. Examples of several BBA's and decisions made (no constraint case).

$X \in 2^{\Theta}$	$m_1(\cdot)$	$m_2(\cdot)$	$m_3(\cdot)$	$m_4(\cdot)$	$m_5(\cdot)$	$m_6(\cdot)$	$m_7(\cdot)$
A	0.9	0.5	0.8	0.1	0.4	0.9	0.1
B	0.1	0.5	0.1	0.1	0.4	0	0
$A \cup B$	0	0	0.1	0.8	0.2	0.1	0.9
$d_{BI}^{\min}(m_i, m_X)$	0.1000	0.2887	0.1528	0.0577	0.2309	0.0577	0.0577
$q(\hat{X}^{d_{BI}})$	0.9330	0.7760	0.8939	0.9502	0.8134	0.9622	0.9513
$\hat{X}^{d_{BI}}$	A	$A \cup B$	A	$A \cup B$	$A \cup B$	A	$A \cup B$
$d_J^{\min}(m_i, m_X)$	0.1000	0.5000	0.1581	0.1000	0.4000	0.0707	0.0707
$q(\hat{X}^{d_J})$	0.9390	0.6667	0.8999	0.9276	0.6409	0.9574	0.9501
$\hat{X}^{d_J}$	A	$A, B, A \cup B$	A	$A \cup B$	$A \cup B$	A	$A \cup B$

on the cardinality of decisions. For this m_2 case, one gets a unique decision $\hat{X}^{d_{BI}} = A \cup B$ with a better quality 0.776 which seems more reasonable. We see also that all minimal distance values obtained with d_{BI} are less (or equal in case m_1) to the minimal values obtained with d_J. In fact, when the mass function is distributed symmetrically, it is naturally expected that no real decision can be easily taken (as illustrated for BBA's $m_2(\cdot)$ and $m_5(\cdot)$ in Table 1). Here, the decision $A \cup B$ for BBA's $m_2(\cdot)$ and $m_5(\cdot)$ can be interpreted as a no proper decision, in the sense that $A \cup B$ is the whole universe of discourse, hence we are merely selecting anything (and discarding nothing). Such kind of no proper decision may however be very helpful in some fusion systems because it warns that input information is not rich enough, and that one needs more information to take a proper decision (by including more sensors or more experts reports in the system for instance). For symmetrical mass function, the decision drawn from the new proposed decision rule is consistent with what we can reasonably

Table 2. Average distances and relative closeness indicators for example 1.

$X \in 2^{\Theta}$	$m_1(\cdot)$	$m_2(\cdot)$	$m_3(\cdot)$	$m_4(\cdot)$	$m_5(\cdot)$	$m_6(\cdot)$	$m_7(\cdot)$
A	0.9	0.5	0.8	0.1	0.4	0.9	0.1
B	0.1	0.5	0.1	0.1	0.4	0	0
$A \cup B$	0	0	0.1	0.8	0.2	0.1	0.9
$d_{BI}^{\min}(m_i, m_X)$	0.1000	0.5000	0.1528	0.5508	0.5033	0.0577	0.5196
$q(\hat{X}^{d_{BI}})$	0.9000	0.5000	0.8477	0.5000	0.5000	0.9427	0.5393
$\hat{X}^{d_{BI}}$	A	A, B	A	A, B	A, B	A	A
$d_J^{\min}(m_i, m_X)$	0.1000	0.5000	0.1581	0.6403	0.5099	0.0707	0.6364
$q(\hat{X}^{d_J})$	0.9000	0.5000	0.8434	0.5000	0.5000	0.9308	0.5276
$\hat{X}^{d_J}$	A	A, B	A	A, B	A, B	A	A

get because. To make a proper decision we will always need to introduce some possibly arbitrary additional constraints.

Table 2 shows the decisions made for same examples when we force the decision to be a singleton, that is when the constraint is $c(X) \equiv$ "$|X| = 1$". One sees that the decisions restricted to the set of singletons using $d_{BI}(m, m_X)$ or $d_J(m, m_X)$ are the same but the quality indicators are a bit better when using $d_{BI}(m, m_X)$ with respect to $d_J(m, m_X)$. The values of the quality indicators in Table 2 are different to those of Table 1 which is normal because we use the constraint $c(X)$ in the denominator of the formula (7).

4.2   Examples with $\Theta = \{A, B, C\}$

Table 3 shows the decisions made when there is no constraint on the cardinality of the decision $\hat{X}$, whereas Table 4 shows the results for the same examples when the decisions made are restricted to singletons. As shown in the tables all minimal distance values obtained with d_{BI} are less (or equal) to the minimal values obtained with d_J and the quality indicator decisions is better when computed with d_{BI} (except in case m_1 of Table 3). The decisions results obtained with d_J are mostly consistent with those obtained with d_{BI} (except in case m_2 and m_3 of Table 3) where a larger set of decisions (tie) is obtained using d_J. If the decisions are restricted to singletons (see Table 4), then the decision-making based on d_{BI} and on d_J provides the same results with a better quality of decisions using d_{BI}.

Table 3. Average distances and relative closeness indicators for example 2.

$X \in 2^{\Theta}$	$m_1(\cdot)$	$m_2(\cdot)$	$m_3(\cdot)$	$m_4(\cdot)$	$m_5(\cdot)$	$m_6(\cdot)$	$m_7(\cdot)$	$m_8(\cdot)$
A	0.9	0.5	1/3	0.5	0	0	0	0.2
B	0.1	0.5	1/3	0	0	0	0	0.1
$A \cup B$	0	0	0	0.5	0.5	2/3	1/3	0.05
C	0	0	1/3	0	0	0	0	0.05
$A \cup C$	0	0	0	0	0	0	1/3	0.1
$B \cup C$	0	0	0	0	0.5	1/3	1/3	0.2
$A \cup B \cup C$	0	0	0	0	0	0	0	0.3
$d_{BI}^{\min}(m_i, m_X)$	0.1000	0.2887	0.4082	0.2887	0.2887	0.1925	0.2357	0.2227
$q(\hat{X}^{d_{BI}})$	0.9776	0.9242	0.8787	0.9271	0.9120	0.9421	0.9241	0.9280
$\hat{X}^{d_{BI}}$	A	$A \cup B$	$2^{\Theta} \setminus \{\emptyset, A, B, C\}$	$A, A \cup B$	$A \cup B, B \cup C, \Theta$	$A \cup B$	$A \cup B \cup C$	$A \cup B \cup C$
$d_J^{\min}(m_i, m_X)$	0.1000	0.5000	0.5774	0.3536	0.4082	0.2722	0.3333	0.3149
$q(\hat{X}^{d_J})$	0.9798	0.8870	0.8571	0.9225	0.8989	0.9337	0.9111	0.9152
$\hat{X}^{d_J}$	A	$A, B, A \cup B$	$2^{\Theta} \setminus \{\emptyset\}$	$A, A \cup B$	$A \cup B, B \cup C, \Theta$	$A \cup B$	$A \cup B \cup C$	$A \cup B \cup C$

Table 4. Examples of several BBA's and decisions made (restricted to singletons).

$X \in 2^{\Theta}$	$m_1(\cdot)$	$m_2(\cdot)$	$m_3(\cdot)$	$m_4(\cdot)$	$m_5(\cdot)$	$m_6(\cdot)$	$m_7(\cdot)$	$m_8(\cdot)$
A	0.9	0.5	1/3	0.5	0	0	0	0.2
B	0.1	0.5	1/3	0	0	0	0	0.1
$A \cup B$	0	0	0	0.5	0.5	2/3	1/3	0.05
C	0	0	1/3	0	0	0	0	0.05
$A \cup C$	0	0	0	0	0	0	1/3	0.1
$B \cup C$	0	0	0	0	0.5	1/3	1/3	0.2
$A \cup B \cup C$	0	0	0	0	0	0	0	0.3
$d_{BI}^{min}(m_i, m_X)$	0.1000	0.5000	0.5774	0.2887	0.5000	0.5092	0.6236	0.5770
$q(\hat{X}^{d_{BI}})$	0.9488	0.7321	0.6667	0.8531	0.7388	0.7364	0.6667	0.6855
$\hat{X}^{d_{BI}}$	A	A, B	A, B, C	A	B	B	A, B, C	A
$d_J^{min}(m_i, m_X)$	0.1000	0.5000	0.5774	0.3536	0.5774	0.5932	0.6667	0.6117
$q(\hat{X}^{d_J})$	0.9488	0.7321	0.6667	0.8300	0.7257	0.7229	0.6667	0.6836
$\hat{X}^{d_J}$	A	A, B	A, B, C	A	B	B	A, B, C	A

5   Conclusions

We have presented a new method for decision-making with belief functions which truly exploits the belief interval value of each focal element of a BBA. It is easy to implement and can be applied with any strict distance metric between two BBAs. We have considered and compared the well-known Jousselme's distance and the recent belief interval distance. This method is general because the decision can be made not only on singletons, but also on any other compound focal elements (if needed and allowed). It also provides a quality indicator of the decision made.

References

1. Shafer, G.: A Mathematical Theory of Evidence. Princeton University Press, Princeton (1976)
2. Dempster, A.: Upper and lower probabilities induced by a multivalued mapping. Ann. Math. Stat. **38**, 325–339 (1967)
3. Smets, P.: Practical uses of belief functions. In: Laskey, K.B., Prade, H. (eds.) Uncertainty in Artificial Intelligence 15, Stockholm, Sweden, pp. 612–621 (1999)
4. Zadeh, L.A.: On the validity of Dempster's rule of combination. Memo M79/24, University of California, Berkeley, USA (1979)
5. Lemmer, J.: Confidence factors, empiricism and the Dempster-Shafer theory of evidence. In: Proceedings of the 1st Conference on Uncertainty in Artificial Intelligence (UAI-85), pp. 160–176 (1985)
6. Pearl, J.: Reasoning with belief functions: an analysis of compatibility. IJAR **4**, 363–389 (1990). with Rejoinder in IJAR, vol. 6, pp. 425–443 (1992)

7. Voorbraak, F.: On the justification of Dempster's rule of combination. Department of Philosophy, University of Utrecht, The Netherlands, Logic Group Preprint Series, No. 42 (1988)

8. Wang, P.: A defect in Dempster-Shafer theory. In: Proceedings of 10th Conference on Uncertainty in AI, pp. 560–566 (1994)

9. Gelman, A.: The boxer, the wrestler, and the coin flip: a paradox of robust Bayesian inference and belief functions. Am. Stat. **60**(2), 146–150 (2006)

10. Dezert, J., Wang, P., Tchamova, A.: On the validity of Dempster-Shafer theory. In: Proceedings of Fusion 2012, Singapore (2012)

11. Tchamova, A., Dezert, J.: On the behavior of Dempster's rule of combination and the foundations of Dempster-Shafer theory. In: Proceedings of IEEE IS 2012 Conference, Sofia, Bulgaria (2012)

12. Dezert, J., Tchamova, A., Han, D., Tacnet, J.-M.: Why Dempster's rule doesn't behave as Bayes rule with informative priors. In: Proceedings of 2013 IEEE INISTA 2013, Albena, Bulgaria (2013)

13. Dezert, J., Tchamova, A.: On the validity of Dempster's fusion rule and its interpretation as a generalization of Bayesian fusion rule. IJIS **29**(3), 223–252 (2014)

14. Smarandache, F., Dezert, J.: Advances and applications of DSmT for information fusion, vol. 1–4, ARP, USA (2004–2015). http://www.onera.fr/fr/staff/jean-dezert

15. Srivastava, R.P.: Decision making under ambiguity: a belief-function perspective. Arch. Control Sci. **6 (XLII)**(1–2), 5–27 (1997)

16. Nguyen, H.T., Walker, E.A.: On decision making using belief functions. In: Yager, R.R., Fedrizzi, M., Kacprzyk, J. (eds.) Advances in the Dempster-Shafer Theory of Evidence. Wiley, New York (1994)

17. Jaffray, J.-Y.: Utility theory for belief functions. Oper. Res. Lett. **8**, 107–112 (1989)

18. Strat, T.M.: Decision analysis using belief functions. IJAR **4**(5), 6 (1990)

19. Yager, R.R.: Decision making under Dempster-Shafer uncertainties. Int. J. Gen. Syst. **20**, 233–245 (1992)

20. Smets, P., Kennes, R.: The transferable belief model. Artif. Int. **66**, 191–234 (1994)

21. Cobb, B.R., Shenoy, P.P.: On the plausibility transformation method for translating belief function models to probability models. IJAR **41**(3), 314–330 (2006)

22. Dezert, J., Smarandache, F.: A new probabilistic transformation of belief mass assignment. In: Proceedings of the Fusion 2008, Cologne, Germany (2008)

23. Han, D., Dezert, J., Yang, Y.: New distance measures of evidence based on belief intervals. In: Proceedings of the Belief 2014, Oxford, UK (2014)

24. Han, D., Dezert, J., Yang, Y.: Belief interval based distance measures in the theory of belief functions (2016, submitted)

25. Irpino, A., Verde, R.: Dynamic clustering of interval data using a wasserstein-based distance. Pattern Recogn. Lett. **29**, 1648–1658 (2008)

26. Essaid, A., Martin, A., Smits, G., Ben Yaghlane, B.: A distance-based decision in the credal level. In: International Conference AISC 2014, Sevilla, Spain (2014)

27. Jousselme, A.-L., Grenier, D., Bossé, É.: A new distance between two bodies of evidence. Inf. Fusion **2**(2), 91–101 (2001)

28. Jousselme, A.-L., Maupin, P.: Distances in evidence theory: comprehensive survey and generalizations. IJAR **53**(2), 118–145 (2012)

29. Bouchard, M., Jousselme, A.-L., Doré, P.-E.: A proof for the positive definiteness of the Jaccard index matrix. IJAR **54**, 615–626 (2013)

The BF-TOPSIS Approach for Solving Non-classical MCDM Problems

Jean Dezert[1(✉)], Deqiang Han[2], Jean-Marc Tacnet[3], Simon Carladous[3,4,5], and Hanlin Yin[2]

[1] The French Aerospace Lab, 91761 Palaiseau, France
jean.dezert@onera.fr
[2] CIESR, Xi'an Jiaotong University, Xi'an 710049, China
deqhan@gmail.com, iverlon1987@stu.xjtu.edu.cn
[3] UGA, Irstea, UR ETGR,
2 rue de la Papeterie-BP 76, 38402 St-Martin-d'Hères, France
{jean-marc.tacnet,simon.carladous}@irstea.fr
[4] AgroParisTech, 19 avenue du Maine, 75732 Paris, France
[5] ENSMSE - DEMO, 29, rue Ponchardier, 42100 Saint-Etienne, France

Abstract. In this paper we show how the Belief-Function based Technique for Order Preference by Similarity to Ideal Solution (BF-TOPSIS) approach can be used for solving non-classical multi-criteria decision-making (MCDM) problems. We give simple examples to illustrate our presentation.

Keywords: Multi-criteria decision-making · Belief functions · TOPSIS · BF-TOPSIS

1 Introduction

Classical Multi-Criteria Decision-Making (MCDM) consists in choosing an alternative among a known set of alternatives based on their quantitative evaluations (numerical scores) obtained with respect to different criteria. A typical example could be the selection of a car to buy among a given set of cars based on different criteria (cost, engine robustness, fuel economy, CO_2 emission, etc.). The classical MCDM problem, although easily formulated, have no solution at all in general due to the fact that no alternative exists that optimizes all criteria jointly. Thus MCDM problems are generally not *solved*, but a decision is found by means of ranking, compromises etc. The difficulty of MCDM problems is also because the scores are usually expressed in different (physical) units with different scales which generally necessitates an ad-hoc choice of a normalization step that may lead to many problems, e.g. rank reversal.

Many methods have been developed to address the classical MCDM. AHP[1] [1] and its extensions in belief function frameworks [2–6], ELECTRE[2] [7],

---

[1] Analytic hierarchy process.
[2] Elimination and choice translating reality.

© Springer International Publishing Switzerland 2016
J. Vejnarová and V. Kratochvíl (Eds.): BELIEF 2016, LNAI 9861, pp. 75–83, 2016.
DOI: 10.1007/978-3-319-45559-4_8

TOPSIS[3] [8,9] methods are the most well-known and widely used MCDM methods in applications. These methods have already been extended in the belief function framework in our previous works [2,10,11] to take into account epistemic uncertainty, missing scores' values as well as conflicting information between sources[4]. In this work, we show how the BF-TOPSIS methods proposed recently in [11] (with application in [12]), can be directly used for solving also non-classical multicriteria decision-making problems where not only alternatives are scored (with possibly missing values), but also any element of the power set of alternatives.

In the sequel, we assume the reader to be familiar with the theory of belief functions [13] and its definitions and notations, mainly the basic belief assignment (BBA) $m(\cdot)$, the belief function $Bel(\cdot)$ and the plausibility function $Pl(\cdot)$ defined with respect to a discrete finite frame of discernment (FoD).

2   Non-classical MCDM Problem Formulation

We consider a given set of alternatives $\mathcal{A} \triangleq \{A_1, A_2, \ldots, A_M\}$ $(M > 2)$ representing the FoD of our problem under consideration, and we denote $2^{\mathcal{A}}$ the power set[5] of $\mathcal{A}$. In our approach, we work with Shafer's classical model of FoD and we do not allow the empty set to be a focal element[6] because in our opinion it does not make sense to compare an alternative with respect to the empty set from the decision-making standpoint. The cardinality of the (non empty) elements of the power set varies from 1 to $2^M - 1$. We also consider a given set of criteria $\mathcal{C} \triangleq \{C_1, C_2, \ldots, C_N\}$ $(N \geq 1)$, where each criterion C_j is characterized by a relative importance weighting factor $w_j \in [0,1]$, $j = 1, \ldots, N$ such that $\sum_{j=1}^{N} w_j = 1$. The set of normalized weighting factors is denoted by $\mathbf{w} = \{w_1, w_2, \ldots, w_N\}$. The score[7] value is a number $S_{ij} = S_j(X_i)$ related to the evaluation of an element $X_i \in 2^{\mathcal{A}} \setminus \{\emptyset\}$ from a given criterion C_j. If the score value $S_j(X_i)$ is not available (or missing), we denote it by the "varnothing" symbol $\varnothing$. The non-classical MCDM problem can be formulated as follows in the worst case (i.e. when scores apply to all elements of $2^{\mathcal{A}}$): given the $(2^M - 1) \times N$ score matrix $\mathbf{S} = [S_j(X_i)]$ whose elements take either a numerical value or a $\varnothing$ value (if the value is not available) and knowing the set $\mathbf{w}$ of the relative importance weights of criteria, how to rank the elements of $2^{\mathcal{A}} \setminus \{\emptyset\}$ to make the final decision?

---

[3] Technique for order preference by similarity to ideal solution.

[4] In the MCDM context, a source of information consists in the list of scores values of alternatives related to a given criterion.

[5] The power set $2^{\mathcal{A}}$ is the set of all subsets of $\mathcal{A}$, empty set $\emptyset$ and $\mathcal{A}$ included.

[6] As proposed in Smets Transferable Belief Model for instance.

[7] Depending on the context of the MCDM problem, the score can be interpreted either as a cost/expense or as a reward/benefit. In the sequel, by convention and without loss of generality, we will interpret the score as a reward having monotonically increasing preference. Thus, the best alternative with respect to a given criterion will be the one providing the highest reward/benefit.

Example: Let us consider the ranking of five students $A_1, \ldots, A_5$ based on two criteria C_1 and C_2. The criterion C_1 is their long jump performance (in meters), and the criteria C_2 is a realization of a small project to collect funds (in euros) to help a bigger nature protection project. Highest scores values mean better results in this particular context. Let us assume that students were allowed to realize their project in joint collaboration (no more than three students are allowed in a group), or alone. At the end term of the project, suppose that one has the two following evaluations (scoring)

$$
\mathbf{S_{C_1}} = \begin{array}{c} A_1 \\ A_3 \\ A_4 \\ A_5 \end{array} \begin{pmatrix} 3.7\,m \\ 3.6\,m \\ 3.8\,m \\ 3.7\,m \end{pmatrix} \quad \text{and} \quad \mathbf{S_{C_2}} = \begin{array}{c} A_5 \\ A_1 \cup A_2 \\ A_3 \cup A_4 \end{array} \begin{pmatrix} 640\,\text{€} \\ 600\,\text{€} \\ 650\,\text{€} \end{pmatrix} \tag{1}
$$

The scores' values listed in $\mathbf{S_{C_1}}$ indicate in fact that the student A_2 has not been able to pass the long jump test for some reason (medical, familial or whatever), so his score is missing. The scores' values listed in $\mathbf{S_{C_2}}$ indicate that A_5 did choose to realize his project alone with a pretty good performance, and the project realized by the collaboration of students A_3 with A_4 has obtained the best performance (the highest amount of collected funds). In this very simple example, one sees that the score evaluation can be done not only on single alternatives (as for criterion C_1) but also on a subset of elements of 2^A (as for criterion C_2). All the elements having a score are called scoring focal elements. In general, these focal elements can differ from one criterion C_j to another criterion C_k for $k \neq j$ and the score matrix cannot be built by a simple (horizontal) stacking of scoring lists. In general, one must identify all focal elements of each scoring list to determine the minimum number of rows necessary to define the scoring matrix. As mentioned, we use the symbol $\varnothing$ to identify all values that are missing in the scoring matrix. Note that we do not set missing values to zero number (or any other chosen number) to make explicit distinction between the known precise numerical value zero and a missing value. In this example, the scoring matrix will be defined as

$$
\mathbf{S} = \begin{array}{c} A_1 \\ A_3 \\ A_4 \\ A_5 \\ A_1 \cup A_2 \\ A_3 \cup A_4 \end{array} \begin{pmatrix} 3.7\,m & \varnothing \\ 3.6\,m & \varnothing \\ 3.8\,m & \varnothing \\ 3.7\,m & 640\,\text{€} \\ \varnothing & 600\,\text{€} \\ \varnothing & 650\,\text{€} \end{pmatrix} \tag{2}
$$

The question we want to address is how to rank the students based on such a kind of scoring information including disjunctions of alternatives and missing values, taking into account the relative importance weight of each criterion. Is it possible to solve such type of non-classical MCDM problems, and how?

3 The BF-TOPSIS Approach

The BF-TOPSIS approach has been proposed recently in [11] in a classical MCDM context where the focal elements of the scoring function $S_j(\cdot)$ $(j = 1, \ldots, N)$ are only the singletons A_i $(i = 1, \ldots, M)$ of the frame of discernment $\mathcal{A}$. BF-TOPSIS is initially based on belief functions for MCDM support which exploits only the $M \times N$ score matrix $\mathbf{S} = [S_j(A_i)]$ and the relative importance weighting factors of criteria. The first main step of BF-TOPSIS is the construction of an $M \times N$ BBA matrix $\mathbf{M} = [m_{ij}(\cdot)]$ from the score matrix $\mathbf{S}$, and then the combination of components of $\mathbf{M}$ to make a final decision thanks to the Euclidean belief interval distance, denoted by d_{BI}, defined in [14,15].

In fact, the BF-TOPSIS approach can also be directly applied to solve the non-classical MCDM problems because the belief interval $[Bel_{ij}(X_i), Pl_{ij}(X_i)]$ of each proposition (i.e. each focal element which is not necessarily a singleton) X_i based on a criteria C_j can be established in a consistent manner[8] from the score matrix $\mathbf{S} = [S_j(X_i)]$ as follows

$$[Bel_{ij}(X_i); Pl_{ij}(X_i)] \triangleq [\frac{Sup_j(X_i)}{X_{\max}^j}; 1 - \frac{Inf_j(X_i)}{X_{\min}^j}] \qquad (3)$$

where the $Sup_j(X_i)$ and $Inf_j(X_i)$ are computed from the score matrix $\mathbf{S}$ by

$$Sup_j(X_i) \triangleq \sum_{Y \in 2^{\mathcal{A}} | S_j(Y) \leq S_j(X_i)} |S_j(X_i) - S_j(Y)| \qquad (4)$$

$$Inf_j(X_i) \triangleq - \sum_{Y \in 2^{\mathcal{A}} | S_j(Y) \geq S_j(X_i)} |S_j(X_i) - S_j(Y)| \qquad (5)$$

$Sup_j(X_i)$ is called the "positive support" of X_i because it measures how much X_i is better than other propositions according to criterion C_j, and $Inf_j(X_i)$ is called the "negative support" of X_i because it measures how much X_i is worse than other propositions according to criterion C_j. The length of interval $[0, Sup_j(X_i)]$ measures the support in favor of X_i as being the best proposition with respect to all other ones, and the length of $[Inf_j(X_i), 0]$ measures the support against X_i based on the criterion C_j.

The denominators involved in (3), are defined by $X_{\max}^j \triangleq \max_i Sup_j(X_i)$ and $X_{\min}^j \triangleq \min_i Inf_j(X_i)$, and they are supposed different from zero[9]. From the belief interval $[Bel_{ij}(X_i); Pl_{ij}(X_i)]$, we obtain the BBA $m_{ij}(\cdot)$ defined by

$$m_{ij}(X_i) \triangleq Bel_{ij}(X_i) \qquad (6)$$

$$m_{ij}(\bar{X}_i) \triangleq Bel_{ij}(\bar{X}_i) = 1 - Pl_{ij}(X_i) \qquad (7)$$

$$m_{ij}(X_i \cup \bar{X}_i) \triangleq Pl_{ij}(X_i) - Bel_{ij}(X_i) \qquad (8)$$

---

[8] Indeed, $Bel_{ij}(X_i)$ and $Bel_{ij}(\bar{X}_i)$ (where $\bar{X}_i$ is the complement of X_i in the FoD $\mathcal{A}$) belong to $[0, 1]$ and they are consistent because the equality $Pl_{ij}(X_i) = 1 - Bel_{ij}(\bar{X}_i)$ holds. The proof is similar to the one given in [11].

[9] If $X_{\max}^j = 0$ then $Bel_{ij}(X_i) = 0$, and if $X_{\min}^j = 0$ then $Pl_{ij}(X_i) = 1$, so that $Bel_{ij}(\bar{X}_i) = 0$.

If a numerical value $S_j(X_i)$ is missing in the score matrix $\mathbf{S}$ (it is equal to $\varnothing$), one chooses $m_{ij}(\cdot)$ equals $(0, 0, 1)$, i.e., one takes a vacuous belief assignment. In [11], we have proposed four methods (called BF-TOPSIS1, ..., BFTOPSIS4) to make a decision from the BBA matrix $\mathbf{M} = [m_{ij}(\cdot)]$. Due to space restriction constraint, we just recall the principle of the BF-TOPSIS1 method because it is the simplest one. Applications of BFTOPSIS2–BFTOPSIS4 methods to non-classical MCDM problems is also possible without difficulty. The proposed transformation of score values to BBAs and basis of BF-TOPSIS method are theoretically justified in [11].

Before presenting succinctly the BF-TOPSIS1 method, we need to recall the definition of Belief Interval-based Euclidean distances $d_{BI}(m_1, m_2)$ introduced in [14] between two BBAs $m_1(\cdot)$ and $m_2(\cdot)$ defined on a same FoD Θ. Mathematically, $d_{BI}(m_1, m_2)$ is defined by

$$d_{BI}(m_1, m_2) \triangleq \sqrt{N_c \cdot \sum_{X \in 2^\Theta} d_W^2(BI_1(X), BI_2(X))} \qquad (9)$$

where $N_c = 1/2^{|\Theta|-1}$ is a normalization factor to have $d_{BI}(m_1, m_2) \in [0, 1]$, and $d_W(BI_1(X), BI_2(X))$ is the Wassertein distance [16] between belief intervals $BI_1(X) \triangleq [Bel_1(X), Pl_1(X)] = [a_1, b_1]$ and $BI_2(X) \triangleq [Bel_2(X), Pl_2(X)] = [a_2, b_2]$. More specifically,

$$d_W([a_1, b_1], [a_2, b_2]) \triangleq \sqrt{\left[\frac{a_1 + b_1}{2} - \frac{a_2 + b_2}{2}\right]^2 + \frac{1}{3}\left[\frac{b_1 - a_1}{2} - \frac{b_2 - a_2}{2}\right]^2} \qquad (10)$$

In [14], we have proved that $d_{BI}(x, y)$ is a true distance metric.

Principle of BF-TOPSIS1: From the BBA matrix $\mathbf{M}$ and for each proposition (focal element) X_i, one computes the Belief Interval-based Euclidean distances $d_{BI}(m_{ij}, m_{ij}^{\text{best}})$ defined in (9) between the BBA $m_{ij}(\cdot)$ and the ideal best BBA defined by $m_{ij}^{\text{best}}(X_i) = 1$, and the distance $d_{BI}(m_{ij}, m_{ij}^{\text{worst}})$ between $m_{ij}(\cdot)$ and the ideal worst BBA defined by $m_{ij}^{\text{worst}}(\bar{X}_i) = 1$.

Then, one computes the weighted average of $d_{BI}(m_{ij}, m_{ij}^{\text{best}})$ values with relative importance weighting factor w_j of criteria C_j. Similarly, one computes the weighted average of $d_{BI}(m_{ij}, m_{ij}^{\text{worst}})$ values. More specifically, one computes

$$d^{\text{best}}(X_i) \triangleq \sum_{j=1}^{N} w_j \cdot d_{BI}(m_{ij}, m_{ij}^{\text{best}}) \qquad (11)$$

$$d^{\text{worst}}(X_i) \triangleq \sum_{j=1}^{N} w_j \cdot d_{BI}(m_{ij}, m_{ij}^{\text{worst}}) \qquad (12)$$

The relative closeness of the proposition X_i with respect to ideal best solution X^{best} defined by

$$C(X_i, X^{\text{best}}) \triangleq \frac{d^{\text{worst}}(X_i)}{d^{\text{worst}}(X_i) + d^{\text{best}}(X_i)} \qquad (13)$$

is used to make the preference ordering according to the descending order of $C(X_i, X^{\text{best}}) \in [0, 1]$, where a larger $C(X_i, X^{\text{best}})$ value means a better proposition X_i.

Note that once the BBA matrix is computed from Eqs. (6), (7) and (8), we can also apply (if we prefer) BF-TOPSIS2, BF-TOPSIS3 or BFTOPSIS4 methods to make the final decision. Their presentation is out of the scope of this paper.

4   Apply BF-TOPSIS to Non-classical MCDM Problems

Due to space limitation restriction, we present the results of the BF-TOPSIS1 method only for two simple non-classical MCDM problems.

Example 1: This example is given by the score matrix of Eq. (2). We consider the relative importance weights $w_1 = 1/3$ and $w_2 = 2/3$ of criteria C_1 and C_2 respectively. Applying BBA construction formulas (6), (7) and (8) for this example[10], we get the BBA matrix $\mathbf{M} = [(m_{ij}(X_i), m_{ij}(\bar{X}_i), m_{ij}(X_i \cup \bar{X}_i))]$ with

$$
\mathbf{M} = \begin{array}{c} \\ A_1 \\ A_3 \\ A_4 \\ A_5 \\ A_1 \cup A_2 \\ A_3 \cup A_4 \end{array}
\begin{array}{c} C_1 \\ \left(\begin{array}{c} (0.25, 0.25, 0.50) \\ (0, 1, 0) \\ (1, 0, 0) \\ (0.25, 0.25, 0.50) \\ (0, 0, 1) \\ (0, 0, 1) \end{array} \right. \end{array}
\begin{array}{c} C_2 \\ \left. \begin{array}{c} (0, 0, 1) \\ (0, 0, 1) \\ (0, 0, 1) \\ (0.6667, 0.1111, 0.2222) \\ (0, 1, 0) \\ (1, 0, 0) \end{array} \right) \end{array} \quad (14)
$$

From this matrix $\mathbf{M}$, we compute the distances $d_{BI}(.,.)$ with respect to ideal best and worst solutions shown in Table 1. Table 2 provides $d^{\text{best}}(X_i)$, $d^{\text{worst}}(X_i)$ and $C(X_i, X^{\text{best}})$ values computed from the formulas (11), (12) and (13). Based on $C(X_i, X^{\text{best}})$ values sorted in descending order, we finally get the preference order $(A_3 \cup A_4) \succ A_5 \succ A_4 \succ A_1 \succ (A_1 \cup A_2) \succ A_3$. If we restrict the preference order to only singletons, we will get $A_5 \succ A_4 \succ A_1 \succ A_3$ (i.e. student A_5 is the best one). Note that student A_2 alone cannot be ranked with respect to the other students, which is normal based on the non-specific input (scoring) information one has for him. Of course ad-hoc ranking solutions to rank all five students can always be developed[11], but without necessarily preserving the compatibility with the rank obtained previously.

Example 2: In mountains, protecting housing areas against torrential floods is based on a lot of alternatives at the watershed scale such as check dams' series, sediment traps, dikes, and individual protections [12]. Moreover, alternatives can be the maintenance of existing structures or the construction of new ones to

---

[10] When a score value is missing for some proposition X_i (i.e. if $S_j(X_i) = \varnothing$), then we take the vacuous BBA $m_{ij}(X_i \cup \bar{X}_i) = 1$.

[11] For instance by normalizing the $C(X_i, X^{\text{best}})$ values (the most right column of Table 2) and interpret it as a BBA, and then apply a decision method described in [15].

Table 1. Distances to ideal best and worst solutions.

Focal elem. X_i	$d_{BI}(m_{i1}, m^{best})$	$d_{BI}(m_{i1}, m^{worst})$	$d_{BI}(m_{i2}, m^{best})$	$d_{BI}(m_{i2}, m^{worst})$
A_1	0.6016	0.2652	0.7906	0.2041
A_3	0.8416	0	0.7906	0.2041
A_4	0	0.8416	0.7906	0.2041
A_5	0.6016	0.2652	0.2674	0.5791
$A_1 \cup A_2$	0.5401	0.3536	0.6770	0
$A_3 \cup A_4$	0.5401	0.3536	0	0.6770

Table 2. Average distances and relative closeness indicators.

Focal elem. X_i	$d^{best}(X_i)$	$d^{worst}(X_i)$	$C(X_i, X^{best})$	Ranking
A_1	0.7276	0.2245	0.2358	4
A_3	0.8076	0.1361	0.1442	6
A_4	0.5270	0.4166	0.4415	3
A_5	0.3788	0.4745	0.5561	2
$A_1 \cup A_2$	0.6314	0.1179	0.1573	5
$A_3 \cup A_4$	0.1800	0.5692	0.7597	1

increase the protection level. Final propositions generally involve several of previous individual alternatives. We propose here a simplified case of application. Within a given watershed, a check-dams' series already exists. Older than one century years old, its maintenance (alternative A_1) is questioned. Some experts propose to abandon it and to build a sediment trap upstream the alluvial fan (alternative A_2) or to limit damage on buildings through individual protections (alternative A_3). The Decision-Maker (DM), here the local municipality, must decide the best proposition taking into account several criteria: the investment cost (C_1 in €, in negative values), the risk reduction in 50 years between the current situation and the expected situation after each proposition implementation (C_2 in €), the impact on environment (C_3 is a grade from 1 to 10), and the land-use areas needed in privates (C_4 in m^2, in negative values). For each criterion, the higher is the score, the better is the proposition. The DM gives the same importance weight to C_1 and C_2 ($w_1 = w_2 = 0.33$), but they are more important than C_3 ($w_3 = 0.20$) which is more important than C_4 ($w_4 = 0.14$). The score matrix is given in Eq. (15). In this case, the problem is not to have no knowledge on some scores but is that they are not cumulative in the same way for each criterion. For C_1 and C_4, the score of the disjunction of two alternatives is the sum of individual scores whereas it is not the case for C_2 and C_3.

$$\mathbf{S} = \begin{matrix} A_1 \\ A_2 \\ A_3 \\ A_1 \cup A_2 \\ A_1 \cup A_3 \\ A_2 \cup A_3 \\ A_1 \cup A_2 \cup A_3 \end{matrix} \begin{pmatrix} C_1 & C_2 & C_3 & C_4 \\ -150000 & 100000 & 10 & 0 \\ -500000 & 200000 & 2 & -20000 \\ -550000 & 250000 & 10 & -5000 \\ -650000 & 230000 & 2 & -20000 \\ -700000 & 250000 & 10 & -5000 \\ -1050000 & 250000 & 2 & -25000 \\ -1200000 & 250000 & 2 & -25000 \end{pmatrix} \qquad (15)$$

The BBA matrix based on **S** using (3), (4), (5), (6), (7) and (8) (rounded to 2 decimal points) is

$$
M = \begin{array}{c} A_1 \\ A_2 \\ A_3 \\ A_1 \cup A_2 \\ A_1 \cup A_3 \\ A_2 \cup A_3 \\ A_1 \cup A_2 \cup A_3 \end{array}
\begin{array}{cccc}
C_1 & C_2 & C_3 & C_4 \\
(1,0,0) & (0,1,0) & (1,0,0) & (1,0,0) \\
(0.44,0.10,0.46) & (0.45,0.28,0.27) & (0,1,0) & (0.10,0.67,0.23) \\
(0.37,0.13,0.50) & (1,0,0) & (1,0,0) & (0.70,0.07,0.23) \\
(0.27,0.21,0.52) & (0.73,0.10,0.17) & (0,1,0) & (0.10,0.67,0.23) \\
(0.23,0.26,0.51) & (1,0,0) & (1,0,0) & (0.70,0.07,0.23) \\
(0.04,0.75,0.21) & (1,0,0) & (0,1,0) & (0,1,0) \\
(0,1,0) & (1,0,0) & (0,1,0) & (0,1,0)
\end{array} \qquad (16)
$$

The weighted distances to the ideal best and worst solutions and the relative closeness indicator are listed in Table 3. Based on relative closeness indicator sorted in descending order, the final preference order is $(A_1 \cup A_3) \succ A_3 \succ A_1 \succ (A_1 \cup A_2) \succ (A_2 \cup A_3) \succ A_2 \succ (A_1 \cup A_2 \cup A_3)$: maintaining the existing check dams' series and implementing individual protections is the best option. If the preferences are restricted to single alternatives, one will get as final preference order $A_3 \succ A_1 \succ A_2$, i.e. option A_3 (only individual protections) should be preferred by the DM.

Table 3. Average distances and relative closeness indicators.

Focal elem. X_i	$d^{\text{best}}(X_i)$	$d^{\text{worst}}(X_i)$	$C(X_i, X^{\text{best}})$	Ranking
A_1	0.3012	0.6116	0.6700	3
A_2	0.5668	0.3677	0.3935	6
A_3	0.1830	0.7483	0.8035	2
$A_1 \cup A_2$	0.4476	0.4901	0.5226	4
$A_1 \cup A_3$	0.1555	0.7775	0.8333	1
$A_2 \cup A_3$	0.5562	0.3614	0.3938	5
$A_1 \cup A_2 \cup A_3$	0.8328	0.2694	0.2444	7

5 Conclusions

In this paper, we have shown how the BF-TOPSIS approach can be exploited to solve non-classical MCDM problems. This method is relatively easy to use. It does not require the normalization of data and offers a consistent construction of basic belief assignments from the available scoring values. It can also deal with missing scoring values and different criteria weights as well. In this paper only the BF-TOPSIS1 method has been presented, but other more sophisticate BF-TOPSIS methods could be also used to solve non-classical problems, but at the price of a higher complexity. The application of this new BF-TOPSIS approach to solve non-classical MCDM problems for natural risk prevention is currently under evaluation, and it will be reported in a forthcoming publication.

References

1. Saaty, T.: The Analytic Hierarchy Process. McGraw-Hill, New York (1980)
2. Dezert, J., Tacnet, J.-M., Batton-Hubert, M., Smarandache, F.: Multi-criteria decision making based on DSmT/AHP. In: Proceedings of the International Workshop on Belief Functions, Brest, France (2010)
3. Dezert, J., Tacnet, J.-M.: Evidential reasoning for multi-criteria analysis based on DSmT-AHP. In: Proceedings of the ISAHP 2011, Italy (2011)
4. Tacnet, J.-M., Dezert, J., Batton-Hubert, M.: AHP and uncertainty theories for decision making using the ER-MCDA methodology. In: Proceedings of the ISAHP 2011, Italy (2011)
5. Ennaceur, A., Elouedi, Z., Lefevre, E.: Multi-criteria decision making method with belief preference relations. Int. J. Uncertainty Fuzziness Knowl. Based Syst. (IJUFKS) **22**(4), 573–590 (2014)
6. Ennaceur, A., Elouedi, Z., Lefevre, E.: Belief AHP method: AHP method with the belief function framework. Int. J. Inf. Technol. Decis. Making (IJITDM) **15**(3), 553–573 (2016)
7. Wang, X., Triantaphyllou, E.: Ranking irregularities when evaluating alternatives by using some ELECTRE methods. Omega **36**(1), 45–63 (2008)
8. Hwang, C.L., Yoon, K.: Multiple Attribute Decision Making. Lecture Notes in Economics and Mathematical Systems, vol. 186. Springer-Verlag, Berlin (1981)
9. Lai, Y.J., Liu, T.Y., Hwang, C.L.: TOPSIS for MODM. Eur. J. Oper. Res. **76**(3), 486–500 (1994)
10. Dezert, J., Tacnet, J.-M.: Soft ELECTRE TRI outranking method based on belief functions. In: Proceedings of the 15th Fusion Conference, Singapore (2012)
11. Dezert, J., Han, D., Yin, H.: A new belief function based approach for multi-criteria decision-making support. In: Proceedings of the 19th International Fusion Conference, Heidelberg, Germany (2016)
12. Carladous, S., Tacnet, J.-M., Dezert, J., Han, D., Batton-Hubert, M.: Evaluation of efficiency of torrential protective structures with new BF-TOPSIS methods. In: Proceedings of the 19th Fusion Conference, Heidelberg, Germany (2016)
13. Shafer, G.: A Mathematical Theory of Evidence. Princeton University Press, Princeton (1976)
14. Han, D., Dezert, J., Yang, Y.: New distance measures of evidence based on belief intervals. In: Proceedings of the 3rd Belief International Conference, Oxford (2014)
15. Dezert, J., Han, D., Tacnet, J.-M., Carladous, S., Yang, Y.: Decision-making with belief interval distance. In: Proceedings of the 4th Belief International Conference, Prague, Czech Republic (2016)
16. Irpino, A., Verde, R.: Dynamic clustering of interval data using a wasserstein-based distance. Pattern Recogn. Lett. **29**, 1648–1658 (2008)

Use of Evidence Theory in Fault Tree Analysis for Road Safety Inspection

Nopadon Kronprasert[(✉)] and Nattika Thipnee

Excellence Center in Infrastructure Technology and Transportation
Engineering (ExCITE), Department of Civil Engineering,
Chiang Mai University, Chiang Mai, Thailand
nopkron@eng.cmu.ac.th

Abstract. Road traffic accidents are among the most pressing transportation-related issues; they have not yet been addressed in a satisfactory way in many countries. They can be viewed as failures of road safety systems caused by a set of contributing components. This paper proposes a belief fault tree analysis model based on road safety inspection for identifying road infrastructure deficiencies that influence an accident occurrence and guiding highway professionals in the implementation of proper correction actions. Fault Tree Analysis is used as a risk assessment technique to diagnose the failures of road safety systems, while evidence theory is used to represent the probabilistic-based information under uncertainty gathered from expert opinions. The proposed approach is applied to analyse a real-world high-accident intersection location. It provides a means for road safety engineers to elucidate the cause of accident occurrence and to conduct road safety inspection under uncertainty.

Keywords: Fault tree analysis · Evidence theory · Uncertainty · Road accident · Road safety inspection · Decision making

1 Introduction

Road traffic accidents have been acknowledged as one of the most serious phenomena due to the problem of life loss and economic loss. Many national and international attempts have been made in order to alleviate the road accident situations. However, they have not yet been addressed in a satisfactory way. Among various road safety improvement programs, Road Safety Inspection (RSI) program is a proactive tool to prevent the accident occurrence. RSI is a site review of hazardous conditions and an identification of road infrastructure failures and deficiencies that influence an accident loss. It needs expert opinions and experience in road safety, but does not require in-depth data input [1].

The study considers a road as a system and road accidents are the consequence of road safety system failure. Road traffic accidents are the chain of event caused by three contributing elements, which are (i) the roadway and environmental system; (ii) the driver system; and (iii) the vehicle system. [2] This study proposes a systemic approach by using an evidence theory in Fault Tree Analysis (FTA) as a mean to identify road safety deficiencies and recommend safety measures. Fault Tree Analysis (FTA) is used

© Springer International Publishing Switzerland 2016
J. Vejnarová and V. Kratochvíl (Eds.): BELIEF 2016, LNAI 9861, pp. 84–93, 2016.
DOI: 10.1007/978-3-319-45559-4_9

as a risk and reliability analysis technique to diagnose the failures of the road safety system, while evidence theory is used to represent the probabilistic-based information under ignorance from expert opinions.

The study approaches the road safety inspection as decisions under uncertainty of which safety experts have ambiguous and conflicting opinions about the possible risk of accidents. The new approach for road safety inspection is proposed that models decision systems based on fault tree analysis and employs uncertain knowledge in supporting decision-making. The study selects a right-turn angled collision at a high-accident intersection location as a case study to demonstrate the application of evidence theory and FTA to road safety inspection.

2 Literature Review

Fault Tree Analysis (FTA) is a well-known risk analysis technique to diagnose the failures of many engineering systems. FTA helps determine the combinations of hardware component failures and human errors that result in the occurrence of undesired outcome [3–5]. Figure 1 shows the typical structure of fault tree. Under the fault tree structure, an undesired outcome is referred to a "top event", causes are referred to "basic events" (e.g. E1–E6 in Fig. 1), and the intermediate events (e.g. G1–G3 in Fig. 1).

The traditional FTA calculates the probability of the top event based on the probabilistic-based information. It assumes that a probability distribution of each basic event is known and complete. Such information can be derived from either database or expert knowledge.

In real-world risk and reliability analyses, the information is incomplete or imprecise. It has been argued that traditional probabilities are no longer appropriate to represent uncertainty associated with ignorance particularly where probabilities of basic events are not known or sufficient past statistical data are not completed. [6, 7] During the last decade, a number of studies have been made to apply the concept of fuzzy logic to the fault-tree analysis in several systems [8–10]. Their results showed the

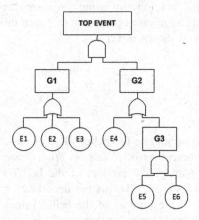

Fig. 1. Structure of fault tree

compatibility of fuzzy logic with the fault-tree analysis. However, the fuzzy set theory is limited to deal with data under vagueness.

Recent developments in evidence theory, also known as Dempster-Shafer Theory (DST), have revealed how probability can be used to represent incomplete or imprecise information, especially information that is based on human judgment or human-machine interaction. DST was developed by Dempster and Shafer as an extension of probability theory. [6, 11–13] DST has been applied in reliability analyses in engineering systems where several states cannot be distinguished from one another or the state of "I don't know" exists. [13–18] This paper employs the basic concepts of DST including the Dempster Rule of Combination (DRC), the method of defining the basic probability assignment (bpa), and the calculation of the lower and upper probabilities (belief and plausibility measures.)

3   Evidence Theory in Fault Tree Analysis

The study proposes the fault tree analysis with evidence theory for examining factors that affect the occurrence of road traffic accidents. The steps of analysis are as follows.

Step 1. Construct a logical fault-tree diagram consisting of a top event and basic events, and determine the minimum cut sets of the fault tree.

Step 2. Interview experts to assign the basic probability assignment (or belief value) associated with the truth of individual basic events. Each basic event has three outcomes (X_i) and their associated belief value are: $m_k(T)$ for *True*, $m_k(F)$ for *False*, and $m_k(T \cup F)$ for *I don't know*. Two basic questions are asked: how much does the expert believe that the basic event leads to the accident occurrence; and how much are they confident about their belief value. In other words, the lower and upper probabilities for basic event k are assigned.

$$\sum_{X_i \subseteq X} m_k(X_i) = m_k(T) + m_k(F) + m_k(T \cup F) = 1 \tag{1}$$

Step 3. Aggregate experts' opinions by using the Dempster's rule of combination (DRC). DRC is an aggregate operator in evidence theory used for combining two belief values as shown in Eq. (2).

$$m_k(X_i) = \frac{\displaystyle\sum_{X_U, X_V | X_U \cap X_V = X_p} m_{k,1}(X_U) \cdot m_{k,2}(X_V)}{1 - \displaystyle\sum_{X_U, X_V | X_U \cap X_V = \varnothing} m_{k,1}(X_U) \cdot m_{k,2}(X_V)} \tag{2}$$

where $m_{k,1}(X)$ and $m_{k,2}(X)$ be the belief value of basic event k from experts 1 and 2 where the outcomes of X can be *True*, *False*, or *I don't know*. The numerator is the sum of the product of the belief values that supports set X assigned by each expert, whereas the denominator is a normalizing factor which is the sum of the product of the belief values associated with all the possible combinations of opinions that are not in conflict.

Step 4. Calculate the basic probability assignment of the intermediate and top events of the fault tree. The basic probability assignment of the event is calculated by Eqs. (3)–(5) for the "OR" gate and by Eqs. (6)–(8) for the "AND" gate. Let $\{m_k(T),\ m_k(F),\ m_k(T \cup F)\}$ and $\{m_l(T),\ m_l(F),\ m_l(T \cup F)\}$ denote the basic probability assignment of the event k and l, respectively.

For the OR gate

$$
\begin{aligned}
m(T) = {}& m_k(T)m_l(T) + m_k(T)m_l(F) + m_k(T)m_l(T \cup F) \\
& + m_k(F)m_l(T) + m_k(T \cup F)m_l(T)
\end{aligned}
\tag{3}
$$

$$
m(F) = m_k(F)m_l(F)
\tag{4}
$$

$$
\begin{aligned}
m(T \cup F) = {}& m_k(F)m_l(T \cup F) + m_k(T \cup F)m_l(F) \\
& + m_k(T \cup F)m_l(T \cup F)
\end{aligned}
\tag{5}
$$

For the AND gate

$$
m(T) = m_k(T)m_l(T)
\tag{6}
$$

$$
\begin{aligned}
m(F) = {}& m_k(T)m_l(F) + m_k(F)m_l(T) + m_k(F)m_l(F) \\
& + m_k(F)m_l(T \cup F) + m_k(T \cup F)m_l(F)
\end{aligned}
\tag{7}
$$

$$
\begin{aligned}
m(T \cup F) = {}& m_k(T)m_l(T \cup F) + m_k(T \cup F)m_l(T) \\
& + m_k(T \cup F)m_l(T \cup F)
\end{aligned}
\tag{8}
$$

Step 5. Once the basic probability assignment of the top event $m_{top}(X)$ of the fault tree is calculated, then compute the Belief measure (*Bel*) and Plausibility measure (*Pl*) of the top event by Eqs. (9) and (10), which indicate the lower (conservative) and upper (optimistic) failure probabilities.

$$
Bel_{top} = m_{top}(T)
\tag{9}
$$

$$
Pl_{top} = m_{top}(T) + m_{top}(T \cup F)
\tag{10}
$$

Step 6. Recalculate the basic probability assignment and Belief measure of the top event when each basic event is unavailable, $Bel_{top}\{E_k = 0\}$. In this step, the basic event E_k is removed one at a time from the fault tree, and then repeat Steps 4 and 5.

Step 7. Compute importance measures (I_k) for individual basic events and minimum cut sets. The importance measure is calculated by the difference between failure probabilities (belief values) of top events when all basic events exist (from Step 5) and when each event k does not exist (from Step 6)

$$
I_k = Bel_{top} - Bel_{top}(E_k = 0)
\tag{11}
$$

Step 8. Set the priority among the basic events based on the importance measure (I_k) and then propose corrective actions to minimize the failure of accident occurrence according to the highly important minimum cut sets.

4   Application to Road Safety Inspection

The proposed approach, belief fault tree analysis, was applied to road safety inspection program at a high accident location in Chiang Mai, Thailand. The location is the unsignalized T-intersection between 6-lane divided major road (north-south) and 4-lane minor road (west-east) controlled by stop operations. Figure 2 shows the layout of this unsignalized T-intersection. There are storage right-turn lanes on both directions of

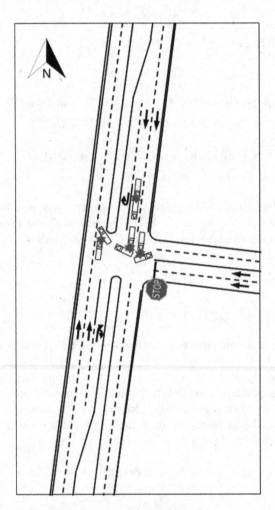

Fig. 2. Layout of intersection area

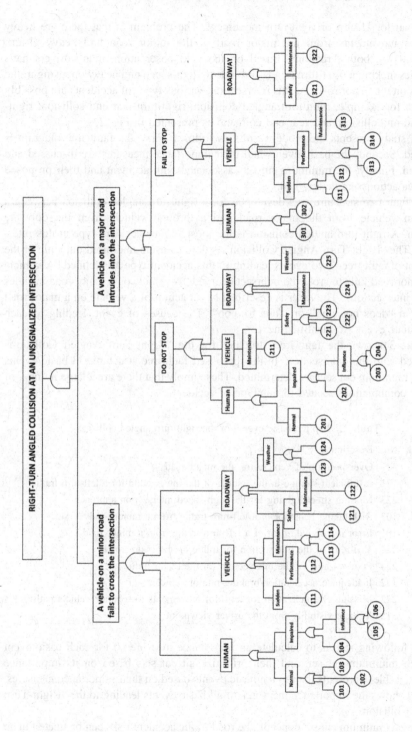

Fig. 3. Fault tree diagram for "right-turn angled collision" case

major road for U-turn or right-turn movement. The problem is that there are heavy right-turn movements from the major road to the minor road and heavy U-turn movements on both directions. Based on the field observation, many drivers have difficulties making a right-turn or a U-turn due to high-speed and heavy opposing traffic volumes on the major road. At this intersection, various types of accidents are possibly occurred; for example, right-turn angled collision, right-turn rear end collision, right-turn head-on collision, and rear-end collision as presented in Fig. 2.

This study presents the model results as follows. First, the fault tree diagram is presented. Second, the basic events and their importance measures are discussed and compared. Finally, the minimum cut sets associated with accident and their proposed corrective actions are determined.

The fault tree structure was developed for a right-turn angled collision between a right-turn vehicle from the major road and a through vehicle from the opposite direction. A right-turn angled collision is the most serious accident type at this intersection. The "Right-Turn Angled Collision" is defined as an undesired outcome or the top event of fault tree. Two events leading to this accident type are defined "A vehicle on a minor road fails to cross the intersection" and "A vehicle on a major road intrudes into the intersection." The latter is described by an action of a vehicle on a major road whether it "does not stop" or "fails to stop". The causes of event, leading to each intermediate event are identified next.

Figure 3 shows the fault-tree structure for the "Right-Turn Angled Collision" associated with this intersection. In this proposed fault-tree structure, 33 basic events and 285 minimum cut sets are determined. These imply that there are a large number of possible combinations related to this type of accident.

Table 1. Top ten basic events of the right-turn angled collision

Rank	No.	Description
1	301	Overspeeding of vehicles on the major road
2	121	Insufficient storage in the middle of the intersection for a left-turn traffic
3	223	Missing street lighting for the high-speed intersection approach
4	102	Risk-taking behavior of a left-turn traffic from a minor road
5	101	Error in gap judgment of a left-turn traffic from a minor road
6	221	Visibility of the intersection for traffic on the major road
7	224	Poor warning of the intersection for the major traffic
8	122	Inadequate acceleration/braking rate of vehicles
9	222	Missing channelization for left-turn movements to separate vehicle paths
10	315	Vehicle visibility from the driver viewpoint

The following step is to calculate an importance measure (I) for each basic event and each minimum cut set, and then prioritize all cut sets based on its importance measure. Table 1 presents the top ten basic events based on their importance measures. Figure 4 shows the importance measures of all basic events leading to the "Right-Turn Angled Collision."

Using a minimum cut set concept, the road traffic accident risks can be treated in an effective manner by prioritizing the minimum cut sets and recommending corrective

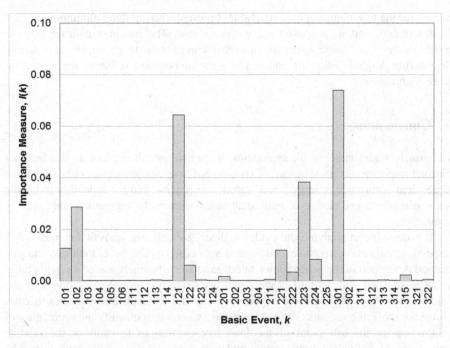

Fig. 4. Importance measure of basic events leading to a right-turn angled collision

Table 2. Minimum cut sets of the right-turn angled collision and their proposed preventive actions

Rank	Minimum Cut Set	Description	Preventive Actions
1	Minor road: insufficient storage Major road: overspeed	Spaces in the middle of the intersection are not adequate to accommodate right-turn vehicles from the minor road waiting to merge the northbound traffic. In particular, when a long heavy vehicle stops and waits to merge, its trailer may intrude into the through lane in the southbound direction	• Provide an acceleration lane to separate through northbound maneuvers on a major road and right-turn maneuvers from a minor road • Redesign or consider other traffic control operations to reduce this type of conflict at an unsignalized intersection • Relocate or close the median U-turn intersection
2	Minor road: error in gap judgment Major road: overspeed	The driver of right-turn vehicle has difficulty judging gap sizes before deciding to make a turn. Such driver decides to proceed when high-speed oncoming vehicles are close	• Increase availability of gaps in through traffic on a major road by properly coordinating with an upstream intersection • Assist right-turn drivers in judging gap sizes by providing visual information for right-turn vehicles from a minor road (e.g. traffic information system)
3	Minor road: risk-taking driving Major road: overspeed	The risk-taking driver from the minor road is likely to cross the intersection even though there is a small headway between two vehicles on the major road. The situation is more severe when the vehicles on the major road approach with the high speed	• Improve the visibility of traffic on a major road for drivers making right-turn from a minor road • Reduce vehicle speeds on northbound so that vehicles approach the intersection as a platoon from the adjacent intersection

actions for the top minimum cut sets. Table 2 presents the top three minimum cut sets, its description, and its proposed preventive actions. The rankings indicate that the higher order of the basic event has a higher contribution to an undesired outcome (Right-Turn Angled Collision), and hence, some immediate treatments are needed for those high rankings.

5 Conclusions

The principal advantages of the application of the evidence theory to fault tree analysis for road safety inspection program are (i) potential to systematically identify the causes of accident occurrence or inspect road safety deficiencies; and (ii) capability to handle ignorance where knowledge of individual safety experts is fragmented and possibly conflicting.

It is desirable in applying the evidence theory to fault tree analysis for road safety inspection program in which several experts are involved. The belief fault tree analysis method developed in the paper allows safety experts to genuinely assign the probability values associated with individual causes of accident. The proposed method uses the evidence theory to represent the expert opinions and the fault tree structure to categorize the roots of accidents. The evidence theory is used to quantify the probability of occurrence for the top event of the fault tree as well as to evaluate the relative importance of individual basic events and minimum cut sets of the fault tree. The rankings of basic events and minimum cut sets are obtained based on the importance values, while their respective preventive measures are proposed to reduce the risks of accident.

To handle uncertainty in road safety inspection program, it is essential to preserve uncertainty as much as possible, and be flexible to use mathematical framework that are most fit to the nature of information available.

References

1. PIARC: Road safety inspection guidelines for safety checks of existing roads (2012)
2. Kuzminski, P., Eisele, J.S., Garber, N., Schwing, R., Haimes, Y.Y., Li, D.: Improvement of highway safety i: identification of causal factors through fault-tree modeling. Risk Anal. 15(3), 293–312 (1995)
3. Geymayr, J.A.B., Ebecken, N.F.F.: Fault-tree analysis: a knowledge-engineering approach. IEEE Trans. Reliab. 14(1), 37–45 (1995)
4. Liu, T., Zhao, T.: Study on fault tree analysis model of road transport safety supervision system and control strategies. In: Proceedings of the ICMIC, pp. 448–453 (2012)
5. Zhang, M., Kecojevic, V., Komljenovic, D.: Investigation of haul truck related fatal accidents in surface coal mining using fault tree analysis. Safety Sci. 65, 106–117 (2014)
6. Guth, M.A.: A probabilistic foundation for vagueness & imprecision in fault-tree analysis. IEEE Trans. Reliab. 40(5), 563–571 (1991)
7. Almond, R.G.: Graphical Belief Models. Chapman and Hall, London (1995)

8. Gmytrasiewicz, P., Hassberger, J.A., Lee, J.C.: Fault tree based diagnostics using fuzzy logic. IEEE Trans. Pattern Anal. Mach. Intell. **12**(11), 1115–1119 (1990)
9. Guimarees, A., Ebecken, N.: FuzzyFTA: a fuzzy fault tree system for uncertainty analysis. Ann. Nucl. Energy **26**, 523–532 (1999)
10. Mohan, S., Elango, K., Sivakumar, S.: Evaluation of risk in canal irrigation systems due to non-maintenance using fuzzy fault tree approach. In: Proceedings of the IEEE International Conference on Industrial Informatics, pp. 351–357 (2003)
11. Chang, Y.: Uncertainties in fault tree analysis. J. Appl. Sci. Eng. **3**(1), 23–29 (2000)
12. Kay, R.U.: Fundamentals of the Dempster-Shafer theory and its application to system safety and reliability modeling. RTA **3**(4), 173–185 (2007)
13. Jacob, C., Dubois, D., Cardoso, J.: Uncertainty handling in quantitative BDD-based fault-tree analysis by interval computation. In: Benferhat, S., Grant, J. (eds.) SUM 2011. LNCS, vol. 6929, pp. 205–218. Springer, Heidelberg (2011)
14. Martinez, F.A., Sallak, M., Schon, W.: An efficient method for reliability analysis of systems under epistemic uncertainty using belief function theory. IEEE Trans. Reliab. **64**(3), 893–909 (2015)
15. Sallak, M., Schoen, W., Aguirre, F.: Extended component importance measures considering aleatory and epistemic uncertainties. IEEE Trans. Reliab. **62**(1), 49–64 (2013)
16. Sallak, M., Schoen, W., Aguirre, F.: Transferable belief model for reliability analysis of systems with data uncertainties and failure dependencies. Proc. Inst. Mech. Eng. Part O: J. Risk Reliab. **24**(4), 264–276 (2010)
17. Sallak, M., Schoen, W., Aguirre, F.: Extended component importance measures considering aleatory and epistemic uncertainties. IEEE Trans. Reliab. **62**(1), 49–65 (2013)
18. Dempster, A.P., Kong, A.: Uncertain evidence and artificial analysis. J. Stat. Plan. Infer. **20**(3), 355–368 (1988)

Classification

Characterization of Experts
in Crowdsourcing Platforms

Amal Ben Rjab[1], Mouloud Kharoune[2], Zoltan Miklos[2], and Arnaud Martin[2(✉)]

[1] LARODEC Laboratory, University of Tunis, Tunis, Tunisia
benrjabamal.ihec@gmail.com
[2] University of Rennes 1/IRISA, Rennes, France
{Mouloud.Kharoune,Arnaud.Martin}@univ-rennes1.fr,
zoltan.miklos@irisa.fr

Abstract. Crowdsourcing platforms enable to propose simple human intelligence tasks to a large number of participants who realise these tasks. The workers often receive a small amount of money or the platforms include some other incentive mechanisms, for example they can increase the workers reputation score, if they complete the tasks correctly. We address the problem of identifying experts among participants, that is, workers, who tend to answer the questions correctly. Knowing who are the reliable workers could improve the quality of knowledge one can extract from responses. As opposed to other works in the literature, we assume that participants can give partial or incomplete responses, in case they are not sure that their answers are correct. We model such partial or incomplete responses with the help of belief functions, and we derive a measure that characterizes the expertise level of each participant. This measure is based on precise and exactitude degrees that represent two parts of the expertise level. The precision degree reflects the reliability level of the participants and the exactitude degree reflects the knowledge level of the participants. We also analyze our model through simulation and demonstrate that our richer model can lead to more reliable identification of experts.

Keywords: Crowdsourcing · Expert · Expertise level · Exactitude and precision degrees

1 Introduction

Crowdsourcing is term for *"the act of a company or institution taking a function once performed by employees and outsourcing it to an undefined (and generally large) network of people in the form of an open call"* [4]. Crowdsourcing platforms are used more and more often to execute tasks that are hard for computers but easy for humans. This form of realizing small human intelligence tasks through a large number of individuals has been used in various domains; and plays a more and more important role. It is also considered as a style of future work [10] that can be crucial for example in the context of decision support [2]. Controlling the

© Springer International Publishing Switzerland 2016
J. Vejnarová and V. Kratochvíl (Eds.): BELIEF 2016, LNAI 9861, pp. 97–104, 2016.
DOI: 10.1007/978-3-319-45559-4_10

quality of obtained data and identifying the workers who tend to give correct answers in this environment still a major problem. The absence of quality control of participants (and their responses) reduces the efficiency of these platforms [5].

One often refers to a participant who gives exact and precise answers as an expert [12]. Several works [5,8,9,11] were proposed to identify the experts in this context. These methods assume that if a worker accepts to complete a task, he will give an answer, even if he is not sure about it. In other words, they make the assumption that a worker does not skip a question. Also, existing crowdsourcing platforms do not allow to give partial results. For example, if the tasks involve a multiple choice question with answers A, B, C and D, a worker cannot say that the correct answer either A or B (he is not sure about), but certainly not C or D.

Some works use first "gold" data on which real answers are known [6]. In that case, a degree of exactitude (the percentage of answers that is not wrong) and a degree of precision (the percentage of answers that is not partial) could be learn to measure the expertise level. Here, we assume we that do not have such data.

In our work, we construct a model where we allow situations where a worker skips some questions or answers them partially. In our model we make use of belief functions that is a powerful framework to take into account such imperfection of data. We propose a novel expert identification technique that by calculating a degree of exactitude (based on a level of answers that is not wrong) and a degree of precision (based on a level of answers that is not partial). The "ideal" worker has a high degree of exactitude and a high degree of precision. For example, in the multiple choice question case, if the correct answer is A then clearly the answer A is better than an answer A or B (higher degree of precision).

The degrees of exactitude and precision are complementary, so using both of them together can lead to better expert identification methods. The rest of the paper is organized as follows. Section 2 formulates the expert identification problem more precisely, together with some relevant related work. We present our approach in Sect. 3. The experimental evaluation is presented in Sect. 4.

2   Expert Identification in the Context of Crowdsourcing

2.1   Notions of an Expert

An expert in the context of crowdsourcing, is the person who provides a large number of correct, complete and reliable answers. The person who acquired a set of knowledge and skills about a particular area. He can extract knowledge and relevant responses with a minimum cognitive effort. He is identified in crowdsourcing platforms by: the precision and the exactitude of responses, the capability to detect the tasks *a priori*, the knowledge, skills and learning level.

2.2   Expert Identification Methods

Evaluating quality of workers and identifying experts in crowdsourcing represents a standing problem. Many authors found that taking randomly workers is a good choice [1] and others found that establishing a good strategy for selecting experts is more interesting [5]. Several researches have been exploring this area, but essentially there are two basic approaches to identify the experts: *Use "gold" data:* Provide participants the questions that we already know the answers and identify the workers who give the correct responses as the experts. *Use multiple workers:* Give a score for each participant which represents his qualities and skills. In this context, Ipeirotis *et al.* improved in [5] the expectation maximization algorithm (EM) to generate a scalar score representing the quality of each worker. [9] proposed an evaluation of the participants by the set of labels. [8] based on behavioral observation to define a typology of workers. [11] proposed an algorithm based on the graphs (SPEAR) to classify the users and to identify the experts. Various methods proposed to identify the experts. But, all these methods have a such level of imprecision and inaccuracy results. In order to ensure a certain identification, we propose to model this imperfection. We proposed an identification of experts with using the theory of belief functions [3,13] which represents a mathematical theory for representing imperfect information and gives a complete framework to model the participant's answers.

3   Identification of the Experts

We would like to identify the experts in a crowdsourcing platform. We assume that the questions (tasks) and a list of answers from the crowd workers available. However, we do not assume any access to a "gold" data that would contain all the correct answers. Such a ground truth would clearly largely simplify the identification of experts. Therefore, we develop novel techniques - based on the theory of belief functions - to calculate the exactitude and precision degrees.

We use the following formalism. We note the responses r_{U_j} proposed by each participant U_j with a mass of belief $m_{U_j}^{\Omega_k}$. Each response is specific for each question Q_k ($k = \{1, \cdots, K\}$) which has a specific frame of discernment Ω_k with $\Omega_k = \{\omega_1^{Q_k}, \ldots, \omega_{n_k}^{Q_k}\}$. The frame Ω_k is the set of all possible responses of Q_k question. Therefore, we obtain a matrix of mass of belief of size s participants/lines and K questions/columns given by:

$$
\begin{array}{c}

\end{array}
\begin{array}{c}
Q_1 \ldots Q_k \ldots Q_K
\end{array}
$$

$$
\begin{array}{c}
U_1 \\ \vdots \\ U_j \\ \vdots \\ U_s
\end{array}
\begin{bmatrix}
m_{U_1}^{\Omega_1} & \ldots & m_{U_1}^{\Omega_k} & \ldots & m_{U_1}^{\Omega_K} \\
\vdots & & \vdots & & \vdots \\
m_{U_j}^{\Omega_1} & \ldots & m_{U_j}^{\Omega_k} & \ldots & m_{U_j}^{\Omega_K} \\
\vdots & & \vdots & & \vdots \\
m_{U_s}^{\Omega_1} & \ldots & m_{U_s}^{\Omega_k} & \ldots & m_{U_s}^{\Omega_K}
\end{bmatrix}
\tag{1}
$$

3.1   Exactitude Degree

The exactitude degree is based on the average of the distance between the response proposed by the participant $m_{U_j}^{\Omega_k}$ and all the responses of the other participants $m_{U_{\varepsilon_{s-1}}}^{\Omega_k}$. This representation of all other participants is obtained by the average of the responses proposed by the $s - 1$ participants for the kth question, such as:

$$m_{U_{\varepsilon_{s-1}}}^{\Omega_k}(X) = \frac{1}{s-1}\sum_{j=1}^{s-1} m_j(X) \tag{2}$$

The distance is then calculated by the distance of Jousselme et al. [7]: $d_J(m_{U_i}^{\Omega_k}, m_{U_{\varepsilon_{s-1}}}^{\Omega_k})$. According to this distance, we calculate the exactitude degree for each participant U_j as follows:

$$IE_{U_j} = 1 - \frac{1}{r_{(U_j)}}\sum_{k=1}^{K} d_{U_j}^{\Omega_k} \tag{3}$$

The assumption behind this method is the majority of participants give a correct answer. This assumption is currently made in information fusion and crowdsourcing.

The exactitude degree can be used to identify the experts. For this purpose, we use the k-means algorithm (with $k = 2$ for expert/non expert). The set of experts is given by the cluster with the higher average of exactitude degree.

3.2   Precision Degree

Based on the model of responses given by the mass functions $m_{U_j}^{\Omega_k}$, we can define a degree of precision.

We recall that we allow the participants to give partial answers, that is crucial for calculating the precision degree. The usual model of responses (that is, the worker must give a complete answer), we could not define a such degree.

We note $\delta_{U_j}^{\Omega_k}$ the specificity degree of the mass function $m_{U_j}^{\Omega_k}$. It is defined by [14] as follows:

$$\delta_{U_j}^{\Omega_k} = 1 - \sum_{X \in 2^{\Omega_k}} m_{U_j}^{\Omega_k}(X) \frac{\log_2(|X|)}{\log_2(|\Omega_k|)} \tag{4}$$

This specificity degree allows to translate the precision level of each response independently of the other participant's responses. To measure the degree of precision of each participant IP_{U_j}, we propose to calculate the average of the specificity degrees for all the kth questions. Such as:

$$IP_{U_j} = \frac{1}{r_{(U_j)}}\sum_{k=1}^{K} \delta_{U_j}^{\Omega_k} \tag{5}$$

We determine the experts by using k-means (with $k = 2$). We do not need the assumption on the majority of participant's answers.

3.3 Global Degree

In order to obtain a global degree, we combine both degrees in a single degree for each participant. The global degree is given by a weighted average as follows:

$$GD_{U_j} = \beta_{U_j} IE_{U_j} + (1 - \beta_{U_j}) IP_{U_j} \qquad (6)$$

The weight β_{U_j} is introduced to give more or less importance for each degree. Hereafter, we do not make any difference between the participants in the crowd.

4 Experimentation

In the following, we generate some mass functions in order to evaluate our approach in the context where there is not use of gold data. We generate three kinds of participants. The **experts** are those who provide precise and exact responses, in the generation of the masses a *singleton* is expected on the correct answer. However, if the expert is not totally sure of him, the *ignorance* is also a focal element. The **imprecise experts** are those who provide exact but imprecise answers, the correct *singleton* can be in a disjunction and the *ignorance* can also be a focal element. The **ignorants** (sometimes called spammers) are those who give random responses with mass functions taken randomly. To verify the efficiency of our approach we make several experiments with 100 participants, 100 questions where each experiment is repeated 10 times.

The precision or the exactitude degree alone is insufficient to identify the experts. The global degree of the equation (6) allows to identify precise and exact responses simultaneously. In a first experiment (with results illustrated in Fig. 1), we vary the experts' number, without generating imprecise experts, from 10 % to 90 % with the global degree in order to prove the ability of our method to identify precise and exact responses simultaneously. In order to demonstrate the importance of each degree we vary in each case the weight β_{U_j} from 0.1 to 0.9. 100 % Good classification rate with $\beta_{U_j} = 0.5$ reflects that both exactitude and precision degrees have the importance to identify experts. Our algorithm identifies correctly the experts and puts all the other participants in the class of the ignorant.

To verify the stability of the good classification rates, we vary in the next experiment (with results illustrated in Fig. 2) the number of questions with 35 % of experts, 35 % of imprecise experts and 30 % of ignorants for 10 iterations, we calculate the three degrees. We measure this stability with a perturbation rate calculated by the standard deviation between the different good classification rate exchange on 10 iterations. This experiment shows that it is necessary to have a certain number of questions in order to ensure a better identification.

We can found that 30 questions provide a reliable good classification rate. All the previous experiments show the ability of our method to identify the experts in the context of uncertain and imprecise responses. The recourse to the theory of belief functions ensures a reliable identification. It solves the problem of imperfection and provides a certain frame of characterization. With both

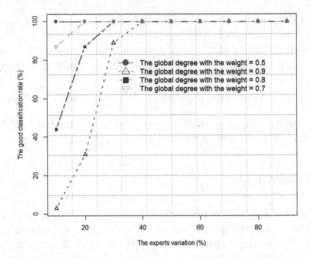

Fig. 1. Variation of the good classification rate according to the percentages of experts

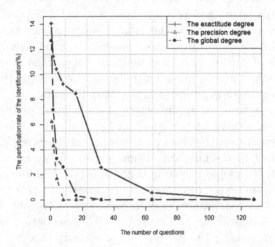

Fig. 2. The variation of the perturbation rate according to the different degrees

degrees, we detect the exactitude and precision level of each participant and we correctly identify the experts in the crowd. To confirm the interest of the theory of the belief functions, we compare our belief approach with the probabilistic approach corresponding to the mass function $m_{U_j}^{\Omega_k}$ which models the responses proposed by each participant U_j given by the pignistic probability:

$$BetP_{m_{U_j}^{\Omega_k}}(\omega_k) = \sum_{X \subseteq \Omega_k, \omega_k \in X} \frac{m_{U_j}^{\Omega_k}(X)}{(1 - m_{U_j}^{\Omega_k}(\emptyset))|X|} \qquad (7)$$

With the same principle in Sect. 3, we calculate the exactitude degree as follows:

$$EP(U_j) = 1 - \frac{1}{r_{(U_j)}} \sum_{k=1}^{K} d_{U_j}^{\Omega_k} \tag{8}$$

where $d_{U_j}^{\Omega_k}$ is the Euclidean distance on the probabilities. We have to do the same assumption on the majority of correct answers. We use k-means to characterize the experts. In this way, we obtain a probabilistic approach available to detect experts. We limit the comparison by the exactitude degree, due to the impossibility to determine the specificity degree with the probability. We vary in this experiment the percentage of experts and imprecise experts at the same time. The results are illustrated in Fig. 3. This figure shows the interest of the use of the belief functions theory to identify the experts and imprecise experts. The probabilistic approach cannot identify the experts from the imprecise experts, it loose the information of exactitude and could not model the imprecision. The regression of the good classification rate to 0 % reflects this inability. Whereas with the belief approach the precise and imprecise experts are better discriminated with all the variations. In complex environment like the crowdsourcing, the theory of belief functions can consider all the imperfection of the participant's responses.

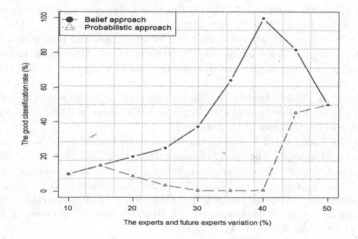

Fig. 3. Comparison between belief function and probability function

5   Conclusion

We introduced a new technique for characterizing the experts in a crowdsourcing platform by using the belief functions theory, to improve the quality of data that one could obtain from such platforms. We use a model where the crowd workers are allowed to skip a question or provide partial answers. Based on a belief model of the participant's responses, we calculated two complementary degrees: An exactitude degree translates the knowledge level of the participants and a precision degree reflects their reliability level. We showed the ability of these degrees to help for the expert identification and we demonstrated the interest of the theory of the belief functions in a comparison with the probability theory.

References

1. Bozzon, A., Brambilla, M., Ceri, S., Silvestri, M., Vesci, G.: Choosing the right crowd: expert finding in social networks. In: Proceedings of the 16th International Conference on Extending Database Technology, pp. 637–648. ACM (2013)
2. Chiu, C.-M., Liang, T.-P., Turban, E.: What can crowdsourcing do for decision support? Decis. Support Syst. **65**, 40–49 (2014)
3. Dempster, A.P.: Upper and lower probabilities induced by a multivalued mapping. Ann. Math. Stat. **38**, 325–339 (1967)
4. Howe, J.: The rise of crowdsourcing. Wired Mag. **14**(6), 1–4 (2006)
5. Ipeirotis, P.G., Provost, F., Wang, J.: Quality management on amazon mechanical turk. In: Proceedings of the ACM SIGKDD Workshop on Human Computation, pp. 64–67. ACM (2010)
6. Ipeirotis, P.: Worker evaluation in crowdsourcing: gold data or-multipleworkers? (2010)
7. Jousselme, A.-L., Grenier, D., Bossé, É.: A new distance between two bodies of evidence. Inf. Fusion **2**(2), 91–101 (2001)
8. Kazai, G., Kamps, J., Milic-Frayling, N.: Worker types and personality traits in crowdsourcing relevance labels. In: Proceedings of the 20th ACM International Conference on Information and Knowledge Management, pp. 1941–1944. ACM (2011)
9. Khattak, F.K., Salleb-Aouissi, A.: Quality control of crowd labeling through expert evaluation. In: Proceedings of the NIpPS 2nd Workshop on Computational Social Science and the Wisdom of Crowds (2011)
10. Kittur, A., Nickerson, J.V., Bernstein, M., Gerber, E., Shaw, A., Zimmerman, J., Lease, M., Horton, J.: The future of crowd work. In: Proceedings of the 2013 Conference on Computer Supported Cooperative Work, pp. 1301–1318. ACM (2013)
11. Noll, M.G., Au Yeung, C., Gibbins, N., Meinel, C., Shadbolt, N.: Telling experts from spammers: expertise ranking in folksonomies. In: Proceedings of the 32nd International ACM SIGIR Conference on Research and Development in Information Retrieval, pp. 612–619. ACM (2009)
12. Rjab, A.B., Kharoune, M., Miklos, Z., Martin, A., Yaghlane, B.B.: Caractérisation d'experts dans les plate-formes de crowdsourcing. In: 24ème Conference sur la Logique Floue et ses Applications (LFA), Poitiers, France, no. 13 (2015)
13. Shafer, G., et al.: A Mathematical Theory of Evidence, vol. 1. Princeton University Press, Princeton (1976)
14. Smarandache, F., Martin, A., Osswald, C.: Contradiction measures and specificity degrees of basic belief assignments. In: International Conference on Information Fusion, Chicago, USA (2011)

k-EVCLUS: Clustering Large Dissimilarity Data in the Belief Function Framework

Orakanya Kanjanatarakul[1], Songsak Sriboonchitta[2], and Thierry Denœux[3]([✉])

[1] Faculty of Management Sciences,
Chiang Mai Rajabhat University, Chiang Mai, Thailand
orakanyaa@gmail.com
[2] Faculty of Economics, Chiang Mai University, Chiang Mai, Thailand
songsakecon@gmail.com
[3] Sorbonne Universités, Université de Technologie de Compiègne,
CNRS, UMR 7253, Heudiasyc, France
tdenoeux@utc.fr

Abstract. In evidential clustering, the membership of objects to clusters is considered to be uncertain and is represented by mass functions, forming a credal partition. The EVCLUS algorithm constructs a credal partition in such a way that larger dissimilarities between objects correspond to higher degrees of conflict between the associated mass functions. In this paper, we propose to replace the gradient-based optimization procedure in the original EVCLUS algorithm by a much faster iterative row-wise quadratic programming method. We also show that EVCLUS can be provided with only a random sample of the dissimilarities, reducing the time and space complexity from quadratic to linear. These improvements make EVCLUS suitable to cluster large dissimilarity datasets.

Keywords: Evidential clustering · Dempster-Shafer theory · Evidence theory · Unsupervised learning

1 Introduction

Evidential clustering extends both hard and fuzzy clustering by modeling cluster-membership uncertainty using Dempster-Shafer mass functions. The collection of mass functions for n objects is called a *credal partition*. The first evidential clustering algorithm, called EVCLUS, was introduced in [4]. This algorithm constructs a credal partition from a dissimilarity matrix, in such a way that more dissimilar objects are assigned mass functions with greater degrees of conflict. This method was shown to perform as well as or better than other relational clustering algorithms on a variety of datasets, even when the dissimilarities are

---

This research was supported by the Labex MS2T, which was funded by the French Government, through the program "Investments for the future" by the National Agency for Research (reference ANR-11-IDEX-0004-02). It was also supported by the Center of Excellence in Econometrics at Chiang Mai University.

J. Vejnarová and V. Kratochvíl (Eds.): BELIEF 2016, LNAI 9861, pp. 105–112, 2016.
DOI: 10.1007/978-3-319-45559-4_11

not Euclidean distances [4]. However, as other relational clustering algorithms, EVCLUS requires to store the whole dissimilarity matrix; the space complexity is thus $O(n^2)$, where n is the number of objects, which precludes application to datasets containing more than a few thousand objects. Also, each iteration of the gradient-based optimization algorithm used in [4] requires $O(f^3 n^2)$ operations, where f is the number of focal sets of the mass functions, i.e., the number of subsets of clusters being considered. This computational complexity of EVCLUS further restricts its use to relatively small datasets.

After EVCLUS, other evidential clustering algorithms were introduced. The Evidential c-means algorithm (ECM) [7] is an evidential version of the hard and fuzzy c-means; it is only applicable to attribute data. A version of ECM for dissimilarity data (Relational Evidential c-means, RECM) was later proposed in [8]. This algorithm is faster than EVCLUS, but it can fail to converge when the dissimilarities are not Euclidean distances. In [11], Zhou et al. introduced another variant of ECM, called the Median Evidential c-means (MECM), which is an evidential counterpart to the median c-means and median fuzzy c-means algorithms. MECM can be used with non-metric dissimilarity data. Yet, it still requires to store the whole dissimilarity matrix. Recently, we introduced another evidential clustering procedure, called EK-NNclus [3]. This method uses only the k nearest neighbors of each object: it thus has lower storage requirements than EVCLUS, RECM or MECM, and it is considerably faster. However, it can generate only very simple credal partitions, in which masses are assigned only to singletons $\{\omega_k\}$ and to the set Ω of clusters.

In this paper, we propose two improvements of EVCLUS, which make it applicable to very large dissimilarity datasets. First, the gradient-based optimization procedure in the original EVCLUS algorithm is replaced by an adaptation of the much faster iterative row-wise quadratic programming method proposed in [10]. Secondly, and even more importantly, we show that EVCLUS does not need to be provided with the whole dissimilarity matrix, reducing the time and space complexity from quadratic to roughly linear. The rest of this paper is organized as follows. The basic notions of evidential clustering and the EVCLUS algorithm will first be recalled in Sect. 2. The improvements to EVCLUS will then be introduced in Sect. 3, and simulation results will be presented in Sect. 4. Finally, Sect. 5 will conclude the paper.

2   Evidential Clustering

The notion of credal partition will first be recalled in Sect. 2.1. The EVCLUS algorithm will then be summarized in Sect. 2.2.

2.1   Credal Partition

Assume that we have a set $\mathcal{O} = \{o_1, \ldots, o_n\}$ of n objects, each one belonging to one and only one of c groups or clusters. Let $\Omega = \{\omega_1, \ldots, \omega_c\}$ denote the set of clusters. If we know for sure which cluster each object belongs to, we can provide a partition of the n objects. Such a partition may be represented by binary variables u_{ik} such that $u_{ik} = 1$ if object o_i belongs to cluster ω_k, and $u_{ik} = 0$ otherwise. If objects cannot be assigned to clusters with certainty, then it is natural to quantify cluster-membership uncertainty by mass functions $m_1, \ldots, m_n$, where each mass function m_i is defined on Ω and describes the uncertainty about the cluster of object i. The n-tuple $\mathcal{M} = (m_1, \ldots, m_n)$ is called a *credal partition* [4]. The notion of credal partition is very general, in the sense that it boils down to several alternative clustering structures when the mass functions composing the credal partition have some special forms [2]. Hard, fuzzy, possibilistic and rough partitions may also be computed from a credal partition as by-products [2,7]. Recently, evidential clustering has been successfully applied in various domains such as machine prognosis [9], medical image processing [6] and analysis of social networks [11].

2.2   EVCLUS

The EVCLUS algorithm, introduced in [4], constructs a credal partition for dissimilarity data. Let $\boldsymbol{D} = (d_{ij})$ be an $n \times n$ dissimilarity matrix, where d_{ij} denotes the dissimilarity between objects o_i and o_j. Dissimilarities may be distances computed from attribute data, or they may be provided directly, in which case they need not satisfy the axioms of a distance function. To derive a credal partition $\mathcal{M} = (m_1, \ldots, m_n)$ from $\boldsymbol{D}$, we assume that the plausibility pl_{ij} that two objects o_i and o_j belong to the same class is a decreasing function of the dissimilarity d_{ij}: the more similar are two objects, the more plausible it is that they belong to the same cluster. Now, it can be shown [4] that the plausibility pl_{ij} is equal to $1 - \kappa_{ij}$, where κ_{ij} is the *degree of conflict* between m_i and m_j. The credal partition $\mathcal{M}$ should thus be determined in such a way that similar objects have mass functions m_i and m_j with low degree of conflict, whereas highly dissimilar objects are assigned highly conflicting mass functions. This can be achieved by minimizing a *stress function* measuring the discrepancy between the pairwise degrees of conflict and the dissimilarities, up to some increasing transformation. Here, we consider the following stress function,

$$J(\mathcal{M}) = \eta \sum_{i < j} (\kappa_{ij} - \delta_{ij})^2, \tag{1}$$

where $\eta = \left(\sum_{i<j} \delta_{ij}^2 \right)^{-1}$ is a normalizing constant, and the $\delta_{ij} = \varphi(d_{ij})$ are transformed dissimilarities, for some fixed increasing function φ from $[0, +\infty)$ to $[0, 1]$. For instance, φ can be chosen as $\varphi(d) = 1 - \exp(-\gamma d^2)$, where γ is a user-defined parameter. Parameter γ can be fixed as follows. For $\alpha \in (0, 1)$, let $d_0 = \varphi^{-1}(1 - \alpha)$ be the dissimilarity value such that two objects whose dissimilarity exceeds d_0 have a plausibility at least equal to $1 - \alpha$. For φ defined as above, we have $\gamma = -\log \alpha / d_0^2$. In the simulations presented in this paper, we used $\alpha = 0.05$, leaving d_0 as the only parameter to be adjusted.

3   Improvements to EVCLUS

In this section, we introduce two improvements to the original EVCLUS algorithm. First, in Sect. 3.1, we show that the special form of stress function (1) makes it possible to use an Iterative Row-wise Quadratic Programming (IRQP) algorithm, such as introduced in [10] for latent-class clustering. In Sect. 3.2, we then propose to use only a subset of the dissimilarities, allowing for a drastic reduction in computing time.

3.1   Optimization Algorithm

To simplify the presentation of the IRQP algorithm, let us rewrite (1) using matrix notations. Let us assume that the f focal sets $F_1, \ldots, F_f$ of mass functions $m_1, \ldots, m_n$ have been ordered in some way. We can then represent each mass function m_i by a vector $\boldsymbol{m}_i = (m_1(F_1), \ldots, m_i(F_f))^T$ of length f. The credal partition $\mathcal{M} = (m_1, \ldots, m_n)$ can then be represented by a matrix $\boldsymbol{M} = (\boldsymbol{m}_1^T, \ldots, \boldsymbol{m}_n^T)^T$ of size $n \times f$. The degree of conflict between two mass functions m_i and m_j can be written as $\kappa_{ij} = \boldsymbol{m}_i^T \boldsymbol{C} \boldsymbol{m}_j$, where $\boldsymbol{C}$ is the square matrix of size f, with general term $C_{k\ell} = 1$ if $F_k \cap F_\ell = \emptyset$ and $C_{k\ell} = 1$ otherwise. With these notations, the stress function (1) can be written as

$$J(\boldsymbol{M}) = \eta \sum_{i<j} (\boldsymbol{m}_i^T \boldsymbol{C} \boldsymbol{m}_j - \delta_{ij})^2. \tag{2}$$

In [4], we proposed to minimize J using a gradient-based algorithm. Another approach, which better exploits the particular form of (1), is to minimize $J(\boldsymbol{M})$ with respect to each row of $\boldsymbol{M}$ at a time, keeping the other rows constant [10]. Minimizing $J(\boldsymbol{M})$ with respect to $\boldsymbol{m}_i$ is equivalent to minimizing

$$g(\boldsymbol{m}_i) = \|\boldsymbol{M}_{-i} \boldsymbol{C} \boldsymbol{m}_i - \boldsymbol{\delta}_i\|^2, \tag{3}$$

where $\boldsymbol{M}_{-i}$ is the matrix obtained from $\boldsymbol{M}$ by deleting row i, and $\boldsymbol{\delta}_i$ is the vector of transformed dissimilarities δ_{ij} between object o_i and all other objects o_j, $j \neq i$. Minimizing $g(\boldsymbol{m}_i)$ under the constraints $\boldsymbol{m}_i^T \boldsymbol{1} = 1$ and $\boldsymbol{m}_i \geq \boldsymbol{0}$ is a linearly constrained positive least-squares problem, which can be solved using efficient algorithms. By iteratively updating each row of $\boldsymbol{M}$ as described above, as long as the overall function value decreases, the algorithm converges to a stable function value, which is at least a local minimum.

3.2   kEVCLUS

As mentioned in Sect. 1, the $O(n^2)$ complexity of EVCLUS, where n is the number of objects, makes it inapplicable to large dissimilarity data. The fundamental reason for this high complexity is the fact that the calculation of stress criterion (1) requires the full dissimilarity matrix. However, there is usually some redundancy in a dissimilarity matrix, even if the dissimilarity measure is not a distance. In particular, if two objects o_1 and o_2 are very similar, then any object o_3 that is dissimilar from o_1 is usually also dissimilar from o_2. Because of such redundancies, it might be possible to compute the differences between degrees of conflict and dissimilarities, for *only a subset of randomly sampled dissimilarities*.

More precisely, let $j_1(i), \dots, j_k(i)$ be k integers sampled at random from the set $\{1, \dots, i-1, i+1, \dots, n\}$, for $i = 1, \dots, n$. Let J_k the following stress criterion,

$$J_k(\mathcal{M}) = \eta \sum_{i=1}^{n} \sum_{r=1}^{k} (\kappa_{i,j_r(i)} - \delta_{i,j_r(i)})^2, \tag{4}$$

where, as before, η is a normalizing constant, $\eta = \left(\sum_{i,r} \delta_{i,j_r(i)}^2 \right)^{-1}$. Obviously, $J(\mathcal{M})$ is recovered as a special case when $k = n - 1$. However, in the general case, the calculation of $J_k(\mathcal{M})$ requires only $O(nk)$ operations. If k can be kept constant as n increases, or, at least, if k increases slower than linearly with n, then significant gains in computing time and storage requirement could be achieved. In the experiments below, we show that this version of EVCLUS (hereafter referred to as k-EVCLUS) is more scalable than the original version, and applicable to large dissimilarity datasets.

4 Experiments

In this section, we first report some results showing the superiority of IRQP over the gradient-based optimization procedure in Sect. 4.1. Experiments with k-EVCLUS are then reported in Sect. 4.2. For all the experiments reported in this section, we used the version of EVCLUS with the empty set $\emptyset$, the singletons $\{\omega_k\}$, and Ω as focal sets. The k-EVCLUS algorithm, as well as other evidential clustering procedures, has been implemented in the R package[1] evclust [1].

4.1 Comparison Between IRQP and Gradient-Based Optimization

The Protein dataset [4] consists of a dissimilarity matrix derived from the structural comparison of 213 protein sequences. Each of these proteins is known to belong to one of four classes of globins. We ran the Gradient and IRQP algorithms on the Protein dataset with $c = 4$, and parameter d_0 set to the largest dissimilarity value. Both algorithms were run 20 times from 20 random initial values. In each run, both algorithms were started from the same initial conditions. Figure 1, which shows boxplots of the stress values at convergence and computing times, for both algorithms. We can see that, on this data, the IRQP algorithm converges more than 10 times faster than the Gradient algorithm. The stress values at convergence for IRQP also have lower variability and are consistently smaller than those obtained by the Gradient algorithm.

---

[1] Available from the CRAN web site at https://cran.r-project.org/web/packages.

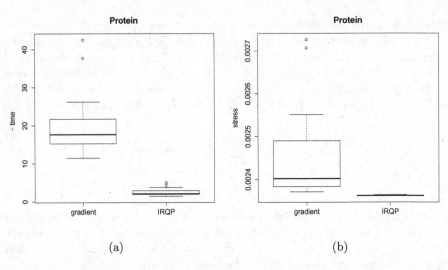

Fig. 1. Boxplots of computing time (a) and stress value at convergence (b) for 20 runs of the Gradient and IRQP algorithms on the Protein data.

4.2   Evaluation of k-EVCLUS

In this section, we report experiments with artificial datasets composed of four clusters of $n/4$ two-dimensional vectors, generated from a multivariate t distribution with five degrees of freedom and centered, respectively, on $[0, 0]$, $[0, 5]$, $[5, 0]$ and $[5, 5]$. The dissimilarities were computed as the Euclidean distances between the data points. Algorithm k-EVCLUS was run with d_0 equal to the 0.9-quantile of distances and $c = 4$. Figure 2 shows the Adjusted Rand Index (ARI) and computing time[2] as functions of k for a simulated dataset with $n = 2000$. The ARI was computed after transforming the credal partition into a hard partition by selecting, for each object, the cluster with the largest plausibility. The values of k were chosen as 10, 20, 50, 100, 200, 500 and 1999. When $k = 1999 = n - 1$, the whole distance matrix is used, and k-EVCLUS boils down to EVCLUS. As we can see, k-EVCLUS performs as well as EVCLUS ($k = 1999$) according to the ARI (Fig. 2(a)), as long as $k \geq 100$, with a significant gain in training time (Fig. 2(b)). We observe that the computing time is higher for $k = 10$ than it is for $k = 20$, which is due to the fact that the algorithm took more time to converge for $k = 10$.

To compare k-EVCLUS with RECM and EK-NN on this clustering problem, we let n vary in from 1000 to 5000 (by 1000 increments), and we generated 10 datasets of each size, from the same distribution. We then recorded the computing times and ARI values for for k-EVCLUS (with $k = 100$ and d_0 equal to the 0.9-quantile of the distances), RECM (with the same parameters as above), and EK-NNclus with $K = 3\sqrt{n}$ and $q = 0.95$. The results are reported in Fig. 3.

---

[2] All simulations reported in this paper were performed on an Apple MacBook Pro computer with a 2.5 GHz Intel Core i7 processor.

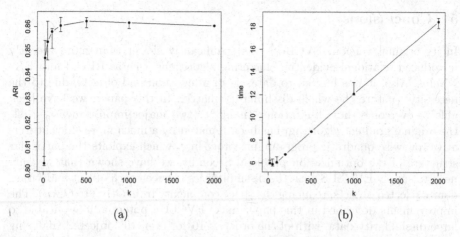

(a)   (b)

Fig. 2. Adjusted Rand Index (a) and computing time (b) of *k*-EVCLUS as a function of k, as a function of k, for the simulated data with $n = 2000$. The error bars show the median as well as the lower and upper quartiles over 10 runs of the algorithm.

From Fig. 3(a), we can see that *k*-EVCLUS and E*K*-NNclus are comparable in terms of computing time for different values of n, whereas the time complexity of RECM seems to be considerably higher. On the other hand, *k*-EVCLUS and RECM yield comparable results in terms of ARI (see Fig. 3(b)), whereas the partitions obtained by E*K*-NNclus have higher variability. It must be noticed that the number c of clusters is specified for *k*-EVCLUS and RECM, but it is not for E*K*-NNclus. Overall, *k*-EVCLUS seems to provide the best results (for correctly specified c) in the least amount of time. More extensive results with several synthetic and real datasets are reported in [5].

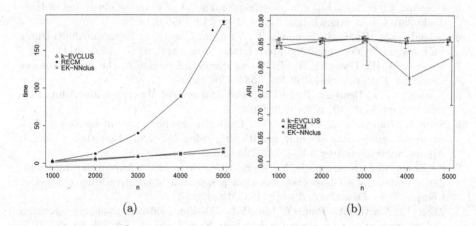

(a)   (b)

Fig. 3. Computing time (a) and ARI (b) for *k*-EVCLUS, RECM and E*K*NNclus for simulated datasets with different values of n.

5   Conclusions

In its original version, EVCLUS was significantly slower than more recently introduced relational evidential clustering algorithms such as RECM and EK-NNclus. Also, it was limited to datasets of a few thousand objects, due to the necessity to store the whole dissimilarity matrix. In this paper, we have been able to overcome these limitations, thanks to two major improvements. First, the original gradient algorithm has been replaced by a much more efficient iterative row-wise quadratic programming procedure, which exploits the particular structure of the optimization problem. Secondly, we have shown that we only need to supply EVCLUS with the dissimilarities between each object and k randomly selected objects, reducing the space complexity from $O(n^2)$ to $O(kn)$. The improvements described in this paper make EVCLUS potentially applicable to large dissimilarity data, with of the order of 10^4 or even 10^5 objects. Analyzing even larger datasets (with millions of objects, as arising in social network studies, for instance), would probably require to sample the rows of the dissimilarity matrix. This issue requires further investigation.

References

1. Denœux, T.: EVCLUST: Evidential Clustering, R package version 1.0.2. (2016)
2. Denoeux, T., Kanjanatarakul, O.: Beyond fuzzy, possibilistic and rough: an investigation of belief functions in clustering. In: 8th International Conference on Soft Methods in Probability and Statistics (SMPS 2016), Rome, Italy, September 2016
3. Denœux, T., Kanjanatarakul, O., Sriboonchitta, S.: EK-NNclus: a clustering procedure based on the evidential k-nearest neighbor rule. Knowl.-Based Syst. **88**, 57–69 (2015)
4. Denœux, T., Masson, M.-H.: Evidential clustering of proximity data. IEEE Trans. Syst. Man Cybern. B **34**(1), 95–109 (2004)
5. Denœux, T., Sriboonchitta, S., Kanjanatarakul, O.: Evidential clustering of large dissimilarity data. Knowl.-Based Syst. **106**, 179–195 (2016)
6. Lelandais, B., Ruan, S., Denœux, T., Vera, P., Gardin, I.: Fusion of multi-tracer PET images for dose painting. Med. Image Anal. **18**(7), 1247–1259 (2014)
7. Masson, M.-H., Denoeux, T.: ECM: an evidential version of the fuzzy c-means algorithm. Pattern Recogn. **41**(4), 1384–1397 (2008)
8. Masson, M.-H., Denœux, T.: RECM: relational evidential c-means algorithm. Pattern Recogn. Lett. **30**, 1015–1026 (2009)
9. Serir, L., Ramasso, E., Zerhouni, N.: Evidential evolving Gustafson-Kessel algorithm for online data streams partitioning using belief function theory. Int. J. Approximate Reasoning **53**(5), 747–768 (2012)
10. ter Braak, C.J., Kourmpetis, Y., Kiers, H.A., Bink, M.C.: Approximating a similarity matrix by a latent class model: a reappraisal of additive fuzzy clustering. Comput. Stat. Data Anal. **53**(8), 3183–3193 (2009)
11. Zhou, K., Martin, A., Pan, Q., Liu, Z.-G.: Median evidential c-means algorithm and its application to community detection. Knowl.-Based Syst. **74**, 69–88 (2015)

SVM Classifier Fusion Using Belief Functions: Application to Hyperspectral Data Classification

Marie Lachaize[1,2], Sylvie Le Hégarat-Mascle[1(✉)], Emanuel Aldea[1],
Aude Maitrot[2], and Roger Reynaud[1]

[1] SATIE, Université Paris-Sud, Université Paris-Saclay, 91405 Orsay, France
{marie.lachaize,sylvie.le-hegarat,emanuel.aldea,roger.reynaud}@u-psud.fr
[2] Veolia Recherche & Innovation, 291 Av. Dreyfous Ducas, Limay, France
{marie.lachaize,aude.maitrot}@veolia.com

Abstract. Hyperspectral imagery is a powerful source of information
for recognition problems in a variety of fields. However, the resulting
data volume is a challenge for classification methods especially considering industrial context requirements. Support Vector Machines (SVMs),
commonly used classifiers for hyperspectral data, are originally suited
for binary problems. Basing our study on [12] bbas allocation for binary
classifiers, we investigate different strategies to combine two-class SVMs
and tackle the multiclass problem. We evaluate the use of belief functions regarding the matter of SVM fusion with hyperspectral data for a
waste sorting industrial application. We specifically highlight two possible ways of building a fast multi-class classifier using the belief functions
framework that takes into account the process uncertainties and can use
different information sources such as complementary spectra features.

Keywords: Hyperspectral classification · Belief Function Theory ·
Waste sorting

1 Introduction

Hyperspectral imaging acquires an almost continuous sampling of the spectral
data in each pixel of a scene. The large number of narrow and contiguous bands
allows us to detect even minor variations in a spectrum and provides a significant
advantage for the distinction of different materials (natural or artificial). Hyperspectral imaging popularity has thus increased during the last decade, due both
to the increase in computing power (that allows us to process these voluminous
data) and to the need of separation of increasingly specific classes, e.g. different
kinds of polymers for industrial application or different mineralogical composi-
tions of surfaces for remote sensing applications. The acquisition of numerous
wavebands enables the identification of fine classes belonging to various fields:
atmosphere analysis, ecosystems monitoring, military applications and industrial
applications (e.g. [5]).

Recently, hyperspectral imaging industrial applications appeared in waste
sorting field. This latter needs new automated processes to improve the working

© Springer International Publishing Switzerland 2016
J. Vejnarová and V. Kratochvíl (Eds.): BELIEF 2016, LNAI 9861, pp. 113–122, 2016.
DOI: 10.1007/978-3-319-45559-4_12

conditions and decrease the cost of recycled materials. This requires sensors able to discriminate among waste materials as close (in terms of spectral response) as different kinds of plastics or different fibrous materials. Then, some efficient classification methods should be defined to use the full potential of hyperspectral data in this industrial context: methods adapted to waste material classes, robust to significant object occlusion (objects stacked on one another), and fast enough to match the waste flow.

Hyperspectral imagery provides detailed spectral information for each pixel of the picture. This information richness comes with an obvious drawback: the huge amount of data to process. Indeed, it involves significant computing resources (time, memory...) that may be an issue in an industrial context. In addition to spectral information, several works also propose to include spatial information in their classification process, e.g. [13]. However, in this study, we focus on blind classification, i.e. classification of each pixel independently (not taking into account the neighbouring pixels that provide the spatial information). For our industrial application, it is a first step towards a classification process at object level which couples blind classification and spatial segmentation using others sensors.

Support vector machines (SVMs) are classically used to meet the challenge of hyperspectral classification, see [7,8,10] for instance. Basically, they project data into a higher dimensional space in which classes can be separated using (optimal) hyperplanes. SVMs are widely used in a probabilistic framework (e.g. through logistic regression). However, probabilities are not able to distinguish between uncertainty (in decision process) due to ambiguity, e.g. because of overlapping between classes, and uncertainty due to imprecision, e.g. because of low number of samples for some score values during the SVM training and calibration processes. Thus, [12] has extended several classical regressions used for SVM binary classifiers to the Belief Function Theory framework.

As SVMs are well suited for 2-class problems, several strategies have been proposed to address the multiclass case. Classical approaches are: (i) the *one-versus-one* strategy, where a classifier is trained on each class pair and (ii) the *one-versus-all* strategy, where a classifier is trained to distinguish one class against all the others. For each strategy, the merging of these 2-class classifiers is an important issue. In this study, we propose and evaluate three strategies to combine binary SVM outputs in the BFT framework. We also show that the use of belief functions allows us to combine the information contained into different input data derived from the whole spectrum data, and that it is an efficient way to deal with the complexity involved by the high dimensionality of the hyperspectral data.

2   Strategies from Binary to Multiclass Belief Functions

Addressing a multiclass problem from binary SVMs (*one-versus-one* or *one-versus-all*), we have to combine their binary decisions while taking into account the imprecision of each SVM (classes overlapping, number of samples, ...).

We choose to perform this combination in BFT framework considering SVM outputs as logical sources. The way an observed score generates a basic belief assignment (bba) is defined by the calibration step proposed by [12]. It is briefly recalled in Appendix. Then, in the following, we assume that each cluster of SVM produces as many bbas as there are SVMs in the cluster, and that each bba represents our belief in each of the two classes handled by the considered SVM as well as the ignorance left by this classifier.

Notation are as follows. For any *one-versus-one* SVM dealing with the pair of classes ω_j and ω_k, $\Omega_{j,k}^b$ denotes the associated discernment frame and $m^{\Omega_{j,k}^b}$ the bba derived from calibration. For any *one-versus-all* SVM dealing with the pair of classes ω_j and its complementary $\bar{\omega}_j$, Ω_j^b denotes the associated discernment frame and $m^{\Omega_j^b}$ the bba derived from calibration. In both cases, the upperscript b recalls that SVM was binary and the cardinality of $\Omega_{j,k}^b$ or Ω_j^b is 2. Then, the transition from binary classification to a multiclass one implies a change of discernment frame from $\Omega_{j,k}^b$ or Ω_j^b to $\Omega = \{\omega_1, \ldots, \omega_n\}$, the multiclass set.

2.1   Case of *one-versus-one* SVMs

In the *one-versus-one* strategy, $\Omega_{j,k}^b = \{\omega_j, \omega_k\}$ and $m^{\Omega_{j,k}^b}$ is interpreted as the result of a conditioning of a multiclass bba m^Ω on $\Omega_{j,k}^b$, noted $m^\Omega \left[\Omega_{j,k}^b\right]$. Then, from these conditioned estimations of the bba, [9] proposes to derive m^Ω by solving the optimization problem:

$$\min_{m^\Omega} \sum_{k>j} \sum_{\emptyset \neq A \subseteq \Omega} \left(m^\Omega \left[\Omega_{j,k}^b\right](A) - m^{\Omega_{j,k}^b}(A)\left(1 - m^\Omega \left[\Omega_{j,k}^b\right](\emptyset)\right)\right)^2, \quad (1)$$

under the constraints: (i) $m^\Omega(A) \geq 0, \forall A \in 2^\Omega$, (ii) $m^\Omega(\emptyset) = 0$ and (iii) $\sum_{A \in 2^\Omega} m^\Omega(A) = 1$. In Eq. (1), the factor $1 - m^\Omega \left[\Omega_{j,k}^b\right](\emptyset)$ is due to the fact that $m^{\Omega_{j,k}^b}$ is a normal bba which may not be the case for $m^\Omega \left[\Omega_{j,k}^b\right]$. To solve such a constrained system, we have noticed that it can also be written as a matrix system $\min_X |\mathbf{AX} - \mathbf{B}|^2$.

In this study, we propose an alternative to derive m^Ω that consists in simply performing a deconditioning of every bba $m^{\Omega_{j,k}^b}$ on the frame of discernment Ω and then combining the deconditioned bbas $m^{\Omega_{j,k}^b \Uparrow \Omega}$ using a conjunctive rule: denoting $B = \bar{A}$ the complementary in Ω of hypothesis A,

$$m^\Omega(A) = \bigcirc_{(j,k)\in[1,n]^2} m^{\Omega_{j,k}^b \Uparrow \Omega}(A), \ \forall A \in 2^\Omega, \quad (2)$$

with

$$m^{\Omega_{j,k}^b \Uparrow \Omega}\left(A \cup \bar{\Omega}_{j,k}\right) = m^{\Omega_{j,k}^b}(A), \ \forall A \in \{\omega_j, \omega_k, \{\omega_j, \omega_k\}\}. \quad (3)$$

This second way is much simpler than the first one and it is theoretically founded on the independence between the binary SVM outputs. Now, it could provide an interesting approximation of the solution and even, it outperforms the optimization proposed by [9] in our application case. Therefore, on this latter at least, there are only advantages in using the proposed alternative.

2.2 Case of *one-versus-all* SVMs

In the *one-versus-all* strategy, the binary discernment frames Ω_j^b are some coarsenings of discernment frame Ω, or equivalently Ω is a common refinement of the different $\Omega_j^b = \{\omega_j, \bar{\omega}_j\}$. Then, the bbas defined on Ω_j^b are refined on Ω using classical refinement operator, before combination using Dempster's rule:

$$m^\Omega(A) = \oplus_{j \in [1,n]} m^{\Omega_j^b \uparrow \Omega}(A), \ \forall A \in 2^\Omega, \tag{4}$$

with

$$m^{\Omega_j^b \uparrow \Omega}(A) = m^{\Omega_j^b}(A), \ \forall A \in \{\omega_j, \bar{\omega}_j, \Omega\}. \tag{5}$$

Here, we use the orthogonal sum instead of the conjunctive combination rule since, due to the existence of singleton focal elements and to the high number of combinations (as much as the number of classes), conflict becomes very important even in standard cases.

2.3 Case of Hybrid Strategy

Each of the two previous strategies handles a given kind of binary SVMs, either *one-versus-one* or *one-versus-all*. Each of these strategies has some advantages: better separability of the classes for the *one-versus-one* SVMs, simplicity and speed for the *one-versus-all* SVMs. Then, in order to benefit from both advantages, we propose a hybrid strategy that handles SVMs belonging to both kinds of binary SVMs.

The proposed solution is based on some metaknowledge on the classes used to choose the considered SVMs. Let us first present the particular case of a hierarchical strategy through a toy example with only 4 classes: $\Omega = \{\omega_1, \omega_2, \omega_3, \omega_4\}$, and assume ω_3 and ω_4 classes are difficult to separate. According to the proposed strategy, one will focus on most performing SVMs, i.e. SVMs 'ω_1 against $\{\omega_2, \omega_3, \omega_4\}$', '$\omega_2$ against $\{\omega_1, \omega_3, \omega_4\}$', '$\{\omega_3, \omega_4\}$ against $\{\omega_1, \omega_2\}$' and 'ω_3 against ω_4'. In a more general way, the classes of Ω are 'wisely' grouped to form a new coarsened discernment frame on which the *one-versus-all* approach performs well ('good' enough class separability, such as for $\{\omega_1, \omega_2, \{\omega_3, \omega_4\}\}$ in the example). Then, the considered classifiers are: the *one-versus-all* SVMs for classes corresponding to singleton hypotheses of the coarsened discernment frame (i.e. some of them are compound classes, e.g. hypothesis $\{\omega_3, \omega_4\}$ in the example) and the *one-versus-one* SVMs for classes belonging to a compound class of the coarsened discernment frame (e.g. SVM ω_3 versus ω_4 in the example). The bbas derived from outputs of previously cited SVMs that have been either refined or deconditioned on Ω are combined using conjunctive rule (or Dempster's orthogonal rule).

This hierarchical strategy appears as a compromise in terms of number of used (and thus trained) classifiers: if $n = |\Omega|$, with the pure *one-versus-one* strategy, we have to consider $\binom{n}{2} = \frac{n(n-1)}{2}$ classifiers, with the pure *one-versus-all* strategy, we have to consider n classifiers and with the hierarchical strategy involving l groups of n_i indistinguishable classes, we have to consider

$n - \sum_{i=1}^{l} (n_i - 1))$ *one-versus-all* classifiers and $\sum_{i=1}^{l} \frac{n_i(n_i-1)}{2}$ *one-versus-one* classifiers.

With respect to the hierarchical strategy, the hybrid strategy can in addition consider few other classifiers in order to increase the redundancy between classifiers and then provide more robust results. However, this number of additional classifiers should remain low to keep an interest in terms of complexity.

Finally, if the derivation of the metaknowledge is a subject beyond the scope of this article (here we simply assume that it can be either known *a priori* or learnt from training samples), let us underline that it is the crucial point for the proposed hybrid strategy since it allows us to add *prior* information (metaknowledge) that should be carefully chosen.

2.4   Decision

Independently of the strategy used, at the end, we have a bba resulting from the combination of the information pieces provided by different binary SVMs taking into account their own features (in particular the learning step conditions and results). From this bba, we can take a decision or, as seen in the experimental part, combine it with other bba(s) and then take the decision.

The belief function framework offers many possibilities for decision making [3]. Among them, pessimistic and optimistic strategies consist in maximizing, over the singleton hypotheses, the belief or plausibility function, respectively. A decision according to the pignistic probability provides intermediate results.

Here, specific to the *one-versus-one* strategy based optimization [9], we also test the following criterion: the decided singleton class ω_i maximizes the conflict generated by conditioning on binary subsets not including ω_i:

$$\omega_i = \arg\max_i \sum_{j,k \neq i} m^{\Omega} \left[\Omega_{j,k}^{b} \right] (\emptyset) . \tag{6}$$

3   Experiments

3.1   Industrial Context and Data Preprocessing

We applied the proposed classification strategies to waste sorting. Despite the use of some sorting components exploiting the mechanical properties of the waste materials in order to separate them, this industrial application has still several issues such as the automatic identification of some resembling materials or the detection of some 'intruders' in a set of similar wastes (e.g. paper, cardboard and plastic waste). For such purposes, the hyperspectral sensor appears relevant since it provides some information about the nature of the material itself that should help us to discriminate among different fibrous materials and polymers with high throughput and a reliability and robustness suitable for an industrial context.

As with any classification method, the performance of a SVM classifier strongly depends on the input data. Classical preprocessing on the spectrum involves a filtering and derivation at different orders. Specifically, the Savitsky-Golay filter is widely used for hyperspectral data analysis [6,11]. This filter fits a low degree polynomial on data within a sliding window having fixed size. It allows us to smooth the data and to compute the derivatives from the fitted polynoms. The fact of considering different derivative orders (typically 0, 1 and 2) appears all the more justified since, for classification, not the whole spectrum is considered but only some selected features, in order to reduce both the data complexity and the correlation between the bands. Then, a classical way is to perform a Principal Component Analysis (PCA) on the filtered spectra, e.g. [1,2]. In our case, the number of selected components is set to represent 99 % of the information. It varies between 3 to about 20 whereas the whole spectrum dimensionality was about 275.

In summary, preprocessing involves the computation of different derivative orders (0, 1 and 2) of the spectrum by the Savitsky-Golay filter and then, for each of these derivatives, the computation of the PCA that provides the input data for the SVM classifiers. In the following, these input data are denoted S_0, S_1 and S_2 where subscript denotes the derivation order. The results obtained using these inputs will be compared in terms of classification performance. We also propose to use them as different logical sources so that, we combine the multiclass (defined on Ω) bbas derived for given input data (S_0, S_1 and S_2). Assuming that the PCA process makes input data cognitively independent, bba combination will be done through the conjunctive rule.

3.2 Experimental Results

The sample sets used for these experiments have been collected in the Veolia laboratories on a hyperspectral sensor (whose spectra contains about 275 wavelengths) via specimen boards with small material samples: four boards called *Paper, Plastic1, Plastic2a, Plastic2b*. Samples are divided in 9 classes, namely 7 polymers classes (not listed here for paper shortness) and 2 fibrous classes (paper and cardboard). From specimen boards, three different datasets were extracted. The first one, called training set, has 1000 samples per class and is used for SVM training. The second one, called calibration set, has 200 samples per class and is used for bba calibration. The last one has 1000 samples per class and is used for test and performance estimation. In addition to this test dataset, another board, exclusively used for testing and called *Superposition*, presents real objects stacked on top of each other to provide more realistic conditions.

Then, the training set allows for the estimation of each SVM classifier parameters, determined by cross validation and grid search, using Gaussian kernels. The calibration set allows for the estimation of sigmoid parameters and contour function defined for any score value (see Appendix for details). It also allows us to determine the classes to group for the hybrid strategy. Then, using the test set and the *Superposition* board, the first analysis (not presented here) puts forward some complementarity of classification performance for the input data S_1 and S_2, in particular for the 'difficult' pixels such as those present in the shadows or pixels corresponding to the superposition of two objects. The initial

Table 1. Correct classification rate (in %) for the 5 test sample boards (each one having 13500 pixels). Results are given for S_1 source, considering different strategies and decisions for the *one-versus-one* strategy.

Strategy→	*One-versus-one*			*One-versus-all*	Hybrid
↓Boards	Score vote	Optimization	Deconditioning		
Paper	95.3	95.2	**95.5**	91.6	94.1
Plastic1	90.2	87.3	**91.4**	85.2	91.0
Plastic2a	79.1	83.7	**84.1**	77.5	79.5
Plastic2b	87.2	89.3	**89.7**	83.9	87.8
Superposition	82.8	88.0	**88.4**	79.5	80.1
Whole data	86.9	88.8	**89.8**	83.5	86.5

analysis also revealed that the S_0 input data provides results of little interest (low performance and lower complementarity) so that it has not been considered in the results presented further.

3.3 Comparison of the Different Strategies

The comparison of the different strategy is presented here in the case of S_1 data that prompts better results than S_0 or S_2. Considering S_1, the hybrid strategy was instantiated introducing two coarse classes: one grouping paper and cardboard and another grouping two classes of polymers (among the 7). A supplementary *one-versus-one* classifier is also considered to remove ambiguities between two other classes of polymers.

Classification results are analyzed in the perspective between comparison of (i) different multi-class strategies (*one-versus-one*, *one-versus-all*, hybrid), (ii) different decision making processes for the *one-vs-one* strategy. Quantitative results, computed on the whole datasets, are shown in Table 1. Our main conclusions are:

- In the case of the *one-versus-one* strategy, solving Eq. (1), the computation time increases dramatically with the number of classes (factor about 200 with the *one-vs-all* strategy computation time). Performing deconditioning (Eq. (2)) as proposed provides slightly better results for a much lower computation time.
- Comparison with classic decision rules, either score voting (shown in Table 1) or probabilistic decision (not shown) shows that the optimistic decision on bba obtained using either optimization or deconditioning (Eq. (2)) is better in every cases.
- The *one-vs-one* strategy always outperforms the *one-vs-all* strategy and the hybrid one, which is a standard result due to the better separability of the classes and much higher number of considered classifiers.

Fig. 1. Example of the fusion impact on classification rate (superposition board). From left to right: test board image, binary representations of the well classified pixels (in white) considering S_1, S_2 and their evidential fusion, respectively.

Table 2. Correct classification rate (in %) for the 5 test sample boards. Results are given for the $S_1 \& S_2$ fusion, considering different strategies.

Boards→	Paper	Plastic1	Plastic2a	Plastic2b	Superposition	Whole data
One-versus-one	93.3	**93.4**	**82.2**	**87.9**	**89.9**	**89.3**
One-versus-all	92.3	91.8	80.1	87.1	87.3	87.7
Hybrid	**95.9**	92.2	78.4	87.3	86.1	88.0

- The hybrid strategy shows intermediate results between the *one-vs-one* strategy and the *one-vs-all* one: depending on the considered test dataset, the improvement relatively to the *one-vs-all* strategy varies between 0.6 % and 5.8 %.

3.4   Combination of Sources S_1 and S_2

In this subpart, classification results are analyzed versus different input data, namely both S_1 and S_2 (combined by fusion) or only S_1 (shown in Table 1). Quantitative results are shown on Table 2. Our main conclusions are:

- The fusion of S_1 and S_2 sources provides no or low improvement compared to the *one-vs-one* strategy, however the complementarity is very beneficial to the *one-versus-all* strategy and narrows the gap between the classification results of the two strategies (from 6.3 % to 1.5 % on the whole dataset).
- Fig. 1 presents the *Superposition* results illustrating that the fusion improves particularly the classification of the difficult pixels, such as at the top of the bottle and the caps stacked on paper.
- The hybrid strategy still provides intermediate results between *one-versus-one* strategy and *one-versus-all* one, but the interest relatively to the *one-versus-all* is reduced (relatively to the case of the only-S_1 data) due to the high improvement of performance of *one-versus-all* strategy provided by fusion.

4   Conclusion and Perspectives

This study has investigated the possibility in BFT to build a multiclass classifier which would be fast and efficient enough to be considered in the industrial context of waste sorting. We compare different ways to achieve it: using the deconditioning operator on bbas derived from *one-vs-one* classifiers, using the refinement operator on bbas derived from *one-vs-all* classifiers or a using hybrid strategy. According to our tests, using *one-vs-one* leads to better performance but requires more classifiers to train than using *one-vs-all* classifiers. Using optimization [9] to derive the multiclass bba from bbas derived from *one-vs-one* classifiers can be advantageously replaced by the proposed deconditioning and conjunctive combination in terms of computation time. Hybrid strategy seems a good compromise between pure *one-vs-one* and pure *one-vs-all* strategies, presenting both reasonable number of classifiers and interesting performance results. Combining multiclass bbas associated to different features of the hyperspectral spectra (different orders of derivative) enhances the classification results in a noticeable way.

A main perspective to our work is the automatic derivation of the meta-knowledge on data used to build the hybrid strategy. We saw that the results provided by hybrid strategy are encouraging. However, the impact of the meta-knowledge has to be investigated and this also indirectly raises the question of the calibration quality of the binary classifiers. Then, we also intend to investigate some evidential criteria that will allow us to analyze training calibration sets, for instance to group automatically some classes and make the most of the hybrid strategy.

Appendix: Evidential Calibration

Handling binary classifiers, the discernment frame is $\Omega^b = \{\{0\}, \{1\}\}$. Then, for a given SVM having its own features in terms of number of samples, learning step performance, we aim at defining a belief function for each score that reflects the confidence we may have in each class. Indeed, this belief function will be used for forecasting taking into account the whole training set specificities. Explicitly, for each score s, the mass function, denoted m, is derived from the contour function: $\omega \rightarrow pl_X(\omega, s)$, where $\omega = P(y = 1|s)$ (note that, ω is not a class but a probability).

To build the contour function on ω, [12] uses the idea behind the logistic regression: approximating the probability $P(y = 1|s)$ by a sigmoid $sig_s(\theta) = [1 + exp(\theta_0 + \theta_1 s)]^{-1}$, where the parameter $\hat{\theta} = (\theta_0, \theta_1)$ is determined by maximizing the likelihood function $L_X(\theta)$ over the training set $X = \{(s_1, y_1), \ldots, (s_N, y_N)\}$ where, for each sample number i, $s_i \in \mathbb{R}$ is the score given by the considered classifier and $y_i \in \{0, 1\}$ is its true label. Then, the contour function of interest is drawn for a given value of score. It derives from the 2D function plotting the relative value of the likelihood function $\frac{L_X(\theta)}{L_X(\hat{\theta})}$ versus $\theta = (\theta_0, \theta_1)$. Then, for any given pair (s, ω), the set of θ (i.e. $sig_s^{-1}(\omega)$) values is a straight line in $\mathbb{R}^2$. Then, the contour function value can be determined as the maximum value over this straight line:

$$pl_X^{\Omega_{j,k}^b}(\omega) = \begin{cases} 0 & \text{if } \omega \in \{0, 1\}, \\ \sup_{sig_s^{-1}(\omega)} \frac{L_X(\theta)}{L_X(\hat{\theta})} & \text{otherwise,} \end{cases} \tag{7}$$

with $L_X(\theta) = \prod_{i=1}^{N} p_i^{y_i}(1-p_i)^{1-y_i}$ where $p_i = \frac{1}{1+exp(\theta_0+\theta_1 s_i)}$. Finally, from each $pl_X^{\Omega_{j,k}^b}$, the corresponding mass function $m^{\Omega_{j,k}^b}$ on binary discernment frame $\Omega_{j,k}^b$ is derived using the 'likelihood based' belief function for statistical inference approach proposed by Shafer and further justified by Denœux [4].

References

1. Cavalli, R., Licciardi, G., Chanussot, J.: Archaeological structures using nonlinear principal component analysis applied to airborne hyperspectral image. IEEE J. Sel. Top. Appl. Earth Obs. Remote Sens. **6**(2), 659–669 (2013)
2. Chen, G., Qian, S.-E.: Denoising of hyperspectral imagery using principal component analysis and wavelet shrinkage. IEEE Trans. Geosci. Remote Sens. **49**(3), 973–980 (2011)
3. Denoeux, T.: Analysis of evidence-theoretic decision rules for pattern classification. Pattern Recogn. **30**(7), 1095–1107 (1997)
4. Denœux, T.: Likelihood-based belief function: justification and some extensions to low-quality data. Int. J. Approx. Reason. **55**(7), 1535–1547 (2014)
5. Grahn, H., Geladi, P.: Techniques and Applications of Hyperspectral Image Analysis. Wiley, New York (2007)
6. King, R.L., Ruffin, C., LaMastus, F., Shaw, D.: The analysis of hyperspectral data using Savitzky-Golay filtering-practical issues. 2. In: Proceedings of IGARSS 1999, vol. 1, pp. 398–400. IEEE (1999)
7. Kuo, B.-C., Ho, H.-H., Li, C.-H., Hung, C.-C., Taur, J.-S.: A kernel-based feature selection method for SVM with RBF kernel for hyperspectral image classification. IEEE J. Sel. Top. Appl. Earth Obs. Remote Sens. **7**(1), 317–326 (2014)
8. Melgani, F., Bruzzone, L.: Classification of hyperspectral remote sensing images with support vector machines. IEEE Trans. Geosci. Remote Sens. **42**(8), 1778–1790 (2004)
9. Quost, B., Denœux, T., Masson, M.-H.: Pairwise classifier combination using belief functions. Pattern Recogn. Lett. **28**(5), 644–653 (2007)
10. Samiappan, S., Prasad, S., Bruce, L.M.: Non-uniform random feature selection, kernel density scoring with SVM based ensemble classification for hyperspectral image analysis. IEEE J. Sel. Top. Appl. Earth Obs. Remote Sens. **6**(2), 792–800 (2013)
11. Vaiphasa, C.: Consideration of smoothing techniques for hyperspectral remote sensing. ISPRS J. Photogram. Remote Sens. **60**(2), 91–99 (2006)
12. Xu, P., Davoine, F., Zha, H., Denoeux, T.: Evidential calibration of binary SVM classifiers. Int. J. Approx. Reason. **72**, 55–70 (2016)
13. Yang, J.-H., Wang, L.-G., Qian, J.-X.: Hyperspectral image classification based on spatial and spectral features and sparse representation. Appl. Geophys. **11**(4), 489–499 (2014)

Semi-supervised Evidential Label Propagation Algorithm for Graph Data

Kuang Zhou[1,2($\boxtimes$)], Arnaud Martin[2], and Quan Pan[1]

[1] Northwestern Polytechnical University,
Xi'an 710072, Shaanxi, People's Republic of China
kzhoumath@163.com, quanpan@nwpu.edu.cn
[2] DRUID, IRISA, University of Rennes 1, Rue E. Branly, 22300 Lannion, France
Arnaud.Martin@univ-rennes1.fr

Abstract. In the task of community detection, there often exists some useful prior information. In this paper, a Semi-supervised clustering approach using a new Evidential Label Propagation strategy (SELP) is proposed to incorporate the domain knowledge into the community detection model. The main advantage of SELP is that it can take limited supervised knowledge to guide the detection process. The prior information of community labels is expressed in the form of mass functions initially. Then a new evidential label propagation rule is adopted to propagate the labels from labeled data to unlabeled ones. The outliers can be identified to be in a special class. The experimental results demonstrate the effectiveness of SELP.

Keywords: Semi-supervised learning · Belief function theory · Label propagation · Community detection

1 Introduction

With the increasing size of networks in real world, community detection approaches should be fast and accurate. The Label Propagation Algorithm (LPA) [5] is known to be one of the near-linear solutions and benefits of easy implementation, thus it forms a good basis for efficient community detection methods. The behavior of LPA is not stable because of the randomness. Different communities may be detected in different runs over the same network. Moreover, by assuming that a node always adopts the label of the majority of its neighbors, LPA ignores any other structural information existing in the neighborhood.

Semi-supervised classification has been widely studied for classical data sets, but there has been little work on semi-supervised community detection. In many scenarios a substantial amount of prior knowledge about the graph structure may be available. It can reflect the application-specific knowledge about cluster membership to some extent. For instance, in a co-authorship community network, it

J. Vejnarová and V. Kratochvíl (Eds.): BELIEF 2016, LNAI 9861, pp. 123–133, 2016.
DOI: 10.1007/978-3-319-45559-4_13

may be possible to label a small subset of scholars based on their research interests. In a social network application, it may be desirable to label some nodes according to their affinity to some products.

In [4] the authors considered the individual labels as prior knowledge, *i.e.* the true community assignments of certain nodes are known in advance. In their work the traditional LPA is adapted, allowing a few nodes to have true community labels, but the rest nodes are unlabeled. In face the presented semi-supervised community detection approach is an application of the semi-supervised classification algorithm proposed by [7] on graph data sets.

In this paper, we enhance the original LPA by introducing new update and propagation strategies using the theory of belief functions. The Semi-supervised version of Evidential Label Propagation (SELP) algorithm is presented. SELP can take advantage of the limited amount of supervised information and consequently improve the detection results.

The remainder of this paper is organized as follows. Some basic knowledge is briefly introduced in Sect. 2. The SELP algorithm is presented in detail in Sect. 3. In order to show the effectiveness of the proposed community detection approach, in Sect. 4 SELP algorithm is tested on different graph data sets. Conclusions are drawn in the final section.

2 Background

In this section some related preliminary knowledge will be presented. Some basis of belief function theory will be recalled first. As this work is inspired from the LPA [5] and EK-NNclus [2] clustering, the two algorithms will also be briefly introduced.

2.1 Theory of Belief Functions

Let $\Omega = \{\omega_1, \omega_2, \ldots, \omega_c\}$ be the finite domain of X, called the discernment frame. The belief functions are defined on the power set $2^\Omega = \{A : A \subseteq \Omega\}$.

The function $m : 2^\Omega \to [0, 1]$ is said to be the Basic Belief Assignment (bba) on 2^Ω, if it satisfies:

$$\sum_{A \subseteq \Omega} m(A) = 1. \tag{1}$$

Every $A \in 2^\Omega$ such that $m(A) > 0$ is called a focal element. The credibility and plausibility functions are defined in Eqs. (2) and (3) respectively:

$$Bel(A) = \sum_{B \subseteq A, B \neq \emptyset} m(B) \ \forall A \subseteq \Omega, \tag{2}$$

$$Pl(A) = \sum_{B \cap A \neq \emptyset} m(B), \ \forall A \subseteq \Omega. \tag{3}$$

Each quantity $Bel(A)$ measures the total support given to A, while $Pl(A)$ represents potential amount of support to A.

If bbas $m_j, j = 1, 2, \cdots, S$ describing S distinct items of evidence on Ω, the DS rule of combination [6] of S bbas can be mathematically defined as

$$(m_1 \oplus m_2 \oplus \cdots \oplus m_S)(X) =$$

$$\begin{cases} 0 & \text{if } X = \emptyset, \\ \dfrac{\sum\limits_{Y_1 \cap \cdots \cap Y_S = X} \prod_{j=1}^{S} m_j(Y_j)}{1 - \sum\limits_{Y_1 \cap \cdots \cap Y_S = X} \prod_{j=1}^{S} m_j(Y_j)} & \text{otherwise.} \end{cases} \tag{4}$$

2.2 EK-NNclus Clustering

Recently, a new decision-directed clustering algorithm for relational data sets, named EK-NNclus, is put forward based on the evidential K nearest-neighbor (EK-NN) rule [2]. Starting from an initial partition, the algorithm, called EK-NNclus, iteratively reassigns objects to clusters using the EK-NN rule [1], until a stable partition is obtained. After convergence, the cluster membership of each object is described by a mass function assigning a mass to each specific cluster and to the whole set of clusters.

2.3 Label Propagation

Let $G(V, E)$ be an undirected network, V is the set of N nodes, E is the set of edges. Each node $v(v \in V)$ has a label c_v. Denote by N_v the set of neighbors of node v. The Label Propagation Algorithm (LPA) uses the network structure alone to guide its process. It starts from an initial configuration where every node has a unique label. Then at every step one node (in asynchronous version) or each node (in a synchronous version) updates its current label to the label shared by the maximum number of its neighbors. For node v, its new label can be updated to ω_j with

$$j = \arg\max_{l} \{|u : c_u = l, u \in N_v|\}, \tag{5}$$

where $|X|$ is the cardinality of set X, and N_v is the set of node v's neighbors. When there are multiple maximal labels among the neighbors labels, the new label is picked randomly from them. By this iterative process densely connected groups of nodes form consensus on one label to form communities, and each node has more neighbors in its own community than in any of other community. Communities are identified as a group of nodes sharing the same label.

3 Semi-supervised Label Propagation

Inspired from LPA and EK-NNclus [2], we propose here SELP algorithm for graph data sets with prior information. The problem of semi-supervised community detection will be first described in a mathematical way, and then the proposed SELP algorithm will be presented in detail.

3.1 Problem Restatement and Notions

Let $G(V, E)$ denote the graph, where V is the set of n nodes and $E \subseteq V \times V$ is the set of edges. Generally, a network can be expressed by its adjacent matrix $\boldsymbol{A} = (a_{ij})_{n \times n}$, where $a_{ij} = 1$ indicates that there is a direct edge between nodes i and j, and 0 otherwise.

Assume that there are c communities in the graph. The set of labels is denoted by $\Omega = \{\omega_1, \omega_2, \cdots, \omega_c\}$. In addition, in order to make sure that the solution is unique, we assume that there must be at least one labeled vertex in each community. The n nodes in set V can be divided into two parts:

$$V_L = \{(n_1, y_1), (n_2, y_2), \cdots, (n_l, y_l)\}, \quad y_j \in \Omega$$

for the labeled nodes, and

$$V_U = \{n_{l+1}, n_{l+2}, \cdots, n_n\}$$

for the unlabeled ones. The main task of the semi-supervised community detection is to make models propagating the labels from nodes in V_L to those in V_U, and further determine the labels of those unlabeled vertices.

3.2 The Dissimilarities Between Nodes

Like the smooth assumption in the semi-supervised graph-based learning methods [8], here we assume that the more common neighbors the two nodes share, the larger probability that they belong to the same community. Thus in this work, the index considering the number of shared common neighbors is adopted to measure the similarities between nodes.

Definition 1. Let the set of neighbors of node n_i be N_i, and the degree of node n_i be d_i. The similarity between nodes n_i and n_j ($n_i, n_j \in V$) is defined as

$$s_{ij} = \begin{cases} \frac{|N_i \cap N_j|}{d_i + d_j}, & \text{if } a_{ij} = 1 \\ 0, & \text{otherwise.} \end{cases} \tag{6}$$

Then the dissimilarities associated with the similarity measure can be defined as

$$d_{ij} = \frac{1 - s_{ij}}{s_{ij}}, \ \forall \, n_i, n_j \in V. \tag{7}$$

3.3 Evidential Label Propagation

For a labeled node $n_j \in V_L$ in community ω_k, the initial bba can be defined as a Bayesian categorical mass function:

$$m^j(A) = \begin{cases} 1 & \text{if } A = \{\omega_k\} \\ 0 & \text{otherwise.} \end{cases} \tag{8}$$

For an unlabeled node $n_x \in V_U$, the vacuous mass assignment can be used to express our ignorance about its community label:

$$m^x(A) = \begin{cases} 1 & \text{if } A = \Omega \\ 0 & \text{otherwise.} \end{cases} \tag{9}$$

To determine the label of node n_x, its neighbors can be regarded as distinct information sources. If there are $|N_x| = r_x$ neighbors for node n_x, the number of sources is r_x. The reliability of each source depends on the similarities between nodes. Suppose that there is a neighbor n_t with label ω_j, it can provide us with a bba describing the belief on the community label of node n_x as [2]

$$\begin{aligned} m_t^x(\{\omega_t\}) &= \alpha * m^t(\{\omega_j\}), \\ m_t^x(\Omega) &= m^t(\Omega) + (1 - \alpha) * m^t(\{\omega_j\}), \\ m_t^x(A) &= 0, \quad \text{if } A \neq \{\omega_j\}, \Omega, \end{aligned} \tag{10}$$

where α is the discounting parameter such that $0 \leq \alpha \leq 1$. It should be determined according to the similarity between nodes n_x and n_t. The more similar the two nodes are, the more reliable the source is. Thus α can be set as a decreasing function of d_{xt}. In this work we suggest to use

$$\alpha = \alpha_0 \exp\{-\gamma d_{xt}^\beta\}, \tag{11}$$

where parameters α_0 and β can be set to be 1 and 2 respectively as default, and γ can be set to

$$\gamma = 1/\text{median}\left(\left\{d_{ij}^\beta, \ i = 1, 2, \cdots, n, \ j \in N_i\right\}\right). \tag{12}$$

After the r_x bbas from its neighbors are calculated using Eq. (10), the fused bba of node n_x can be got by the use of Dempster's combination rule:

$$m^x = m_1^x \oplus m_2^x \oplus \cdots \oplus m_{r_x}^x. \tag{13}$$

The label of node n_x can be determined by the maximal value of m^x. The main principle of semi-supervised learning is to take advantage of the unlabeled data. It is an intuitive way to add node n_x (previously in set V_U but already be labeled now) to set V_l to train the classifier. However, if the predicted label of n_x is wrong, it will have very bad effects on the accuracy of the following predictions. Here a parameter η is introduced to control the prediction confidence of the nodes that to be added in V_l. If the maximum of m^x is larger than η, it indicates that the belief about the community of node n_x is high and the prediction is confident. Then we remove node n_x in V_U and add it to set V_L. On the contrary, if the maximum of m^x is not larger than η, it means that we can not make a confident decision about the label of n_x based on the current information. Thus the node n_x should be remained in set V_U. This is the idea of self-training [3].

In order to propagate the labels from the labeled nodes to the unlabeled ones in the graph, a classifier should be first trained using the labeled data in V_l.

For each node n_x in V_U, we find its direct neighbors and construct bbas through Eq. (10). Then the fused bba about the community label of node n_x is calculated by Eq. (13). The subset of the unlabeled nodes, of which the maximal bba is larger than the given threshold η, are selected to augment the labeled data set. The predicted labels of these nodes are set to be the class assigned with the maximal mass. Parameter η can be set to 0.7 by default in practice.

After the above update process, there may still be some nodes in V_U. For these nodes, we can find their neighbors that are in V_L, and then use Eqs. (10) and (13) to determine their bbas.

4   Experiment

In order to verify the efficiency and effectiveness of the proposed SELP algorithm, some experiments on graph data sets will be conducted in this section, and the results by the use of different methods will be reported. The semi-supervised community detection algorithm using label propagation (SLP) [4] and the unsupervised label propagation algorithm will be used to compare the performance. The parameters in SELP are all set to the default values in the experiments.

4.1   Real World Networks

A. Karate Club Network. In this experiment we tested on the widely used benchmark in detecting community structures, "Karate Club". The network consists of 34 nodes and 78 edges representing the friendship among the members of the club. During the development, a dispute arose between the club's administrator and instructor, which eventually resulted in the club split into two smaller clubs. The first one was an instructor-centered group covering 16 vertices: 1–8, 11–14, 17–18, 20 and 22, while the second administrator centered group consisted of the remaining 18 vertices.

In the first test, the labeled node in community ω_1 was set to node 5, while that in community ω_2 was set to node 24. After five steps, SELP algorithm stopped. The detailed update process is displayed in Fig. 2. It can be seen from the figure that two outliers, nodes 10 and 12 are detected by SELP. From the original graph, we can see that node 10 has two neighbors, nodes 3 and 34. But neither of them shares a common neighbor with node 10. For node 12, it only connects to node 1, but has no connection with any other node in the graph. Therefore, it is very intuitive that both the two nodes are regarded as outliers of the graph.

The detection results on Karate Club network by SELP and SLP algorithms with different labeled nodes are shown in Table 1. The labeled vertices and its corresponding misclassified vertices are clearly presented in the table. As can be seen from the table, nodes 10 and 12 are detected as outliers in all the cases by SELP, and the two communities can be correctly classified most of the time. The performance of SLP is worse than that of SELP when there is only one labeled data in each community. For the nodes which are connected to both communities

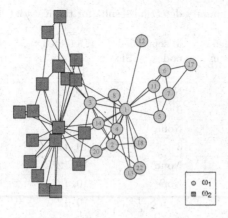

Fig. 1. Karate Club network.

and located in the overlap, such as nodes 3 and 9, they are misclassified most frequently. If the number of labeled data in each community is increased to 2, the exact community structure can be got by both methods. It is indicated that the more prior information (*i.e.* labeled vertices) we have, the better the performance of SELP is (Fig. 1).

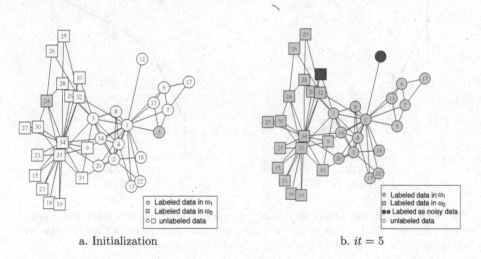

a. Initialization   b. *it* = 5

Fig. 2. The results on Karate Club network. The nodes marked with color red are the outliers detected by SELP. (Color figure online)

B. American Football Network. As a further test of our algorithm, the network we investigated in this experiment was the world of American college football games.

Table 1. Community detection results for the Karate Club network.

Labeled nodes in ω_1	Labeled nodes in ω_2	Misclassified nodes by SELP	Detected outliers by SELP	Misclassified nodes by SLP
1	34	None	10, 12	None
1	32	9	10, 12	9, 10, 27, 31, 34
2	33	None	10, 12	None
6	31	3	10, 12	2, 3, 8, 14, 2
8	31	None	10, 12	10
8	32	None	10, 12	None
17	31	3, 4, 8, 14	10, 12	2, 3, 4, 8, 13, 14, 18, 20, 22
1, 2	33, 34	None	10, 12	None
1, 2	33, 9	None	10, 12	None
3, 18	26, 30	None	10, 12	None
17, 4	31, 9	None	10, 12	None

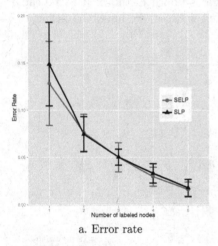

a. Error rate

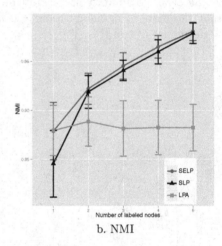

b. NMI

Fig. 3. The results on American football network. The two figures show the average error rates and NMI values (plus and minus one standard deviation) for 50 repeated experiments, as a function of the number of labeled samples.

Let the number of labeled nodes in each community to be fixed. Then SELP and SLP algorithms were evoked 50 times respectively with randomly selected labeled nodes. The average error rates and NMI values (plus and minus one standard deviation) of the 50 experiments are displayed in Figs. 3a and b respectively. As can be seen from the figures, with the increasing number of labeled samples, the performance of both SELP and SLP becomes better. The NMI values of the detected communities by SELP and SLP are significantly better than those by LPA. It indicates that the semi-supervised community detection methods could take advantage of the limited amount of prior information and consequently improve the accuracy of the detection results. The behavior of SELP is better than that of SLP in terms of both error rates and NMI values.

4.2   LFR Network

In this subsection, LFR benchmark networks were used to test the ability of the algorithm to identify communities. The experiments here included evaluating the performance of the algorithm with various amounts of labeled nodes and different values of parameter μ in the benchmark networks. The original LPA [5] and the semi-supervised community detection approach SLP [4] were used to compare.

In LFR networks, the mixing parameter μ represents the ratio between the external degree of each vertex with respect to its community and the total degree of the node. The larger the value of μ is, the more difficult the community structure will be correctly detected. The values of the parameters in LFR benchmark networks in this experiment were set as follows: $n = 1000, \xi = 15, \tau_1 = 2, \tau_2 = 1, cmin = 20, cmax = 50$.

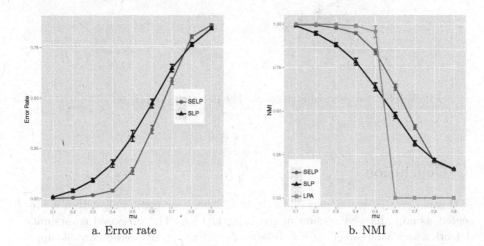

a. Error rate   b. NMI

Fig. 4. The results on LFR network. The number of labeled nodes in each community is 3.

The performance of different methods with various values of μ is shown in Fig. 4. As expected, the error rate is very high and the NMI value is low when μ is large. It demonstrates the fact that the community structure is not very clear and consequently difficult to be identified correctly. It can be seen from Fig. 4a that the error rates by SELP are smaller than those by SLP generally.

SELP performs better than SLP. This conclusion could also be got in terms of the NMI values displayed in Fig. 4b.

The original LPA could not work at all when μ is larger than 0.5. The results of SELP and SLP are significantly improved in these cases compared with LPA. As shown in Fig. 5b, even when there is only one labeled data in each community, the behavior of SELP is much better than that of LPA. This confirms the fact that the semi-supervised community detection approaches can effectively take advantage of the limited amount of labeled data. From Fig. 5, we can also see that the performance of SELP and SLP becomes better with the increasing number of labeled nodes.

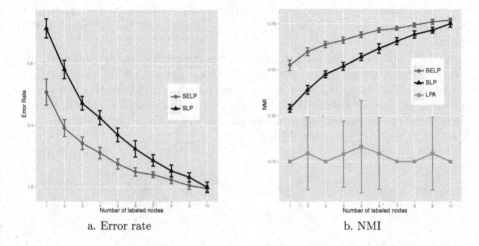

a. Error rate   b. NMI

Fig. 5. The results on LFR network. The parameter of μ is set to be 0.6.

5   Conclusion

In this paper, the semi-supervised evidential label propagation algorithm is presented as an enhanced version of the original LPA. The proposed community detection approach can effectively take advantage of the limited amount of supervised information. This is of practical meaning in real applications as there often exists some prior knowledge for the analyzed graphs. The experimental results show that the detection results will be significantly improved with the help of limited amount of supervised information.

References

1. Denœux, T.: A k-nearest neighbor classification rule based on Dempster-Shafer theory. IEEE Trans. Syst. Man Cybern. **25**(5), 804–813 (1995)
2. Denœux, T., Kanjanatarakul, O., Sriboonchitta, S.: EK-NNclus: a clustering procedure based on the evidential k-nearest neighbor rule. Knowl. Based Syst. **88**, 57–69 (2015)
3. Li, M., Zhou, Z.-H.: SETRED: self-training with editing. In: Ho, T.-B., Cheung, D., Liu, H. (eds.) PAKDD 2005. LNCS (LNAI), vol. 3518, pp. 611–621. Springer, Heidelberg (2005)
4. Liu, D., Bai, H.-Y., Li, H.-J., Wang, W.-J.: Semi-supervised community detection using label propagation. Int. J. Mod. Phys. B **28**(29), 1450208 (2014)
5. Raghavan, U.N., Albert, R., Kumara, S.: Near linear time algorithm to detect community structures in large-scale networks. Phys. Rev. E **76**(3), 036106 (2007)
6. Shafer, G.: A Mathematical Theory of Evidence. Princeton University Press, Princeton (1976)
7. Wang, F., Zhang, C.: Label propagation through linear neighborhoods. IEEE Trans. Knowl. Data Eng. **20**(1), 55–67 (2008)
8. Zhu, X., Lafferty, J., Rosenfeld, R.: Semi-supervised learning with graphs. Language Technologies Institute, School of Computer Science, Carnegie Mellon University (2005)

Information Fusion

Conjunctive Rules in the Theory of Belief Functions and Their Justification Through Decisions Models

Andrey G. Bronevich[1(✉)] and Igor N. Rozenberg[2]

[1] National Research University Higher School of Economics,
Myasnitskaya 20, 101000 Moscow, Russia
brone@mail.ru
[2] JSC Research, Development and Planning Institute for Railway Information
Technology, Automation and Telecommunication,
Orlikov Per.5, Building 1, 107996 Moscow, Russia
I.Rozenberg@gismps.ru

Abstract. In the paper we argue that aggregation rules in the theory of belief functions should be in accordance with underlying decision models, i.e. aggregation produced in conjunctive manner has to produce the order embedded to the union of partial orders constructed in each source of information; and if we take models based on imprecise probabilities, then such aggregation exists if the intersection of underlying credal sets is not empty. In the opposite case there is contradiction in information and the justifiable functional to measure it is the functional giving the smallest contradiction by applying all possible conjunctive rules. We give also the axiomatics of this contradiction measure.

Keywords: Belief functions · Contradiction measures · Aggregation rules · Conjunctive rules

1 Introduction

The theory of belief functions gives us many methods of information fusion. This procedure can be characterized as an aggregation of information sources that allows us to improve its reliability, precision, etc. There are many rules for aggregation of information in the frame of the belief function theory [7]. If each source of information is considered to be reliable then we can use conjunctive rules [2,8] of aggregation that should decrease uncertainty. Because belief functions have various interpretations, the optimal conjunctive rule does not exist. Therefore, in the first part of the paper we propose to justify the application of conjunctive rules based on the underlying decision models. This can be shortly described as follows. Suppose that by using each source of information we can construct the corresponding model of decision making described by a partial preference order on decisions. The union of these orders can be understood as the result of their conjunction. If orders do not contradict each other, then their

© Springer International Publishing Switzerland 2016
J. Vejnarová and V. Kratochvíl (Eds.): BELIEF 2016, LNAI 9861, pp. 137–145, 2016.
DOI: 10.1007/978-3-319-45559-4_14

conjunction can be embedded to a partial order. This way also explains when contradiction among sources of information exists or does not. We show that if we choose decisions based on models of imprecise probabilities then sources of information are contradictory if the intersection of the corresponding credal sets is not empty. We show that in this case the contradiction measure giving the smallest contradiction after applying possible conjunctive rules is justifiable, and we propose a number of axioms that leads to its unique choice.

The paper has the following structure. We give first the basic constructions concerning belief functions in Sect. 2. Then we describe some aggregation rules in Sect. 3, in particular, conjunctions rules that generalize the non-normalized Dempster's rule. In Sect. 4 we analyze the relation between decision models based on imprecise probabilities and aggregation rules, and finally, in Sect. 5 we give the axiomatics of the contradiction measure justified in the theory of imprecise probabilities.

2   Some Facts and Notions from the Theory of Belief Functions

Let $X = \{x_1, ..., x_n\}$ be a finite set also called the *frame of discernment* and let 2^X be the powerset of X. Any *belief function* [9] $Bel : 2^X \to [0, 1]$ can be defined by a *basic belief assignment* (bba) $m : 2^X \to [0, 1]$ with $\sum_{B \in 2^X} m(B) = 1$ as

$$Bel(A) = \sum_{B \in 2^X | B \subseteq A} m(B).$$

A belief function is called *normalized* if $Bel(\emptyset) = 0$. The value $Bel(\emptyset)$ shows the *amount of contradiction* in information described by a belief function. Let Bel be a belief function on 2^X with bba m. Then a set $B \in 2^X$ is called a *focal element* if $m(B) > 0$. The set of all focal elements for a belief function Bel is called the *body of evidence*. If the body of evidence has only one focal element B, then the belief function is called *categorical* and it is denoted by $\eta_{\langle B \rangle}$. Obviously,

$$\eta_{\langle B \rangle}(A) = \begin{cases} 1, \ B \subseteq A, \\ 0, \ B \nsubseteq A. \end{cases}$$

Any belief function Bel on 2^X can represented as a sum of categorical belief functions as

$$Bel = \sum_{B \in 2^X} m(B) \eta_{\langle B \rangle},$$

where obviously m is the bba of Bel.

In the next we will use the following notations:

- M_{bel} is the set of all normalized belief functions on 2^X and the set of all belief functions including non-normalized ones is denoted by $\bar{M}_{bel}$;
- M_{pr} is the set of all probability measures on 2^X, i.e. normalized belief functions, for which $m(A) = 0$ if $|A| \geqslant 2$.

3   Aggregation Rules in the Theory of Belief Functions

The application of aggregation rules depends on prior information about information sources. We will discuss in detail the conjunctive rules. They are used if each source of information is assumed to be reliable. The following scheme gives us the general approach to construction of conjunctive rules [2,8]. Suppose we have two sources of information described by belief functions $Bel_i = \sum_{A \in 2^X} m_i(A)\eta_{\langle A \rangle}$, $i = 1, 2$. Then the general conjunctive rule can be defined with the help of a joint belief assignment $m : 2^X \times 2^X \to [0,1]$ that satisfies the following conditions:

$$\begin{cases} \sum_{A \in 2^X} m(A, B) = m_2(B), \\ \sum_{B \in 2^X} m(A, B) = m_1(A). \end{cases} \tag{1}$$

The result of the conjunctive rule is defined as

$$Bel = \sum_{A, B \in 2^X} m(A, B)\eta_{\langle A \cap B \rangle}.$$

Let us notice that if we assume that the sources of information are independent, then the joint belief assignment m is defined as $m(A, B) = m_1(A)m_2(B)$, $A, B \in 2^X$. In the next the last rule of aggregation is referred as the classical conjunctive rule. Dempster's and Yager's rules of aggregation defined as

(1) Dempster's rule [4,9]: $Bel = \frac{1}{1-k} \sum_{A \cap B \neq \emptyset} m_1(A)m_2(B)\eta_{\langle A \cap B \rangle}$, where $k = \sum_{A \cap B = \emptyset} m_1(A)m_2(B)$;

(2) Yager's rule [10]: $Bel = \sum_{A \cap B \neq \emptyset} m_1(A)m_2(B)\eta_{\langle A \cap B \rangle} + k\eta_{\langle X \rangle}$, where k is defined as in (1);

are closely related to the classical conjunctive rule. As one can see they show how the result of the classical conjunctive rule can be transformed to the normalized belief function.

In the theory of belief functions you can find also other rules of aggregation. The *disjunctive rule* [7] is used if at least one source of information is reliable. The result of its application is defined through the joint belief assignment obeying the conditions (1) as

$$Bel = \sum_{A, B \in 2^X} m(A, B)\eta_{\langle A \cup B \rangle}.$$

If the sources of information are independent, then $m(A, B) = m_1(A)m_2(B)$ for all $A, B \in 2^X$, and also $Bel(A) = Bel_1(A)Bel_2(A)$ for all $A \in 2^X$.

The *mixture rule* is used if we can evaluate the reliability of each source of information. Let us assume that we have m sources of information described by belief functions Bel_i, $i = 1, ..., m$, and reliability of i-th source, $i = 1, ..., m$, is evaluated by a non-negative real number r_i and $\sum_{i=1}^{m} r_i = 1$, then the result of the mixture rule is defined as $Bel = \sum_{i=1}^{m} r_i Bel_i$. There are other approaches for accounting reliability of information sources, see for example, Shafer's rule [9]. Let us notice that one can find other rules of aggregation in the theory of belief functions [7] but they can be represented as a combination of the above basic aggregation rules.

4   Aggregation Rules and Decision Models

We will consider decision models in a view of probabilistic interpretation of normalized belief functions. Suppose that each decision is identified with a real valued function (gamble) f on X. The set of all such functions is denoted by K. Let the available information be described by a probability measure $P \in M_{pr}$. Then the preference order $\prec$ on K, based on suspected utility

$$E_P(f) = \sum_{i=1}^{n} f(x_i) P(\{x_i\}),$$

is defined as: decision f_2 is more preferable than decision f_1 ($f_1 \prec f_2$) iff $E_P(f_1) < E_P(f_2)$. If the available information is imprecise then it can be described by a belief function $Bel \in M_{bel}$ or the corresponding credal set $\mathbf{P} = \{P \in M_{pr} | P \geqslant Bel\}$, and we can use several decision rules from the theory of imprecise probabilities [1]:

(a) $f_1 \prec f_2$ iff $E_P(f_1) < E_P(f_2)$ for all $P \in \mathbf{P}$;
(b) $f_1 \prec f_2$ iff $\underline{E}_\mathbf{P}(f_1) < \underline{E}_\mathbf{P}(f_2)$, where $\underline{E}_\mathbf{P}(f) = \inf_{P \in \mathbf{P}} E_P(f)$;
(c) $f_1 \prec f_2$ iff $\bar{E}_\mathbf{P}(f_1) < \bar{E}_\mathbf{P}(f_2)$, where $\bar{E}_\mathbf{P}(f) = \sup_{P \in \mathbf{P}} E_P(f)$;
(d) $f_1 \prec f_2$ iff $\underline{E}_\mathbf{P}(f_1) < \underline{E}_\mathbf{P}(f_2)$ and $\bar{E}_\mathbf{P}(f_1) < \bar{E}_\mathbf{P}(f_2)$.

Let us notice that the relation $\prec$ is a strict partial order, and this seems to be natural that we cannot choose an optimal decision if we do not have sufficient information. In the next we will focuse on the rule (a) and analyze its behavior w.r.t. applying aggregation rules.

Assume that we have m information sources described by belief functions $Bel_i \in M_{bel}$, $i = 1, ..., m$. Assume also that each source of information is characterized by the preference order $\rho_i \subseteq K \times K$. Then the result of applying the conjunctive rule to orders ρ_i should be also the preference order $\rho \subseteq K \times K$ and obey the consensus condition $\rho_i \subseteq \rho$, $i = 1, ..., m$, with the meaning that each source of information is reliable. The application of the disjunction rule should give us an order ρ obeying the condition $\rho_i \supseteq \rho$, $i = 1, ..., m$, meaning that $(f_1, f_2) \in \rho$ if this preference is confirmed in each source of information. Observe that the conjunctive rule is not defined if an order $\rho \subseteq K \times K$ with

$\rho_i \subseteq \rho$, $i = 1, ..., m$, does not exist. In this case we say that sources of information are contradictory. The disjunctive rule always exists and it can be defined as $\rho = \bigcap\limits_{i=1}^{m} \rho_i$.

Let us analyze how the above definitions agree with the aggregation rules in the theory of belief functions.

Lemma 1. *Let $Bel \in M_{bel}$ be the result of the conjunctive rule to belief functions $Bel_1, Bel_2 \in M_{bel}$. Let us consider preference orders ρ, ρ_1, ρ_2 that correspond to belief functions Bel, Bel_1, Bel_2 by decision rule (a). Then the preference order ρ for Bel agrees with orders ρ_1 and ρ_2.*

Proof. Clearly, $\mathbf{P}(Bel) \subseteq \mathbf{P}(Bel_i)$, $i = 1, 2$. Thus, applying decision rule (a) implies that $\rho_i \subseteq \rho$, $i = 1, 2$.

Lemma 2. *Let $Bel \in M_{bel}$ be the result of the disjunctive rule to belief functions $Bel_1, Bel_2 \in M_{bel}$. Then $\rho_i \supseteq \rho$, $i = 1, 2$.*

Proof. It is easy to see that $Bel \leqslant Bel_i$, $i = 1, 2$. Thus, $\mathbf{P}(Bel_i) \subseteq \mathbf{P}(Bel)$ and $\rho_i \supseteq \rho$, $i = 1, 2$.

Proposition 1. *Sources of information described by belief functions Bel_1, $Bel_2 \in M_{bel}$ are not contradictory iff $\mathbf{P}(Bel_1) \cap \mathbf{P}(Bel_2) \neq \emptyset$. In this case there is a conjunctive rule with the result $Bel \in M_{bel}$.*

Proof. Sufficiency. Assume that there exists a $P \in \mathbf{P}(Bel_1) \cap \mathbf{P}(Bel_2)$. Consider the preference order ρ, generated by a probability measure P. Obviously, $\rho_i \subseteq \rho$, $i = 1, 2$, where ρ_i is the preference order, generated by Bel_i.

Necessity. Let $\mathbf{P}(Bel_1) \cap \mathbf{P}(Bel_2) = \emptyset$. We will use the well known fact that if we have two disjoint closed convex sets in $\mathbb{R}^n$, then there is a hyperplane separating them. This fact for credal sets $\mathbf{P}(Bel_1)$ and $\mathbf{P}(Bel_2)$ can be formulated as: there is a $f \in K$ such that $E_P(f) > 0$ for all $P \in \mathbf{P}(Bel_1)$ and $E_P(f) < 0$ for all $P \in \mathbf{P}(Bel_1)$. Thus, f is more preferable than $-f$ according to the order ρ_1 and $-f$ is more preferable than f according to the order ρ_2. Clearly, a partial order ρ does not exist, because the above preferences contradict to its asymmetry property.

The existence of the conjunctive rule with properties indicated in the proposition follows from the results in [2].

5   The Axiomatics of Contradiction Measure

Let us consider the measure of contradiction, analyzed in [2,3,5]. Let $R(Bel_1, Bel_2)$ be the set of possible belief functions obtained by the conjunctive rules applied to $Bel_1, Bel_2 \in M_{bel}$. Then the measure of contradiction $Con : M_{bel} \times M_{bel} \to [0, 1]$ is defined as

$$Con(Bel_1, Bel_2) = \inf \{Bel(\emptyset) | Bel \in R(Bel_1, Bel_2)\}.$$

Let us consider its properties indicated in [2]. Further we will use the order $\preccurlyeq$ on $\bar{M}_{bel}$ called *specialization*. Let $Bel_1, Bel_2 \in \bar{M}_{bel}$, then $Bel_1 \preccurlyeq Bel_2$ iff there are representations $Bel_1 = \sum_{i=1}^{N} a_i \eta_{\langle A_i \rangle}$ and $Bel_2 = \sum_{i=1}^{N} a_i \eta_{\langle B_i \rangle}$, such that $\sum_{i=1}^{N} a_i = 1$, $a_i \geqslant 0$, $B_i \subseteq A_i$, $i = 1, ..., n$. It easy to see that $Bel_1 \preccurlyeq Bel_2$ implies $Bel_1 \leqslant Bel_2$ ($Bel_1(A) \leqslant Bel_2(A)$ for all $A \in 2^X$), but the opposite is not true in general [6].

Proposition 2. *The measure of contradiction* $Con : M_{bel} \times M_{bel} \to [0,1]$ *has the following properties:*

A1. $Con(Bel_1, Bel_2) = 0$ for $Bel_1, Bel_2 \in M_{bel}$ iff $\mathbf{P}(Bel_1) \cap \mathbf{P}(Bel_2) \neq \emptyset$.

A2. Let $Bel_1, Bel_2 \in M_{bel}$, and let $\mathcal{A}_i$ be their corresponding bodies of evidence, then $Con(Bel_1, Bel_2) = 1$ iff $A \cap B = \emptyset$ for all $A \in \mathcal{A}_1$ and $B \in \mathcal{A}_2$.

A3. $Con(Bel_1, Bel_2) = Con(Bel_2, Bel_1)$ for all $Bel_1, Bel_2 \in M_{bel}$;

A4. Let $Bel_1 \preccurlyeq Bel_1'$ and $Bel_2 \preccurlyeq Bel_2'$, then $Con(Bel_1, Bel_2) \leqslant Con(Bel_1', Bel_2')$;

A5. Let $Bel_1 = (1-a)Bel_1^{(1)} + aBel_1^{(2)}$ and $Bel_2 = (1-a)Bel_2^{(1)} + aBel_2^{(2)}$, where $a \in [0,1]$ and $Bel_i^{(k)} \in M_{bel}$, $i,k = 1,2$. Then $Con(Bel_1, Bel_2) \leqslant (1-a)Con(Bel_1^{(1)}, Bel_2^{(1)}) + aCon(Bel_1^{(2)}, Bel_2^{(2)})$.

A6. Let $Con(Bel_1, Bel_2) = a$, where $a \in [0,1]$ and $Bel_1, Bel_2 \in M_{bel}$, then there exist $Bel_i^{(k)} \in M_{bel}$, $i,k = 1,2$, such that $Bel_i = (1-a)Bel_i^{(1)} + aBel_i^{(2)}$, $i = 1,2$, $Con(Bel_1^{(1)}, Bel_2^{(1)}) = 0$, and $Con(Bel_1^{(2)}, Bel_2^{(2)}) = 1$.

In addition,

(a) $Con(P_1, P_2) = 1 - \sum_{i=1}^{n} \min\{P_1(x_i), P_2(x_i)\}$, $P_i \in M_{pr}$, $i = 1,2$;

(b) $Con(Bel_1, Bel_2) = \inf\{Con(P_1, P_2)|P_1 \in \mathbf{P}(Bel_1), P_2 \in \mathbf{P}(Bel_2)\}$.

We will consider properties A1–A6 as axioms for a measure of contradiction. We will show later that the measure of contradiction is uniquely defined by this system of axioms. Let us notice that axioms A1–A4 are considered in [5]. Axiom A1 describes the case when sources of information are non-contradictory, and similarly in axiom A2 we describe the case, when information sources are absolutely contradictory. In the last case any evidence (focal element) $A \in \mathcal{A}_1$ taken from the first source of information contradicts to any evidence $B \in \mathcal{A}_2$ from the second source of information. Axiom A3 is the symmetry axiom that follows from the problem statement. Let us observe that axiom A4 reflects the following. If $Bel_i \preccurlyeq Bel_i'$, then Bel_i' describes the same information but with higher precision. Therefore, axiom A4 says that increasing precision can lead to higher contradiction. Axioms A5 and A6 describe how we can evaluate contradiction by dividing information in each source on two parts: axiom A5 says that evaluation produced by dividing on two parts can gives us the result with the higher value of contradiction. Axiom A6 says that it is possible to divide information in each source on two parts such that we can extract parts of information that do not contradict each other and parts that are absolutely contradictory, and this separation defines the value of contradiction.

Lemma 3. *Belief functions $Bel_1, Bel_2 \in M_{bel}$ are absolutely contradictory, i.e. they obey the condition A2, iff there are disjoint sets $A, B \in 2^X$ $(A \cap B = \emptyset)$ such that $Bel_1(A) = Bel_2(B) = 1$.*

Proof. Necessity. Let we use notations from A2 and assume Bel_1, Bel_2 are absolutely contradictory. Let us choose $A = \bigcup_{C \in \mathcal{A}_1} C$ and $B = \bigcup_{C \in \mathcal{A}_2} C$. Then obviously $A \cap B = \emptyset$ and $Bel_1(A) = Bel_2(B) = 1$.

Sufficiency. Assume that there are $A, B \in 2^X$ such that $Bel_1(A) = Bel_2(B) = 1$ and $A \cap B = \emptyset$. Then $\sum_{C \subseteq A} m_1(C) = 1$ and $\sum_{C \subseteq B} m_1(C) = 1$. This means that any focal element for Bel_1 is a subset of A and any focal element for Bel_2 is a subset of B, i.e. belief functions Bel_1, Bel_2 are absolutely contradictory.

Lemma 4. *Let a functional $\Phi : M_{pr} \times M_{pr} \rightarrow [0,1]$ obey axioms A1, A2 and A6. Then*

$$\Phi(P_1, P_2) = 1 - \sum_{i=1}^{n} \min\{P_1(x_i), P_2(x_i)\}, P_1, P_2 \in M_{pr}.$$

Proof. In the case of probability measures in possible representations $P_i = (1 - a)P_i^{(1)} + aP_i^{(2)}$, where $P_i^{(k)} \in M_{pr}$, $i, k = 1, 2$, $P_1^{(1)} = P_1^{(2)}$, and $P_2^{(1)}, P_2^{(2)}$ are absolutely contradictory, the parameter a is uniquely defined as

$$a = 1 - \sum_{i=1}^{n} \min\{P_1(x_i), P_2(x_i)\}.$$

The probability measures used in these representations can be chosen as

(1) $P_i^{(1)}(\{x_k\}) = \frac{1}{1-a} \min\{P_1(x_k), P_2(x_k)\}$, $i = 1, 2$, for $a \in [0, 1)$;
(2) $P_i^{(2)}(\{x_k\}) = \frac{1}{a}\left(P_i(\{x_k\}) - \min\{P_1(\{x_k\}), P_2(\{x_k\})\}\right)$ for $a \in [0, 1)$;
(3) if $a = 1$, then a probability measure $P_1^{(1)} = P_1^{(2)}$ can be chosen arbitrarily;
(4) if $a = 0$, then absolutely contradictory probability measures $P_2^{(1)}, P_2^{(2)} \in M_{pr}$ can be chosen arbitrary.

Thus, the result from the lemma is proved.

Theorem 1. *Let a functional $\Phi : M_{bel} \times M_{bel} \rightarrow [0,1]$ obey axioms A1, A2, A4, and A6. Then it coincides with the contradiction measure Con on $M_{bel} \times M_{bel}$.*

Proof. Let us notice that Lemma 4 implies that functionals Φ and Con coincide on $M_{pr} \times M_{pr}$. Let us show first that $\Phi(Bel_1, Bel_2) \leqslant Con(Bel_1, Bel_2)$ for all $Bel_1, Bel_2 \in M_{bel}$. Property (b) implies that there exist $P_i \in M_{pr}$, $i = 1, 2$, such that $Con(Bel_1, Bel_2) = Con(P_1, P_2)$ and $Bel_i \preccurlyeq P_i$, $i = 1, 2$. Because $\Phi(P_1, P_2) = Con(P_1, P_2)$, axiom A4 implies that $\Phi(Bel_1, Bel_2) \leqslant \Phi(P_1, P_2) = Con(Bel_1, Bel_2)$.

Let us prove that $Con(Bel_1, Bel_2) \leqslant \Phi(Bel_1, Bel_2)$ for all $Bel_1, Bel_2 \in M_{bel}$. Let us assume to the contrary that $Con(Bel_1, Bel_2) > \Phi(Bel_1, Bel_2)$ for some $Bel_1, Bel_2 \in M_{bel}$. Then by axiom A6 there are representations

$$Bel_i = (1-a)Bel_i^{(1)} + aBel_i^{(2)}, i = 1, 2,$$

such that $\Phi(Bel_1, Bel_2) = a$, $\mathbf{P}(Bel_1^{(1)}) \cap \mathbf{P}(Bel_2^{(1)}) \neq \emptyset$, and $\mathbf{P}(Bel_1^{(2)}) \cap \mathbf{P}(Bel_2^{(2)}) = \emptyset$. Consider probability measures

$$P_i = (1-a)P + aP_i^{(2)}, i = 1, 2,$$

where $P \in \mathbf{P}(Bel_1^{(1)}) \cap \mathbf{P}(Bel_2^{(1)})$ and $P_i^{(2)} \in \mathbf{P}(Bel_i^{(2)})$, $i = 1, 2$. Obviously, probability measures $P_1^{(2)}$ and $P_2^{(2)}$ are absolutely contradictory, thus, $\Phi(Bel_1, Bel_2) = Con(P_1, P_2)$. In addition, $P_i \in \mathbf{P}(Bel_i)$, $i = 1, 2$. Thus, by property (b) from Proposition 2, we get $Con(Bel_1, Bel_2) \leqslant Con(P_1, P_2)$, but this contradicts to our assumption.

6   Conclusion

In this paper we show that the choice of aggregation rules has to be in accordance with the underlying decision models, and if we take decision models based on imprecise probabilities then contradiction exists if the intersection of underlying credal sets is not empty. We show that in this case the contradiction measure giving the smallest contradiction by applying possible conjunctive rules is justifiable, and we give the axiomatics of this measure. The important topic of the next research can be the analysis of relations obtained as union of partial preference orders on decisions and how these relations can be used for decision making in case of contradictory information.

References

1. Augustin, A., Coolen, F.P.A., de Cooman, G., Troffaes, M.C.M. (eds.): Introduction to Imprecise Probabilities. Wiley, New York (2014)
2. Bronevich, A.G., Rozenberg, I.N.: The choice of generalized Dempster-Shafer rules for aggregating belief functions. Int. J. Approx. Reason. **56**, 122–136 (2015)
3. Cattaneo, M.E.G.V.: Combining belief functions issued from dependent sources. In: Proceedings in Informatics, ISIPTA 2003, vol. 18, pp. 133–147. Carleton Scientific, Waterloo (2003)
4. Dempster, A.P.: Upper and lower probabilities induced by a multivalued mapping. Ann. Math. Stat. **38**, 325–339 (1967)
5. Destercke, S., Burger, T.: Toward an axiomatic definition of conflict between belief functions. IEEE Trans. Syst. Man Cybern. **43**, 585–596 (2013)
6. Dubois, D., Prade, H.: A set-theoretic view of belief functions: logical operations and approximations by fuzzy sets. Int. J. Gen. Syst. **12**, 193–226 (1986)
7. Dubois, D., Prade, H.: On the combination of evidence in various mathematical frameworks. In: Flamm, J., Luisi, T. (eds.) Reliability Data Collection and Analysis. Reliability and Risk Analysis, pp. 213–241. Springer, Dordrecht (1992)

8. Dubois, D., Yager, R.: Fuzzy set connectives as combination of belief structures. Inf. Sci. **66**, 245–275 (1992)
9. Shafer, G.: A Mathematical Theory of Evidence. Princeton University Press, Princeton (1976)
10. Yager, R.: On the Dempster-Shafer framework and new combination rules. Inf. Sci. **41**, 93–137 (1987)

A Relationship of Conflicting Belief Masses to Open World Assumption

Milan Daniel(✉)

Prague, Czech Republic
milan.daniel@cs.cas.cz

Abstract. When combining belief functions by conjunctive rules of combination, conflicting belief masses often appear, which are assigned to empty set by the non-normalized conjunctive rule or normalized by Dempster's rule of combination in Dempster-Shafer theory.

This theoretical study analyses processing of conflicting belief masses under open world assumption. It is observed that sum of conflicting masses covers not only a possibility of a non-expected hypothesis out of considered frame of discernment. It also covers, analogously to the case of close world assumption, internal conflicts of individual belief functions and conflict between/among two or several combined belief functions.

Thus, for correct and complete interpretation of open world assumption it is recommended to include extra element(s) into used frame of discernment.

Keywords: Belief functions · Dempster-shafer theory · Uncertainty · Conflicting belief masses · Internal conflict · Conflict between belief functions · Open world assumption · Transferable Belief Model (TBM)

1 Introduction

When combining belief functions by conjunctive rules of combination, conflicting belief masses often appear. This happens whenever combined belief functions (BFs) are not mutually completely consistent. Conflicting masses are originally considered to be caused by a conflict between belief functions [16] and later, alternatively, by a possibility of having a new hypothesis outside of a considered frame of discernment [17]. The later approach is called open world assumption (OWA).

The original Shafer's interpretation of the sum of all conflicting belief masses does not correctly correspond to the real nature of conflicts between belief functions [1,13], this has motivated a theoretical research and a series of papers on the topic of conflicts of BFs, e.g., [3,6,9–15].

Smets' idea of open world assumption is usually accepted by papers on the Transferable Belief Model (TBM) and on TBM based approaches. Nevertheless Smets' OWA approach hides the real nature of conflicting masses and conflicts of BFs; it mixes conflicts with a possibility of existence of a hypothesis outside of a considered frame of discernment.

J. Vejnarová and V. Kratochvíl (Eds.): BELIEF 2016, LNAI 9861, pp. 146–155, 2016.
DOI: 10.1007/978-3-319-45559-4_15

Motivated by a discussion after presentation of author's recent approach to conflicts of BFs [9], we discuss a relationship of the sum of conflicting belief masses and OWA approach in this study, in order to uncover a real nature of the sum of all conflicting masses and to present and analyse interpretations of conflicting belief masses under OWA.

Important basic notions are briefly recalled in Sect. 2. Section 3 presents normalized belief functions under OWA, whereas non-normalized belief functions under OWA are analysed in Sect. 4. Section 5 summarizes the analysed interpretations of OWA approach. Utilizing the presented results, Smets' TBM based on OWA is compared with the classic Shafer's approach to belief functions.

2 Preliminaries

We assume classic definitions of basic notions from the theory of *belief functions* (BFs) [16] on a finite frame of discernment $\Omega_n = \{\omega_1, \omega_2, ..., \omega_n\}$. An exhaustive frame of discernment is considered in the classic Shafer's approach; this is called *closed world assumption*. Alternatively Smets [17] admits a possibility of appearance of a new hypothesis outside of the considered frame of discernment, thus the frame is not exhaustive there; this is called *open world assumption (OWA)*. The sum of conflicting belief masses is interpreted as a mass of a hypothesis(-es) outside of the original frame, BFs are not assumed to be normalized there.

A *basic belief assignment (bba)* is a mapping $m : \mathcal{P}(\Omega) \longrightarrow [0,1]$ such that $\sum_{A \subseteq \Omega} m(A) = 1$; the values of the bba are called *basic belief masses (bbm)*. $m(\emptyset) = 0$ is assumed in the classic approach; $m(\emptyset) \geq 0$ in Smets' OWA approach. A *belief function (BF)* is a mapping $Bel : \mathcal{P}(\Omega) \longrightarrow [0,1]$, $Bel(A) = \sum_{\emptyset \neq X \subseteq A} m(X)$. There is a unique correspondence between m and corresponding Bel thus we often speak about m as of belief function.

A BF is *normalized* if $m(\emptyset) = 0$, thus if $\sum_{\emptyset \neq X \subseteq \Omega} m(X) = Bel(\Omega) = 1$. A BF is *non-normalized* if $m(\emptyset) > 0$, thus if $\sum_{\emptyset \neq X \subseteq \Omega} m(X) = Bel(\Omega) < 1$.

A *focal element* is a subset X of the frame of discernment, such that $m(X) > 0$. If all focal elements are nested, we speak about *a consonant belief function*; if all focal elements have a non-empty intersection, we speak about *a consistent belief function*.

Dempster's (conjunctive) rule of combination $\oplus$ is given as $(m_1 \oplus m_2)(A) = \sum_{X \cap Y = A} K m_1(X) m_2(Y)$ for $A \neq \emptyset$, where $K = \frac{1}{1-\kappa}$, $\kappa = \sum_{X \cap Y = \emptyset} m_1(X) m_2(Y)$, and $(m_1 \oplus m_2)(\emptyset) = 0$, see [16]; putting $K = 1$ and $(m_1 \, \copyright m_2)(\emptyset) = \kappa$ we obtain the *non-normalized conjunctive rule of combination* $\copyright$, which is used in OWA approach, see e.g., original Smets' Transferable Belief Model (TBM) [18].

3 Normalized Examples Against a Simple Interpretation of OWA Approach

Let us present several examples in this section. We will start with an extremely illustrative Almond's example [1,6], assuming OWA here.

Example 1. Let us suppose six-element frame of discernment, results of a six-sided die and two independent believers with the same beliefs[1] expressing that the six-sided die is fair: $\Omega_6 = \{\omega_1, ..., \omega_6\} = \{1, 2, 3, 4, 5, 6\}$, $m_j(\{\omega_i\}) = 1/6$ for $i = 1, ..., 6$, $j = 1, 2$, $m_j(X) = 0$ otherwise. Let $m = m_1 \otimes m_2$. We obtain $m(\{\omega_i\}) = 1/36$ for $i = 1, ..., 6$, $m(\emptyset) = 5/6$, $m(X) = 0$ otherwise. Supposing the usual simple OWA interpretation we obtain big belief mass $m(\emptyset) = 5/6$ for a non-expected hypothesis outside of our frame Ω_6, e.g. the die stands on one of its edges or vertices. It seems obvious that such an interpretation is not correct.

An analogous example is presented by W. Liu in [13] on a five-element frame of discernment. We can modify these examples, where both believers have same positive arguments for all hypotheses, by decreasing belief masses of singletons by the same value and putting the removed belief masses to the frame of discernment, or by taking any classic (i.e., normalized with $m(\emptyset) = 0$) non-vacuous[2] symmetric BFs, i.e., by some kind of discounting. Nevertheless, we always obtain positive $m(\emptyset) = 0$, which is hardly interpretable as a belief mass of an unexpected hypothesis, when zero belief mass is assigned to a hypothesis outside of the frame by both of the believers, which are in full accord.

More generally, we can take any couple of numerically same classic non-consistent BFs under OWA, e.g., Example 2 from [6], tossing a coin. We again obtain $m(\emptyset) = 0$, from two believers in full accord with $m_j(\emptyset) = 0$. This is again hardly interpretable as a belief mass of unexpected hypotheses, e.g., coin stands on its edge.

Example 2. Let us suppose for simplicity $\Omega_2 = \{\omega_1, \omega_2\}$ now. Let $m_j(\{\omega_1\}) = 0.5$, $m_j(\{\omega_2\}) = 0.4$, $m_j(\{\omega_1, \omega_2\}) = 0.1$ for $j = 3, 4$, $m_j(X) = 0$ otherwise. Let $m = m_3 \otimes m_4$ now. We obtain $m(\{\omega_1\}) = 0.35$, $m(\{\omega_2\}) = 0.24$, $m(\{\omega_1, \omega_2\}) = 0.01$, $m(\emptyset) = 0.4$, $m(X) = 0$ otherwise.

Both believers have same beliefs, they are in full agreement, there is no conflict between them. Assuming OWA the believers have a possibility to assign some belief mass to a new hypothesis unexpected in the frame of discernment using non-normalized BF(s). But they did not use this option, they assigned all the belief masses to non-empty subsets of the considered frame. Thus the positive resulting $m(\emptyset)$ expresses, in accordance with [6], rather *internal conflict* of input BFs than a belief mass assigned to a new hypothesis unexpected in the frame of discernment.

Let us suppose classic internally non-conflicting BFs, thus consonant or more generally consistent BFs now. There is no issue when the BFs are mutually

---

[1] Do not forget that the equality of BFs is not equivalent to their dependence: dependent BFs, BFs from dependent believers should be same or somehow similar, dependence implies similarity, but same (or very similar) BFs do not imply their dependence.

[2] Combining two vacuous BFs gives $m(\Omega) = 1$, thus $m(\emptyset) = 0$, but vacuous BF does not express the same positive arguments for all hypotheses, it expresses the full ignorance.

consistent, i.e., if common intersection of all their focal elements is non-empty, there is $m(\emptyset) = 0$ in such a case. On the other hand, if our consistent BFs are not mutually consistent, we can obtain the following example:

Example 3. Let us suppose $\Omega_6 = \{\omega_1, ..., \omega_6\}$ again and two simple internally non-conflicting BFs: $m_5(\{\omega_2, \omega_4, \omega_6\}) = 1$, $m_6(\{\omega_1\}) = 1/3$, $m_6(\{\omega_1, \omega_3\}) = 2/3$, $m_i(X) = 0$, otherwise. Combining $m = m_5 \textcircled{\odot} m_6$ we obtain $m(\emptyset) = 1$.

Example 3 (Modified). Let us suppose Ω_6 again and two modified BFs Bel_5', Bel_6':

X :	$\{\omega_1\}$	$\{\omega_1, \omega_3\}$	$\{\omega_2, \omega_4, \omega_6\}$	Ω_6	$\emptyset$
$m_5(X)$:			2/3	1/3	
$m_6(X)$:	2/9	4/9		3/9	
$(m_5 \textcircled{\odot} m_6)(X)$:	2/27	4/27	6/27	3/27	12/27

A situation is much more complicated here. Both the input BFs are consistent, thus internally non-conflicting. On the other hand the BFs are not mutually consistent, there is high conflict between them, they are even completely conflicting in the case of the original Example 3. Some part of $m(\emptyset)$ represents conflict between BFs here. Of course another part of $m(\emptyset)$ may be caused by OWA. Because both of the believers assign all their belief masses to non-empty subsets of the frame, even if OWA is considered, we can hardly interpret entire $m(\emptyset)$ as a belief mass assigned to a new hypothesis outside of the frame.

Thus we rather have to consider entire $m(\emptyset)$ or its part to be a *conflict between* BFs (external conflict [11]) than to consider a belief mass of an unexpected hypothesis (or unexpected hypotheses) only.

4   Non-normalized Belief Functions Under OWA

Let us turn our attention to non-normalized BFs in this section. Input BFs explicitly assume or at least admit existence of a new hypothesis unexpected in the considered frame of discernment.

Let us start with an analogy of Example 1, but the believers want to admit the existence of a new hypothesis, thus they assign belief mass $\frac{1}{10}$ outside of the considered frame Ω_6 frame thus to the $\emptyset$:

Example 4. Let us again suppose a six-sided fair die, thus Ω_6, but modified bbms m_1', m_2' this time:

X :	$\{\omega_1\}$	$\{\omega_2\}$	$\{\omega_3\}$	$\{\omega_4\}$	$\{\omega_5\}$	$\{\omega_6\}$	$\emptyset$
$m_1'(X)$:	0.15	0.15	0.15	0.15	0.15	0.15	0.10
$m_2'(X)$:	0.15	0.15	0.15	0.15	0.15	0.15	0.10
$(m_1' \textcircled{\odot} m_2')(X)$:	0.0225	0.0225	0.0225	0.0225	0.0225	0.0225	0.8650

The result is better this time, positive belief masses same for all singletons are obtained. Nevertheless, both believers assign greater masses to any element from the frame than to a new hypothesis. But the resulting belief mass of the empty set is significantly greater than masses assigned to the singletons, even significantly greater than the sum of belief masses assigned to all the singletons from the frame of discernment ($0.865 = m'(\emptyset) > \sum_{i=1}^{6} m'(\{\omega_i\}) = 0.135$). When believers decrease their belief masses assigned to the empty set (see the following modification of the example), the resulting belief mass assigned to the empty set remains almost the same. Thus (a possibility of appearing of) a new hypothesis outside of the frame of discernment is significantly preferred to any hypothesis from the frame, even to the entire frame (as $m(\emptyset) > Bel(\Omega)$).

Example 4 (Modified). Let us suppose Ω_6 again, with different modification of bbms m_1'', m_2'' this time:

X :	$\{\omega_1\}$	$\{\omega_2\}$	$\{\omega_3\}$	$\{\omega_4\}$	$\{\omega_5\}$	$\{\omega_6\}$	$\emptyset$
$m_j''(X)$:	0.16	0.16	0.16	0.16	0.16	0.16	0.04
$(m_1'' \, \textcircled{\tiny\bigcirc} m_2'')(X)$:	0.0256	0.0256	0.0256	0.0256	0.0256	0.0256	0.8464

There is a simple mathematical explanation: $m(\emptyset)$ is absorbing element with respect to conjunctive combination, i.e., $m_i(X)m_j(\emptyset)$ goes to $(m_i \, \textcircled{\tiny\bigcirc} m_j)(\emptyset)$ for any $X \subseteq \Omega$, as there always holds that $X \cap \emptyset = \emptyset$.

There is also an interpretational explanation: in accord with the classic cases studied in [6] the sum of conflicting belief masses $m_{\textcircled{\tiny\bigcirc}}(\emptyset)$ contains also internal conflicts of input belief masses (and conflict between BFs if they are mutually conflicting).

When we want to admit a possibility of an unexpected hypothesis and we do not like to assign positive belief masses directly to the empty set we can either explicitly add a new element(s) representing some unexpected hypothesis(es) into the considered frame of discernment or we can add empty set to the frame.

Let us start with the later option, i.e., addition of the empty set to the frame of discernment. Thus we obtain $\Omega_n^\emptyset = \Omega_n \cup \{\emptyset\} = \{\omega_1, \omega_2, ..., \omega_n, \emptyset\}$, especially $\Omega_6^\emptyset = \{\omega_1, \omega_2, ..., \omega_6, \emptyset\}$. We can express a possibility of unexpected hypothesis by positive $m(\Omega_n^\emptyset)$ now. Let us look at Example 5 and its modification applied to $\Omega_6^\emptyset$:

Example 5. A six-sided fair die again; and modified bbms on $\Omega_6^\emptyset$ this time:

X :	$\{\omega_1\}$	$\{\omega_2\}$	$\{\omega_3\}$	$\{\omega_4\}$	$\{\omega_5\}$	$\{\omega_6\}$	Ω_6	$\Omega_6^\emptyset$	$\emptyset$
$m_1'''(X)$:	0.15	0.15	0.15	0.15	0.15	0.15		0.10	
$m_2'''(X)$:	0.15	0.15	0.15	0.15	0.15	0.15		0.10	
$(m_1''' \, \textcircled{\tiny\bigcirc} m_2''')(X)$:	0.0525	0.0525	0.0525	0.0525	0.0525	0.0525		0.01	0.6750
$m_j''''(X)$:	0.16	0.16	0.16	0.16	0.16	0.16		0.04	
$(m_1'''' \, \textcircled{\tiny\bigcirc} m_2'''')(X)$:	0.0384	0.0384	0.0384	0.0384	0.0384	0.0384		0.0016	0.7680

We can observe a high belief mass assigned to the empty set at $m_1''' \, \textcircled{\tiny\bigcirc} m_2'''$ and $m_1'''' \, \textcircled{\tiny\bigcirc} m_2''''$, especially in the later case where less masses are assigned to $\Omega_6^\emptyset$ in input BFs m_1'''', m_2''''. Thus, the problem of preference of an unexpected hypothesis seems to be solved here, but interpretation of high $(m_1 \, \textcircled{\tiny\bigcirc} m_2)(\emptyset)$

remains an open issue. Moreover, when we interpret $m(\emptyset)$ or its part as belief mass of an unexpected hypothesis, the unexpected hypothesis is preferred again, as its belief mass comes from two parts: $m(\emptyset)$ and $m(\{\emptyset\})$ (the later is zero in Example 5).

We are going to investigate addition of a new classic element $N(ew)$ representing unexpected hypotheses now. We obtain $\Omega_n^+ = \Omega_n \cup \{N\} = \{\omega_1, \omega_2, ..., \omega_n, N\}$, especially $\Omega_6^+ = \{\omega_1, \omega_2, ..., \omega_6, N\}$. Let us look at Example 4 and its modification 6 applied to Ω_6^+. We can directly assign a belief mass to the additional element N, see Example 6, or analogously to the previous case to entire Ω_6^+ (we obtain numerically same results as in the previous case), see Example 6 (modified). The combination of these two options is of course also a possibility.

Example 6. A six-sided fair die again; and modified bbms on Ω_6^+ this time:

X :	$\{\omega_1\}$	$\{\omega_2\}$	$\{\omega_3\}$	$\{\omega_4\}$	$\{\omega_5\}$	$\{\omega_6\}$	$N(ew)$	Ω_6^+	$\emptyset$
$m_1^v(X)$:	0.15	0.15	0.15	0.15	0.15	0.15	0.10		
$m_2^v(X)$:	0.15	0.15	0.15	0.15	0.15	0.15	0.10		
$(m_1^v \otimes m_2^v)(X)$:	0.0225	0.0225	0.0225	0.0225	0.0225	0.0225	0.01		0.8550
$m_j^{vi}(X)$:	0.16	0.16	0.16	0.16	0.16	0.16	0.04		
$(m_1^{vi} \otimes m_2^{vi})(X)$:	0.0256	0.0256	0.0256	0.0256	0.0256	0.0256	0.0016		0.8448

Example 6 (Modified). A six-sided fair die; and modified bbms on Ω_6^+ this time:

X :	$\{\omega_1\}$	$\{\omega_2\}$	$\{\omega_3\}$	$\{\omega_4\}$	$\{\omega_5\}$	$\{\omega_6\}$	$N(ew)$	Ω_6^+	$\emptyset$
$m_1^{vii}(X)$:	0.15	0.15	0.15	0.15	0.15	0.15		0.10	
$m_2^{vii}(X)$:	0.15	0.15	0.15	0.15	0.15	0.15		0.10	
$(m_1^{vii} \otimes m_2^{vii})(X)$:	0.0525	0.0525	0.0525	0.0525	0.0525	0.0525		0.01	0.6750
$m_j^{viii}(X)$:	0.16	0.16	0.16	0.16	0.16	0.16		0.04	
$(m_1^{viii} \otimes m_2^{viii})(X)$:	0.0384	0.0384	0.0384	0.0384	0.0384	0.0384		0.0016	0.7680

We can see a high belief mass assigned to the empty set also in the case of Ω_6^+ but this time it does not represent a belief mass of unexpected hypotheses. Belief mass directly assigned to unexpected hypotheses is represented by $m(\{N\})$ and plausibly also by any $m(X)$ for $N \in X$, while $m_i \otimes m_j(\emptyset)$ represents conflicts inside and between m_i and m_j as under the close world assumption. If it is useful for a given domain, we can use several additional elements for several unexpected hypotheses, or just one as coarsening of all unexpected hypotheses together. We can see that belief mass of an unexpected hypothesis (of element N) which is less than belief mass of any element of Ω_6 in individual BFs remains less also after combination. Thus an unexpected hypothesis in not preferred now.

Let us suppose an observer which knows European animals only and a frame of discernment Ω_{EA} containing the European animals. Let us move our observer (without any previous knowledge of African animals) to Africa now. When observing a zebra, an assignment of positive belief mass explicitly to a new element N is probably not necessary, as belief masses may be assigned to focal elements $H = \{horse, N\}$ and $H \cup X$ for $X \subseteq \Omega_{EA}$. Observing a crocodile or an elephant some positive belief mass should be probably assigned to N (where its size would be related to a quality of the observation). For some applications one element N for all unknown animals is sufficient, for other applications several new elements, e.g., NM (new mammal), NB (new bird), NR (new reptile), etc., would fit better.

Using additional element N for unexpected hypothesis, we can either make normalization as in classic Shafer's approach; or we can use non-normalized BFs as in Smets' approach, considering that $m(\emptyset)$ represents a size of conflict (both internal and external) of BFs. From the decisional point of view both the options are the same as an element with the highest value of some probabilistic transformation[3] of BFs is usually selected. Usually Smets' pignistic probability [19] or normalized plausibility of singletons [4] (i.e., normalized contour function) is used. For an analysis[4] of probabilistic transformations see, e.g., [4,5].

5   A Comparison of the Approaches

5.1   A Summary of the Presented OWA Approaches

Using just a non-negative $m(\emptyset)$: This is a simple idea and performance. But simple interpretation of $m(\emptyset)$ hides internal conflict(s) of BF(s) and conflict between BFs in results of their combination. Interpreting $m(\emptyset)$ only as belief mass assigned to new unexpected hypotheses significantly prefers possibility of unexpected hypotheses to those which are included in the considered frame of discernment.

Extension of Ω by $\{\emptyset\}$, where belief masses are assigned only to classic focal elements and entire extended $\Omega_n^\emptyset$: This simple extension, unfortunately does not cover the issue of interpretation of $m(\emptyset)$, see Example 5.

Extension of Ω by new element(s): Ω^+. This approach increases the size of the frame, thus it also a little bit increases complexity of computation (especially when several new elements are added in a small frame). On the other hand, this approach distinguishes belief masses of unexpected hypothesis(es) from both internal and external conflicts caused by conflicting masses of disjoint focal elements from the frame and also from conflicts caused by conflicting masses of original focal elements and unexpected hypotheses. Moreover, both original and additional hypotheses are managed analogously in this approach, none of them is preferred.

---

[3] Note, that the pignistic probability gives numerically same results under close and open world assumptions, as normalization is part of pignistic transformation; and that TBM with non-normalized $\odot$ under OWA gives same decisional results as classic Shafer's approach with $\oplus$ and pignistic transformation does. The only difference is that TBM explicitly keeps in $m(\emptyset)$ value of conflict (internal and external conflict together with masses of unexpected hypotheses) until the moment of decision.

[4] Note, that normalized plausibility is consistent with conjunctive combination (they mutually commute), while pignistic transformation is not. Pignistic transformation commutes instead of conjunctive combination with linear combination of BFs.

5.2   When Do the OWA Approaches Coincide?

When there is no necessity or reason to assign belief mass directly to sets of considered hypotheses, we obtain an unexpected hypothesis N in all focal elements in the extended approach. Thus all intersections of focal elements contain N again. There is no reason to assign a positive belief mass to the empty set in the extended approach. Intersections are non-empty under our assumption, thus $\emptyset$ is not a focal element in the extended approach under our assumption. Hence we obtain the following equivalence of focal elements, thus also of the approaches: $X^+ \equiv X$, where $X \subseteq \Omega$, $X^+ \subseteq \Omega^+$, $X^+ = X \cup \{N\}$, and $\{N\} \equiv \emptyset$.

E.g., for two-element frame $\{H(ead), T(ail)\}$ we obtain under our assumption the following equivalence with extended version of the frame $\{H, T, N\}$:

$$\{N\} \equiv \emptyset,$$
$$\{H, N\} \equiv \{H\},$$
$$\{T, N\} \equiv \{T\},$$
$$\{H, T, N\} \equiv \{H, T\}.$$

We can see that $Bel(\Omega)$ is not only ≤ 1, but it is just $Bel(\Omega) = 0$ under the assumption. We can see that N is preferred in this case as $Bel(\{N\}) \geq 0$. It may be zero in initial BFs, but it may obtain a positive belief mass within combination of two BFs which are not mutually consistent.

We have to notice that we cannot assign any positive belief mass to any focal element from the considered frame Ω in this case which is equivalent to simple interpretation of OWA. Even if we have a fully reliable believer (observer, sensor) and 100% clear argument (observation, measurement) in favour of an element or a subset of the frame ($\omega_X \in \Omega$ or $X \subseteq \Omega$), focal elements should always contain N, thus they are $\{\omega_X, N\}$ or $X \cup \{N\}$ and $m(\{\omega_X\}) = m(X) = 0$ hence always also $Bel(\{\omega_X\}) = Bel(X) = 0$.

Assuming a criminal example analogous to Smets' Peter, Paul and Mary case, any (partially of fully) contradictive testimonies give (multiples of) their contradictive masses to a person which is out of the frame, thus to unknown person, which is still not suspicious to be an assassin. On the other hand, belief of the entire frame is zero, thus $Bel(\{Peter, Paul, Mary\}) = 0$.

This always holds true under the above assumption and due to the equivalence it also holds true in the simple interpretation of OWA in general.

5.3   A Comparison of Smets' OWA and Classic Shafer's Approaches

A Decisional Point of View. Based on commutativity of normalization with conjunctive combination, i.e., on the fact that $n(n(m_1) \odot n(m_2)) = n(m_1 \odot m_2) = m_1 \oplus m_2$, where $(n(m))(X) = \frac{m(X)}{\sum_{\emptyset \neq Y \subseteq \Omega} m(Y)}$, $\odot$ non-normalized, and $\oplus$ normalized conjunctive combinations, we can see that TBM gives the same results as classic Shafer's approach produces, when pignistic probability is used. This holds true because the first step of the pignistic transformation (generating of $BetP$) is just a normalization. Possibly different results may arise when different probabilistic approaches are used in the approaches: e.g., pignistic transformation in TBM, and plausibility transformation (generation of normalized plausibility of singletons) in the classic approach.

Belief Mass of the Empty Set: $m(\emptyset)$. A positive belief mass of the empty set is a feature which really distinguishes TBM form the classic approach. It is hidden on the normalization step when two or more BFs are combined in the same time in Shafer's approach. It is not even computed there, when input BFs are combined gradually one by one. We have to recall that $m(\emptyset)$ includes not only belief mass of a possible unexpected hypothesis, but also internal conflicts of input BFs, conflict between two or among several input BFs.

If we want correctly use the simple interpretation of $m(\emptyset)$ only as a belief mass of an unexpected hypothesis, then we have to assume that all focal elements include the unexpected hypothesis, hence that $m(X) = Bel(X) = 0$ for any subset X of Ω $(X \subseteq \Omega)$, which does not contain the unexpected hypothesis.

Definition Domains. Non-normalized conjunctive rule is defined for any couple (n-tuple) of BFs. Classic Dempster rule is not defined $\sum_{X \cap Y \neq \emptyset} m_1(X)m_2(Y) = 0$, i.e., if $\sum_{X \cap Y = \emptyset} m_1(X)m_2(Y) = 1$. On the other hand in this case we know $m(\emptyset) = 1$ even in the classic approach.

6   Conclusion

In this study, we have studied the nature of conflicting belief masses under open world assumption. Simple interpretation of sum of all conflicting masses from the Transferable Belief Model was analysed. Several variants of extension of frame of discernment with additional element(s) representing unexpected hypothesis(es) was suggested here. Finally, simple interpretation and extension approaches were mutually compared, and condition of their coincidence described.

We have to always keep in mind that the sum of all conflicting belief masses $(m(\emptyset))$ contains not only belief mass which should be assigned to new unexpected hypothesis(es), but also internal conflicts of single belief functions and conflict between belief functions (external conflict) whenever m is a basic belief assignment corresponding to a result of combination of two or more belief functions.

For a correct and complete interpretation of open world assumption it is recommended to include extra element(s) into used frame of discernment.

The presented theoretical results improve general understanding of both the sum of all conflicting masses and conflicts of belief functions under open world assumption. This, consequently, may improve combination of conflicting belief functions and interpretation of results of combination in practical applications under open world assumption.

Acknowledgments. This study is a continuation of author's research previously conducted at the Institute of Computer Science, The Czech Academy of Sciences.

References

1. Almond, R.G.: Graphical Belief Modeling. Chapman & Hall, London (1995)
2. Ayoun, A., Smets, P.: Data association in multi-target detection using the transferable belief model. Int. J. Intell. Syst. **16**(10), 1167–1182 (2001)
3. Burger, T.: Geometric views on conflicting mass functions: from distances to angles. Int. J. Approx. Reason. **70**, 36–50 (2016)
4. Cobb, B.R., Shenoy, P.P.: On the plausibility transformation method for translating belief function models to probability models. Int. J. Approx. Reason. **41**(3), 314–330 (2006)
5. Daniel, M.: Probabilistic transformations of belief functions. In: Godo, L. (ed.) ECSQARU 2005. LNCS (LNAI), vol. 3571, pp. 539–551. Springer, Heidelberg (2005)
6. Daniel, M.: Conflicts within and between belief functions. In: Hüllermeier, E., Kruse, R., Hoffmann, F. (eds.) IPMU 2010. LNCS, vol. 6178, pp. 696–705. Springer, Heidelberg (2010)
7. Daniel, M.: Non-conflicting and conflicting parts of belief functions. In: Proceedings of the 7th ISIPTA, ISIPTA 2011, pp. 149–158. Studia Universitätsverlag, Innsbruck (2011)
8. Daniel, M.: Properties of plausibility conflict of belief functions. In: Rutkowski, L., Korytkowski, M., Scherer, R., Tadeusiewicz, R., Zadeh, L.A., Zurada, J.M. (eds.) ICAISC 2013, Part I. LNCS, vol. 7894, pp. 235–246. Springer, Heidelberg (2013)
9. Daniel, M.: Conflict between belief functions: a new measure based on their non-conflicting parts. In: Cuzzolin, F. (ed.) BELIEF 2014. LNCS, vol. 8764, pp. 321–330. Springer, Heidelberg (2014)
10. Daniel, M., Ma, J.: Conflicts of belief functions: continuity and frame resizement. In: Straccia, U., Calì, A. (eds.) SUM 2014. LNCS, vol. 8720, pp. 106–119. Springer, Heidelberg (2014)
11. Destercke, S., Burger, T.: Toward an axiomatic definition of conflict between belief functions. IEEE Trans. Cybern. **43**(2), 585–596 (2013)
12. Lefèvre, E., Elouedi, Z.: How to preserve the conflict as an alarm in the combination of belief functions? Decis. Support Syst. **56**(1), 326–333 (2013)
13. Liu, W.: Analysing the degree of conflict among belief functions. Artif. Intell. **170**, 909–924 (2006)
14. Martin, A.: About conflict in the theory of belief functions. In: Denœux, T., Masson, M.H. (eds.) Belief Functions: Theory and Applications. AISC, vol. 164, pp. 161–168. Springer, Heidelberg (2012)
15. Schubert, J.: The internal conflict of a belief function. In: Denœux, T., Masson, M.H. (eds.) Belief Functions: Theory and Applications. AISC, vol. 164, pp. 169–176. Springer, Heidelberg (2012)
16. Shafer, G.: A Mathematical Theory of Evidence. Princeton University Press, Princeton (1976)
17. Smets, P.: Belief functions. In: Smets, P., et al. (eds.) Non-standard Logics for Automated Reasoning, chap. 9, pp. 253–286. Academic Press, London (1988)
18. Smets, P., Kennes, R.: The transferable belief model. Artif. Intell. **66**, 191–234 (1994)
19. Smets, P.: Decision making in the TBM: the necessity of the pignistic transformation. Int. J. Approx. Reason. **38**(2), 133–147 (2005)
20. Smets, P.: Analyzing the combination of conflicting belief functions. Inf. Fusion **8**, 387–412 (2007)

Idempotent Conjunctive Combination of Belief Functions by Distance Minimization

John Klein[1]([✉]), Sebastien Destercke[2], and Olivier Colot[1]

[1] University of Lille, CNRS, Centrale Lille, UMR 9189 - CRIStAL - Centre de
Recherche en Informatique Signal et Automatique de Lille, 59000 Lille, France
{john.klein,olivier.colot}@univ-lille1.fr
[2] Technologic University of Compiegne, CNRS, UMR 7253 - Heudiasyc,
Centre de Recherche de Royallieu, Compigne, France
sebastien.destercke@hds.utc.fr

Abstract. When combining multiple belief functions, designing a combination rule that selects the least informative belief function among those more informative than each of the combined ones is a difficult task. Such rules, commonly depicted as "cautious", are typically required to be idempotent, since when one is cautious, combining identical information should not lead to the reinforcement of some hypothesis. However, applying the least commitment principle using partial orders is in general not straightforward, mainly due to the non-uniqueness of solutions. Building upon previous work, this paper investigates the use of distances compatible with such partial orders to determine a unique solution to the combination problem. The obtained operators are conjunctive, idempotent and commutative, but lack associativity. They are, however, quasi-associative allowing sequential combinations at no extra complexity.

Keywords: Conjunctive combination · Idempotence · Belief function · Distance · Optimization

1 Introduction

Combining pieces of evidence coming from different sources of information is one of the most frequently studied problem in the belief function theory. In particular, there exist a rich literature proposing alternatives to Dempster's rule when this latter does not apply, that is when sources of information are either unreliable or non-independent, or both. This paper deals with the second issue, that is the one concerning source independence, and more particularly with the case where this dependence is ill-known and hard to assess.

Under such an assumption, it is common to adopt a cautious approach, also known under least-commitment principle [7] (LCP). A natural consequence of this principle is that if all the sources provide the same mass function, then the result of the combination should be this very mass function, or in other words the combination should be idempotent. However, if idempotence is a consequence of the LCP, satisfying idempotence does not imply satisfying the LCP.

© Springer International Publishing Switzerland 2016
J. Vejnarová and V. Kratochvíl (Eds.): BELIEF 2016, LNAI 9861, pp. 156–163, 2016.
DOI: 10.1007/978-3-319-45559-4_16

As shown by Dubois and Yager [8], there is virtually an infinity of ways to derive idempotent combination rules, not all of them necessarily following a least-commitment principle. For instance, Cattaneo [2] provides an idempotent rule following a conflict-minimization approach, which may lead to non-least committed results [4].

To satisfy the LCP, we therefore must add additional constraints on the combination results. One such natural constraint is to consider a partial order over informative content of mass functions, and to require the combination result to be one of the maximal element of this partial order within the subset of possible combination results. Unfortunately, such an approach will very often lead to multiple solutions corresponding to all possible maximal elements [6]. Denœux [3] shows that using the canonical decomposition and the associated partial order leads to a unique LCP, idempotent solution, yet this solution has two limitations: the set of possible combination results is much reduced, leading to a not so conservative behavior (as we will see on a simple example in Sect. 4, and as already pointed out in [4]), and the combination only apply to specific (i.e., non-dogmatic) mass functions.

In this paper, we take inspiration from some of our previous work [9] studying the consistency of distances with partial orders comparing informative contents to propose a new way to derive cautious combination rules. Our approach departs from previous ones, as it is formulated as an optimization problem that naturally satisfies the LCP principle (similarly to what is done by Cattaneo [2] for conflict minimization). The interest of this approach is that if the distance is chosen so as to minimize a strictly convex objective function, we are guaranteed to have a unique solution that satisfies the LCP and is easy to compute. The bulk of the proposal is contained in Sect. 3, where we present the combination approach and study its properties. Sections 2 and 4 respectively recalls the basics needed in this paper and (briefly) compares our proposal with respect to existing ones.

2   Preliminaries and Problem Statement

This section briefly recalls the basics of evidence theory (due to space limitations, we will provide references for details).

2.1   Basic Concepts

A body of evidence $\mathcal{E}_i$ defined on the space $\Omega = \{\omega_1, \ldots, \omega_n\}$ will be modeled by a mass function $m_i : 2^\Omega \to [0, 1]$ that sums up to one, $i.e.$, $\sum_{E \subseteq \Omega} m(E) = 1$. In evidence theory, this basic tool models our uncertainty about the true value of some quantity (parameter, variable) lying in Ω. The cardinality of 2^Ω is denoted by $N = 2^n$. A set A is a **focal element** of m_i iff $m_i(A) > 0$. A mass function assigning a unit mass to a single focal element A is called **categorical** and denoted by m_A: $m_A(A) = 1$. If $A \neq \Omega$, the mass function m_A is equivalent to providing the set A as information, while the **vacuous** mass function m_Ω represents ignorance.

Several alternative set functions are commonly used in the theory of belief functions and encode the same information as a given mass function m_i. The **belief, plausibility** and **commonality** functions of a set A are defined as

$$bel_i(A) = \sum_{E \subseteq A, E \neq \emptyset} m_i(E), \quad pl_i(A) = \sum_{E \cap A \neq \emptyset} m_i(E), \quad q_i(A) = \sum_{E \supseteq A} m_i(E)$$

and respectively represent how much A is implied, consistent and common by the actual evidence.

In this paper, we will also use the **conjunctive weight function** denoted by w_i introduced by Smets [10]. It is only defined for mass functions with $m_i(\Omega) \neq 0$ (*i.e.* non-dogmatic mass functions). We refer to Denœux [3] for a thorough presentation of the conjunctive weight function.

2.2 Comparing Mass Functions with Respect to Informative Content

When considering two mass functions m_1 and m_2 providing information about the same quantity, a natural question is to wonder if one of these two is more informative than the other one. This question can be answered if the **mass space** $\mathcal{M}$, *i.e.* the set of mass functions over Ω, is endowed with a relevant partial order $\sqsubseteq$ with $m_1 \sqsubseteq m_2$ when m_1 is more informative than m_2. Informative content related partial orders should extend set inclusion, since when $A \subseteq B$, A is more informative than B. Such partial orders[1] can be directly obtained by considering inequality between the set functions $f \in \{pl, q, w\}$, by stating that m_1 is f-**included** in m_2, denoted $m_1 \sqsubseteq_f m_2$, if $f_1 \leq f_2$ where $\leq$ is the element-wise inequality.

Each of these orders is partial in the sense that in general there are some incomparable pairs (m_1, m_2), *i.e.* $m_1 \not\sqsubseteq m_2$ and $m_2 \not\sqsubseteq m_1$. There exist implications between them, as we have

$$m_1 \sqsubseteq_w m_2 \Rightarrow \begin{cases} m_1 \sqsubseteq_{pl} m_2 \\ m_1 \sqsubseteq_q m_2 \end{cases}. \tag{1}$$

2.3 Distances and Partial Orders Compatibility

Another way to compare mass functions is by measuring how distant they are. An **evidential distance** is a function $d : \mathcal{M} \times \mathcal{M} \to [0, \infty]$ that satisfies the symmetry, definiteness and triangle inequality properties. In [9], we have formalized the idea of compatibility between a distance and a partial order in the following way:

Definition 1. *Given a partial order $\sqsubseteq_f$ defined over $\mathcal{M}$, an evidential distance d is said to be $\sqsubset_f$-compatible (in the strict sense) if for any mass functions m_1, m_2 and m_3 such that $m_1 \sqsubset_f m_2 \sqsubset_f m_3$, we have:*

$$\max \{d(m_1, m_2); d(m_2, m_3)\} < d(m_1, m_3), \tag{2}$$

---

[1] There are others, but due to limited space, we will only deal with these ones.

For some family of set-functions f that are in bijective correspondence with mass functions, an interesting distance $d_{f,k}$ is defined as

$$d_{f,k}(m_1, m_2) = \left(\sum_{A \subseteq \Omega} |f_1(A) - f_2(A)|^k \right)^{\frac{1}{k}}.$$

In particular, we showed that for any $k \in \mathbb{N}^* \setminus \{\infty\}$, $d_{pl,k}$ are $\sqsubseteq_{pl}$-compatible and $d_{q,k}$ is $\sqsubseteq_q$-compatible (in the strict sense for all of them).

3   A Distance-Based Cautious Conjunctive Aggregation

In this section, we introduce the main idea of our new combination operator, relying on distances compatible with the partial orders comparing informative content.

3.1   Conjunctive Combination Using Partial Orders

In this paper, rather than seeing a conjunctive combination $\mathcal{E}_1, \ldots, \mathcal{E}_\ell$ as a particular operator defined either on the mass functions $m_1, \ldots, m_\ell$ or on the weight functions $w_1, \ldots, w_\ell$, we simply consider that a mass function m^* resulting from a conjunction should be (1) more informative (in the sense of some partial order $\sqsubseteq_f$) than any $m_1, \ldots, m_\ell$ and (2) should be among the least committed elements (in terms of information) among those, in accordance with the LCP. Formally speaking, if we denote by

$$S_f(m_i) := \{m \in \mathcal{M} \mid m \sqsubseteq_f m_i\} \tag{3}$$

the set of mass functions more informative than m_i, then we should have:

1. $m^* \in S_f(m_1) \cap \ldots \cap S_f(m_\ell)$,
2. $\nexists m' \in S_f(m_1) \cap \ldots \cap S_f(m_\ell)$ such that $m^* \sqsubset_f m'$.

The first constraint expresses the conjunctive behavior of such an approach. The second constraint says that m^* is a maximal element (*i.e.* a least committed solution) for admissible solutions subject to the first constraint.

The interest of such a solution is that it is rather generic, and does not require any explicit model of dependence. However, it should be noted that the choice of the partial order to consider is not without consequence. Considering those mentioned in Sect. 2.2, Eq. (1) tells us that for a same mass function m, $S_w(m) \subseteq S_{pl}(m)$, hence the space of solutions will be potentially much smaller when choosing $\sqsubseteq_w$ rather than $\sqsubseteq_{pl}$. In practice and in accordance with the LCP, it seems safer to choose the most conservative partial orders, *i.e.*, in our case $\sqsubseteq_{pl}$ or $\sqsubseteq_q$. We will see in Sect. 4 that it can have an important impact on the combination results, even for simple examples.

While our definition of the cautious result of a conjunctive combination appears natural, it still faces the problem that many different solutions m^* could actually fit the two constraints, as $\sqsubseteq$ is a partial order. One idea to solve this problem is to use distances that are compatible with $\sqsubseteq$.

3.2   New Conjunctive Operators from Soft LCP

To derive new conjunctive operators, we consider a weaker form of least commitment principle which we call **soft LCP**. This principle states that when there are several candidate mass functions compliant with a set of constraints, the one with minimal distance value from the vacuous mass function should be chosen for some $\sqsubseteq$-compatible distance. According to Corollary 4 in [9], we know that the problem induced by the soft LCP is a convex optimization problem with a unique solution if the chosen distance $d_{f,k}$ is $\sqsubseteq_f$-compatible and if $2 \leq k < \infty$. Let $\star_{k,f}$ denote this operator, for any set of ℓ functions $\{m_1, .., m_\ell\}$, we have

$$m_1 \star_{f,k} .. \star_{f,k} m_l = \underset{m \in \mathcal{S}_f(m_1) \cap .. \cap \mathcal{S}_f(m_\ell)}{\arg\min} d_{f,k}(m, m_\Omega). \qquad (4)$$

The commutativity of the set-intersection and the symmetry property of distance give that $\star_{f,k}$ is commutative. Each operator $\star_{f,k}$ is also idempotent: for any possible solution $m \in \mathcal{S}_f(m_1) \setminus \{m_1\}$, we have $d_{f,k}(m_1, m_\Omega) < d_{f,k}(m, m_\Omega)$ because $d_{f,k}$ is $\sqsubseteq_f$-compatible and $m \sqsubseteq_f m_1 \sqsubseteq_f m_\Omega$, hence $m_1 \star_{f,k} m_1 = m_1$. Each of these operators are also conjunctive by construction, in the sense that the output mass function is more informative than any of the initial mass functions. Indeed if m_i states that ω is not a possible value of the unknown quantity $(pl_i(\omega) = 0)$, then any function in $\mathcal{S}(m_i)$ also states so. Since the combination result belongs to $\mathcal{S}(m_i)$, then this piece of information is propagated by $\star_{f,k}$.

This operator is, however, not associative because we can have

$$\mathcal{S}_f(m_1 \star_{f,k} m_2) \subsetneq \mathcal{S}_f(m_1) \cap \mathcal{S}_f(m_2).$$

Consequently, the optimization constraints are not deducible from an output mass function $m_1 \star_{f,k} m_2$. Fortunately, these constraints can be stored and updated iteratively, meaning that the complexity of the combination does not increase with ℓ. In practice, one needs to be able to compute combinations iteratively without storing the whole set of mass functions $\{m_1, \ldots, m_\ell\}$ and restart the combination from scratch when a new function $m_{\ell+1}$ arrives. This property is often referred to as **quasi-associativity**. Let c denote a set function from 2^Ω to $[0; 1]$ which is meant to store the problem constraints. Algorithm 1 allows to compute combinations using $\star_{q,k}$ sequentially. The same algorithm works for $\star_{pl,k}$. In practice, what we simply do is storing, for each set A, the lowest commonality (resp. plausibility) value encountered in $\{m_1, \ldots, m_\ell\}$.

4   A Brief Comparison with Related Works

As said earlier, there are many works that have dealt with the problem of either cautious conjunctive rules or of conjunctive rules not relying on independence. They depart from the classical conjunctive rule $\odot$ that assume independence of the sources, and whose formula for a pair (m_1, m_2) of mass functions is

$$m_{1 \odot 2}(A) = \sum_{\substack{A_1, A_2 \in 2^X \\ \text{s.t. } A_1 \cap A_2 = A}} m_1(A_1) m_2(A_2), \text{ for all } A \subseteq \Omega. \qquad (5)$$

Algorithm 1. Sequential combination using $\star_{q,k}$

entries : $\{m_1, .., m_\ell\}$, $k \geq 2$.
$c \leftarrow \min\{q_1; q_2\}$ (entrywise minimum).
$m \leftarrow m_1 \star_{q,k} m_2$.
for i from 3 to ℓ **do**
    $c \leftarrow \min\{c; q_i\}$ (entrywise minimum).
    $m \leftarrow \arg\min_{m'} d_{q,k}(m', m_\Omega)$ subject to $q' \leq c$.
end for
return m.

Dempster's rule $\oplus$ corresponds to the normalized version of this rule where the mass of the empty set is forced to zero. Choosing an alternative to them is however not so easy. A principled and common approach is to rely on a set of axiomatic properties [5] or to adapt existing rules from other frameworks [4]. In practice, such axioms seldom lead to a unique solution, and it is then necessary to advocate more practical solutions. Our rule can be seen as an instance of such an approach, where the axiom consists in using the LCP over sets of f-included mass functions, and the practical solution is to use a distance compliant with such an axiom. Cattaneo's solution [1] as well as Denoeux [3] cautious rules can also be seen as instances of the same principle. The former defends the fact of reducing the conflict rather than minimizing the informative content, while the latter focuses on using the set $\mathcal{S}_w(m_1) \cap \ldots \cap \mathcal{S}_w(m_\ell)$ and the order $\sqsubseteq_w$, and demonstrates that in this case there is a unique LCP solution known in closed form. This cautious rule is usually denoted by $\oslash$. Due to lack of space, we will focus on comparing our approach with the most well-known, that is with rules $\cap$, $\oplus$ and $\oslash$.

Table 1 summarizes some basic theoretical properties satisfied by operators $\cap$, $\oplus$, $\oslash$ and $\star_{f,k}$. From a practical point of view, let us stress that combinations using $\star_{f,k}$ for $f \in \{pl, q\}$ and $k = 2$ are really easy to compute. Indeed, quadratic programming techniques can solve equation (4) in a very few iterations. The function $m_\emptyset$ can be used to initialize the minimization as we are sure that it belongs to $\mathcal{S}_f(m_1) \cap .. \cap \mathcal{S}_f(m_\ell)$.

Table 1. Basic properties of operators $\cap$, $\oplus$, $\oslash$ and $\star_{f,k}$.

Operator	Condition for use	Commutativity	Associativity	Idempotence
$\cap$	None	Yes	Yes	No
$\oplus$	$m_{1 \cap 2}(\emptyset) < 1$	Yes	Yes	No
$\oslash$	$m_1(\Omega) > 0$ and $m_2(\Omega) > 0$	Yes	Yes	Yes
$\star_{f,k}$	None	Yes	Quasi	Yes

Let us illustrate the operator discrepancies on a simple situation inspired from Zadeh's counter-example [11]. Suppose $m_1 = \alpha m_{\{b\}} + (1 - \alpha) m_{\{a\}}$ and $m_2 = \alpha m_{\{b\}} + (1 - \alpha) m_{\{c\}}$ are two mass functions on a frame $\Omega = \{a, b, c\}$.

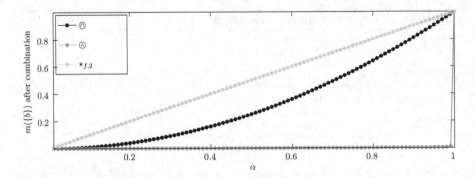

Fig. 1. Mass assigned to $\{b\}$ after combination of $m_1 = \alpha m_{\{b\}} + (1-\alpha)\, m_{\{a\}}$ and $m_2 = \alpha m_{\{b\}} + (1-\alpha)m_{\{c\}}$ with $\bigcirc$, $\bigwedge$ and $\star_{f,2}$.

Figure 1 shows the mass assigned to $\{b\}$ after combination by $\bigcirc$, $\bigwedge$ and $\star_{f,2}$. The same masses are obtained for $f \in \{pl, q\}$. A very small mass was assigned to Ω when using $\bigwedge$ to circumvent the non-dogmatic constraint.

As could be expected, our rule tries to maintain as much evidence on $\{b\}$ as possible. A striking fact is that we have obviously $m_1 \star_{f,2} m_2 (\{b\}) = \alpha$. More precisely, we have $m_1 \star_{f,2} m_2 = (1-\alpha)\, m_\emptyset + \alpha m_{\{b\}}$.

This result can be proved for any finite $k \geq 2$ when $f = q$. Let $q_{1 \wedge 2}$ denote the entrywise minimum of functions q_1 and q_2. In this particular setting, $q_{1 \wedge 2}$ happens to be a valid commonality function. Consequently, $m_{1 \wedge 2} \in \mathcal{S}_q (m_1) \cap \mathcal{S}_q (m_2)$. By definition of the partial order $\sqsubseteq_q$, for any function $m \in \mathcal{S}_q (m_1) \cap \mathcal{S}_q (m_2)$, we have $m \sqsubseteq_q m_{1 \wedge 2}$. Since we also have $m_{1 \wedge 2} \sqsubseteq_q m_\Omega$ and $d_{q,k}$ is $\sqsubseteq_q$-compatible, then $m_1 \star_{q,k} m_2 = m_{1 \wedge 2}$. In other words, our approach coincides with the minimum rule applied to commonalities in this case.

When $f = pl$, the result can also be proved. For any $m \in \mathcal{S}_{pl} (m_1) \cap \mathcal{S}_{pl} (m_2)$, the constraints $pl(\{a\}) = pl(\{c\}) = 0$ imply that only $\{b\}$ and $\emptyset$ are possible focal sets for m. More precisely, this actually implies that $\mathcal{S}_{pl} (m_1) \cap \mathcal{S}_{pl} (m_2)$ is a segment $(1-\beta)\, m_\emptyset + \beta m_{\{b\}}$ in $\mathcal{M}$ parametrized by $\beta \in [0; \alpha]$. $\sqsubseteq_{pl}$ is a total order for this segment and obviously $m_1 \star_{pl,k} m_2 = (1-\alpha)\, m_\emptyset + \alpha m_{\{b\}}$.
In this example, the behavior of Denœux's cautious rule $\bigwedge$ is more questionable, as it keeps almost no mass on $\{b\}$ except when $\alpha = 1$. This is an unconservative behavior, due partly to the fact that $\mathcal{S}_w$ induces stronger constraints than $\mathcal{S}_{pl}$ or $\mathcal{S}_q$. Finally, the conjunctive rule appears to have an intermediate behavior as compared to the two others.

5   Conclusion

This paper introduces an idea allowing cautious conjunctive combinations of mass functions by relying on constraints inducing a more informative mass function than the combined ones on one hand, and on the minimization of distances to total ignorance on the other hand. The metrics used in the minimization procedure must be compatible with partial orders comparing informative contents.

This idea can generate several commutative, idempotent and quasi-associative combination operators that are in line with the LCP principle. This procedure allows these operators to be easily interpretable and to rely on sound justifications. Preliminary experimental results show that they have very regular behavior as compared to standard approaches, and comply with some user's expectations.

This study is a start, but the interesting results we obtained call for several possible extensions, for instance by adapting the approach to other combination types (starting with disjunction), and by fully investigating its connection with other rules trying to solve the same problem. Moreover, it would be also interesting to check if our distance-based approach is to some extent compliant with other operations such as conditioning or refining. Finally, these new operators rely on L_k norms ($k \geq 2$) and the influence of parameter k must be studied.

References

1. Cattaneo, M.E.G.V.: Combining belief functions issued from dependent sources. In: Bernad, J.M., Seidenfeld, T., Zaffalon, M. (eds.) Third International Symposium on Imprecise Probabilities and Their Applications (SIPTA 2003), pp. 133–147. Carleton Scientific, Lugano (Switzerland) (2003)
2. Cattaneo, M.E.G.V.: Belief functions combination without the assumption of independence of the information sources. Int. J. Approx. Reason. **52**(3), 299–315 (2011). Dependence Issues in Knowledge-Based Systems
3. Denœux, T.: Conjunctive and disjunctive combination of belief functions induced by nondistinct bodies of evidence. Artif. Intell. **172**, 234–264 (2008)
4. Destercke, S., Dubois, D.: Idempotent conjunctive combination of belief functions: extending the minimum rule of possibility theory. Inf. Sci. **181**(18), 3925–3945 (2011)
5. Dubois, D., Liu, W., Ma, J., Prade, H.: The basic principles of uncertain information fusion. An organised review of merging rules in different representation frameworks. Inf. Fusion **32**, 12–39 (2016)
6. Dubois, D., Prade, H.: Consonant approximations of belief functions. Int. J. Approx. Reason. **4**(56), 419–449 (1990)
7. Dubois, D., Prade, H., Smets, P.: A definition of subjective possibility. Int. J. Approx. Reason. **48**(2), 352–364 (2008). In Memory of Philippe Smets (19382005)
8. Dubois, D., Yager, R.R.: Fuzzy set connectives as combinations of belief structures. Inf. Sci. **66**(3), 245–276 (1992)
9. Klein, J., Destercke, S., Colot, O.: Interpreting evidential distances by connecting them to partial orders: application to belief function approximation. Int. J. Approx. Reason. **71**, 15–33 (2016)
10. Smets, P.: The canonical decomposition of a weighted belief. In: 14th International Joint Conference on Artificial Intelligence, vol. 2, pp. 1896–1901 (1995)
11. Zadeh, L.A.: A simple view of the Dempster-Shafer theory of evidence, its implication for the rule of combination. Artif. Intell. Mag. **7**, 85–90 (1986)

IPFP and Further Experiments

Václav Kratochvíl and Jiřina Vejnarová[✉]

Institute of Information Theory and Automation,
Czech Academy of Sciences, Prague, Czech Republic
{velorex,vejnar}@utia.cas.cz

Abstract. Iterative Proportional Fitting Procedure is commonly used in probability theory for construction of a joint probability distribution from a system of its marginals. A similar idea can be used in case of belief functions thanks to special operators of composition defined in this framework. In this paper, a formerly designed IPF procedure is further studied. We propose a modification of composition operator (for the purpose of the procedure), compare the behavior of the modified procedure with the previous one and prove its convergence.

1 Introduction

The marginal problem, as one of the most challenging problem types in probability theory, addresses the question whether or not a common extension exists for a given system of marginals. The challenges lie not only in a wide range of the relevant theoretical problems, but also in its applicability to various problems of statistics [1], computer tomography [8], relational databases [10] and artificial intelligence [12]. In the last case, it is the problem how to obtain a global knowledge (represented by a multidimensional probability distribution) from pieces of local knowledge (represented by low-dimensional probability distributions).

To solve a discrete marginal problem, one can use Iterative Proportional Fitting Procedure (IPFP), introduced by Deming and Stephan already in 1940 [5]. Its convergence was finally proven by Csiszár [6] in 1975. Note that both the EM and the Newton-Raphson algorithms converge towards the same limit. However, in most cases, IPFP is preferred due to its computational speed, numerical stability and algebraic simplicity [13]. A possibilistic version of this procedure (parametrized by a continuous t-norm) was studied in [11].

A possible application of IPFP in the framework of belief functions was studied in [2]. Knowing that the probabilistic IPFP can be easily (and elegantly) expressed with the help of the so-called *operator of composition* [7], the same idea was applied in this framework. Two different composition operators for bpas were discussed in the above-mentioned paper: the first one has already been introduced in [3], the second one was based on *Dempster's combination rule* [9]. Let us note that the operator based Dempster's rule appeared as inappropriate for IPFP (for more details see [2]). That is why, in this paper, we focus on the original operator only. We illustrate one undesirable aspect of its behavior and suggest a possible modification to solve the problem.

© Springer International Publishing Switzerland 2016
J. Vejnarová and V. Kratochvíl (Eds.): BELIEF 2016, LNAI 9861, pp. 164–173, 2016.
DOI: 10.1007/978-3-319-45559-4_17

The paper is organized as follows. After a brief overview of necessary concepts and notation (Sect. 2), in Sect. 3 we recall the concept of evidential IPF procedure and present its modification. Section 4 is devoted to the discussion of experimental results. The proof of convergence is given is Sect. 5.

2   Basic Concepts and Notation

In this section we will briefly recall basic concepts from evidence theory [9] concerning sets and set functions as well as the concept of the operator of composition [4].

2.1   Set Projections and Joins

In this paper $\mathbb{X}_N = \mathbb{X}_1 \times \mathbb{X}_2 \times \ldots \times \mathbb{X}_n$ denotes a finite multidimensional space, and its subspaces (for all $K \subseteq N$) are denoted by $\mathbb{X}_K = \times_{i \in K} \mathbb{X}_i$. For a point $x = (x_1, x_2, \ldots, x_n) \in \mathbb{X}_N$, its *projection* into subspace $\mathbb{X}_K$ is denoted $x^{\downarrow K} = (x_i)_{i \in K}$, and for $A \subseteq \mathbb{X}_N$ $A^{\downarrow K} = \{y \in \mathbb{X}_K : \exists x \in A, x^{\downarrow K} = y\}$.

By a *join* of two sets $A \subseteq \mathbb{X}_K$ and $B \subseteq \mathbb{X}_L$ we understand a set $A \bowtie B = \{x \in \mathbb{X}_{K \cup L} : x^{\downarrow K} \in A \ \& \ x^{\downarrow L} \in B\}$. Let us note that if K and L are disjoint, then $A \bowtie B = A \times B$, if $K = L$ then $A \bowtie B = A \cap B$. Generally, for $C \subseteq \mathbb{X}_{K \cup L}$, C is a subset of $C^{\downarrow K} \bowtie C^{\downarrow L}$, which may be proper.

2.2   Basic Assigments

A *basic assignment* (bpa) m on $\mathbb{X}_K$ ($K \subseteq N$) is a real non-negative function on power set of $\mathbb{X}_K$, for which $\sum_{\emptyset \neq A \subseteq \mathbb{X}_K} m(A) = 1$. If $m(A) > 0$, then A is said to be a *focal element* of m.

A bpa is called vacuous, if it contains only one focal element, namely $\mathbb{X}_K$. In accordance with [2] we call a bpa *uniform* if $m(A) = 1/(2^{|\mathbb{X}_K|} - 1)$ for each $A \subseteq \mathbb{X}_K, A \neq \emptyset$.

Considering two bpas m_1, m_2 on the same space $\mathbb{X}_K$, we say that m_1 is *dominated* by m_2, if for all $A \subseteq \mathbb{X}_K$: $m_1(A) > 0 \implies m_2(A) > 0$.

Having a bpa m on $\mathbb{X}_K$ one can consider its *marginal assignments*. On $\mathbb{X}_L$ (for $L \subseteq K$) it is defined (for each $\emptyset \neq B \subseteq \mathbb{X}_L$) as follows $m^{\downarrow L}(B) = \sum_{A \subseteq \mathbb{X}_K : A^{\downarrow L} = B} m(A)$.

Having two bpas m_1 and m_2 on $\mathbb{X}_K$ and $\mathbb{X}_L$, respectively ($K, L \subseteq N$), we say that these assignments are *projective* if $m_1^{\downarrow K \cap L} = m_2^{\downarrow K \cap L}$, which occurs if and only if there exists a bpa m on $\mathbb{X}_{K \cup L}$ such that both m_1 and m_2 are its marginal assignments.

2.3   Operator of Composition

Let us recall the definition of operator of composition $\triangleright$ introduced in [3].

Definition 1. *Consider two arbitrary basic assignments m_1 on $\mathbb{X}_K$ and m_2 on $\mathbb{X}_L$ ($K \neq \emptyset \neq L$). A composition $m_1 \triangleright m_2$ is defined for each $C \subseteq \mathbb{X}_{K \cup L}$ by one of the following expressions:*

[a] *if $m_2^{\downarrow K \cap L}(C^{\downarrow K \cap L}) > 0$ and $C = C^{\downarrow K} \bowtie C^{\downarrow L}$ then*

$$(m_1 \triangleright m_2)(C) = \frac{m_1(C^{\downarrow K}) \cdot m_2(C^{\downarrow L})}{m_2^{\downarrow K \cap L}(C^{\downarrow K \cap L})};$$

[b] *if $m_2^{\downarrow K \cap L}(C^{\downarrow K \cap L}) = 0$ and $C = C^{\downarrow K} \times \mathbb{X}_{L \setminus K}$ then*

$$(m_1 \triangleright m_2)(C) = m_1(C^{\downarrow K});$$

[c] *in all other cases $(m_1 \triangleright m_2)(C) = 0$.*

3 Iterative Proportional Fitting Procedure

Let us start this section by recalling the original design of evidential version of IPF procedure [2].

3.1 Original Design

Assume a system of n low-dimensional bpas $m_1, m_2, \ldots, m_n$ defined on $\mathbb{X}_{K_1}, \mathbb{X}_{K_2}, \ldots, \mathbb{X}_{K_n}$, respectively. During the computational process, an infinite sequence of bpas $\mu_0, \mu_1, \mu_2, \mu_3, \ldots$ is computed, each of them defined on $\mathbb{X}_{K_1 \cup \ldots \cup K_n}$. If this sequence is convergent, its limit is the result of this process. For simplicity reason let us suppose that $K_1 \cup K_2 \cup \cdots \cup K_n = N$.

Algorithm IPFP. Define the starting bpa μ_0 on $\mathbb{X}_{K_1 \cup K_2 \cup \ldots \cup K_n}$. Then compute sequence $\{\mu_i\}_{i \in 1,2,3,\ldots}$ in the following way:

$$\mu_1 = m_1 \triangleright \mu_0 \qquad \mu_{n+1} = m_1 \triangleright \mu_n \qquad \mu_{2n+1} = m_1 \triangleright \mu_{2n}$$
$$\mu_2 = m_2 \triangleright \mu_1 \qquad \mu_{n+2} = m_2 \triangleright \mu_{n+1} \qquad \mu_{2n+2} = m_2 \triangleright \mu_{2n+1}$$
$$\vdots \qquad\qquad\qquad \vdots \qquad\qquad\qquad \vdots$$
$$\mu_n = m_n \triangleright \mu_{n-1} \qquad \mu_{2n} = m_n \triangleright \mu_{2n-1} \qquad \mu_{3n} = m_n \triangleright \mu_{3n-1}$$

As already said in the Introduction, if this algorithm is applied to probability distributions, it has nice and useful properties, most of which were proven by Csiszár in his famous paper [6].

Based on the Csiszár's results, two nice properties on convergence were proven in [2].

Theorem 1. *Consider a system of bpas $m_1, m_2, \ldots, m_n$ defined on $\mathbb{X}_{K_1}, \mathbb{X}_{K_2}, \ldots, \mathbb{X}_{K_n}$ and a basic assignment μ_0 on $\mathbb{X}_{K_1 \cup \ldots \cup K_n}$. If there exists a bpa ν on $\mathbb{X}_{K_1 \cup \ldots \cup K_n}$ such that ν is dominated by μ_0, and ν is a common extension of all $m_1, m_2, \ldots, m_n$, then the sequence $\mu_0, \mu_1, \mu_2, \mu_3, \ldots$ computed by the Algorithm IPFP with $\triangleright$ converges.*

Theorem 2. *If the sequence $\mu_0, \mu_1, \mu_2, \mu_3, \ldots$ computed by the Algorithm IPFP converges then the bpa $\mu^* = \lim\limits_{i \to +\infty} \mu_i$ is a common extension of all $m_1, m_2, \ldots, m_n$, i.e., $(\mu^*)^{\downarrow K_j} = m_j$ for all $j = 1, \ldots, n$.*

In experiments performed in [2], the uniform bpa was chosen to be μ_0. It seems to correspond to the probabilistic framework, where the uniform distribution is also used as the starting distribution. Moreover, uniform bpa dominates every other bpa on the same frame. Thus, if one starts the IPFP with uniform basic assignment, Theorem 1 guarantees its convergence whenever the common extension of the given assignments exists.

Nevertheless, there is a big difference between semantics of these two approaches. While in the probabilistic case uniform distribution is considered to be the least specific, nothing similar holds in the evidential framework. Here the vacuous bpa represents the least specific one. However, in this case the assumption of dominance of μ_0 is not valid, and the procedure need not converge (and it does not, in most cases).

3.2   Modification

If the composition operator is applied on projective marginals, part [b] of Definition 1 is never used. On the other hand, if it is not the case, then rule [b] is adding just one focal element of a very specific form. It is, in fact, cylindrical extension of the focal element on $\mathbb{X}_K$ to $\mathbb{X}_{K \cup L}$ (in case of m_1 on $\mathbb{X}_K$, m_2 on $\mathbb{X}_L$, and $m_1 \rhd m_2$).

This led us to the following consideration. Let us start the IPFP procedure with vacuous bpa — reflecting total ignorance about the problem — and rewrite part [b] of the operator of composition in a way to be able to add more focal elements. We decided to add all focal elements that, being marginalized to $\mathbb{X}_K$ have a focal element in m_1. The respective mass is uniformly distributed among them. A lot of unnecessary focal elements may be (and really is) added, but they are left for future removal by rules [a] and [c] of Definition 1 — which remain unchanged.

Definition 2. *Consider two arbitrary bpas m_1 on $\mathbb{X}_K$ and m_2 on $\mathbb{X}_L$ ($K \neq \emptyset \neq L$) an iterative composition $m_1 \rhd' m_2$ is defined for each $C \subseteq \mathbb{X}_{K \cup L}$ by one of the following expressions:*

[a] *if $m_2^{\downarrow K \cap L}(C^{\downarrow K \cap L}) > 0$ and $C = C^{\downarrow K} \bowtie C^{\downarrow L}$ then*

$$(m_1 \rhd' m_2)(C) = \frac{m_1(C^{\downarrow K}) \cdot m_2(C^{\downarrow L})}{m_2^{\downarrow K \cap L}(C^{\downarrow K \cap L})};$$

[b'] *if $m_2^{\downarrow K \cap L}(C^{\downarrow K \cap L}) = 0$ then $\forall D \in \mathcal{D} = \{D \in \mathbb{X}_{K \cup L} : D^{\downarrow K} = C^{\downarrow K}\}$*

$$(m_1 \rhd' m_2)(D) = \frac{m_1(C^{\downarrow K})}{|\mathcal{D}|};$$

[c] *in all other cases $(m_1 \rhd' m_2)(C) = 0$.*

In other words, in [b'] instead of one focal element $C = C^{\downarrow K} \times X_{L \setminus K}$, a system of its subsets is added. The mass of $m_1(C^{\downarrow K})$ is uniformly distributed among them.

This approach has significant impact on the behavior of the IPFP procedure, which seems to behave better (or in the same way, in the worst case) as the one presented in [2] (cf. Sect. 4).

Now, let us summarize three observations concerning both original and modified IPFP, which will, hopefully, help the reader to understand not only the difference between them, but later also the idea of the proof.

Observation 1. *Note that in case of IPFP, $K \subseteq L$ in the definition of the operator of composition and therefore $A = A^{\downarrow K} \bowtie A^{\downarrow L} = A^{\downarrow K} \bowtie A$ for every $A \subseteq \mathbb{X}_N$.*

Note that in case of IPFP, there is a close connection between the notion of dominance and using of rule [b] in the definition of $\triangleright$:

Observation 2. *If ν is dominated by μ_i, then ν is dominated by $\nu^{\downarrow K} \triangleright \mu_i$ as well, and rule [b] from Definition 1 is never used.*

Proof. If it is not the case, then $\exists A \subseteq \mathbb{X}_N$ such that $\nu(A) > 0$ while $(\nu^{\downarrow K} \triangleright \mu_i)(A) = 0$. Since $\mu_i(A) > 0$ by dominance assumption, then, following Observation 1, rule [a] has to be used and therefore $(\nu^{\downarrow K} \triangleright \mu_i)(A) > 0$, which is a contradiction.

Having Observation 2 in mind, one can conclude:

Observation 3. *If ν is dominated by μ_i then $\nu^{\downarrow K} \triangleright \mu_i = \nu^{\downarrow K} \triangleright' \mu_i$.*

4   Experiments

Most experiments discussed in this section deal with cases of consistent bpas, i.e. bpas representing marginals of a multidimensional bpa. We will start with the original IPFP [2] to reveal the problems caused by its application.

4.1   Original Procedure

Let X, Y and Z be three binary variables with values in $\mathbb{X} = \mathbb{Y} = \mathbb{Z} = \{0, 1\}$. Joint basic assignment m on $\mathbb{X} \times \mathbb{Y} \times \mathbb{Z} = \{0, 1\}^3$ is defined in Table 1.

First, we calculate all three two-dimensional marginals of m — denoted by $m_1 = m^{\downarrow XY}$, $m_2 = m^{\downarrow YZ}$, and $m_3 = m^{\downarrow XZ}$ — and we apply them in this order on uniform μ_0 using IPFP. The computational process is illustrated by Table 2.

Notice, that the procedure converges to m' which is not in contradiction with results proven in [2] because both m' and m have the same two-dimensional marginals. This experiment has already been published in [2].

A problem appears if m_Ω is taken into account instead of m (in case of m_Ω — a non-zero mass has been put on the whole frame of discernment — $m_\Omega(\mathbb{X}) = 0.1$). The computational process with respective marginals $m_1 = m_\Omega^{\downarrow XY}$, $m_2 = m_\Omega^{\downarrow YZ}$, and $m_3 = m_\Omega^{\downarrow XZ}$ is illustrated by Table 3.

Table 1. Three-dimensional assignments

(Focal) elements	m	m'	m_Ω	m'_Ω
$\{010, 100\}$	0.2	0.2	0.2	0.2
$\{001, 010\}$	0.3	0.3	0.3	0.3
$\{001, 011, 101, 110\}$	0.5	0.25	0.4	0.2
$\{001, 011, 101, 110, 111\}$	0	0.25	0	0.2
X	0	0	0.1	0.1

Table 2. IPFP with $\triangleright$, two-dimensional marginals of m, and uniform μ_0.

Focal elements	μ_3	μ_4	μ_5	μ_6	μ_7	μ_8	μ_{100}	μ_{1000}
$\{010, 100\}$	0.156	0.200	0.166	0.166	0.200	0.172	0.195	0.199
$\{000, 010, 100, 110\}$	0.043	0.040	0.033	0.033	0.031	0.027	0.004	$4 \cdot 10^{-4}$
$\{001, 010\}$	0.146	0.146	0.300	0.211	0.211	0.300	0.293	0.299
$\{001, 010, 011\}$	0.153	0.153	0.124	0.088	0.085	0.079	0.006	$7 \cdot 10^{-4}$
$\{001, 011, 101, 110\}$	0.250	0.230	0.187	0.250	0.234	0.210	0.250	0.250
$\{001, 011, 101, 110, 111\}$	0.250	0.230	0.187	0.250	0.234	0.210	0.250	0.250

Table 3. IPFP with $\triangleright$, two-dimensional marginals of m_Ω, and uniform μ_0.

Focal elements	μ_3	μ_4	μ_5	μ_6	μ_{100}	μ_{1000}	μ_{10000}
$\{010, 100\}$	0.156	0.195	0.166	0.166	0.188	0.188	0.188
$\{000, 010, 100, 110\}$	0.043	0.040	0.034	0.034	0.011	0.011	0.011
$\{001, 010\}$	0.158	0.158	0.272	0.211	0.257	0.257	0.257
$\{001, 010, 011\}$	0.132	0.132	0.104	0.080	0.038	0.038	0.038
$\{001, 011, 101, 110\}$	0.181	0.167	0.132	0.172	0.170	0.170	0.170
$\{001, 011, 101, 110, 111\}$	0.181	0.167	0.132	0.172	0.170	0.170	0.170
X	0.001	0.0009	0.001	0.001	0.0007	0.0007	0.0007
And 43 other elements	...	...	...	...	...	...	...

IPF procedure does not perform very well in this case. A stabilized state is achieved approximately in μ_{800} and it is far away from m_Ω, with 50 focal elements, although, according to Theorem 1, its two-dimensional marginals coincide with those of m_Ω.

It seems, that the problem consists in the fact that we start with too many focal elements in μ_0. It would be of a special interest to have a procedure that starts with vacuous μ_0. Because the ability of operator $\triangleright$ to add new focal elements is limited, operator $\triangleright'$ will be used instead.

Table 4. Number of focal elements during IPFP

Operator	Assignment	IPFP ordering	μ_0	μ_1	μ_2	μ_3	μ_4	μ_5	μ_6
$\triangleright$	m	$m_1; m_2; m_3;$	255	99	15	6	6	6	6
		$m_2; m_1; m_3;$	255	45	15	6	6	6	6
		$m_3; m_1; m_2;$	255	45	17	6	6	6	6
	m_Ω	$m_1; m_2; m_3$	255	99	66	50	50	50	50
		$m_2; m_1; m_3$	255	126	66	50	50	50	50
		$m_3; m_1; m_2$	255	126	82	50	50	50	50
$\triangleright'$	m	$m_1; m_2; m_3$	1	19	6	30	11	5	5
		$m_1; m_3; m_2$	1	19	9	3	84	11	6
		$m_2; m_1; m_3$	1	45	15	6	6	6	6
	m_Ω	$m_1; m_2; m_3$	1	19	9	33	14	11	11
		$m_2; m_1; m_3$	1	46	16	11	11	11	11
		$m_3; m_1; m_2$	1	46	18	11	11	11	11

4.2 Modified Procedure

Note that in case of IPFP with $\triangleright'$ and vacuous μ_0, only eleven focal elements are taken into the account. Respective elements are depicted in Table 5. Note that the sequence $\{\mu_i\}_{i \to \infty}$ tends to m'_Ω from Table 1 which is not in conflict, because it has the same two-dimensional marginals as m_Ω.

Starting with vacuous assignment, potentially necessary focal elements have to be added. Operator $\triangleright'$ seems to be a reasonable choice. See Table 4 to compare the development of the number of focal elements for both operators $\triangleright$ and $\triangleright'$. Note that for $\triangleright$, the uniform assignment is solely used as μ_0 in respective IPFP.

Table 5. IPFP with $\triangleright'$, two-dimensional marginals of m_Ω, and vacuous μ_0.

Focal elements	μ_5	μ_{100}	μ_{1000}	μ_{10000}
$\{010, 100\}$	0.200	0.199	0.199	0.199
$\{001, 010\}$	0.155	0.292	0.299	0.299
$\{001, 010, 011\}$	0.143	0.007	10^{-4}	10^{-5}
$\{001, 011, 101, 110\}$	0.159	0.198	0.199	0.199
$\{001, 011, 101, 110, 111\}$	0.159	0.198	0.199	0.199
$\{010, 011, 100, 101\}$	0.001	0.001	10^{-4}	10^{-6}
$\{000, 001, 010, 011\}$	0.001	10^{-6}	10^{-9}	10^{-10}
$\{001, 011, 100, 101, 110\}$	0.026	0.001	10^{-4}	10^{-6}
$\{001, 011, 100, 110, 111\}$	0.026	0.001	10^{-4}	10^{-6}
$\{001, 011, 100, 101, 110, 111\}$	0.026	0.001	10^{-4}	10^{-6}
X	0.098	0.099	0.099	0.099

Similarly, $\triangleright'$ is associated with vacuous assignment as its starting point. This is highlighted in Table 4 — in the number of focal elements in column corresponding to μ_0. The number of focal elements stabilizes in μ_i for $i \geq 6$ in this case (some of them may disappear later by having mass converging to zero).

4.3 Inconsistent Marginals

In case of inconsistent marginals and IPFP based on $\triangleright'$ and vacuous μ_0, we observe the same behavior as for $\triangleright$ and uniform μ_0: After several cycles, the iteration process goes through cyclical changes. The length of the cycle corresponds to the number of basic assignments entering the computational process. The subsequences converge.

5 Proof of Convergence

To prove the convergence of the IPFP starting with vacuous bpa and using operator $\triangleright'$ from Definition 2 it is enough to show that the sequence $\mu_0, \mu_1, \mu_2, \dots$ can be divided into two parts. In the first part, a bpa μ_k dominating ν (a common extension of given system of marginals) is found. Then, the second part converges because of Theorem 1 and Observations 2 and 3.

We work in a discrete space, therefore the number of focal elements is finite. We cope with a system of marginals $m_1, m_2, \dots, m_n$ (of a joint (unknown) bpa on $\mathbb{X}_N = \mathbb{X}_{K_1 \cup \dots \cup K_n}$) defined on $\mathbb{X}_{K_1}, \mathbb{X}_{K_2}, \dots, \mathbb{X}_{K_n}$, respectively, and an infinite sequence of bpas $\mu_0, \mu_1, \mu_2, \mu_3, \dots$ computed using IPFP algorithm and operator $\triangleright'$ from Definition 2, where μ_0 is vacuous bpa on $\mathbb{X}_N$.

Lemma 1. *Having a bpa on $\mathbb{X}_N$ and a system of its marginals $\{m_j\}_{j=1}^n$, create sequence $\mu_0, \mu_1, \mu_2, \dots$ using IPFP starting with vacuous μ_0 and using $\triangleright'$. Let $A \subseteq \mathbb{X}_N$ be a focal element of μ_i such that $A^{\downarrow K_j}$ is a focal element of m_j $\forall j = 1, \dots, n$, respectively. Then $\forall k \geq i$, A is a focal element in μ_k.*

Proof. Take an arbitrary $j = 1, \dots, n$. Let $\mu_{i+1} = m_j \triangleright' \mu_i$. To prove the lemma, one has to realize that in case of IPFP, $K \subseteq L$ in the definition of the operator of composition and $A = A^{\downarrow K_j} \bowtie A$ for every A (Observation 1). Then, using lemma assumption, rule [a] from the definition of the composition operator is used in case of A. Because $A^{\downarrow K_j}$ is a focal element in m_j, then we multiply non-zero numbers and A is a focal element in μ_{i+1} as well. This reasoning can be iteratively repeated which finishes the proof.

Observation 4. *Let $K_j \subset N$, $A \subseteq \mathbb{X}_{K_j}$ and $\mathcal{B} = \{B \subseteq \mathbb{X}_N | B^{\downarrow K_j} = A\}$. If none $B \in \mathcal{B}$ is a focal element of μ_i and A is a focal element of m_j then $\mathcal{B}$ is a subset of focal elements of $\mu_{i+1} = m_j \triangleright' \mu_i$.*

Indeed, rule [b'] from Definition 2 is used in this case.

Theorem 3. *Consider a system of bpas $m_1, m_2, \ldots, m_n$ defined on $\mathbb{X}_{K_1}, \mathbb{X}_{K_2},$ $\ldots, \mathbb{X}_{K_n}$, respectively, and a vacuous bpa μ_0 on $\mathbb{X}_{K_1 \cup \ldots \cup K_n}$. If a common extension of $\{m_j\}_{j=1}^n$ exists then the sequence $\mu_0, \mu_1, \mu_2, \mu_3, \ldots$ computed using IPFP with $\triangleright'$ converges to one of them.*

Proof. First, let us prove that in a finite number of steps we get bpa μ_i that dominates a common extension of $\{m_j\}_{j=1}^n$. To prove that, is sufficient to realize three simple facts:

(i) following Lemma 1, once a focal element of a common extension is added, it cannot be removed,

(ii) focal elements are added if necessary (Observation 4) — note that at least of them has to be a focal element of a common extension and therefore it cannot be removed by Lemma 1, and

(iii) there is a finite number of focal elements.

Once a μ_i dominating a common extension is obtained, then, using Observation 3, Theorem 1 can be applied and such a sequence converges. Moreover, it converges to a common extension by Theorem 2 (using Observation 3, again).

6   Conclusions and Future Work

We studied recently designed IPF procedure for bpas based on the evidential composition operator in more detail and realized that its behavior is not satisfactory, especially in case of partial ignorance. Deeper study revealed the fact, that although starting from uniform distribution allows an elegant proof of convergence, the procedure produces a great number of focal elements.

We suggested an alternative approach starting with vacuous basic assignment and consisting in adding of potentially interesting focal elements and subsequent removing of the unimportant ones. Several experiments showed that this procedure behaves much better than the previous one.

Following Table 5, the computational complexity of the new approach seems to be lower. This is caused not only by the fact that the new approach is producing bpas with generally less focal elements, but also by the fact that it does not start with all possible focal elements in μ_0. This could be further improved by excluding the first part of the IPFP responsible for finding dominating bpa. Note that we are not interested in "probability" masses laid on focal elements in this part, but on the shape of focal elements only. This is a topic of further research.

Acknowledgments. This work was supported by GAČR under the grant No. 16-12010S.

References

1. Janžura, M.: Marginal problem, statistical estimation, and Möbius formula. Kybernetika **43**, 619–631 (2007)

2. Jiroušek, R., Kratochvíl, V.: On open problems connected with application of the iterative proportional fitting procedure to belief functions. In: Proceedings of the 8th Symposium on Imprecise Probabilities and their Applications, Compiegne, pp. 149–158 (2013)

3. Jiroušek, R., Vejnarová, J., Daniel, M.: Compositional models of belief functions. In: de Cooman, G., Vejnarová, J., Zaffalon, M. (eds.) Proceedings of the 5th Symposium on Imprecise Probabilities and their Applications, Praha, pp. 243–252 (2007)

4. Jiroušek, R., Vejnarová, J.: Compositional models and conditional independence in evidence theory. Int. J. Approx. Reason. **52**, 316–334 (2011)

5. Deming, W.E., Stephan, F.F.: On a least square adjustment of a sampled frequency table when the expected marginal totals are known. Ann. Math. Stat. **11**, 427–444 (1940)

6. Csiszár, I.: I-divergence geometry of probability distributions and minimization problems. Ann. Probab. **3**, 146–158 (1975)

7. Jiroušek, R.: Foundations of compositional model theory. Int. J. Gen. Syst. **40**(6), 623–678 (2011)

8. Pougazaa, D.-B., Mohammad-Djafaria, A., Berchera, J.-F.: Link between copula and tomography. Pattern Recogn. Lett. **31**, 2258–2264 (2010)

9. Shafer, G.: A Mathematical Theory of Evidence. Princeton University Press, Princeton (1976)

10. Malvestuto, F.M.: Existence of extensions and product extensions for discrete proability distributions. Discret. Math. **69**, 61–77 (1988)

11. Vejnarová, J.: Design of iterative proportional fitting procedure for possibility distributions. In: Bernard, J.-M., Seidenfeld, T., Zaffalon, M. (eds.) 3rd International Symposium on Imprecise Probabilities and their Applications ISIPTA 2003, pp. 577–592. Carleton Scientific, Canada (2003)

12. Vomlel, J.: Integrating inconsistent data in a probabilistic model. J. Appl. Nonclass. Log. **14**, 367–386 (2004)

13. Wikipedia Contributors.: Iterative proportional fitting. Wikipedia, The Free Encyclopedia, 4 July 2016. Web, 14 July 2016

Entropy-Based Counter-Deception
in Information Fusion

Johan Schubert[✉]

Department of Decision Support Systems,
Division of Defence and Security, Systems and Technology,
Swedish Defence Research Agency, Stockholm, Sweden
schubert@foi.se
http://www.foi.se/fusion

Abstract. In this paper, we develop an entropy-based degree of falsity and combine it with a previously developed conflict-based degree of falsity in order to grade all belief functions. The new entropy-based degree of falsity is based on observing changes in entropy that are not consistent with combining only truthful information. With this measure, we can identify deliberately deceptive information and exclude it from the information fusion process.

Keywords: Deception · Counter-deception · Information fusion · Entropy · Conflict · Belief function · Dempster-Shafer theory

1 Introduction

Managing false and possibly deliberately deceptive information is, in general, an important issue within an information fusion process. If false and deceptive information is not actively managed, it becomes impossible to trust any conclusions that is based on combining information from several different sources without knowing if one is deceptive. Conclusions that are drawn based on a combination of information from all sources may become degraded or false when truthful information is combined with deceptive information that supports untrue possibilities.

We previously developed methods within the theory of belief functions [1–6] for clustering information regarding several different subproblems that should be managed separately when the information regarding different subproblems might be mixed up [7–11]. When we know that all information concerns only one problem at hand, this method could be used to identify false pieces of information and allow us to calculate a conflict-based degree of falsity for each piece of evidence [12]. These approaches use a function of the conflict [13, 14] in Dempster's rule [2] as criterion function.

Smets [15] developed a methodology for managing a special case of deception where a deceiver may observe a truthful report and send the complement of a truthful belief function as deception instead of the truthful report itself. Pichon *et al.* [16] later developed a correction scheme that generalizes Shafer's discounting rule [4] by taking into account uncertain meta-knowledge regarding the source relevance and truthfulness. This model now subsumes Smets' model. Furthermore, they recently introduced a contextual correction mechanism [17] for [16].

© Springer International Publishing Switzerland 2016
J. Vejnarová and V. Kratochvíl (Eds.): BELIEF 2016, LNAI 9861, pp. 174–181, 2016.
DOI: 10.1007/978-3-319-45559-4_18

However, the approach taken by Smets is a special case where the deceiver always sends the complement of what is observed from a truthful source. We think that this is not a realistic strategy by the deceiver, as it is easily countered by the counter-deception technique developed in Smets' approach [15]. Instead, we would allow the deceiver to act in any way it chooses and assume it might want to deceive us by supporting some focal elements of the frame of discernment that are wrong but we already somewhat believe. We think that this might be a more realistic approach.

In this paper, we develop an entropy-based measure of degree of falsity based on the change in entropy when truthful belief functions are combined with a deceptive belief function. The aim is that this new approach should be able to manage more generic types of deception than Smets' approach. As we have previously developed a conflict-based measure of degree of falsity [12] we will here combine these two approaches into one method for recognizing and managing deceptive information.

In Sect. 2, we discuss approaches to analyzing belief functions for their likelihood of being false due to deception. In Sect. 3, we review a previous approach to grading pieces of evidence for their degree of falsity based on their contribution to the conflict [13, 14] received from Dempster's rule [2]. We then develop a new complimentary approach for grading pieces of evidence based on such changes in entropy that are not consistent with adding truthful evidence into the combination of all belief functions (Sect. 4). In Sect. 5, we combine the previously developed conflict-based degree of falsity with the new entropy-based degree of falsity into a combined degree of falsity. We use this approach to reason about which pieces of evidence might be false and should be either discounted or eliminated from the combination of information from all sources. Finally, in Sect. 6, we present the study's conclusions.

2 Analyzing Belief Functions

A belief function that is constructed to be deliberately false may be discovered in two different ways. Such a belief function is aimed to change the conclusion when analyzing the combination of all belief functions. Thus, it must be different from truthful belief functions.

One way to find this is by observing the conflict when combining a new belief function with all previous belief functions. For each belief function at hand, we may observe the change in conflict if we remove this particular belief function from the entire set of all available belief functions [7, 18]. This will either lower the conflict or leave it unchanged. From the change in conflict, we can derive a degree of falsity for the belief function in question and, for example, use that to discount this particular belief function [12].

A second approach is to observe the change in entropy when receiving a new belief function. If we receive a good belief function about the problem at hand we should assume that it will further reduce both the scattering and the nonspecificity of the basic belief by focusing it on small focal sets containing the ground truth. Thus, the belief of the ground truth will gradually become more believed and the entropy of the combined belief function will approach zero. On the other hand, if we receive a false belief function that incrementally changes the belief function a small step towards a uniform mass function, then the entropy of the combined belief function will increase. A very strong false belief function may swap the preferred order of the focal sets and leave the entropy unchanged or increased.

We will use both of these approaches to identify which belief functions may be deceptive in order to manage or eliminate them completely from the combination.

3 Conflict-Based Degree of Falsity

We interpret the conflict received when combining a set of basic belief assignments (bbas) χ, as if there is at least one bba in χ that violates the representation of the frame of discernment Θ. Such a bba is interpreted as if it does *not* belong to the evidence that refer to the problem at hand [18].

A conflict when combining all bbas may thus be interpreted as a piece of evidence on a metalevel stating that at least one bba does not belong to χ.

We have,

$$m_\chi(\exists j.e_j \notin \chi) = c_0,$$
$$m_\chi(\Theta) = 1 - c_0, \tag{1}$$

where χ is the set of all bbas, c_0 is the conflict when combining all bbas, e_j is bba number j, and Θ is the frame of discernment.

Let us study one particular piece of evidence e_q in χ. If e_q is removed from χ, the conflict when combining all remaining bbas in χ decreases from c_0 to c_q. This decrease is interpreted as if there exists some evidence on the metalevel indicating that e_q does not belong to χ [12],

$$m_{\Delta\chi}(e_q \notin \chi),$$
$$m_{\Delta\chi}(\Theta), \tag{2}$$

where $\Delta\chi$ is a label for this piece of evidence.

The conflict that remains c_q after e_q has been removed from χ is interpreted as evidence on the metalevel that there is at least one other bba e_j, $j \neq q$, that does not belong to $\chi - \{e_q\}$.

We have,

$$m_{\chi-\{e_q\}}(\exists j \neq q.e_j \notin (\chi - \{e_q\})) = c_q,$$
$$m_{\chi-\{e_q\}}(\Theta) = 1 - c_q. \tag{3}$$

Using Eqs. (1) and (3), we can derive Eq. (2) by stating that the belief in the proposition that there is at least one bba that does not belong to χ, $\exists j.e_j \notin \chi$, must be equal, regardless of whether we base that belief on (1) before e_q is taken out from χ, or on the combination of (2) and (3) after e_q is taken out from χ.

That is,

$$\text{Bel}_\chi(\exists j.e_j \notin \chi) = \text{Bel}_{\Delta\chi\oplus(\chi-\{e_q\})}(\exists j.e_j \notin \chi). \tag{4}$$

On the left hand side (LHS) of Eq. (4) we have,

$$\text{Bel}_\chi(\exists j.e_j \notin \chi) = m_\chi(\exists j.e_j \notin \chi) = c_0 \tag{5}$$

and, on the right hand side (RHS) Eq. (4) we have,

$$\text{Bel}_{\Delta\chi\oplus(\chi-\{e_q\})}(\exists j.e_j \notin \chi) = c_q + m_{\Delta\chi}(e_q \notin \chi)(1 - c_q). \tag{6}$$

By stating that LHS = RHS, we derive the basic belief number (bbn) of Eq. (2) as,

$$m_{\Delta\chi}(e_q \notin \chi) = \frac{c_0 - c_q}{1 - c_q},$$

$$m_{\Delta\chi}(\Theta) = \frac{1 - c_0}{1 - c_q}. \tag{7}$$

We call this the conflict-based degree of falsity of e_q. For additional details, see [12].

4   Entropy-Based Degree of Falsity

Let us measure the change in entropy by observing the change in the aggregated uncertainty functional (*AU*) of the combination of all belief functions, both with and without the particular belief function in question e_q.

4.1   Aggregated Uncertainty Functional

The aggregated uncertainty functional *AU* was discovered by several authors around the same time [19–21]. *AU* is defined as

$$AU(\text{Bel}) = \max_{\{p_x\}_{x\in\Theta}}\left\{-\sum_{x\in\Theta}p(x)\log_2 p(x)\right\} \tag{8}$$

where $\{p_x\}_{x\in\Theta}$ is the set of all probability distributions such that $p_x \in [0, 1]$ for all $x \in \Theta$,

$$\sum_{x\in\Theta}p(x) = 1 \tag{9}$$

and

$$\text{Bel}(A) \leq \sum_{x \in A} p(x) \tag{10}$$

for all $A \subseteq \Theta$. For an overview, see [22]. The AU measure corresponds to measures of nonspecificity and scattering that generalize Hartley information [23] and Shannon entropy [24].

An algorithm for numeric computation of AU was found by Meyerowitz $et\ al.$ [25]. See [26] for implementation.

We define the entropy as a normalization of AU [27, 28],

$$Ent(\{m_j\}) = \frac{AU(\bigoplus\{m_j\})}{\log_2|\Theta|} \tag{11}$$

where m_j is the set of all bbas under combination, $AU \in [0, \log_2|\Theta|]$ and $Ent \in [0, 1]$.

Using Ent and AU, we may define an entropy-based degree of falsity for a deceptive piece of evidence as

$$m_{\Delta Ent}(e_q \notin \chi) = Ent_q\left(\{m_j|j \neq q\}_j\right) - Ent_0\left(\{m_j\}_j\right),$$
$$m_{\Delta Ent}(\Theta) = 1 - m_{\Delta Ent}(e_q \notin \chi), \tag{12}$$

where Ent_0 is the entropy with e_q included in the combination, and Ent_q is the entropy without e_q, under the assumption that $m_{\Delta Ent}(e_q \notin \chi) \geq 0$. Provided that the difference in Eq. (12) is positive and that there is no change in the bbn of the top focal element, this may serve as an adequate measure of falsity for a deceptive piece of evidence based on change of entropy. For a deceptive piece of evidence that changes the order of focal elements we may have a negative difference. For truthful evidence we expect a negative difference and would like to define the degree of falsity as zero. For a general and incremental approach that takes these situations into account see Sect. 4.2.

4.2   Incremental Steps of Entropy Change

Let us focus on e_q, which we want to evaluate by changes in entropy Ent. Because the entropy might increase when we remove e_q we will study a series of incremental changes. We will discount mass function m_q at different rates and observe the incremental changes in entropy. We have [2],

$$m_q(A) = \begin{cases} \alpha m_q(A), & A \subset \Theta \\ 1 - \alpha + \alpha m_q(A), & A = \Theta \end{cases} \tag{13}$$

where $0 \leq \alpha \leq 1$. Let α be defined as

$$\alpha = \frac{i}{n}, \tag{14}$$

where n is a parameter of choice with $0 \leq i \leq n$.

We have,

$$m_q^i(A) = \begin{cases} \frac{i}{n} m_q(A), & A \subset \Theta \\ 1 - \frac{i}{n} + \frac{i}{n} m_q(A), & A = \Theta \end{cases}. \tag{15}$$

Let $\Delta Ent_q^{k+1,k}$ be the incremental change in entropy between two situations using m_q^{k+1} and m_q^k, respectively, in the calculation of $\Delta Ent_q^{k+1,k}$.

We have,

$$\Delta Ent_q^{k+1,k} = Ent_q\left(\left\{m_q^{k+1}, m_j | j \neq q\right\}_j\right) - Ent_q\left(\left\{m_q^k, m_j | j \neq q\right\}_j\right). \tag{16}$$

We may extend Eq. (12) to define an incremental entropy-based degree of falsity as

$$m_{\Delta Ent}(e_q \notin \chi) = \frac{1}{2} \sum_{k=0}^{n-1} \begin{cases} 0, & \forall 0 \leq l \leq k.\ \Delta Ent_q^{l+1,l} \leq 0 \\ \left|\Delta Ent_q^{k+1,k}\right|, & \text{otherwise} \end{cases}, \tag{17}$$

$$m_{\Delta Ent}(\Theta) = 1 - m_{\Delta Ent}(e_q \notin \chi),$$

using Eq. (16).

As long as we receive a sequence of negative incremental changes, we consider m_q to be true. However, if there is a positive incremental change this is interpreted (to a degree) that this piece of evidence is false. The sequential inclusion of m_q may eventually cause a flip in the preferred focal element, followed by a series of negative incremental changes that must be counted towards the degree of falsity when the distribution becomes more and more focused around false focal elements.

This information, $m_{\Delta Ent}(e_q \notin \chi)$, can serve as an indication that m_q might be deliberately false, and may function as an indication even if the direct conflict with the main body of truthful evidence is low.

5   Combine Degree of Falsity with Change of Entropy

In order to find which pieces of evidence might be false, we combine $m_{\Delta\chi}(e_q \notin \chi)$ with $m_{\Delta Ent}(e_q \notin \chi)$ by Dempster's rule; i.e., $m_{\Delta\chi}(e_q \notin \chi) \oplus m_{\Delta Ent}(e_q \notin \chi)$. This is a conflict-free combination as both mass functions have the same foci.

We get,

$$m_{\Delta\chi \oplus \Delta Ent}(e_q \notin \chi) = m_{\Delta\chi}(e_q \notin \chi) + m_{\Delta Ent}(e_q \notin \chi)$$
$$- m_{\Delta\chi}(e_q \notin \chi) \cdot m_{\Delta Ent}(e_q \notin \chi), \tag{18}$$
$$m_{\Delta\chi \oplus \Delta Ent}(\Theta) = 1 - m_{\Delta\chi \oplus \Delta Ent}(e_q \notin \chi),$$

by using Eq. (7) and Eqs. (11), (15)–(17) and the algorithm in [26] to compute Eq. (8).

Based on this results (of Eq. (18)) we can manage all m_q ($\forall q$) in one of several different ways:

1. We may discount all m_q based on $m_{\Delta\chi\oplus\Delta Ent}(e_q \notin \chi)$ using Eq. (13) with $\alpha = 1 - m_{\Delta\chi\oplus\Delta Ent}(e_q \notin \chi)$. Evidence with a high degree of combined conflict-based and entropy-based falsity will be discounted to its degree with a low α. Subsequently, we handle all evidence with whatever mass remains after discounting as if it is true. This approach is somewhat crude and may not be the most preferable way to manage all evidence.
2. A more refined approach is to perform sequential incremental discounts using increments of $\alpha = 1 - m_{\Delta\chi\oplus\Delta Ent}(e_q \notin \chi)$ as was suggested in [12]. With that approach it is possible to manage the conflict by appropriate discounts that bring the conflict down to an acceptable level.
3. A third approach is to evaluate and rank all m_q based on $m_{\Delta\chi\oplus\Delta Ent}(e_q \notin \chi)$ and if there is a natural partition of all m_q into two groups (corresponding to true and false reports) we eliminate the false group from the combination.

We think that managing all evidence in an interactive and incremental way using Eq. (18) and Approach 3 above whenever possible is a good way to find and manage deceptive information in an information fusion process.

6 Conclusions

We have developed an approach for counter-deception in information fusion. This method combines the study of conflict in Dempster's rule with observation of changes in entropy to determine which belief functions are deceptive. With this methodology, we can prevent deceptive information from being included in the information fusion process.

References

1. Dempster, A.P.: Upper and lower probabilities induced by a multivalued mapping. Ann. Math. Stat. **38**, 325–339 (1967)
2. Dempster, A.P.: A generalization of Bayesian inference. J. R. Stat. Soc. Ser. B **30**, 205–247 (1968)
3. Dempster, A.P.: The Dempster-Shafer calculus for statisticians. Int. J. Approx. Reason. **48**, 365–377 (2008)
4. Shafer, G.: A Mathematical Theory of Evidence. Princeton University Press, Princeton (1976)
5. Yager, R.Y., Fedrizzi, M., Kacprzyk, J. (eds.): Advances in the Dempster-Shafer Theory of Evidence. Wiley, New York (1994)
6. Smets, P., Kennes, R.: The transferable belief model. Artif. Intell. **66**, 191–234 (1994)
7. Schubert, J.: On nonspecific evidence. Int. J. Intell. Syst. **8**, 711–725 (1993)
8. Schubert, J.: Managing inconsistent intelligence. In: 3rd International Conference on Information Fusion, pp. TuB4/10-16 (2000)

9. Schubert, J.: Clustering belief functions based on attracting and conflicting metalevel evidence using potts spin mean field theory. Inf. Fusion **5**, 309–318 (2004)
10. Schubert, J.: Clustering decomposed belief functions using generalized weights of conflicts. Int. J. Approx. Reason. **48**, 466–480 (2008)
11. Schubert, J., Sidenbladh, H.: Sequential clustering with particle filtering - estimating the number of clusters from data. In: 8th International Conference on Information Fusion, paper A4-3 (2005)
12. Schubert, J.: Conflict management in Dempster-Shafer theory using the degree of falsity. Int. J. Approx. Reason. **52**, 449–460 (2011)
13. Smets, P.: Analyzing the combination of conflicting belief functions. Inf. Fusion **8**, 387–412 (2007)
14. Schubert, J.: The internal conflict of a belief function. In: Denoeux, T., Masson, M.-H. (eds.) Belief Function: Theory and Applications. AISC, vol. 164, pp. 169–177. Springer, Heidelberg (2012)
15. Smets, P.: Managing deceitful reports with the transferable belief model. In: 8th International Conference on Information Fusion, pp. 893–899 (2005)
16. Pichon, F., Dubois, D., Denœux, T.: Relevance and truthfulness in information correction and fusion. Int. J. Approx. Reason. **53**, 159–175 (2012)
17. Pichon, F., Mercier, D., Lefèvre, É., Delmotte, F.: Proposition and learning of some belief function contextual correction mechanisms. Int. J. Approx. Reason. **72**, 4–42 (2016)
18. Schubert, J.: Specifying nonspecific evidence. Int. J. Intell. Syst. **11**, 525–563 (1996)
19. Chau, C.W.R., Lingras, P., Wong, S.K.M.: Upper and lower entropies of belief functions using compatible probability functions. In: Komorowski, J., Raś, Z.W. (eds.) ISMIS 1993. LNCS, vol. 689, pp. 306–315. Springer, Heidelberg (1993)
20. Maeda, Y., Ichihashi, H.: An uncertainty measure with monotonicity under the random set inclusion. Int. J. Gen Syst **21**, 379–392 (1993)
21. Harmanec, D., Klir, G.J.: Measuring total uncertainty in Dempster-Shafer theory: a novel approach. Int. J. Gen Syst **22**, 405–419 (1994)
22. Klir, G.J.: Uncertainty and Information: Foundation of Generalized Information Theory. Wiley, Hoboken (2006)
23. Hartley, R.V.L.: Transmission of information. Bell Syst. Tech. J. **7**, 535–563 (1928)
24. Shannon, C.E.: A mathematical theory of communication. Bell Syst. Tech. J. **27**(379–423), 623–656 (1948)
25. Meyerowitz, A., Richman, F., Walker, E.: Calculating maximum-entropy probability for belief functions. Int. J. Uncertain. Fuzziness Knowl.-Based Syst. **2**, 377–389 (1994)
26. Harmanec, D., Resconi, G., Klir, G.J., Pan, Y.: On the computation of uncertainty measure in Dempster-Shafer theory. Int. J. Gen Syst **25**, 153–163 (1996)
27. Schubert, J.: Constructing multiple frames of discernment for multiple subproblems. In: Hüllermeier, E., Kruse, R., Hoffmann, F. (eds.) IPMU 2010. CCIS, vol. 80, pp. 189–198. Springer, Heidelberg (2010)
28. Schubert, J.: Constructing and evaluating alternative frames of discernment. Int. J. Approx. Reason. **53**, 176–189 (2012)

Identification of Elastic Properties Based on Belief Function Inference

Liqi Sui[1]([✉]), Pierre Feissel[1], and Thierry Denœux[2]

[1] Sorbonne Universités, Université de Technologie de Compiègne, CNRS 7337,
Laboratoire Roberval, 60203 Compiègne, France
{liqi.sui,pierre.feissel}@utc.fr
[2] Sorbonne Universités, Université de Technologie de Compiègne, CNRS 7253,
Laboratoire Heudiasyc, 60203 Compiègne, France
thierry.denoeux@utc.fr

Abstract. In this paper, we consider parameter identification from measurement fields in an uncertain environment. An approach based on the
theory of belief functions is developed to take into account all possible sources of information. Information from measurements is described
through likelihood-based belief functions, while consonant random sets
are used to handle prior information on the model parameters. Next, we
construct the posterior random set by combining measurement and prior
information using Dempster's rule. To summarize the posterior random
sets, we propose to find the minimal-area region in the parameter space,
whose belief and plausibility values exceed given thresholds. This approach was applied to identify the elastic properties of a 2D plate from a
measured kinematic field.

Keywords: Identification · Measurement field · Prior information ·
Aleatory uncertainty · Epistemic uncertainty · Likelihood-based belief
function · Belief function theory

1 Introduction

In recent years, full field measurements (e.g., kinematic fields) have been increasingly used for the characterization of the mechanical behavior of materials and
structures. They allow one to tackle the challenge of identification from heterogeneous tests thanks to their very rich information contents. However, the measurements are always uncertain and the identification problems can be ill-posed.
A way to solve this problem is to take advantage of available prior information. Nevertheless, similarly to measurement information, prior information is
also tainted with uncertainty. Furthermore, measurement uncertainty and prior
information uncertainty have different natures. Measurement uncertainty can be
considered as aleatory, whereas prior information uncertainty is epistemic [1,2].
The uncertainty on prior information can be represented by various approaches,
such as intervals [3], possibility theory [4], or imprecise probability [5]. We aim
at proposing a unified framework to describe all uncertainties, and a strategy to
propagate them.

© Springer International Publishing Switzerland 2016
J. Vejnarová and V. Kratochvíl (Eds.): BELIEF 2016, LNAI 9861, pp. 182–189, 2016.
DOI: 10.1007/978-3-319-45559-4_19

This paper focuses on developing a method to identify material parameters from kinematic fields. There are two challenges: firstly, taking into account both measurement and prior information; secondly, quantifying the different kinds of uncertainty and propagating them through models. Belief function theory, also referred to as Evidence theory [6–8], offers a suitable framework to encode and quantify both epistemic and aleatory uncertainty. Moreover it includes a comprehensive information merging mechanism for combination and conditioning. Some previous studies using belief function theory have focused on the conversion of available information and the propagation of uncertainty through mechanical models [9,10]. However, very few studies have been devoted to handling uncertainty in identification based on belief functions. In this paper, we explore the possibility of using belief functions theory to quantify uncertainty in identification.

2   Identification Strategy

We consider the identification of elastic parameters of a 2D body (plain stress) under loading based on displacement field data. The body shown in Fig. 1 is considered as a 2D domain Ω. The main unknowns are the material parameters collected in $\boldsymbol{\theta}$; the stress field $\boldsymbol{\sigma}$ and the displacement field $\boldsymbol{u}$ are secondary unknowns.

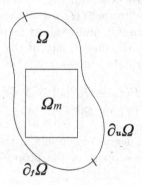

Fig. 1. Mechanical model for identification.

We sum up the equation corresponding to the available information as follows:

– On Ω:

Equilibrium: $\qquad\qquad\qquad\qquad \mathrm{div}\boldsymbol{\sigma} = \boldsymbol{0},$ $\qquad\qquad\qquad\qquad\qquad$ (1)

Constitutive equation: $\qquad \boldsymbol{\sigma} = \boldsymbol{C}(\boldsymbol{\theta})\boldsymbol{\varepsilon}$ with $\boldsymbol{\varepsilon} = \dfrac{1}{2}(\nabla\boldsymbol{u} + \nabla^T\boldsymbol{u}),$ $\quad$ (2)

where $\boldsymbol{u}$, $\boldsymbol{\varepsilon}$ and $\boldsymbol{\sigma}$ are, respectively, the displacement, strain and stress fields;

- On $\partial_u \Omega$: $u = u_d$, where u_d is a known Dirichlet boundary condition;
- On $\partial_f \Omega$: $\sigma \cdot n = f_s$, where f_s is a known Neumann boundary condition;
- On Ω_m: $u = \tilde{u}$. The displacement is measured in $\Omega_m \subset \Omega$.

We consider the simple case where $\partial_u \Omega \cup \partial_f \Omega = \partial \Omega$ and $\partial_u \Omega \cap \partial_f \Omega = \emptyset$. The purpose of the identification is to find the elastic parameters θ that are compatible with the above equations, taking into account uncertainty. The available information can be split into three categories:

- Theoretical information, which is considered as reliable and deterministic. We substitute Eq. (2) into Eq. (1) and obtain an implicit function about u and θ: $g(u, \theta) = 0$. Considering the boundary conditions, a well-posed direct problem, whose solution is denoted $u = u(\theta)$ for any given θ, can then be defined.
- Experimental information, with mainly aleatory uncertainty. Hence the displacement measurement can be written as

$$\tilde{u} = u(\theta) + e, \tag{3}$$

   where e is the measurement error.
- Background information corresponding to prior knowledge on θ; it is tainted with epistemic uncertainty.

   In the following, we will use belief functions and random sets to model uncertainty. Considering a probability space $(\Omega, \sigma_\Omega, P)$, a non-empty set Θ, its power set 2^Θ and a strongly measurable multi-valued mapping $\Gamma: \Omega \longrightarrow 2^\Theta$, Γ is a random set. For all $A \subseteq \Theta$, the uncertainty of the proposition $\theta \in A$ can be quantified by belief and plausibility function [6,11]:

$$Bel(A) = P(\{\omega \in \Omega | \Gamma(\omega) \subseteq A, \Gamma(\omega) \neq \emptyset\}), \tag{4}$$
$$Pl(A) = P(\{\omega \in \Omega | \Gamma(\omega) \cap A \neq \emptyset\}). \tag{5}$$

$Bel(A)$ is interpreted as the degree of support in the proposition $\theta \in A$, while $Pl(A)$ measures the lack of support in the proposition $\theta \notin A$. The contour function $pl : \Theta \to [0, 1]$ is defined as

$$pl(\theta) = Pl(\{\theta\}) \quad \text{for all} \quad \theta \in \Theta. \tag{6}$$

2.1   Measurement Information

The measurement $\tilde{u}$ is assumed to be known with some aleatory uncertainty (see Eq. (3)). The error is assumed to be a random Gaussian noise, with known covariance $e \sim \mathcal{N}(0, D)$. Based on [6,8], the uncertainty about θ is represented by a consonant likelihood-based belief function, whose contour function equals the normalized likelihood function:

$$pl(\theta; \tilde{u}) = \frac{L(\theta; \tilde{u})}{\sup_\theta L(\theta; \tilde{u})}, \tag{7}$$

where $L(\boldsymbol{\theta}; \widetilde{\boldsymbol{u}})$ is the likelihood function,

$$L(\boldsymbol{\theta}; \widetilde{\boldsymbol{u}}) = (2\pi \det \boldsymbol{D})^{-1/2} \exp\left[-\frac{1}{2}(\boldsymbol{u}(\boldsymbol{\theta}) - \widetilde{\boldsymbol{u}})^T \boldsymbol{D}^{-1}(\boldsymbol{u}(\boldsymbol{\theta}) - \widetilde{\boldsymbol{u}})\right]. \qquad (8)$$

The contour function $pl(\boldsymbol{\theta}; \widetilde{\boldsymbol{u}})$ in Eq. (7) is normalized. It is equivalent to a possibility distribution, and corresponds to a consonant random set.

2.2 Prior Information

Prior information with epistemic uncertainty is represented by a possibility distribution $\pi(\boldsymbol{\theta})$, which induces the consonant random set

$$\Gamma(\omega) = \{\boldsymbol{\theta} \in \boldsymbol{\Theta} | \pi(\boldsymbol{\theta}) \geq \omega\}. \qquad (9)$$

The consonant random set shown in Fig. 2 expresses an expert opinion about $\boldsymbol{\theta}$: values of $\boldsymbol{\theta}$ outside interval $[a, d]$ are considered as impossible, while values inside interval $[b, c]$ are considered as fully possible. Indeed, $\Gamma(\omega) \subseteq [a, d]$ and $[b, c] \subseteq \Gamma(\omega)$ for any $\omega \in [0, 1]$. In this paper, we assume that $\omega \sim \mathcal{U}[0, 1]$.

Moreover, in the framework of belief function theory, the discounting operation allows us to express the degree of confidence in a source of information. Assume, for instance, that an expert uses the possibility distribution of Fig. 2 to represent their opinion about a parameter, and we have a degree of confidence $m_\Theta \in [0, 1]$ in this opinion. We can then assign the value m_Θ to the whole set $\boldsymbol{\Theta}$, i.e., $P(\{\omega \in \Omega | \Gamma(\omega) = \boldsymbol{\Theta}\}) = m_\Theta$. When $m_\Theta = 0$, we fully trust the expert's opinion; when $m_\Theta = 1$, we totally doubt it. The discounted possibility distribution is shown in Fig. 3. We notice that it has an infinite support.

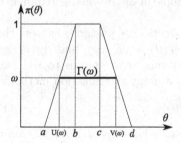
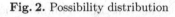
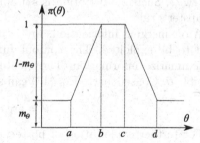

| Fig. 2. Possibility distribution | Fig. 3. Discounted possibility distribution |

2.3 Dempster's Rule

Measurement and prior information typically induce two random sets represented by possibility distributions. Aggregation of information from multiple sources is an important step in the modeling of uncertainty. Dempster's rule [6] is a combination mechanism in belief function theory. This rule is often used to combine belief functions defined on finite sets. Here, we reformulate it in the infinite setting. Consider two random sets $(\Omega_k, \sigma_{\Omega_k}, P_k, \Gamma_k)$, $k = 1, 2$. Let $\Omega = \Omega_1 \times \Omega_2$ be the product space, $P = P_1 \otimes P_2$ the product measure on $\sigma_\Omega = \sigma_{\Omega_1} \otimes \sigma_{\Omega_2}$, and Γ_p the multi-valued mapping defined by: $\forall (\omega_1, \omega_2) \in \Omega_p$, $\Gamma_p(\omega_1, \omega_2) = \Gamma_1(\omega_1) \cap \Gamma_2(\omega_2)$. The combined random set is $(\Omega, \sigma_\Omega, P, \Gamma_p)$. It induces the following belief and plausibility functions: for any $A \subset \Theta$,

$$Bel(A) = \frac{P(\{(\omega_1, \omega_2) \in \Omega | \Gamma_p(\omega_1, \omega_2) \subseteq A, \Gamma_p(\omega_1, \omega_2) \neq \emptyset\})}{P(\{(\omega_1, \omega_2) \in \Omega | \Gamma_p(\omega_1, \omega_2) \neq \emptyset\})}, \tag{10}$$

$$Pl(A) = \frac{P(\{(\omega_1, \omega_2) \in \Omega | \Gamma_p(\omega_1, \omega_2) \cap A \neq \emptyset\})}{P(\{(\omega_1, \omega_2) \in \Omega | \Gamma_p(\omega_1, \omega_2) \neq \emptyset\})}. \tag{11}$$

The degree of conflict is:

$$k = P(\{(\omega_1, \omega_2) \in \Omega | \Gamma_p(\omega_1, \omega_2) = \emptyset\}). \tag{12}$$

It is a measure of the compatibility between the two sources of information.

3   Numerical Implementation and Posterior Exploration

In this paper, we use Monte Carlo simulation to implement Dempster's rule for combining information. Considering two possibility distributions $\pi_1(\boldsymbol{\theta})$ and $\pi_2(\boldsymbol{\theta})$, we can draw (ω_1, ω_2) uniformly from $[0, 1]^2$ and cut the two possibility distributions, respectively, at levels ω_1 and ω_2. Then we intersect the two ω-level cuts. After iterating the above process a large number of times, we obtain a collection of subsets or domains with irregular shapes. Therefore, we need a strategy to describe domains of arbitrary shape. Here, we propose to describe a subset using a cloud of points generated by a Halton sequence [12]. For each domain, the value at any point is 1 if the point is inside this domain, and 0 otherwise. Such a description is suitable for Boolean operations as required by Dempster's rule.

After merging information, we obtain a collection of posterior subsets that need to be exploited. The contour function $pl(\boldsymbol{\theta})$ is an easy and direct way to summarize information. The greatest $pl(\boldsymbol{\theta})$ value corresponds to the most possible $\boldsymbol{\theta}$. Consequently Eq. (13) can serve as a point identification method:

$$\widehat{\boldsymbol{\theta}} = \arg\max pl(\boldsymbol{\theta}). \tag{13}$$

For further exploitation of posterior random sets, we search for a minimal subset $\boldsymbol{R} \subseteq \boldsymbol{\Theta}$ such that $Pl(\boldsymbol{R})$ and $Bel(\boldsymbol{R})$ are larger than threshold values δ_{Pl} and δ_{Bel}. Formally, we need to solve the following constrained minimization problem:

$$\widehat{\boldsymbol{R}} = \arg\min_{\boldsymbol{R} \subseteq \boldsymbol{\Theta}} V(\boldsymbol{R}), \tag{14}$$

such that

$$\begin{cases} Pl(\boldsymbol{R}) \geq \delta_{Pl} \\ Bel(\boldsymbol{R}) \geq \delta_{Bel} \end{cases},$$

where $V(\boldsymbol{R})$ is the area or volume of $\boldsymbol{R}$.

4   Application

In this section, we present as a numerical example the identification of the Lamé coefficients $\boldsymbol{\theta} = \{\lambda, \mu\}$ describing the elastic properties of a 2D plate from a tensile test. The measurement is the displacement field on the whole plate and the applied traction. It was created based on a reference finite element calculation with reference value $\{\lambda, \mu\} = \{1, 1\}$ and adding a 5 % Gaussian noise to represent the measurement error.

The prior information, which comes from expert opinions, was expressed by possibility distributions. In order to check the performance of this approach, two scenarios were considered: in the first scenario, the expert possibility distributions are close to the reference values; in the second scenario, they are far from the reference values. We assumed a 80 % degree of confidence in the expert opinions in both scenarios. The possibility distributions considered in both scenarios are shown in Fig. 4.

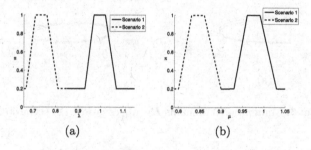

(a)   (b)

Fig. 4. Prior information on λ (a) and μ (b).

Based on the discussion in Sect. 2.3, we used Dempster's rule to combine the information. After computing the ω-level cuts of the two distributions and intersecting the random sets, we obtained a posterior random set. The degrees of conflict in scenarios 1 and 2 were, respectively, $\widehat{k}_1 = 0.3867$ and $\widehat{k}_2 = 0.7996$. If the degree of conflict k is too large, at least one source is likely to provide wrong information.

The estimator $\widehat{pl}(\boldsymbol{\theta})$ of the contour function is shown in Fig. 5. The value $\boldsymbol{\theta}_{max}$ with maximum plausibility can be used as a point estimator. For scenario 1, we obtained $\boldsymbol{\theta}_{max} = \{0.943, 0.939\}$; for scenario 2, $\boldsymbol{\theta}_{max} = \{0.935, 0.937\}$. Thanks to the discounting operation, the contour function keeps the same form as the possibility distribution from the measurement, even when the prior information is inaccurate.

Lastly, we focussed on finding a minimum subset $\boldsymbol{R}$ with $Pl(\boldsymbol{R})$ and $Bel(\boldsymbol{R})$ larger than given threshold values δ_{Bel} and δ_{Pl}. We set (1) $\delta_{Bel} = 0.30$ and $\delta_{Pl} = 0.95$; (2) $\delta_{Bel} = 0.25$ and $\delta_{Pl} = 0.95$ (3) $\delta_{Bel} = 0.25$ and $\delta_{Pl} = 0.90$. The obtained subsets $\widehat{\boldsymbol{R}}$ for the two scenarios are shown in Fig. 6. It is clear that the area of minimum subsets grows as thresholds δ_{Bel} and δ_{Pl} increase.

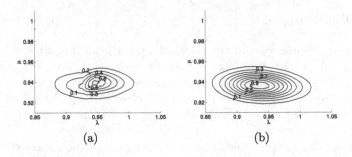

Fig. 5. Contour function $\widehat{pl}(\boldsymbol{\theta})$: (a) scenarios 1; (b) scenarios 2.

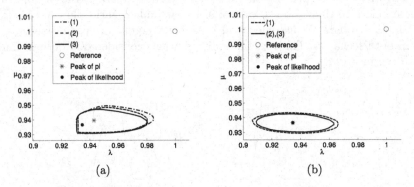

Fig. 6. Minimal-area domains $\widehat{R}$: (a) scenario 1 (b) scenario 2

As compared to those in scenario 2, the minimal subsets in scenario 1 move to top right because of the influence of prior information. In scenario 2, the prior information does not affect the measurement information; consequently, the minimal subsets reflect the form of the likelihood function.

5   Conclusion

In this paper, we have presented an identification strategy based on belief function theory. This approach allows for the representation and combination of prior and measurement information. Point clouds were used to describe multi-dimension random sets. Dempster's rule was used to combine random sets from prior and measurement information. Finally, posterior random sets were obtained and explored. This approach makes it possible to encode and propagate epistemic and aleatory uncertainty in a unified framework. The discounting operation allows us to take into account the reliability of the sources of information; as a result, inaccurate information only marginally affects measurement information. The two functions Bel and Pl provide a rich description of the uncertainty on model parameters, taking into account prior information. In the future, our research will focus on accounting for uncertainty in mechanical models and on the application of this approach to more complex structures.

Acknowledgments. This work was carried out and funded in the framework of the Labex MS2T. It was supported by the French Government, through the program "Investments for the future" managed by the National Agency for Re-search (Reference ANR-11-IDEX-0004-02).

References

1. Ferson, S., Ginzburg, L.R.: Different methods are needed to propagate ignorance and variability. Reliab. Eng. Syst. Saf. **54**(2), 133–144 (1996)
2. Helton, J.C., Burmaster, D.E.: Guest editorial: treatment of aleatory and epistemic uncertainty in performance assessments for complex systems. Reliab. Eng. Syst. Saf. **54**(2), 91–94 (1996)
3. Moore, R.E.: Interval Analysis, vol. 4. Prentice-Hall, Englewood Cliffs (1966)
4. Dubois, D., Kerre, E., Mesiar, R., Prade, H.: Fuzzy interval analysis. In: Dubois, D., Prade, H. (eds.) Fundamentals of Fuzzy Sets. The Handbooks of Fuzzy Sets Series, vol. 7, pp. 483–581. Springer, Heidelberg (2000)
5. Ferson, S., Kreinovich, V., Ginzburg, L., Myers, D.S., Sentz, K.: Constructing Probability Boxes and Dempster-Shafer Structures, vol. 835. Sandia National Laboratories, Albuquerque (2002)
6. Shafer, G.: A Mathematical Theory of Evidence, vol. 1. Princeton University Press, Princeton (1976)
7. Smets, P.: Belief functions on real numbers. Int. J. Approx. Reason. **40**(3), 181–223 (2005)
8. Denoeux, T.: Likelihood-based belief function: justification and some extensions to low-quality data. Int. J. Approx. Reason. **55**(7), 1535–1547 (2014)
9. Tonon, F.: Using random set theory to propagate epistemic uncertainty through a mechanical system. Reliab. Eng. Syst. Saf. **85**(1), 169–181 (2004)
10. Tonon, F., Bae, H.-R., Grandhi, R.V., Pettit, C.L.: Using random set theory to calculate reliability bounds for a wing structure. Struct. Infrastruct. Eng. **2**(3–4), 191–200 (2006)
11. Shafer, G.: Allocations of probability. Ann. Probab. 827–839 (1979)
12. Kocis, L., Whiten, W.J.: Computational investigations of low-discrepancy sequences. ACM Trans. Math. Softw. (TOMS) **23**(2), 266–294 (1997)

D-S Theory for Argument Confidence Assessment

Rui Wang[1]([⊠]), Jérémie Guiochet[1], Gilles Motet[1], and Walter Schön[2]

[1] LAAS-CNRS, Université de Toulouse, CNRS, INSA,UPS, Toulouse, France
{rui.wang,jeremie.guiochet,gilles.motet}@laas.fr
[2] Sorbonne Universités, Université de Technologie de Compiègne,
Heudiasyc UMR CNRS 7253, 60319 Compiègne Cedex, France
wschon@utc.fr

Abstract. Structured arguments are commonly used to communicate to stakeholders that safety, security or other attributes of a system are achieved. Due to the growing complexity of systems, more uncertainties appear and the confidence in arguments tends to be less justifiable by reviewing. In this paper, we propose a quantitative method to assess the confidence in structured arguments, like safety cases. We adopt the Goal Structuring Notation (GSN) to model the safety case and propose to add annotations to identify uncertainties in this model. Three inference types of arguments are proposed according to their impact on confidence. Definition and quantification assessment of confidence are based on the belief function theory. The proposed approach is illustrated with several GSN examples.

Keywords: Safety case · Confidence assessment · Belief function theory · Assurance case

1 Introduction

Structured arguments play important role in communicating a system's attributes with various names: safety case [2,19], assurance case [4], trust case [5], dependability case [3], etc. For safety-critical industries, such arguments are even required by the standards (ISO 26262 [15] for automotive, EN 50129 for railway, etc.).

Furthermore, regulation bodies (such as avionics certification authorities) have to evaluate the system safety based on safety cases in order to produce a justified decision for certification. Nevertheless, some problematic issues has been argued when assessing the structured arguments, especially for computing systems. In [6], authors consider that the excessive growth of argument leads it to be too complex to be analyzed. In [1,14], the authors emphasize the necessity to assess the confidence in these arguments and propose to develop a confidence argument in parallel with the safety argument. Besides, some quantitative assessment of confidence in arguments are provided in [9] (using Bayesian Network), and [6,13] (using belief function theory for confidence definition).

© Springer International Publishing Switzerland 2016
J. Vejnarová and V. Kratochvíl (Eds.): BELIEF 2016, LNAI 9861, pp. 190–200, 2016.
DOI: 10.1007/978-3-319-45559-4_20

This paper aims to propose a quantitative approach to assess the confidence in structured arguments. In order to give an understandable demonstration, a graphical notation, called Goal Structuring Notation (GSN) [19] presented in Sect. 2, is adopted to model the analyzed safety case including its identified uncertainties. Then, the quantified assessment process is developed under the frame of belief function theory in Sect. 3. Belief function theory allows uncertainty to be explicitly modeled and handled. An application of this approach is conducted for some extracts of GSN safety case in Sect. 4.

2   Safety Argumentation

Safety argument, also called safety case, is defined by [2] as "a documented body of evidence that provides a convincing and valid argument that a system is adequately safe for a given application in a given environment". It is used to communicate the rationale of developers for implementing the development or their choices of techniques. Many related research work are available based on the Toulmin's argument model [22]. [17] defined a notation of safety case, called Goal Structuring Notation (GSN), to make the presentation of argumentation more readable and adaptable. GSN allows the representation of the supporting evidence, objectives to be achieved, safety argument, context, etc. An example of GSN is given in Fig. 1, which is derived from the Hazard Avoidance Pattern [18]. The five main elements of GSN are: *goal* (e.g., G1): the claim about the system; *solution* (e.g., Sn1): the reference to evidence item(s); *strategy* (e.g., S1): the nature of inference that exists between a goal and its supporting sub-goal(s); *context* (e.g., C1): a reference to contextual information, or a statement.

GSN provides a qualitative representation. Nevertheless, the confidence in the top claim is not specified in this view. Indeed, the correctness of the inference links, the appropriateness of the context, the sufficiency of the evidence are key factors to make the assertions in safety argument acceptable. However,

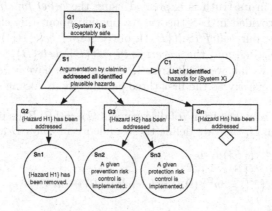

Fig. 1. GSN example adapted from Hazard Avoidance Pattern [18]

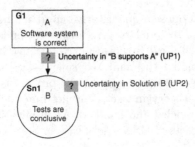

Fig. 2. Uncertainty points in a simple inference

in practice, no precise values can be assigned to these factors. We have to cope with uncertainties. We actually consider two types of uncertainties sources, which are similar to those presented in [14] named "appropriateness" and "trustworthiness". They are illustrated in the simple safety case presented in Fig. 2 as uncertainty points (UPs): UP1 - uncertainty in the fact that B supports A; and UP2 - uncertainty in the fact that B is True.

3   Safety Case Confidence Assessment

This section presents the main contribution of the paper, which is a framework to quantitatively estimate the confidence in a safety case.

3.1   Definition of Confidence in Argument

We adopt the belief function theory, also called Dempster-Shafer theory (D-S theory) [7,8,21], to define the confidence in arguments. It is indeed one of the uncertainty theories with which you can explicitly estimate the uncertainty, and combine several sources of information which is particularly convenient to develop our confidence aggregation rules. For the claim B, ("Tests are conclusive") in Fig. 2, the belief in its truth is expressed using the *belief function* and *plausibility function* provided in D-S theory. An opinion about this claim is assessed with 3 attributes: our *belief* ($bel(\{B\})$), our *disbelief* ($bel(\{\bar{B}\})$) in the conclusiveness of the testing, and the *uncertainty* ($pl(\{B\})$-$bel(\{B\})$) concerning the fact that "we know that we don't know". This leads to have *belief* + *disbelief* + *uncertainty* = 1, exactly as the first three parameters in Jøsang's opinion space [16].

In this paper, a binary frame of discernment $\Omega_B = \{\bar{B}, B\}$ is used to describe the truth of claim B; then we define the confidence in claim B as follows:

$$\begin{cases} bel(\{B\}) = m^{\Omega_B}(\{B\}) = g_B \\ bel(\{\bar{B}\}) = m^{\Omega_B}(\{\bar{B}\}) = f_B \\ pl(\{B\}) - bel(\{B\}) = m^{\Omega_B}(\Omega_B) = 1 - m^{\Omega_B}(\{B\}) - m^{\Omega_B}(\{\bar{B}\}) = 1 - g_B - f_B \end{cases} \tag{1}$$

where $g_P, f_P \in [0, 1]$.

Formalization of Inferences (UP1). To study the inference between B and A, we propose to use a 2-tuple (X_B, X_A) to express the cross product $\Omega_B \times \Omega_A$, where X_B and X_A are elements of Ω_B and Ω_A respectively. Then, the joint frame of discernment is $\Omega_B \times \Omega_A = \{(\bar{B}, \bar{A}), (\bar{B}, A), (B, \bar{A}), (B, A)\}$. For instance, the mass describing the belief that claim A can be inferred from claim B and conversely that the fact that A is false can be inferred from the fact that B is false, is $m^{\Omega_B \times \Omega_A}(\{(B, A), (\bar{B}, \bar{A})\})$. This inference is measured by the *contributing weight* of B to A (w_B). Moreover, it is hard to ensure that the available supporting premises cover all aspects to assert the upper-level claim. Thus, we introduce a discounting factor (v) to represent the completeness of premises. The contributing weight is defined as follows:

$$m_1^{\Omega_B \times \Omega_A}(\{(\bar{B}, \bar{A}), (B, A)\}) = w_B v \qquad m_1^{\Omega_B \times \Omega_A}(\Omega_B \times \Omega_A) = 1 - w_B v \quad (2)$$

Where $m_1^{\Omega_B \times \Omega_A}(\Omega_B \times \Omega_A)$ is used as abbreviation of $m_1^{\Omega_B \times \Omega_A}(\{(\bar{B}, \bar{A}), (\bar{B}, A), (B, \bar{A}), (B, A)\})$. When $v = 1$, it means that B sufficiently support A; When $v = 0$, $m_1^{\Omega_B \times \Omega_A}(\Omega_B \times \Omega_A) = 1$ means that B does not provide any knowledge about A, i.e. a full uncertainty exists in A.

Formalization of the Confidence in Claims (UP2). The measure of confidence in B has been defined as Formula (1). In order to combine UP1 and UP2, we apply the *vacuous extension* [20] (represented by the up arrow $\uparrow$) to m_2, to transform the confidence in B on the frame Ω_B to the frame $\Omega_B \times \Omega_A$. Therefore, the confidence in claim B is:

$$\begin{cases} m_2^{\Omega_B \uparrow \Omega_B \times \Omega_A}(\{B\} \times \Omega_A) = g_B \\ m_2^{\Omega_B \uparrow \Omega_B \times \Omega_A}(\{\bar{B}\} \times \Omega_A) = f_B \\ m_2^{\Omega_B \uparrow \Omega_B \times \Omega_A}(\Omega_B \times \Omega_A) = 1 - f_B - g_B \end{cases} \quad (3)$$

Where $\{B\} \times \Omega_A$ is employed instead of $\{(B, A), (B, \bar{A})\}$ and $\{\bar{B}\} \times \Omega_A$ instead of $\{(\bar{B}, A), (\bar{B}, \bar{A})\}$ to highlight the ignorance in A.

Confidence Aggregation for Simple Inference. Our aim is to deduce the degree of belief in the fact that claim A is true $(m(\{A\}))$ based on the belief placed in (2) and (3). With the help of Dempster's rule [21], these two pieces of information can be combined. The 6 possible combinations and *focal sets* are shown in Table 1, where the conflict factor K [21] in this combination rule is 0, due to no conflict in this case. To calculate $m(\{A\})$ on Ω_A from the combined information on $\Omega_B \times \Omega_A$, we have to use the *marginalization* operation [20]. Accordingly, there is only one focal set ($\{(B,A)\}$ underlined in Table 1) contributing to $m(\{A\})$. Thus, the confidence in A is:

$$bel(\{A\}) = m(A) = g_B w_B v \quad (4)$$

where $g_B, w_B, v \in [0, 1]$.

Table 1. Combination results of confidence measures

$m_{12} = m_1 \oplus m_2$	$m_1^{\Omega_B \times \Omega_A}(\{(\bar{B},\bar{A}),(B,A)\})$	$m_1^{\Omega_B \times \Omega_A}(\Omega_B \times \Omega_A)$
$m_2^{\Omega_B \uparrow \Omega_B \times \Omega_A}(\{B\} \times \Omega_A)$	$\{(B,A)\}$	$\{B\} \times \Omega_A$
$m_2^{\Omega_B \uparrow \Omega_B \times \Omega_A}(\{\bar{B}\} \times \Omega_A)$	$\{(\bar{B},\bar{A})\}$	$\{\bar{B}\} \times \Omega_A$
$m_2^{\Omega_B \uparrow \Omega_B \times \Omega_A}(\Omega_B \times \Omega_A)$	$\{(\bar{B},\bar{A}),(B,A)\}$	$\Omega_B \times \Omega_A$

3.2   Arguments Inference Types

In practice, several premises are used to support one goal. Therefore, a new issue arises: how the contributions of premises are combined while assessing the confidence in a goal? Cyra and Gorski [6] extend the work of Govier [12] and introduce two inference rules, each of which contains 3 sub types of inferences. Nevertheless, there are overlapping among them. We propose another categorization of the argument with three inference types (listed in Table 2):

- Type 1: Dependent inference: premises supporting the same goal have some degree of dependency, denoted with d.
  - $d = 1$: fully dependent inference. B and C are needed as premises of A. For instance, safety engineers often consider that a system is safe if the "test process is correct" as well as the "test results are correct". If one of these two premises is false, no confidence can be placed in the system safety. It is important to emphasize that this "dependence" means only that A depends on B and C (dependence formalized by joint mass function m_1 hereafter). The confidences in sub-claims B and C (formalized by mass functions m_2 and m_3 hereafter) are considered independent (there are independent elements of evidence in experts opinion) and can therefore be combined using Dempter's rule. In cases where this hypothesis would be not ensured, other combination rules like "cautious rule" [10] could be used instead.
  - $d = 0.5$: partial dependent inference. B and C have some impacts on each other when supporting A. For instance, safety engineers also consider that a system is safe if "high-level requirement coverage is achieved", that is, all functions perform correctly, and "low-level requirement coverage is achieved", that is, all components are exercised. If we have high confidence in the function correctness, then we have high confidence in system safety. Then, even if we do not have sufficient evidence in the component exercising, we preserve our confidence in the system safety.
- Type 2: Redundant inference: premises contribute to the top goal with certain degree of redundancy, denoted with r.
  - $r = 1$: fully redundant inference. B or C can be used alone as premises of A. For instance, safety engineers consider that "a failure of a hardware component is acceptable" (goal), if "its probability is low" or "the occurrence of this failure can be detected and handled" (fault tolerance mechanism). These two premises are fully redundant because if we have full confidence in one of them, then we believe that the goal is achieved.

- $r = 0.5$: partial redundant inference. B and C are not fully redundant, and can be used in a complementary way. For instance, safety engineers consider that "a system is acceptably safe" (goal), if "its test is conclusive" or "formal verification is passed". We believe that the two techniques (testing and formal verification) are partially redundant as they both partially contribute to our confidence in system safety.

- Type 3: Independent inference: each of the premises covers part of the conclusion, without redundancy or dependency $r/d = 0$. For instance, safety engineers consider that confidence of system safety is obtained (goal), when all hazards are addressed. Therefore, the belief in each premise "Hazard Hi is addressed" provides an independent contribution to our confidence in system safety.

3.3   Confidence Assessment

The proposed confidence aggregation operator varies according to the type of inference. Due to limited space, we only provide details for the dependent inference in this section. We assess the confidence in A based on the confidence in B and C and their way of contribution. The calculation is similar to Sect. 3.1, except that we need to take into account the argument types.

Formalization of Inferences (UP1). In order to provide a general formula for the dependent inference, the cases with $d = 0,\ 0.5\ and\ 1$ have to be taken into account. The independent contributions of B and C and the contribution of the combinations of B and C has to be considered. The corresponding mass function m_1 is therefore built using:

- A focal set giving the contribution of B to A (see Eq. (3)), using the vacuous extension, to extend it to $\Omega = \Omega_B \times \Omega_C \times \Omega_A$,
- A focal set giving the contribution of C to A built on the same model and also extended to Ω,
- A focal set giving the contribution of B and C to A (traduction of an AND operator in terms of mass function),
- The remaining mass being affected on Ω.

Hence, this joint frame of discernment is expressed as $\Omega = \{(\bar{B}, \bar{C}, \bar{A}), (\bar{B}, \bar{C}, A), (\bar{B}, C, \bar{A}), (\bar{B}, C, A), (B, \bar{C}, \bar{A}), (B, \bar{C}, A), (B, C, \bar{A}), (B, C, A)\}$. According to D-S theory, the sum of masses of all the focal sets is 1. We deduce that the degree of dependency (d_A) is $1 - w_B - w_C$. Also, we introduce the discounting factor v. Then, we obtain:

$$
\begin{cases}
m_1^\Omega(\{\bar{B}\} \times \Omega_C \times \{\bar{A}\} \cup \{B\} \times \Omega_C \times \{A\}) = w_B v \\
m_1^\Omega(\Omega_B \times \{\bar{C}\} \times \{\bar{A}\} \cup \Omega_B \times \{C\} \times \{A\}) = w_C v \\
m_1^\Omega(\{(\bar{B}, \bar{C}, \bar{A}), (\bar{B}, C, \bar{A}), (B, \bar{C}, \bar{A}), (B, C, A)\}) = d_A = (1 - w_B - w_C)v \\
m_1^\Omega(\Omega) = 1 - v
\end{cases}
$$

$$(5)$$

where $v, w_B, w_C \in [0, 1]$, and $w_B + w_C \leq 1$.

Formalization of the Confidence in Claims (UP2). According to the definition of confidence in Formula (1) of Sect. 3.1 and the help of vacuous extension, the measures of confidence in sub-claims B and C are:

$$\begin{cases} m_2^{\Omega}(\{B\} \times \Omega_C \times \Omega_A) = g_B \\ m_2^{\Omega}(\{\bar{B}\} \times \Omega_C \times \Omega_A) = f_B \\ m_2^{\Omega}(\Omega) = 1 - f_B - g_B \end{cases} \qquad (6)$$

$$\begin{cases} m_3^{\Omega}(\Omega_B \times \{C\} \times \Omega_A) = g_C \\ m_3^{\Omega}(\Omega_B \times \{\bar{C}\} \times \Omega_A) = f_C \\ m_3^{\Omega}(\Omega) = 1 - f_C - g_C \end{cases} \qquad (7)$$

Confidence Aggregation for Dependent Argument (Type 1). As explained above, mass functions m_1, m_2 and m_3 are considered as independent pieces of evidence and can therefore legitimately combined using Dempster's rule. According to the associativity of this rule, (6) and (7) are combined firstly, then with (5). Due to the limited scale of this paper, the development is not presented here. Thus, we give the confidence in claim A:

$$bel(\{A\}) = m(\{A\}) = v\big((1 - w_B - w_C)g_B g_C + g_B w_B + g_C w_C\big) \qquad (8)$$

Formula (8) is the confidence aggregation formula for the basic dependent argument for two premises. The general confidence aggregation formula for n-nodes dependent argument derived:

$$m(\{A\}) = v\Big[(1 - \sum_{i=1}^{n} w_i)\prod_{i=1}^{n} g_i + \sum_{i=1}^{n} g_i w_i\Big] \qquad (9)$$

Where $n > 1$, $g_i, w_i, v \in [0, 1]$, and $\sum_{i=1}^{n} w_i \leq 1$.

Confidence Aggregation for Redundant Argument (Type 2). For redundant argument, the confidence aggregation operator has to be changed. The redundant parts of the premises behave as an OR gate. Therefore, the contributing weights are measured in the following way:

$$\begin{cases} m_1^{\Omega}(\{\bar{B}\} \times \Omega_C \times \{\bar{A}\} \cup \{B\} \times \Omega_C \times \{A\}) = w_B v \\ m_1^{\Omega}(\Omega_B \times \{\bar{C}\} \times \{\bar{A}\} \cup \Omega_B \times \{C\} \times \{A\}) = w_C v \\ m_1^{\Omega}(\{(\bar{B},\bar{C},\bar{A}), (\bar{B},C,A), (B,\bar{C},A), (B,C,A)\}) = r_A = (1 - w_B - w_C)v \\ m_1^{\Omega}(\Omega) = 1 - v \end{cases} \qquad (10)$$

Then the developing process is similar to the one used for the dependent argument. We directly give the confidence aggregation formula for the above argument:

$$m(\{A\}) = v\big((1 - w_B - w_C)[1 - (1 - g_B)(1 - g_C)] + g_B w_B + g_C w_C\big) \qquad (11)$$

Table 2. Experimental application of confidence aggregation formulas

Type, r_A/d_A	GSN instances	Confidence in A, $m(A)$	Behaviors
2, $r_A = 1$ (Fully redundant)		$v(g_B + g_C - g_B g_C)$	
2, $r_A = 0.5$ (Partially redundant)		$v(\frac{1-(1-g_B)(1-g_C)}{2} + g_B w_B + g_C w_C)$	
3, $r_A = 0$ (Independent)		$v(g_B w_B + g_C w_C)$	
1, $d_A = 0.5$ (Partially dependent)		$v(\frac{g_B g_C}{2} + g_B w_B + g_C w_C)$	
1, $d_A = 1$ (Fully dependent)		$v g_B g_C$	

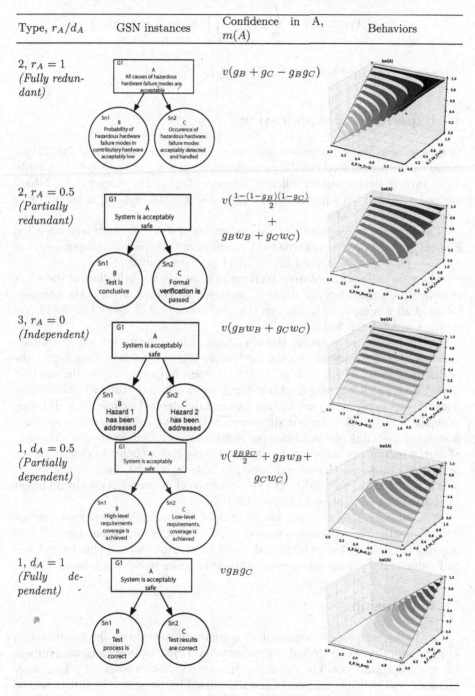

The general formula for n-node redundant argument is deduced. We obtain:

$$m(\{A\}) = v\Big((1 - \sum_{i=1}^{n} w_i)[1 - \prod_{i=1}^{n}(1 - g_i)] + \sum_{i=1}^{n} g_i w_i\Big) \tag{12}$$

Where $n > 1$, $g_i, w_i, v \in [0,1]$, and $\sum_{i=1}^{n} w_i \leq 1$.

4   Experimental Application

In this section, the confidence aggregation formulas are applied to five simple examples with two premises. This application aims to analyze how the confidence evolves depending on different inference types. The examples in Table 2 are extractions of GSN patterns from [23] or objectives required in the avionics standard DO-178C [11].

The formulas corresponding to varied values of d or r are obtained based on Eqs. (8) and (11). Note that when the premises are completely independent, i.e. $r/d = 1 - w_B - w_C = 0$, then Eqs. (8) and (11) are equivalent.

Moreover, we use the contour plotting to illustrate the behaviors of these five cases with several values for d and r, as shown in Table 2. As v is the common factor of all formulas, its impact on the confidence in A is easily estimated. We choose $v = 1$ for this analysis.

In the figures representing the behaviors, light color means low confidence in A. On the contrary, dark color represents high confidence. Comparing the positions of Point M ($g_B = 0, g_C = 1$) and Point N ($g_B = 1, g_C = 0$), the best model, with which it is easy to obtain high confidence, is the fully redundant case (case 1); the opposite is case 5, that is, the fully dependent inference. Looking at cases 2 and 4, the obvious difference is that low confidence in one single premise of partial dependent inference decreases more confidence in A than that of partial redundant inference. Furthermore, this feature helps to determine the right type of inference for an argument. In cases 2, 3 and 4, because the weight of B is higher than the weight of C, the influence of g_B on $bel(A)$ is always larger than g_C (Point M is always higher than Point N).

According to this analysis, the behaviors of the aggregation formulas are consistent with our expectation regarding the confidence variation. The different impacts of contributing weights make explicit the influence of the dependency and redundancy among arguments on the confidence in the top goal.

5   Conclusion

In this paper, we propose a quantitative approach to evaluate the confidence in safety arguments. A graphical safety notation, GSN, is used to clearly present the studied arguments. The definition and aggregation of confidence for simple inference and multiple inferences are all realized by adopting the functions and operations of the belief function theory. We introduce a clear way to categorize three inference types including five cases. This makes it possible to explicitly assess the contributions of premises. We applied our approach to typical examples of arguments in system safety engineering domain, and checked that results of aggregation rules are consistent. A behavior analysis is given to demonstrate the characters of the proposed aggregation formulas. A case study of real system safety case will be our future work. Experts will be inquired to provide the reasonable confidence values with the help of the GSN examples. The issue of decision-making based on confidence levels (see behavior figures in Table 2) will be also considered.

References

1. Ayoub, A., Kim, B.G., Lee, I., Sokolsky, O.: A systematic approach to justifying sufficient confidence in software safety arguments. In: Ortmeier, F., Lipaczewski, M. (eds.) SAFECOMP 2012. LNCS, vol. 7612, pp. 305–316. Springer, Heidelberg (2012)
2. Bishop, P., Bloomfield, R.: A methodology for safety case development. In: Redmill, F., Anderson, T. (eds.) Industrial Perspectives of Safety-Critical Systems, pp. 194–203. Springer, Heidelberg (1998)
3. Bloomfield, R., Littlewood, B., Wright, D.: Confidence: its role in dependability cases for risk assessment. In: 37th Annual IEEE/IFIP International Conference on Dependable Systems and Networks, DSN 2007, pp. 338–346. IEEE (2007)
4. Bloomfield, R.E., Guerra, S., Miller, A., Masera, M., Weinstock, C.B.: International working group on assurance cases (for security). IEEE Secur. Priv. 4(3), 66–68 (2006)
5. Cyra, L., Gorski, J.: Supporting compliance with security standards by trust case templates. In: 2nd International Conference on Dependability of Computer Systems, DepCoS-RELCOMEX 2007, pp. 91–98. IEEE (2007)
6. Cyra, L., Gorski, J.: Support for argument structures review and assessment. Reliab. Eng. Syst. Saf. 96(1), 26–37 (2011)
7. Dempster, A.P.: New methods for reasoning towards posterior distributions based on sample data. Ann. Math. Stat. 37, 355–374 (1966)
8. Dempster, A.P.: Upper and lower probabilities induced by a multivalued mapping. Ann. Math. Stat. 38, 325–339 (1967)
9. Denney, E., Pai, G., Habli, I.: Towards measurement of confidence in safety cases. In: International Symposium on Empirical Software Engineering and Measurement (ESEM), pp. 380–383. IEEE (2011)
10. Denœux, T.: The cautious rule of combination for belief functions and some extensions. In: 9th International Conference on Information Fusion, pp. 1–8. IEEE (2006)
11. DO-178C, ED-12C. Software considerations in airborne systems and equipment certification. RTCA/EUROCAE (2011)
12. Govier, T.: A Practical Study of Argument. Cengage Learning, Wadsworth (2013)
13. Guiochet, J., Do Hoang, Q.A., Kaaniche, M.: A model for safety case confidence assessment. In: Koornneef, F., van Gulijk, C. (eds.) SAFECOMP 2015. LNCS, vol. 9337, pp. 313–327. Springer, Heidelberg (2015). doi:10.1007/978-3-319-24255-2_23
14. Hawkins, R., Kelly, T., Knight, J., Graydon, P.: A new approach to creating clear safety arguments. In: Dale, C., Anderson, T. (eds.) Advances in Systems Safety, pp. 3–23. Springer, Heidelberg (2011)

15. ISO 26262. Software considerations in airborne systems and equipment certification. International Organization for Standardization (ISO) (2011)
16. Jøsang, A.: A logic for uncertain probabilities. Int. J. Uncertainty Fuzziness Knowl.-Based Syst. **9**(03), 279–311 (2001)
17. Kelly, T.: Arguing safety - a systematic approach to safety case management. Ph.D. thesis, Department of Computer Science, University of York (1998)
18. Kelly, T., McDermid, J.: Safety case construction and reuse using patterns. In: Daniel, P. (ed.) Computer Safety, Reliability, and Security (SAFECOMP), pp. 55–69. Springer, Heidelberg (1997)
19. Kelly, T., Weaver, R.: The goal structuring notation-a safety argument notation. In: Proceedings of the Dependable Systems and Networks (DSN) Workshop on Assurance Cases (2004)
20. Mercier, D., Quost, B., Denœux, T.: Contextual discounting of belief functions. In: Godo, L. (ed.) ECSQARU 2005. LNCS (LNAI), vol. 3571, pp. 552–562. Springer, Heidelberg (2005)
21. Shafer, G.: A Mathematical Theory of Evidence, vol. 1. Princeton University Press Princeton, Princeton (1976)
22. Toulmin, S.E.: The Uses of Argument. Cambridge University Press, Cambridge (2003)
23. Robert Andrew Weaver: The safety of software: constructing and assuring arguments. Ph.D. thesis, Department of Computer Science, University of York (2003)

Applications

Evidential Correlated Gaussian Mixture Markov Model for Pixel Labeling Problem

Lin An[1], Ming Li[1], Mohamed El Yazid Boudaren[2],
and Wojciech Pieczynski[3(✉)]

[1] National Laboratory of Radar Signal Processing,
Collaborative Innovation Center of Information Sensing and Understanding,
Xidian University, Xi'an, China
lin.an4579@gmail.com, liming@xidian.edu.cn
[2] Computer Science, Ecole Militaire Polytechnique, Bordj El Bahri, Algeria
boudaren@gmail.com
[3] Telecom SudParis, CITI, Évry, France
wojciech.pieczynski@telecom-sudparis.eu

Abstract. Hidden Markov Fields (HMF) have been widely used in various
problems of image processing. In such models, the hidden process of interest X is
assumed to be a Markov field that must be estimated from an observable process
Y. Classic HMFs have been recently extended to a very general model called
"evidential pairwise Markov field" (EPMF). Extending its recent particular case
able to deal with non-Gaussian noise, we propose an original variant able to deal
with non-Gaussian and correlated noise. Experiments conducted on simulated
and real data show the interest of the new approach in an unsupervised context.

Keywords: Markov random field · Correlated noise model · Gaussian
mixture · Belief functions · Theory of evidence · Image segmentation

1 Introduction

The paper deals with statistical image segmentation. The use of hidden Markov fields
(HMFs) has become popular since the introduction of these models in pioneering
papers [1, 2] with related optimal Bayesian processing. HMFs provide remarkable
results in numerous situations and continue to be used nowadays. On the other hand,
Dempster-Shafer theory of evidence (DST) has been used in different information
fusion problems [3, 4]. However, simultaneous use of both HMFs and DST is rather
rare, and is mainly applied to fuse sensors of different nature [5–8]. Another application
consists of using DST to model images with fine details, and the first results presented
in [9] were encouraging. Calculations presented in [9] were possible because of the fact
that DS fusion in Markov field context can be interpreted as calculation of a marginal
distribution in a "triplet Markov field" (TMF [10]). The model proposed in [9] has been
recently extended to non-Gaussian noise in [11], enjoying the generality of the proposed "Evidential Pairwise Markov Field" (EPMF) models. Such extensions are particularly useful in radar images context, in which noise is not Gaussian in general. The
aim of this paper is to propose a further extension of the model proposed in [11] to the

© Springer International Publishing Switzerland 2016
J. Vejnarová and V. Kratochvíl (Eds.): BELIEF 2016, LNAI 9861, pp. 203–211, 2016.
DOI: 10.1007/978-3-319-45559-4_21

case of correlated noise. This seems to be of interest in radar images processing, as noises are correlated in real situations while they are usually considered independent in different Markov fields based models.

Let S be a finite set, with $Card(S) = N$, let $Y = \{Y_s\}_{s \in S}$ be the observed random field with each Y_s taking its value in $\Re$, and let $X = \{X_s\}_{s \in S}$ be the hidden random label field with each X_s taking its values from a finite set of "classes" or "labels". Realization of such random fields will be denoted using lowercase letters. The labeling problem consists in estimating $X = x$ from $Y = y$.

The reminder of the paper is organized as follows. Section 2 summarizes the theory of evidence and its applicability within Markov models. In Sect. 3, we describe our proposed model. In Sect. 4, we assess the proposed model on image segmentation. Finally, concluding remarks are presented in Sect. 5.

2   Background

In this section, we briefly recall the basics of Dempster-Shafer theory of evidence and discuss its application within Markov field models.

2.1   Hidden Markov Fields

In basic hidden Markov fields (HMFs) context, the field X is assumed Markovian with respect to a system of cliques C, associated to some neighborhood system. The model name "hidden Markov field" stands for the very fact that the hidden field X is Markov. According to the Hammersley-Clifford equivalence, X is then an MRF given by

$$p(x) \propto \exp\left[-\sum_{c \in C} \psi_c(x_c)\right] \tag{1}$$

where $\psi_c(x_c)$ is the potential function associated to clique c, and $x_c = (x_s)_{s \in c}$.

On the other hand, the likelihood distribution $p(y|x)$ is defined by

$$p(y|x) \propto \exp\left[\sum_{s \in S} \log(p(y_s|x_s))\right] \tag{2}$$

The joint distribution of (X, Y) is then given by

$$p(x, y) = p(x)p(y|x). \tag{3}$$

2.2   Theory of Evidence

The class set from which X_s takes its value is defined by $L = \{l_1, \cdots l_K\}$ that is an universe of discourse, also called frame of discernment. Let $\Theta = 2^L = \{\varnothing, l^1, \cdots, L\} = \{\varnothing, \theta_1, \cdots, \theta_Q\}$ be its corresponding powerset, where $l^k = \{l_k\}$ and $Q = 2^K - 1$.

A "basic belief assignment" (*bba*) is a function M from Θ to $[0, 1]$ satisfying $M(\emptyset) = 0$ and $\sum_{i=1}^{Q} m(\theta_i) = 1$. A *bba* M defines then a "plausibility" function Pl and a "credibility" function Cr, both defined from Θ to $[0, 1]$ by $Pl(\theta) = \sum_{\theta \cap \theta' \neq \phi} M(\theta')$ and $Cr(\theta) = \sum_{\theta' \subset \theta} M(\theta')$ respectively. For a given *bba* M, related Pl and Cr are linked by $Pl(\theta) + Cr(\bar{\theta}) = 1$. From this point of view, a probability p can be perceived as a special case for which $p = Pl = Cr$. Moreover, if two *bbas* M_1 and M_2 represent two pieces of evidence, we can merge, or fuse, them using the so called "Dempster-Shafer fusion" (DS fusion), which defines $M = M_1 \oplus M_2$ given by: $M(\theta) = (M_1 \oplus M_2)(\theta) \propto \sum_{\theta' \cap \theta'' = \theta} M_1(\theta') M_2(\theta'')$ for any $\theta \neq \emptyset$. Finally, a *bba* is said "probabilistic" or "Bayesian" when it vanishes outside singletons, and it is said "evidential" otherwise. In this paper, a probabilistic *bba* will be said defined on L and singletons l^k and elements l_k will be handled indifferently.

2.3 Hidden Evidential Markov Field with Gaussian-Mixture Likelihood

Let us consider the fields $X = (X_s)_{s \in S}$, $Y = (Y_s)_{s \in S}$ and let $p_1(x) \propto \exp\left[-\sum_{c \in C} \psi_c(x_c)\right]$ and $p^y(x) \propto \prod_{s \in S} p(y_s | x_s)$. p_1 and p^y will be called "prior" and "likelihood" *bbas* respectively. Then, the posterior distribution $p(x|y)$ given by (3) is itself the DS fusion of p_1 and p^y: $p(x|y) = (p_1 \oplus p^y)(x)$. This is of particular significance since it may offer different possibilities of extensions [9]. More precisely, if either p_1 or p^y is extended to an evidential *bba*, the result of the fusion $p_1 \oplus p^y$ remains a probabilistic distribution, which can then be seen as an extension of the classic posterior probability $p(x|y)$. Additionally, if the "evidential" extension of p_1 or p^y is of a similar Markovian form, the computation of posterior margins $p(x_s|y)$ remains feasible in spite of the fact that the fusion result is no longer necessarily a Markov field [9].

For instance, if p_1 is extended to a Markov *bba* M, we can construct an evidential Markov field (EMF) defined on Θ^N by

$$M(m) \propto \exp\left[-\sum_{c \in C} \psi_c(m_c)\right] \tag{4}$$

In [11], we consider a general situation where the priors are evidential and the noise is blind but not Gaussian. By introducing an auxiliary field $U = (U_s)_{s \in S}$ with $U_s \in \Lambda = \{\lambda_1, \cdots, \lambda_P\}$, the evidential blind Gaussian mixture Markov (EBGMM) model is given by

$$p(m, x, u, y) = 1_{x \in m} \gamma exp \left[-\sum_{c \in C} \psi_c(m_c) - \sum_{s \in S} \eta_s(x_s, u_s) + \sum_{s \in S} Log(p(y_s|x_s, u_s)) \right] \quad (5)$$

Since $p(m, x, y) = \sum\limits_{u \in \Lambda^N} p(m, x, u, y)$, we have

$$p(m, x, y) = \gamma \left[1_{x \in m} \exp \left[-\sum_{c \in C} \psi_c(m_c) \right] \right] \prod_{s \in S} \left[\sum_{u_s \in \Lambda} \exp[-\eta_s(x_s, u_s)] p(y_s|x_s, u_s) \right] \quad (6)$$

and thus $p(m, x, y)$ is a classic EHMF with $p(y_s|x_s)$ being mixtures, $p(y_s|x_s) = \sum\limits_{u_s \in \Lambda} \alpha(u_s) p(y_s|x_s, u_s)$, where the mixture coefficients are $\alpha(u_s) = \exp[-\eta_s(x_s, u_s)]$. As demonstrated in [11], the interest of such models is to make it possible to deal with unknown noise densities $p(y_s|x_s)$.

3   Evidential Correlated Gaussian Mixture Markov Model

The aim of the present paper is to extend the model (5) in such a way that the possible noise correlations can be taken into account. Thus we propose a model in which the noise is non-Gaussian and correlated, and in which all parameters can be estimated by the "iterative conditional estimation" (ICE) method, allowing unsupervised image segmentation.

The distribution of the proposed model, called "evidential correlated Gaussian mixture Markov" (ECGMM) model, is written as

$$p(m, x, u, y) = 1_{x \in m} \gamma \exp \left[-\sum_{c \in C} \psi_c(m_c) - \sum_{c \in C} \phi_c(u_c) - \sum_{s \in S} \eta_s(x_s, u_s) + \sum_{s \in S} Log(p(y_s|x_s, u_s)) \right] \quad (7)$$

Then the likelihood is

$$p(y|x) \propto \sum_{u \in \Lambda^N} \exp \left[-\sum_{c \in C} \phi_c(u_c) - \sum_{s \in S} \eta_s(x_s, u_s) + \sum_{s \in S} Log(p(y_s|x_s, u_s)) \right] \quad (8)$$

Let us notice that this likelihood, which is new with respect to the likelihood in (5), is very different from the latter. Indeed, the likelihood in (5) verifies two classical properties:

(i) $p(y|x) = \prod\limits_{s \in S} p(y_s|x)$;

(ii) $p(y_s|x) = p(y_s|x_s)$ for each $s \in S$,

whereas the likelihood (8) does not verify any of them. Thus the greater complexity of (7) with respect to (5) goes beyond the introduction of the noise correlation.

We have to mention that another way to construct the correlated likelihood is assuming the likelihood to be the Markov field:

$$p(y|x) = \gamma \exp\left[-\sum_{c \in C} \psi_c(y_c, x_c)\right],\tag{9}$$

which captures the contextual information directly [13]. Since the observation y_s takes the value from R, it is such a complex model with so many parameters. When the likelihood is simple Gaussian there are six parameters, it will be much more when we consider the Gaussian mixture. In CGMM, u_s takes the value from a limited data set, so $\psi_c(u_c)$ can be constructed by the well-used Multi-level logistic (MLL) model [14], which keeps the likelihood to be correlated as well as simplify the complexity of the model.

The labeling problem is to find $\hat{x}$ from $Y = y$. Then setting $V = (V_s)_{s \in S}$ with $V_s = (M_s, X_s, U_s)$, we have a standard hidden Markov field (V, Y). The field V is discrete finite, and thus we use the classic "iterated conditional modes" (ICM) algorithm [1, 6], which is an approximation of the optimal Bayesian solution $\hat{v}_B = \arg\max_v p(v|y)$. Having $\hat{v} = (\hat{m}, \hat{x}, \hat{u})$ gives then $\hat{x}$ (in addition, it also gives $(\hat{m}, \hat{u})$, which can be of interest). Let us consider the simplest situation: x_s takes the value from $\{l_1, l_2\}$, and u_s takes the value from $\{\lambda_1, \lambda_2\}$. Then v_s takes the value from $\Omega = \{(l_1, \lambda_1), (l_1, \lambda_2), (l_2, \lambda_1), (l_2, \lambda_2)\} = \{\omega_1, \omega_2, \omega_3, \omega_4\}$. We can estimate the probability $p(v_s|y)$ on Ω by Gibbs sampler. The estimation obtained in this way enables us to compute $p(x_s = l_1|y) = p(v_s = \omega_1|y) + p(v_s = \omega_2|y)$ and $p(x_s = l_2|y) = p(v_s = \omega_3|y) + p(v_s = \omega_4|y)$, which are then used to perform ICM.

4 Experiments

4.1 Simulated Data

The proposed model will be assessed against the existing EBGMM and HMF models on unsupervised segmentation of simulated images in both cases of independent and correlated noise. Let us consider the simulated images "*Nazca bird*", which has already been dealt with in [9, 11], and which is too complex for the simple HMFs models. There are two classes, i.e. X_s takes its value from $L = \{l_1, l_2\}$, M_s takes its values from $\Theta = \{\theta_1, \theta_2, \theta_3\} = \{\{l_1\}, \{l_2\}, \{l_1, l_2\}\}$, and U_s takes its values from $\Lambda = \{\lambda_1, \lambda_2\}$. The non-Gaussian noise used here is the Gamma one. In independent noise case, the two noise densities are Gamma $G_1(0.5, 2)$ and $G_2(3, 1)$, which are quite different from Gaussian densities. The correlated noise is obtained by the following equation:

$$
\begin{aligned}
y_{i,j} = &\left[\frac{\left(y_{i,j}^1 - \mu^1\right) + \left(y_{i-1,j}^1 - \mu^1\right) + \left(y_{i,j-1}^1 - \mu^1\right)}{\sqrt{3}} + \mu^1\right] 1_{a_{i,j} = \omega_1} \\
&+ \left[\frac{\left(y_{i,j}^2 - \mu^2\right) + \left(y_{i-1,j}^2 - \mu^2\right) + \left(y_{i,j-1}^2 - \mu^2\right)}{\sqrt{3}} + \mu^2\right] 1_{a_{i,j} = \omega_2}
\end{aligned}\tag{10}
$$

where i, j is the location of the pixel; y^1 and y^2 are two independent noises with the densities being $G_1(0.5, 2)$ and $G_2(3, 1)$; μ^1 and μ^2 are the means; α is the class image. We obtain a correlation coefficient of 0.23. We show the class image, the observed images, and their corresponding histograms in Fig. 1.

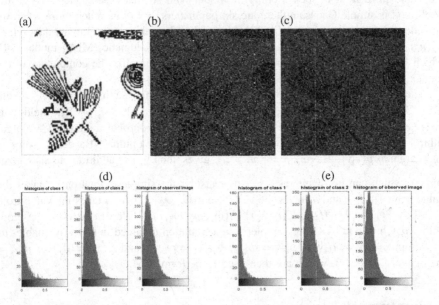

Fig. 1. Simulated noisy *Nazca bird* images (a) class image; (b) image corrupted by independent noise; (c) image corrupted by correlated noise; (d) histogram of independent noise; (e) histogram of correlated noise.

The noisy images are then segmented using HMF, EBGMM and ECGMM respectively. The obtained results are shown in Fig. 2. More precisely, we assess all approaches with respect to the reference map in terms of overall accuracy (OA) and Kappa coefficient (Kappa) [12] and illustrate them in Table 1. The best approach is the one exhibiting the highest OA, and the highest Kappa. The presented results, and other similar results obtained in additional experiments, show that HMFs give very poor results in both independent and correlated noise cases. EBGMM and ECGMM significantly improve HMFs' results in the independent-noise case, and produce equivalent results. Finally, the new ECGMM model based segmentation allows a significant improvement of the EBGMM based one in the case of correlated noise.

4.2   Real Data

In this subsection, we evaluate our method on a real radar image. To this end, we consider the image of Toronto city, shown in Fig. 3(a), obtained in December 2007 by TerraSAR-X SpotLight, which is single HH polarization with a resolution of $1m$.

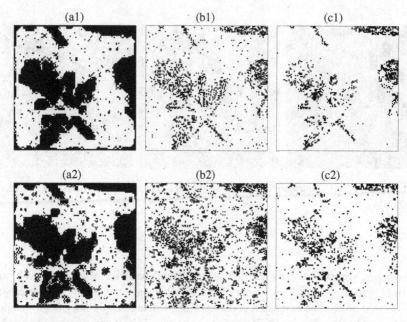

Fig. 2. Results of segmentation of noisy *Nazca bird* images. (a1–a2) by HMF; (b1–b2) by EBGMM; (c1-c2) by ECGMM. (a1–c1) independent noise case; (a2–c2) correlated noise case.

Table 1. Performance evaluation of different approaches on simulated images

OA (%)			
	HMF	EBGMM	ECGMM
Independent noise	73.92	**91.73**	90.28
Correlated noise	69.15	80.22	**90.61**
Kappa			
	HMF	EBGMM	ECGMM
Independent noise	0.3912	**0.5864**	0.5377
Correlated noise	0.3336	0.3405	**0.5864**

We segment the image into three classes by EBGMM and the proposed ECGMM, and show the result in Fig. 3. This data is full of small edges, which is a real challenge for Markov-based methods. Compared with EBGMM, we see that ECGMM seems to perform better in some spots; in particular around the rich-edge area. We can see from the red panels that the segmentation obtained by ECGMM includes more details with respect to the one obtained through EBGMM. The correlated coefficient of this data is about 0.25, which is very close to the simulated image above.

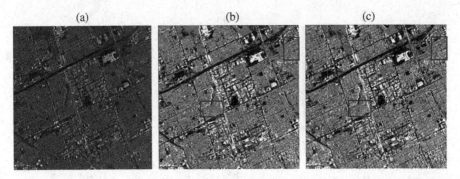

Fig. 3. Unsupervised segmentation of a real SAR image (a) real data, (b) EBGMM's result, and (c) ECGMM's result.

5 Conclusion

In this paper, we extended the particular "evidential pairwise Markov fields" model used in [11] to deal with the segmentation of SAR images containing fine details and non-Gaussian noise. The extension consists of introducing an auxiliary field, making it possible to take the noise correlation into account. The experiments conducted on simulated and real data prove that the new approach can significantly improve the results obtained by the previous one. In future work, one can view an extension of the probabilistic likelihood used here to an evidential one, so that the possible non stationarity of the noise could be taken into account.

References

1. Besag, J.: On the statistical analysis of dirty pictures. J. Roy. Stat. Soc. Ser. B **48**(3), 259–302 (1986)
2. Geman, S., Geman, D.: Stochastic relaxation, Gibbs distributions and the Bayesian restoration of images. IEEE Trans. Pattern Anal. Mach. Intell. **6**(6), 721–741 (1984)
3. Smets, P.: Belief functions: the disjunctive rule of combination and the generalized Bayesian theorem. Int. J. Approximate Reasoning **9**, 1–35 (1993)
4. Shafer, G.: A Mathematical Theory of Evidence. Princeton University Press, Princeton (1976)
5. Bendjebbour, A., Delignon, Y., Fouque, L., Samson, V., Pieczynski, W.: Multisensor images segmentation using dempster-shafer fusion in Markov fields context. IEEE Trans. Geosci. Remote Sens. **39**(8), 1789–1798 (2001)
6. Foucher, S., Germain, M., Boucher, J.-M., Benié, G.B.: Multisource classification using ICM and Dempster-Shafer theory. IEEE Trans. Instrum. Measur. **51**(2), 277–281 (2002)
7. Le Hégarat-Mascle, S., Bloch, I., Vidal-Madjar, D.: Introduction of neighborhood information in evidence theory and application to data fusion of radar and optical images with partial cloud cover. Pattern Recogn. **31**(11), 1811–1823 (1998)

8. Tupin, F., Maitre, H., Bloch, I.: A first step toward automatic interpretation of SAR images using evidential fusion of several structure detectors. IEEE Trans. Geosci. Remote Sens. **37** (3), 1327–1343 (1999)

9. Pieczynski, W., Benboudjema, D.: Multisensor triplet Markov fields and theory of evidence. Image Vis. Comput. **24**(1), 61–69 (2006)

10. Benboudjema, D., Pieczynski, W.: Unsupervised image segmentation using triplet Markov fields. Comput. Vis. Image Underst. **99**(3), 476–498 (2005)

11. Boudaren, M.E.Y., An, L., Pieczynski, W.: Dempster-Shafer fusion of evidential pairwise Markov fields. Int. J. Approximate Reasoning **74**, 13–29 (2016)

12. Poggi, G., Scarpa, G., Zerubia, J.B.: Supervised segmentation of remote sensing images based on a tree-structured MRF model. IEEE Trans. Geosci. Remote Sens. **43**(8), 1901–1911 (2005)

13. Pieczynski, W., Tebbache, A.-N.: Pairwise Markov random fields and segmentation of textured images. Mach. Graph. Vis. **9**, 705–718 (2000)

14. Li, S.Z.: Markov Random Field Modeling in Image Analysis. Springer Science & Business Media, Heidelberg (2009)

The Capacitated Vehicle Routing Problem with Evidential Demands: A Belief-Constrained Programming Approach

Nathalie Helal[1]([⊠]), Frédéric Pichon[1], Daniel Porumbel[2], David Mercier[1], and Éric Lefèvre[1]

[1] University of Artois, EA 3926,
Laboratoire de Génie Informatique et d'Automatique de l'Artois (LGI2A),
62400 Béthune, France
nathalie_helal@ens.univ-artois.fr,
{frederic.pichon,david.mercier,eric.lefevre}@univ-artois.fr
[2] Conservatoire National des Arts et Métiers, EA 4629, Cedric, 75003 Paris, France
daniel.porumbel@cnam.fr

Abstract. This paper studies a vehicle routing problem, where vehicles have a limited capacity and customer demands are uncertain and represented by belief functions. More specifically, this problem is formalized using a belief function based extension of the chance-constrained programming approach, which is a classical modeling of stochastic mathematical programs. In addition, it is shown how the optimal solution cost is influenced by some important parameters involved in the model. Finally, some instances of this difficult problem are solved using a simulated annealing metaheuristic, demonstrating the feasibility of the approach.

Keywords: Vehicle routing problem · Stochastic programming · Chance-constrained programming · Belief functions

1 Introduction

The Capacitated Vehicle Routing Problem with Stochastic Demands (CVRPSD) is a Vehicle Routing Problem (VRP) that asks to determine the set of routes of minimum cost that can serve a set of customers with stochastic demands, while respecting the capacity limit of each vehicle [8]. This stochastic integer linear program can be modeled via the Chance-Constrained Programming (CCP) approach [2,6], which is one of the main approaches to addressing stochastic mathematical programs. Modeling the CVRPSD via CCP amounts to having a constraint, which states that the probability that any route exceeds vehicle capacity, must be below a given (small) value.

Belief function theory [14] is an alternative uncertainty framework to probability theory. Uncertainty on customer demands may be naturally represented by belief functions in various situations; for instance, when sources providing

© Springer International Publishing Switzerland 2016
J. Vejnarová and V. Kratochvíl (Eds.): BELIEF 2016, LNAI 9861, pp. 212–221, 2016.
DOI: 10.1007/978-3-319-45559-4_22

pieces of information on customer demands, are assumed to be partially reliable or biased [12]. In such case, a new VRP is obtained, which may be called the Capacitated VRP with Evidential Demands (CVRPED), where *evidential* means that uncertainty on customer demands is modeled by belief functions.

Few papers [9,10,15] have been dedicated to handling uncertainty within optimization problems using belief functions. These papers only addressed the case of *continuous* linear programs, which are usually far more easier to solve than their discrete counterparts. Most notably, Masri and Ben Abdelaziz [9] generalized the CCP approach to linear programs involving uncertainty represented by belief functions, which they coined the Belief-Constrained Programming (BCP) approach to the belief linear programming problem.

In this paper, we study the extension of the CCP approach to an *integer* linear program involving uncertainty represented by belief functions, which is the CVRPED, leading to what may be called the BCP approach to the CVRPED. Being a derivative from the large class of VRP, which are NP-hard and may be tackled using metaheuristics [3], we adapt a simulated annealing metaheuristic [7] to find solutions to the CVRPED modeled via the BCP approach.

This paper is structured as follows. Section 2 contains a brief reminder of CVRPSD modeled via CCP, and of necessary belief function theory concepts. In Sect. 3, the BCP modeling of CVRPED is presented along with an analysis of how the optimal solution cost is influenced by the parameters involved in the belief-based constraints. Experiments on CVRPED instances built from well-known CVRP instances, are reported in Sect. 4, before concluding in Sect. 5.

2   Background

In this section, the CCP modeling of CVRPSD is first recalled, and then some necessary concepts of belief function theory are reviewed.

2.1   CCP Modeling of CVRPSD

The Capacitated Vehicle Routing Problem (CVRP) is an important variation of VRP where vehicles have identical capacities, and customers have indivisible deterministic demands. It can be formulated as follows:

$$Minimize \sum_{i=1}^{n} \sum_{j=1}^{n} c_{i,j} \sum_{k=1}^{m} w_{i,j,k}, \tag{1}$$

where n is the number of customers including the depot, m the number of vehicles that are initially located at the depot, $c_{i,j}$ the cost for traveling between customers x_i and x_j, and $w_{i,j,k}$ a binary variable that is equal to 1 if vehicle k goes from x_i to x_j and serves them, and 0 if it does not. Besides, routes must be designed so that each route starts and ends at the depot and so that each customer is visited exactly once by exactly one vehicle; due to lack of space, we refer to [1] for a formal description of these constraints. In addition, the sum of the demands of the customers served by a route must not exceed vehicle capacity, which corresponds to the capacity constraints

$$\sum_{i=1}^{n} d_{x_i} \sum_{j=1}^{n} w_{i,j,k} \leq Q, \qquad k = 1, \ldots, m, \qquad (2)$$

where d_{x_i} is the quantity demanded by customer x_i and Q the vehicle capacity.

We are interested by a variation of CVRP, called CVRPSD, which introduces stochastic demands into CVRP, $i.e.$, d_{x_i}, $i = 1, \ldots, n$, are now random variables. A way to address this problem is via the CCP approach, which corresponds to the same optimization problem as CVRP except that constraints represented by (2) are replaced by the following so called chance-constraints:

$$P\left(\sum_{i=1}^{n} d_{x_i} \sum_{j=1}^{n} w_{i,j,k} \leq Q\right) \geq 1 - \beta, \qquad k = 1, \ldots, m,$$

where $1 - \beta$ is the minimum allowable probability that any route respects vehicle capacity and thus succeeds.

2.2   Belief Function Theory

Belief function theory was introduced in [14] as a theory of evidence. In this theory, uncertain knowledge about a variable ω taking its values in a domain Ω, is represented by a *Mass Function* (MF) defined as a mapping $m : 2^{\Omega} \rightarrow [0, 1]$ verifying $\sum_{A \subseteq \Omega} m(A) = 1$ and $m(\emptyset) = 0$. The mass $m(A)$ represents the probability of knowing only that $\omega \in A$. Every $A \subseteq \Omega$ such that $m(A) > 0$, is a *focal element* of m. A mass function is called *Bayesian* if its focal elements are singletons (in which case it is the usual probability mass function) and *categorical* if it has only one focal element. To be consistent with the stochastic case notation and terminology, we will write $m(\omega \in A)$ instead of $m(A)$, and a variable ω whose true value is known in the form of a MF will be called an *evidential variable*.

Equivalent representations of a MF m are the *belief* and *plausibility* functions defined, respectively, as

$$Bel(\omega \in A) = \sum_{B \subseteq A} m(\omega \in B), \quad \forall A \subseteq \Omega, \qquad (3)$$

$$Pl(\omega \in A) = \sum_{B \cap A \neq \emptyset} m(\omega \in B), \quad \forall A \subseteq \Omega.$$

The *degree of belief* $Bel(\omega \in A)$ can be interpreted as the probability that the evidence about ω and represented by m, supports (implies) $\omega \in A$, whereas the *degree of plausibility* $Pl(\omega \in A)$ is the probability that the evidence is consistent with $\omega \in A$. We have $Bel(\omega \in A) \leq Pl(\omega \in A)$, for all $A \subseteq \Omega$. Besides, if m is Bayesian, then $Bel(\omega \in A) = Pl(\omega \in A)$, for all $A \subseteq \Omega$, and this function is a probability measure.

In this paper, belief function theory is used to model uncertain knowledge about customer demands, which we assume to be positive real numbers. Hence, we will be dealing with MF defined on $\Omega = \mathbb{R}^+$. The tools of belief function theory exposed above remain the same in such case, as long as the number of focal sets is finite [11], which will be the case in this study. Besides, focal sets of MF considered in this paper will all be intervals of positive real numbers.

Let us finally recall the definition provided by Yager [17], of the addition of evidential variables, which will also be needed in the next section.

Definition 1. *Let* $[w] = [\underline{w}, \overline{w}]$ *denote the closed interval of all reals* w, *such that* $\underline{w} \leq w \leq \overline{w}$. *Let* σ *and* τ *be two independent evidential variables defined on* $\mathbb{R}^+$, *and having finite numbers of focal sets, which are intervals. Their addition is the evidential variable* $\sigma + \tau$ *with associated mass function*

$$m\left(\sigma + \tau \in [u]\right) = \sum_{[s]+[t]=[u]} m\left(\sigma \in [s]\right) \cdot m\left(\tau \in [t]\right),$$

where the addition of two intervals $[s]$ *and* $[t]$ *is defined by* $[s]+[t] = \left[\underline{s} + \underline{t}, \overline{s} + \overline{t}\right]$.

Remark 1. Let σ and τ be the evidential variables in Definition 1. Let $\overline{\sigma}$ and $\overline{\tau}$ be two independent random variables with associated probability mass functions $p_{\overline{\sigma}}$ and $p_{\overline{\tau}}$ defined by $p_{\overline{\sigma}}(\overline{s}) = m\left(\sigma \in [\underline{s}, \overline{s}]\right)$ and $p_{\overline{\tau}}(\overline{t}) = m\left(\tau \in [\underline{t}, \overline{t}]\right)$ for any focal sets $[\underline{s}, \overline{s}]$ and $[\underline{t}, \overline{t}]$ of σ and τ, respectively. We will refer to $\overline{\sigma}$ and $\overline{\tau}$ as the upper probabilistic versions of σ and τ. It can easily be shown that we have $Bel(\sigma + \tau \leq Q) = P(\overline{\sigma} + \overline{\tau} \leq Q)$, for any $Q \in \mathbb{R}^+$.

3   BCP Modeling of CVRPED

This section formalizes, and then studies, a means to handle the case where uncertainty on customer demands in the CVRP is represented by belief functions.

3.1   Formalization

Let us consider the case where customer demands are no longer deterministic or random, but evidential, *i.e.*, d_{x_i}, $i = 1, \ldots, n$, are now evidential variables. The associated problem is then called CVRPED as already introduced in Sect. 1. Following what has been done in [9] for the case of linear programs under uncertainty, we may generalize the CCP modeling of CVRPSD into a Belief-Constrained Programming (BCP) modeling of CVRPED, which amounts to keeping the same optimization problem as CVRP except that capacity constraints represented by (2) are replaced by the following *belief*-constraints:

$$Bel\left(\sum_{i=1}^{n} d_{x_i} \sum_{j=1}^{n} w_{i,j,k} \leq Q\right) \geq 1 - \underline{\beta}, \qquad k = 1, \ldots, m, \tag{4}$$

$$Pl\left(\sum_{i=1}^{n} d_{x_i} \sum_{j=1}^{n} w_{i,j,k} \leq Q\right) \geq 1 - \overline{\beta}, \qquad k = 1, \ldots, m, \tag{5}$$

with $\beta \geq \overline{\beta}$ and where $1 - \beta$ (resp. $1 - \overline{\beta}$) is the minimum allowable degree of belief (resp. plausibility) that a vehicle capacity is respected on any route. Note that in order to evaluate the belief-constraints (4) and (5), the total demand on every route must be determined by summing all customers demands on that route, which is done using Definition 1.

3.2 Particular Cases of the BCP Modeling of CVRPED

It is interesting to remark that depending on the values chosen for β and $\overline{\beta}$ as well as the nature of the evidential demands d_{x_i}, $i = 1, \ldots, n$, the BC$\overline{P}$ modeling of CVRPED may degenerate into simpler or well-known optimisation problems.

The case $\beta = \overline{\beta}$ is particularly important. In this case, constraints (5) can be dropped, that is, only constraints (4) need to be evaluated (if constraints (4) are satisfied then constraints (5) are necessarily satisfied due to the relation between the belief and plausibility functions). As a matter of fact, the BCP approach originally introduced in [9] is of this form (no constraint based on Pl is considered). Furthermore, we note that due to Remark 1, the BCP modeling of CVRPED can be converted into an equivalent optimisation problem, which is the CCP modeling of a CVRPSD where the stochastic demand of client x_i is defined as the upper probabilistic version $\overline{d_{x_i}}$ of its evidential demand d_{x_i}. In particular, if the evidential demands are Bayesian, *i.e.*, we are dealing really with a CVRPSD, then the BCP modeling clearly degenerates into the CCP modeling of this CVRPSD. In contrast, if the evidential demands are categorical, *i.e.*, we are dealing with a CVRP where each customer demand d_{x_i} is only known to belong to an interval $[\underline{d_{x_i}}, \overline{d_{x_i}}]$, then the belief-constraints reduce to the following constraints

$$\sum_{i=1}^{n} \overline{d_{x_i}} \sum_{j=1}^{n} w_{i,j,k} \leq Q, \qquad k = 1, \ldots, m, \qquad (6)$$

since in the case of categorical demands, the total demand on any given route is also categorical (it corresponds to the interval whose endpoints are obtained by summing the endpoints of the interval demands of the customers on the route) and thus for any $k = 1, \ldots, m$, $Bel(\sum_{i=1}^{n} d_{x_i} \sum_{j=1}^{n} w_{i,j,k} \leq Q)$ either equals 1 or equals 0, with the former occurring iff $\sum_{i=1}^{n} \overline{d_{x_i}} \sum_{j=1}^{n} w_{i,j,k} \leq Q$. In other words, in the case of categorical demands and $\beta = \overline{\beta}$, the BCP modeling amounts to searching the solution which minimizes the overall cost of servicing the customers (1) under constraints (6), *i.e.*, assuming the maximum (worst) possible customer demands, and thus it corresponds to the minimax optimisation procedures encountered in robust optimization [16].

Let us eventually remark that the case $\beta = 1 > \overline{\beta}$ is the converse of the case $\beta = \overline{\beta}$ in the sense that constraints (4) can be dropped (as they are necessarily satisfied) and only constraints (5) need then to be evaluated. Moreover, as in the case $\beta = \overline{\beta}$, the BCP modeling of CVRPED can be converted into an equivalent optimisation problem, which is the CCP modeling of some CVRPSD (this is due to the existence of a counterpart to Remark 1 for the plausibility function, which relies on the lower endpoints of the focal sets rather than the upper endpoints).

3.3   Influence of $\underline{\beta}$, $\overline{\beta}$ and Q on the Optimal Solution Cost

In this section, we study the influence of the parameters $\underline{\beta}$, $\overline{\beta}$ and Q on the cost of the optimal solution of the CVRPED modeled via BCP.

To simplify the presentation, we will denote by $\Sigma_{Q,\underline{\beta},\overline{\beta}}$ the set of solutions to the CVRPED modeled via BCP and $\hat{C}_{Q,\underline{\beta},\overline{\beta}}$ the cost of an optimal solution in $\Sigma_{Q,\underline{\beta},\overline{\beta}}$, for some $\underline{\beta}$, $\overline{\beta}$ and Q.

The following propositions state how the optimal solution cost changes as Q, $\underline{\beta}$ or $\overline{\beta}$ vary.

Proposition 1. *The optimal solution cost is non increasing in Q.*

Proof. Let us consider a set $\mathcal{C} = \{R_1, \ldots, R_m\}$ composed of m routes R_k, $k = 1, \ldots, m$, such that it is not known whether this set respects the belief-constraints (4) and (5), but it is known that it respects all the other constraints of the CVRPED modeled via BCP, in particular each route R_k starts and ends at the depot and each customer is visited exactly once by exactly one vehicle.

It is clear that for any $\underline{\beta}$ and $\overline{\beta}$, as Q increases (starting from 0), it reaches necessarily a value at which $\mathcal{C}$ becomes a solution to the CVRPED modeled via BCP. Hence, $\Sigma_{Q,\underline{\beta},\overline{\beta}} \subseteq \Sigma_{Q',\underline{\beta},\overline{\beta}}$ for $Q' \geq Q$, and thus $\hat{C}_{Q',\underline{\beta},\overline{\beta}} \leq \hat{C}_{Q,\underline{\beta},\overline{\beta}}$. □

Proposition 2. *The optimal solution cost is non increasing in $\underline{\beta}$.*

Proof. Let us consider a set $\mathcal{C} = \{R_1, \ldots, R_m\}$ composed of m routes R_k, $k = 1, \ldots, m$, such that it is not known whether this set respects the belief-constraints (4), but it is known that it respects all the other constraints of the CVRPED modeled via BCP, in particular constraints (5).

It is clear that for any Q, as $\underline{\beta}$ increases from $\overline{\beta}$ to 1, it reaches necessarily a value at which $\mathcal{C}$ becomes a solution to the CVRPED modeled via BCP. Hence, $\Sigma_{Q,\underline{\beta},\overline{\beta}} \subseteq \Sigma_{Q,\underline{\beta}',\overline{\beta}}$ for $\underline{\beta}' \geq \underline{\beta}$, and thus $\hat{C}_{Q,\underline{\beta}',\overline{\beta}} \leq \hat{C}_{Q,\underline{\beta},\overline{\beta}}$. □

Proposition 3. *The optimal solution cost is non increasing in $\overline{\beta}$.*

Proof. The proof is similar to that of Proposition 2.

Informally, Propositions 1–3 show that if a decision maker is willing to buy vehicles with a higher capacity or to have vehicle capacity exceeded on any route more often, then he will obtain at least as good (at most as costly) solutions *in theory*, *i.e.*, if he uses an exact optimization method. Unfortunately, no such method exists yet for the CVRPED modeled via BCP. As a matter of fact, the next section reports an experiment, where solutions to this optimization problem are sought using a metaheuristic.

4   Experimental Study

Section 3 has introduced the CVRPED modeled via BCP, and has studied some of its theoretical properties. In this section, a preliminary experimental study on some CVRPED instances is presented for the case where $\beta = \overline{\beta}$; for notation simplicity we introduce the value β such that $\beta = \underline{\beta} = \overline{\beta}$. These instances are first described, and then the obtained results are discussed. Note that to solve these instances, we adapted a simulated annealing algorithm designed for the CVRP, which was proposed in [5] and that uses a combination of random and greedy operators based on problem knowledge. However, due to space limitations, we must refrain from describing this adaptation.

4.1   CVRPED Instances

We have generated CVRPED instances based on Augerat set A instances for the CVRP [13]. In our instances, the customers coordinates and the capacity constraints are the same as in Augerat's. However, each deterministic customer demand d^{det} in Augerat instances has been replaced by an evidential demand d^{ev} with associated MF

$$m(d^{ev} \in [d^{det}, d^{det}]) = \alpha,$$
$$m(d^{ev} \in [d^{det} - \gamma \cdot d^{det}, d^{det} + \gamma \cdot d^{det}]) = 1 - \alpha, \qquad (7)$$

with $\alpha \in [0, 1]$ and $\gamma \in (0, 1)$. Such a transformation of the original deterministic demand may be relevant if each customer providing his deterministic demand is assumed to be reliable with probability α, and approximately (at $\pm\gamma * 100\%$) reliable with probability $1 - \alpha$ [12].

We note that a deterministic demand is a particular case of an evidential demand, and thus the BCP approach to the CVRPED can also be applied to CVRP instances. Although this latter idea may not be very useful in itself, it leads to an interesting remark based on the following result.

Proposition 4. *For any β and Q, the optimal solution to a CVRPED instance generated from a CVRP instance through transformation (7) and modeled via the BCP approach, has a higher or equal cost to that of the optimal solution of the CVRP instance modeled via the BCP approach.*

Proof. Let $\Sigma_{Q,\beta,\beta}^{ev}$ and $\Sigma_{Q,\beta,\beta}^{det}$ be the sets of solutions to the CVRPED and CVRP instances modeled via BCP, for some Q and β. For any route R_k of any solution $S \in \Sigma_{Q,\beta,\beta}^{ev}$, it can easily be shown that we have $Bel(d_{R_k}^{ev} \leq Q) \leq Bel(d_{R_k}^{det} \leq Q)$, where $d_{R_k}^{ev}$ and $d_{R_k}^{det}$ are evidential variables denoting respectively the sum of the evidential and deterministic demands on R_k, and thus any solution $S \in \Sigma_{Q,\beta,\beta}^{ev}$ also belongs to $\Sigma_{Q,\beta,\beta}^{det}$. We have thus $\Sigma_{Q,\beta,\beta}^{ev} \subseteq \Sigma_{Q,\beta,\beta}^{det}$.   □

The cost difference put forward by Proposition 4 between the optimal solution(s) of a CVRPED instance generated using (7) and the optimal solution(s) of its original generating CVRP instance, represents what a decision maker would loose if the customers were actually totally reliable whereas he was cautious and thought (wrongly) that they were only partially reliable. More specifically, by using (7), the decision maker assumes that the customer demands may be actually higher than they appear, *i.e.*, he believes that the customers may underestimate their needs, and the price to pay by being cautious in that latter way, is that the optimal solution he will obtain may have a higher cost than if he had not made such an assumption.

4.2   Results Using Simulated Annealing

We have generated CVRPED instances using the procedure described in the preceding section, where α was set to 0.8, while γ was set to 0.1. We also chose $\beta = 0.1$. The running time for the algorithm was less than an hour in almost all cases. Each instance was solved 30 times, and the results are given in Table 1.

Table 1. Results of the simulated annealing algorithm on the CVRPED instances

Instance	Best cost CVRP	Best cost CVRPED	Worst cost CVRPED	Avg cost CVRPED	Stand dev CVRPED	Difference with CVRP	Avg runtime CVRPED (seconds)
A-n32-k5	784	802, 07	837, 04	822, 27	8, 3	2.3 %	1919,79
A-n33-k5	661	690, 41	706, 36	696, 33	3, 9	4.45 %	2147,13
A-n33-k6	742	777, 63	782, 80	779, 84	1, 4	4.8 %	2572,64
A-n34-k5	778	800, 96	809, 94	802, 67	2, 8	2.95 %	2727,92
A-n36-k5	799	849, 83	887, 47	866, 67	9, 02	6.36 %	2383,9
A-n37-k5	669	692, 34	740, 17	715, 85	14, 54	3.49 %	2107,05
A-n37-k6	949	1006, 39	1054, 31	1027, 04	12, 4	6.05 %	2131,87
A-n38-k5	730	770, 34	819, 54	796, 9	12, 4	5.53 %	2083,72
A-n39-k5	822	876, 47	934, 18	909, 61	17, 18	6.63 %	2109,3
A-n39-k6	831	855, 18	895, 45	874, 7	8, 8	2.9 %	2479,13
A-n44-k6	937	998, 16	1108, 10	1056, 44	30, 5	6.53 %	2611,04
A-n45-k6	944	1017, 29	1083, 19	1055, 9	17, 12	7.76 %	2276,26
A-n45-k7	1146	1194, 19	1237, 3	1212, 23	12, 08	4.2 %	2917,09
A-n46-k7	914	1014, 87	1060, 3	1034, 81	11, 02	11.03 %	2314,7
A-n48-k7	1073	1150, 32	1201, 80	1174, 61	14, 7	7.2 %	2742,24
A-n53-k7	1010	1145, 46	1233, 65	1181, 39	18, 9	13.4 %	2555,31
A-n54-k7	1167	1297, 98	1409, 6	1336, 05	25, 5	11.22 %	2530,67
A-n61-k9	1034	1121, 58	1162, 52	1142, 31	11, 5	8.47 %	3183,39
A-n62-k8	1288	1392, 68	1448, 29	1414, 21	14, 3	8.13 %	3990,58
A-n63-k9	1616	1835, 86	1959, 45	1890, 48	30, 8	13.61 %	2948,24
A-n65-k9	1174	1326, 63	1400, 09	1366, 96	18, 97	13 %	3097,57
A-n80-k10	1763	2098, 53	2284, 5	2191, 77	48, 3	19.03 %	3459,88

The column "Best cost CVRP" gives the costs of the best solutions reported so far for the CVRP instances [13]. We note that for $\beta \neq 1$, the optimal solutions of the CVRP instances modeled via the BCP approach are the same as the optimal solutions of the CVRP instances, hence the costs in the column "Best cost CVRP" may be taken as the costs of the best solutions for the CVRP instances modeled via the BCP approach.

The "Difference with CVRP" column shows that for all instances the cost of the best solution for the CVRP is better than that of the best solution obtained for the CVRPED. This latter observation may be seen as an approximation of the theoretical difference between the optimal solution cost of a CVRP instance and the optimal solution cost of the CVRPED instance generated from it, which is predicted by Proposition 4; however, one must be careful since it is not possible to quantify the quality of this approximation due to the diversity and complexity of the algorithms involved in computing those values.

5   Conclusions

This paper studied the capacitated vehicle routing problem with evidential demands. We modeled this problem using a belief function based extension of the chance-constrained programming approach to stochastic mathematical programs. Furthermore, theoretical results relating variations of the optimal solution cost with variations of the parameters involved in the model, were provided. Instances of this difficult optimization problem were also solved using a meta-heuristic. Future works includes addressing this problem using a recourse-based approach, which is another main approach to modeling stochastic mathematical programs [3]. Another perspective is to identify the customers whom more knowledge about their demands would lead to better solutions, that is performing a sensitivity analysis [4].

References

1. Bodin, L.D., Golden, B.L., Assad, A.A., Ball, M.O.: Routing and scheduling of vehicles and crews: the state of the art. Comput. Oper. Res. **10**(2), 63–212 (1983)
2. Charnes, A., Cooper, W.W.: Chance-constrained programming. Manag. Sci. **6**(1), 73–79 (1959)
3. Cordeau, J.-F., Laporte, G., Savelsbergh, M.W.P., Vigo, D.: Vehicle routing (Chap. 6). In: Barnhart, C., Laporte, G. (eds.) Transportation, Handbooks in Operations Research and Management Science, vol. 14, pp. 367–428. Elsevier, Amsterdam (2007)
4. Ferson, S., Tucker, W.T.: Sensitivity in risk analyses with uncertain numbers. Technical report, Sandia National Laboratories (2006)
5. Harmanani, H., Azar, D., Helal, N., Keirouz, W.: A simulated annealing algorithm for the capacitated vehicle routing problem. In: 26th International Conference on Computers and their Applications, New Orleans, USA (2011)
6. Kirby, M.J.L.: The current state of chance-constrained programming. In: Kuhn, H.W. (ed.) Proceedings of the Princeton Symposium on Mathematical Programming, pp. 93–111. Princeton University Press (1970)

7. Kirkpatrick, S., Gelatt, C.D., Vecchi, M.P.: Optimisation by simulated annealing. Science **220**(4598), 671–680 (1983)
8. Laporte, G., Louveaux, F.V., van Hamme, L.: An integer l-shaped algorithm for the capacitated vehicle routing problem with stochastic demands. Oper. Res. **50**, 415–423 (2002)
9. Masri, H., Abdelaziz, F.B.: Belief linear programming. Int. J. Approx. Reason. **51**, 973–983 (2010)
10. Mourelatos, Z.P., Zhou, J.: A design optimization method using evidence theory. J. Mech. Design **128**, 901–908 (2006)
11. Nassreddine, G., Abdallah, F., Denoeux, T.: State estimation using interval analysis and belief function theory: application to dynamic vehicle localization. IEEE Trans. Syst. Man Cybern. B **40**(5), 1205–1218 (2010)
12. Pichon, F., Dubois, D., Denoeux, T.: Relevance and truthfulness in information correction and fusion. Int. J. Approx. Reason. **53**(2), 159–175 (2012)
13. Vehicle Routing Data Sets. http://www.coin-or.org/SYMPHONY/branchandcut/VRP/data/index.htm. Accessed 20 Mar 2016
14. Shafer, G.: A Mathematical Theory of Evidence. Princeton University Press, Princeton (1976)
15. Srivastava, R.K., Deb, K., Tulshyan, R.: An evolutionary algorithm based approach to design optimization using evidence theory. J. Mech. Design **135**(8), 081003-1–081003-12 (2013)
16. Sungur, I., Ordónez, F., Dessouky, M.: A robust optimization approach for the capacitated vehicle routing problem with demand uncertainty. IIE Trans. **40**, 509–523 (2008)
17. Yager, R.R.: Arithmetic and other operations on Dempster-Shafer structures. Int. J. Man Mach. Stud. **25**(4), 357–366 (1986)

An Evidential Pixel-Based Face Blurring Approach

Pauline Minary[1,2(✉)], Frédéric Pichon[1], David Mercier[1], Éric Lefèvre[1], and Benjamin Droit[2]

[1] EA 3926, Laboratoire de Génie Informatique et d'Automatique de l'Artois (LGI2A), University of Artois, Béthune 62400, France
pauline.minary@reseau.sncf.fr,
{frederic.pichon,david.mercier,eric.lefevre}@univ-artois.fr
[2] Département des Télécommunications, SNCF Réseau,
La Plaine Saint Denis, France
benjamin.droit@reseau.sncf.fr

Abstract. Blurring faces on images may be required for anonymity reasons. This may be achieved using face detectors that return boxes potentially containing faces. The most direct way to exploit these detectors is to combine them in order to obtain a more efficient face detection system, producing more accurate boxes. However, contrary to detection, blurring is actually a decision problem situated rather at the pixel level than the box level. Accordingly, we propose in this paper a face blurring system based on face detectors, which operates at the pixel-level. First, for each pixel, detector outputs are converted into a common representation known as belief function using a calibration procedure. Then, calibrated outputs are combined using Dempster's rule. This pixel-based approach does not have some shortcomings of a state-of-the-art box-based approach, and shows better performances on a classical face dataset.

Keywords: Belief functions · Information fusion · Image processing · Evidential calibration · Face blurring

1 Introduction

Blurring faces on images may be required for anonymity reasons. Due to the generally large amount of images to process but also the necessity for good performances (in particular, avoiding missed faces), one must resort to semi-automatic blurring systems – typically, a human operator correcting the outputs of an automatic face detection system.

Face detection can be performed using single detectors [6,10], yet since detectors are generally complementary, *i.e.*, they do not detect only the same faces, using multiple detectors is a means to improve overall performance. Within this scope, Faux [3] proposed a face detection system, which consists in combining outputs of the face detector proposed in [10] and a skin colour detector. This step

J. Vejnarová and V. Kratochvíl (Eds.): BELIEF 2016, LNAI 9861, pp. 222–230, 2016.
DOI: 10.1007/978-3-319-45559-4_23

of combination is conducted within a framework for reasoning under uncertainty called evidence theory [8,9]. However, it does not use all available information. Indeed, for a given image, face detectors such as [10] provide a set of bounding boxes corresponding to the assumed positions of the faces, but they provide as well for each of these boxes a confidence score.

In the context of pedestrian detection, Xu *et al.* [11] recently proposed an evidential approach, which uses these confidence scores. Specifically, multiple detectors are used in Xu *et al.* [11], and to be able to combine them, the scores they produce are transposed into a common representation; this latter procedure is called calibration [7]. Of particular interest is that Xu *et al.* [12] subsequently refined this calibration procedure, in order to account explicitly for uncertainties inherent to such process.

Now, although face blurring may be achieved using simply the bounding boxes outputted by a face detection system, we may remark that it is not exactly the same problem as face detection. Indeed, face blurring amounts merely to deciding whether a given pixel belongs to a face, whereas face detection amounts to determining whether a given set of pixels corresponds to the same face. In other words, the richer box-based information provided by detection systems is not strictly necessary for blurring. This remark opens the path for a different approach to reasoning about blurring, which may then be situated at the pixel-level rather than box-level. In particular, face detectors may still be used but their outputs need not be combined so as to produce boxes as is the case in face detection.

Accordingly, we propose in this paper a face blurring system based on face detectors, which operates at the pixel-level. First, for each pixel, detector outputs are calibrated using Xu *et al.* procedure [12]. Then, calibrated outputs are combined using Dempster's rule [8]. We may already remark that this approach does not have some shortcomings of box-based methods, as will be shown later.

This paper is organized as follows. First, Sect. 2 recalls necessary background on evidence theory and calibration. Then, Sect. 3 exposes what may be considered presently as one of the best available blurring system based on multiple detectors, that is, an evidential system relying on face detection performed using Xu *et al.* detection approach [11], applied to faces rather than pedestrians and improved using Xu *et al.* calibration [12]. Our proposed pixel-based system is then detailed in Sect. 4. An experiment comparing these two approaches is reported in Sect. 5, before concluding in Sect. 6.

2 Evidence Theory and Calibration: Necessary Background

2.1 Evidence Theory

The theory of evidence is a framework for reasoning under uncertainty. Let Ω be a finite set called the frame of discernment, which contains all the possible answers to a given question of interest Q. In this theory, uncertainty with respect to the answer to Q is represented using a *Mass Function* (MF) defined as a mapping $m^\Omega : 2^\Omega \to [0,1]$ that satisfies $\sum_{A \subseteq \Omega} m^\Omega (A) = 1$ and $m^\Omega(\emptyset) = 0$. The quantity $m^\Omega(A)$ corresponds to the share of belief that supports the claim that the answer is contained in $A \subseteq \Omega$ and nothing more specific.

Given two independent MFs m_1^Ω and m_2^Ω about the answer to Q, it is possible to combine them using Dempster's rule of combination. The result of this combination is a MF $m_{1 \oplus 2}^\Omega$ defined by

$$m_{1 \oplus 2}^\Omega(A) = \frac{1}{1 - \kappa} \sum_{B \cap C = A} m_1^\Omega(B) m_2^\Omega(C), \tag{1}$$

for all $A \subseteq \Omega$, where $\kappa = \sum_{B \cap C = \emptyset} m_1^\Omega(B) m_2^\Omega(C)$.

Different decision strategies exist to make a decision about the true answer to Q, given a MF m^Ω on this answer [1]. In particular, the answer having the smallest so-called *upper expected cost* may be selected. The upper expected cost $R^*(\omega)$ of some answer $\omega \in \Omega$ is defined as

$$R^*(\omega) = \sum_{A \subseteq \Omega} m^\Omega(A) \max_{\omega' \in A} c(\omega, \omega'), \tag{2}$$

where $c(\omega, \omega')$ is the cost of deciding ω when the true answer is ω'.

2.2 Evidential Calibration of Binary Classifiers

A binary classifier, *e.g.*, a detector, may return a score associated to its classification decision, which is a valuable information because it provides an indication on how confident the classifier is. The range of these scores differs depending on the features and the type of the classification algorithm used. Thus, transposing scores in a common representation is essential in a context of multi-detectors.

This step, called calibration of a classifier, relies on a training set $\mathcal{L}_{cal} = \{(S_1, Y_1), ..., (S_n, Y_n)\}$, with S_i the score provided by the classifier for the ith sample and $Y_i \in \Omega = \{0, 1\}$ its associated true label. Given a new score S, the purpose of calibration is to estimate the posterior probability distribution $p_S^\Omega = p^\Omega(\cdot|S)$ using $\mathcal{L}_{cal}$.

Yet, certain score values may be less present than others in $\mathcal{L}_{cal}$, thus some estimated probabilities may be less accurate than others. To address this issue, Xu *et al.* [12] proposed several evidential extensions of probabilistic calibration methods. Accordingly, given a new score S, any of Xu *et al.* [12] evidential calibration procedures yields a MF m_S^Ω (rather than a probability distribution p_S^Ω) accounting explicitly for uncertainties in the calibration process.

Among the evidential calibration procedures studied in [12], the likelihood-based logistic regression presents overall better performances than other calibrations. Thus, this will be the calibration used in this paper[1].

---

[1] Due to lack of space, we must refrain from recalling the definition of m_S^Ω obtained under this calibration. We refer the interested reader to [12].

3   An Evidential Box-Based Face Detection Approach

Face blurring may be achieved using simply the boxes outputted by a face detection system. In this section, we present such a system, which may be considered as state-of-the-art with respect to face detection. In a nutshell, it is merely Xu et al. [11] evidential box-based detection approach applied to faces rather than pedestrians and whose calibration step has been replaced by the evidential likelihood-based logistic regression calibration procedure proposed in [12].

3.1   Xu et al. [11] Box-Based Detection Approach Applied to Faces

Let us consider a given image and assume that J face detectors are run on this image. Formally, each detector D_j, $j = 1, ..., J$, provides N_j couples $(B_{i,j}, S_{i,j})$, where $B_{i,j}$ denotes the ith box, $i = 1, ..., N_j$, returned by the jth detector and $S_{i,j}$ is the confidence score associated to this box.

Through a calibration procedure, which will be described in Sect. 3.2, score $S_{i,j}$ is transformed into a MF $m^{\mathcal{B}_{i,j}}$ defined over the frame $\mathcal{B}_{i,j} = \{0, 1\}$, where 1 (resp. 0) means that there is a face (resp. no face) in box $B_{i,j}$.

Then, using a clustering procedure detailed in Sect. 3.3, all the boxes $B_{i,j}$ returned by the J detectors for the considered image, are grouped into K clusters C_k, $k = 1, ..., K$, each of these clusters being represented by a single box B_k.

In addition, for each box $B_{i,j} \in C_k$, its associated MF $m^{\mathcal{B}_{i,j}}$ is assumed to represent a piece of evidence regarding the presence of a face in B_k, that is, $m^{\mathcal{B}_{i,j}}$ is converted into a MF $m_{i,j}^{\mathcal{B}_k}$ on $\mathcal{B}_k = \{0, 1\}$ defined by $m_{i,j}^{\mathcal{B}_k}(A) = m^{\mathcal{B}_{i,j}}(A)$, for all $A \subseteq \{0, 1\}$. These pieces of evidence are then combined using Dempster's rule; this can be done as the sources are considered to be independent and reliable. More complex combination schemes are also considered in [11]. However, only Dempster's rule, which besides presents good performance in [11], is considered here. The combination results in a MF $m^{\mathcal{B}_k}$ representing the overall system uncertainty with respect to the presence of a face in B_k.

3.2   Box-Based Score Calibration for a Detector

In order to transform the score $S_{i,j}$ associated to a box $B_{i,j}$ into a MF $m^{\mathcal{B}_{i,j}}$, detector D_j needs to be calibrated. In particular, the evidential likelihood-based logistic regression calibration procedure [12] may be used instead of the cruder procedures used in [11]. As recalled in Sect. 2.2, such procedures require a training set, which we denote by $\mathcal{L}_{cal,j}$. We recall below how $\mathcal{L}_{cal,j}$ is built.

Assume that L images are available. Besides, the positions of the faces really present in each of these images are known in the form of bounding boxes. Formally, this means that for a given image ℓ, a set of M^ℓ boxes G_r^ℓ, $r = 1, ..., M^\ell$, is available, with G_r^ℓ the rth bounding (ground truth) box on image ℓ.

Furthermore, detector D_j to be calibrated is run on each of these images, yielding N_j^ℓ couples $(B_{t,j}^\ell, S_{t,j}^\ell)$ for each image ℓ, where $B_{t,j}^\ell$ denotes the tth box, $t = 1, ..., N_j^\ell$, returned on image ℓ by detector D_j and $S_{t,j}^\ell$ is the confidence score associated to this box.

From these data, training set $\mathcal{L}_{cal,j}$ is defined as the set of couples $(S_{t,j}^{\ell}, YB_{t,j}^{\ell})$, $\ell = 1, ..., L$, and $t = 1, ..., N_j^{\ell}$, with $YB_{t,j}^{\ell} \in \{0, 1\}$ the label obtained by evaluating whether box $B_{t,j}^{\ell}$ "matches" some face in image ℓ, $i.e.$,

$$YB_{t,j}^{\ell} = \begin{cases} 1 \text{ if } \exists G_r^{\ell}, r = 1, ..., M^{\ell}, \text{ such that } ov(G_r^{\ell}, B_{t,j}^{\ell}) \geq \lambda, \\ 0 \text{ otherwise,} \end{cases}$$

where λ is some threshold in $(0, 1)$ and $ov(G_r^{\ell}, B_{t,j}^{\ell})$ is a measure of the overlap between boxes G_r^{ℓ} and $B_{t,j}^{\ell}$ [2]. It is defined by

$$ov(B_1, B_2) = \frac{area(B_1 \cap B_2)}{area(B_1 \cup B_2)}, \tag{3}$$

for any two boxes B_1 and B_2. Informally, $\mathcal{L}_{cal,j}$ stores the scores associated to all the boxes returned by detector D_j on images where the positions of faces are known, and records for each score whether its associated box is a true or false positive. The MF $m^{\mathcal{B}_{i,j}}$ associated to a new score $S_{i,j}$ and obtained from calibration relying on $\mathcal{L}_{cal,j}$ represents thus uncertainty toward box $B_{i,j}$ containing a face.

3.3 Clustering of Boxes

As several detectors are used, some boxes may be located in the same area of an image, which means that different boxes assume that there is a face in this particular area. The step of clustering allows one to group those boxes and to retain only one per cluster. A greedy approach is used in [11]: the procedure starts by selecting the box $B_{i,j}$ with the highest mass of belief on the face hypothesis and this box is considered as the representative of the first cluster. Then, for each box $B_{u,v}$, $\forall (u, v) \neq (i, j)$, such that the overlap $ov(B_{i,j}, B_{u,v})$ is above the threshold λ, the box $B_{u,v}$ is grouped into the same cluster as $B_{i,j}$, and is then no longer considered. Among the remaining boxes, the box $B_{i,j}$ with the highest $m^{\mathcal{B}_{i,j}}(\{1\})$ is selected as representative of the next cluster, and the procedure is repeated until all the boxes are clustered.

4   Proposed Approach

As explained in Sect. 1, for the purpose of blurring, it seems interesting to work at the pixel level rather than box level. This section gives the full particulars of our proposed pixel-based system.

4.1 Overview of the Approach

To each pixel $p_{x,y}$ in an image, we associate a frame of discernment $\mathcal{P}_{x,y} = \{0, 1\}$, where x and y are the coordinates of the pixel in the image and 1 (resp. 0) means that there is a face (resp. no face) in pixel $p_{x,y}$.

The inputs of our approach are the same as for the box-based approach but are treated differently. In particular, if pixel $p_{x,y}$ belongs to a box $B_{i,j}$, the score $S_{i,j}$ associated to this box $B_{i,j}$ is "transferred" to $p_{x,y}$ and then using the evidential likelihood-based logistic regression calibration procedure together with a training set $\mathcal{L}_{calP,j}$ defined in Sect. 4.2, this score is transformed into a MF $m_{i,j}^{P_{x,y}}$. If pixel $p_{x,y}$ does not belong to any of the boxes returned by detector D_j, we take this into account *via* a MF denoted $m_{*,j}^{P_{x,y}}$ and defined in Sect. 4.2.

Eventually, we then obtain for pixel $p_{x,y}$ several MFs on $\mathcal{P}_{x,y}$, which we combine by Dempster's rule, resulting in a MF $m^{P_{x,y}}$ representing the overall system uncertainty with respect to the presence of a face in $p_{x,y}$.

This approach has in theory a high complexity. However, since we have $m_{*,j}^{P_{x,y}}(A) = m_{*,j}^{P_{x',y'}}(A)$, for all $A \subseteq \{0,1\}$ and $x' \neq x$ or $y' \neq y$, i.e., any two pixels that do not belong to a box of D_j are associated MFs with the same definitions, then pixels that do not belong to any of the returned boxes by the detectors have the same resulting MF. Hence, since this latter case happen often in practice, this allows us to have a common processing for a very large number of pixels, which considerably reduces the complexity.

Let us finally remark that this approach presents several advantages over the one of Sect. 3: first, as will be seen in Sect. 4.2, our calibration step avoids the use of the parameter λ, whose value needs to be fixed either *a priori* (but then it is arguably arbitrary) or empirically; second, our approach avoids the use of clustering, which also involves the parameter λ and that may behave non optimally in a multi-object situation, especially when they are close to each other, which may be the case with faces.

4.2   Pixel-Based Score Calibration for a Detector

Let us describe the set $\mathcal{L}_{calP,j}$ underlying the transformation using calibration of a score $S_{i,j}$ associated to a pixel $p_{x,y}$ by a detector D_j, into a MF $m_{i,j}^{P_{x,y}}$.

For a given image ℓ, each couple $(B_{t,j}^\ell, S_{t,j}^\ell)$ introduced in Sect. 3.2 yields, *via* "transfer", $|B_{t,j}^\ell|$ couples $(p_{d,t,j}^\ell, S_{t,j}^\ell)$, with $d = 1, \ldots, |B_{t,j}^\ell|$, and $|B_{t,j}^\ell|$ the number of pixels in box $B_{t,j}^\ell$, and where $p_{d,t,j}^\ell$ denotes the pixel in d^{th} position in box $B_{t,j}^\ell$.

From these data, we define $\mathcal{L}_{calP,j}$ as the set of couples $(S_{t,j}^\ell, YP_{d,t,j}^\ell)$, with $\ell = 1, \ldots, L$, $t = 1, \ldots, N_j^\ell$, and $d = 1, \ldots, |B_{t,j}^\ell|$, with $YP_{d,t,j}^\ell \in \{0,1\}$ the label simply obtained by checking whether pixel $p_{d,t,j}^\ell$ belongs to some ground truth box G_r^ℓ in the image ℓ, *i.e*,

$$YP_{d,t,j}^\ell = \begin{cases} 1 \text{ if } \exists\, G_r^\ell,\ r = 1, \ldots, M^\ell,\ \text{such that } p_{d,t,j}^\ell \in G_r^\ell, \\ 0 \text{ otherwise.} \end{cases}$$

$\mathcal{L}_{calP,j}$ may pose a complexity issue as $|\mathcal{L}_{calP,j}| = \sum_{\ell=1}^{L} \sum_{t=1}^{N_j^\ell} |B_{t,j}^\ell|$. To avoid this, one may use a smaller set $\mathcal{L}'_{calP,j} \subset \mathcal{L}_{calP,j}$, which represents roughly the same information as $\mathcal{L}_{calP,j}$ and built as follows: for each triple (ℓ, t, j), only

10 couples among the couples $(S_{t,j}^{\ell}, YP_{d,t,j}^{\ell})$, $d = 1, \ldots, |B_{t,j}^{\ell}|$, are selected such that the ratio $\frac{|\{YP_{d,t,j}^{\ell}|d=1,\ldots,|B_{t,j}^{\ell}|,YP_{d,t,j}^{\ell}=1\}|}{|\{YP_{d,t,j}^{\ell}|d=1,\ldots,|B_{t,j}^{\ell}|,YP_{d,t,j}^{\ell}=0\}|}$ is preserved. $\mathcal{L}_{calP,j}'$ has then a size of $|\mathcal{L}_{calP,j}'| = 10 \sum_{\ell=1}^{L} N_j^{\ell}$.

Set $\mathcal{L}_{calP,j}$ is useful for pixels that have a score, i.e., are contained in a box. A pixel $p_{x,y}$ that does no belong to any box returned by a given detector D_j, does not have a score for this detector. Yet, it is reasonable to assume that D_j is almost certain that this pixel does not belong to a face, which can be modelled by a MF denoted $m_{*,j}^{\mathcal{P}_{x,y}}$. A first possibility for $m_{*,j}^{\mathcal{P}_{x,y}}$ could be to simply choose some MF representing this kind of knowledge, but this is not a very satisfying solution. Moreover, it should be taken into account that detectors do not present the exact same performances (e.g., some may have many more pixels not in boxes than others). Within this scope, we propose a solution to obtain $m_{*,j}^{\mathcal{P}_{x,y}}$. For each detector D_j, its classification performance on pixels that do not belong to boxes is estimated using L images, where the positions of the faces really present are known. We denote by TN (True Negative) the number of pixels correctly classified on these images as non-face and FN (False Negative) the number of pixels classified as non-face but actually belonging to a face. $m_{*,j}^{\mathcal{P}_{x,y}}$ can then be defined by $m_{*,j}^{\mathcal{P}_{x,y}}(\{0\}) = \frac{TN}{TN+FN+1}, m_{*,j}^{\mathcal{P}_{x,y}}(\{1\}) = \frac{FN}{TN+FN+1}, m_{*,j}^{\mathcal{P}_{x,y}}(\{0,1\}) = \frac{1}{TN+FN+1}$. This definition may be seen as an evidential binning calibration [12] applied to pixels that do not belong to any of the boxes.

Our modeling of box absence is quite different from that of the box-based method, and arguably more consistent. Indeed, in this latter method, for a given area in an image, there are two different modelings of box absence for a detector depending on the situation: either none of the detectors has provided a box, in which case the area is considered as non face, which amounts to considering that the detectors know that there is no face; or only a subset of the detectors has provided a box, in which case the other detectors are ignored, which is equivalent (under Dempster's rule) to considering that these detectors know nothing.

5 Experiment

In this section, the results of the proposed approach on a literature dataset are presented and compared to that of the box-based method presented in Sect. 3.

We selected three face detectors in the light of the availability of an open source implementation. The first detector is the one proposed by Viola and Jones [10], which is based on a classification algorithm called Adaboost and that uses Haar feature extraction. The second detector is a variant of the previous one: the same classification algorithm is used but with Local Binary Patterns (LBP) feature extraction [4]. The third detector relies on Support Vector Machine (SVM) and uses Histogram of Oriented Gradients (HOG) features [6].

For our experiment, we used a literature database called Face Detection Data Set and Benchmark (FDDB) [5]. It contains the annotations (ground truth) for 5171 faces in a set of 2845 images. In this paper, about 2000 images are used for the training of the detectors, and around 200 for calibration. Performance tests are conducted over the last 600 images, containing 1062 ground truth faces.

As our purpose is to minimize the number of non-blurred face pixels, it is worse to consider a face pixel as non-face than the opposite. In other words, using the decision strategy relying on upper expected costs (Sect. 2.1), decisions were made for each test pixel with costs such that $c(1,0) <= c(0,1)$. More specifically, we fixed $c(1,0) = 1$ and gradually increased $c(0,1)$ starting from $c(0,1) = 1$, to obtain different performance points. To quantify performances, we used recall (proportion of pixels correctly blurred among the pixels to be blurred) and precision (proportion of pixels correctly blurred among blurred pixels).

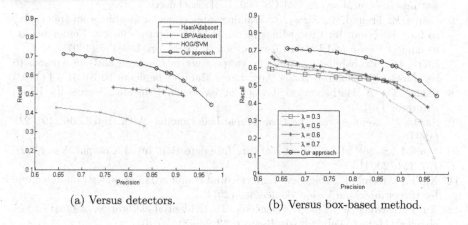

(a) Versus detectors.   (b) Versus box-based method.

Fig. 1. Pixel-based approach vs detectors (1a) and vs box-based approach (1b).

Figure (1a) compare the results of the three selected detectors taken alone with our approach relying on a combination of their outputs. Comparison between the box-based approach used with different values of the overlap threshold λ and our approach is shown in Fig. (1b).

6   Conclusion

In this paper, a pixel-based face blurring system relying on evidential calibration and fusion of several detector outputs was proposed. It brings several advantages over a previous box-based proposal: avoidance of the overlap threshold, of a clustering step, more consistent treatment of box absence, better performances. Several improvements are envisioned such as adding a skin colour detector to the system and refining the calibration and fusion steps. Some experiments are also envisaged on a more challenging database, which presents difficulties such as image quality or low light conditions.

References

1. Denoeux, T.: Analysis of evidence-theoretic decision rules for pattern classification. Pattern Recogn. **30**(7), 1095–1107 (1997)
2. Everingham, M., Van Gool, L., Williams, C.K.I., Winn, J., Zisserman, A.: The PASCAL visual object classes (VOC) challenge. Int. J. Comput. Vis. **88**(2), 303–338 (2010)
3. Faux, F., Luthon, F.: Theory of evidence for face detection and tracking. Int. J. Approximate Reason. **53**(5), 728–746 (2012)
4. Hadid, A., Pietikäinen, M., Ahonen, T.: A discriminative feature space for detecting, recognizing faces. In: Proceedings of the IEEE Computer Society Conference on Computer Vision, Pattern Recognition (CVPR), vol. 2, pp. II-797, 2004 (2011)
5. Jain, V., Learned-Miller, E.: A benchmark for face detection in unconstrained settings. Technical report UM-CS-009, U Massachusetts (2010)
6. Osuna, E., Freund, R., Girosi, F.: Training support vector machines: an application to face detection. In: Proceedings of the IEEE Computer Society Conference on Computer Vision and Pattern Recognition (CVPR), pp. 130–136 (1997)
7. Platt, J.C.: Probabilistic outputs for support vector machines and comparisons to regularized likelihood methods. Adv. Large Margin Classifiers **10**(3), 61–74 (1999)
8. Shafer, G.: A Mathematical Theory of Evidence. Princeton University Press, Princeton (1976)
9. Smets, P., Kennes, R.: The transferable belief model. Artif. Intell. **66**, 191–243 (1994)
10. Viola, P., Jones, M.J.: Robust real-time face detection. Int. J. Comput. Vis. **57**(2), 137–154 (2004)
11. Xu, P., Davoine, F., Denœux, T.: Evidential combination of pedestrian detectors. In: British Machine Vision Conference (2014)
12. Xu, P., Davoine, F., Zha, H., Denoeux, T.: Evidential calibration of binary SVM classifiers. Int. J. Approximate Reason. **72**, 55–70 (2016)

Integrity Preserving Belief Update for Recursive Bayesian Tracking with Non-ideal Sensors

Thanuka L. Wickramarathne[✉]

Department of Electrical and Computer Engineering,
University of Massachusetts Lowell, Lowell, MA 01854, USA
`twickram@nd.edu`

Abstract. The theory of belief functions offers a framework for modeling and reasoning with epistemic uncertainties. While epistemic uncertainties are not well characterized, the Bayesian approaches, such as
the recursive bayesian filtering methods (e.g., Kalman filter) utilize a
sequence of noisy measurements for recursively 'tracking' the behavior
of a dynamic system. While tracking performance is often defined by
the estimation accuracy, the latter in turn depends heavily on what's
being measured by the sensors and how accurately these measurements
are modeled. Characterizing system states and observations solely via
a measurement model may turn out to be inadequate in applications
that involve 'non-ideal' sensors that introduce epistemic uncertainties
into the measurement process, mainly due to the difficulties associated
with capturing highly uncertain, imperfect and subjective nature of these
environments. In this paper, we present a novel approach to utilize belief
theoretic notions to conveniently and accurately model such epistemic
uncertainties that are originated by the use of non-ideal sensors. We
are motivated by the well-understood connection from belief theory to
Bayesian probability to develop this hybrid approach that enables the
utilization of "best of both worlds."

Keywords: Big-data signal processing · Non-ideal sensors · Belief
theory

1 Introduction

The theory of belief functions [1–3] has emerged as one of the most dominant
frameworks for uncertainty processing [4] for decision-making purposes in a wide
variety of application domains [5–18]. While certain types of data uncertainties
may pose several challenges toward probabilistic modeling, the Bayesian probabilistic approaches still form the mainstay of well-understood estimation and
detection techniques. In particular, the Recursive bayesian filtering [19] methods (e.g., Kalman filter [20]), which include perhaps the most widely used and
best-understood 'tracking' technique to-date, utilize a sequence of noisy measurements for recursively 'tracking' the behavior of a dynamic system. While tracking

This work is based on research supported by the U.S. National Science Foundation
via grants IIS-1447795 and EF-1427157.

© Springer International Publishing Switzerland 2016
J. Vejnarová and V. Kratochvíl (Eds.): BELIEF 2016, LNAI 9861, pp. 231–240, 2016.
DOI: 10.1007/978-3-319-45559-4_24

performance in such settings are often defined by the estimation accuracy, the latter in turn depends heavily on what's being measured by the sensors and how accurately these measurements are modeled. In particular, with statistical signal processing community taking an interest in big-data and potential application of recursive bayesian tracking methods therein, one must clearly understand the ramifications of using 'non-ideal' sensors on estimation accuracy. The existing approach to characterizing the system states and observations solely via a measurement model may turn out to be inadequate in these applications, mainly due to the difficulties associated with capturing highly uncertain, imperfect and subjective nature of these environments. Therefore, careful consideration of epistemic uncertainties that originate as result of inability to adequately and accurately (a) take measurements and/or (b) model certain effects that are crucial for the measurement models is of crucial importance in such settings.

In this paper, by deriving from first principles to include explicit sensor reliability terms into estimation equations, we present on-going work on a novel approach to utilize belief theoretic notions to conveniently and accurately model epistemic uncertainties (that are originated by the use of non-ideal sensors) in a recursive bayesian filtering setting. We then introduce an intermediate belief theoretic updating step in order to preserve the 'integrity' of existing evidence, when such updates are carried out with measurements obtained via non-ideal sensors.

2 Preliminaries

2.1 Theory of Belief Functions

Basic Notions. The *frame of discernment (FoD)*, $\Theta = \{\theta_1, \ldots, \theta_n\}$, refers to the set of mutually exclusive and exhaustive propositions of interest; a proposition θ_i represents the lowest level of discernible information.

Definition 1. *The mapping $m : 2^\Theta \mapsto [0,1]$ is a* basic probability assignment (BPA) *or* mass function *for the FoD Θ if $\sum_{B \subseteq \Theta} m(B) = 1$ with $m(\emptyset) = 0$. Consider the proposition $B \subseteq \Theta$. Let $\overline{B} = \Theta \setminus B$.*

(i) *When $m(B) > 0$, B is referred to as a* focal element *and the quantity $m(B)$ is the* mass allocated to B.
(ii) *The set of focal elements is the* core $\mathfrak{F}$; *the triplet $\mathcal{E} \equiv \{\Theta, \mathfrak{F}, m(.)\}$ is the corresponding* body of evidence (BoE).
(iii) *The mapping $\mathrm{Bl} : 2^\Theta \mapsto [0,1]$ where $\mathrm{Bl}(B) = \sum_{C \subseteq B} m(C)$ is the* belief *of B; the mapping $\mathrm{Pl} : 2^\Theta \mapsto [0,1]$ where $\mathrm{Pl}(B) = 1 - \mathrm{Bl}(\overline{B})$ is the* plausibility *of B.*

2.2 Recursive Bayesian Filtering

Problem Statement. Consider a dynamic system $\mathbf{H}$. Let $\mathbf{x}_k \in \Theta_{\mathbf{x}}$ denote the state of $\mathbf{H}$ at time t_k, where $\Theta_{\mathbf{x}}$ represents all possible states. The evolution of $\mathbf{H}$

is given by the *system model,* $\mathbf{x}_k = \mathbf{f}(\mathbf{x}_{k-1}, \mathbf{v}_{k-1})$, where $\mathbf{f}(\textbf{.})$ is a (possibly) non-linear function and $\mathbf{v}_{k-1}$ denotes i.i.d. process noise. The objective of tracking is to recursively estimate $\mathbf{x}_k$ from measurements given by *measurement model,* $\mathbf{z}_k = \mathbf{h}(\mathbf{x}_k, \mathbf{n}_k)$, where $\mathbf{h}(\textbf{.})$ is a (possibly) non-linear function of $\mathbf{x}_k$ and i.i.d. measurement noise $\mathbf{n}_k$.

Optimal Bayesian Formulation. Given the measurements $\mathbf{z}_{1:k}$ up to time t_k and the initial pmf/pdf $p(\mathbf{x}_0|\mathbf{z}_0) \equiv p(\mathbf{x}_0)$, the objective here is to recursively calculate a degree of belief in the state $\mathbf{x}_k$, viz., to recursively construct $p(\mathbf{x}_k|\mathbf{z}_{1:k})$. Now, suppose $p(\mathbf{x}_{k-1}|\mathbf{z}_{1:k-1})$ is available at time t_{k-1}. Then, in principle, $p(\mathbf{x}_k|\mathbf{z}_{1:k})$ can be obtained in two steps:

(a) prediction step: use the system model to obtain the prior pdf of $\mathbf{x}_k$ via

$$p(\mathbf{x}_k|\mathbf{z}_{1:k-1}) = \sum_{\mathbf{x}_{k-1}} p(\mathbf{x}_k|\mathbf{x}_{k-1})p(\mathbf{x}_{k-1}|\mathbf{z}_{1:k-1}). \tag{1}$$

(b) update step: As a measurement $\mathbf{z}_k$ becomes available at t_k, *update* the prior estimate of $\mathbf{x}_k$ via Bayes' rule as

$$p(\mathbf{x}_k|\mathbf{z}_{1:k}) = \frac{1}{p(\mathbf{z}_k|\mathbf{z}_{1:k-1})} \, p(\mathbf{x}_k|\mathbf{z}_{1:k-1})p(\mathbf{z}_k|\mathbf{x}_k), \tag{2}$$

where the normalizing constant is given by,

$$p(\mathbf{z}_k|\mathbf{z}_{1:k-1}) = \sum_{\mathbf{x}_k} p(\mathbf{z}_k|\mathbf{x}_k) \, p(\mathbf{x}_k|\mathbf{z}_{1:k-1}). \tag{3}$$

3 Bayesian Tracking with Non-ideal Sensors

A non-ideal sensor may report a noisy or even an erroneous version of the actual measurement corresponding to the current system state. Such sensing include situations where (a) the sensors are unable to adequately and accurately take measurements and/or (b) the sensing process is not captured by the measurement model. Often times, use of alternative measurement models are also not feasible, since only limited data or knowledge are available to properly characterize sensing process in situations where non-ideal sensors are used, e.g., a faulty sensor making an erroneous mapping or an eye-witness not accurately identifying the target.

Problem Statement. Suppose the non-ideal sensor reports $\hat{\mathbf{z}}_k$ instead of reporting $\mathbf{z}_k$ for system state $\mathbf{x}_k$, where $\mathbf{z}_k$ is now not observable. However, the credibility of each measurement $\hat{\mathbf{z}}_k$ can be indirectly captured via $p(\hat{\mathbf{z}}_k|\mathbf{z}_k)$, which is a probabilistic characterization of sensor reliability estimated over time (alternatively, non-ideal sensor maps $\mathbf{z}_k$ to $\hat{\mathbf{z}}_k$ via $p(\hat{\mathbf{z}}_k|\mathbf{z}_k)$). Then, we are interested in recursively computing $p(\mathbf{x}_k|\hat{\mathbf{z}}_{1:k})$ as measurements $\hat{\mathbf{z}}_k$ become available.

State Estimation. Let $p(\mathbf{x}_0|\hat{\mathbf{z}}_0) \equiv p(\mathbf{x}_0)$ denote the initial pdf. Now, suppose $p(\mathbf{x}_{k-1}|\hat{\mathbf{z}}_{1:k-1})$ is available at time t_{k-1}. Then, let us derive the prediction and update steps as follows.

(a) Prediction step: obtain the prior pdf of state at time t_k via

$$p(\mathbf{x}_k|\hat{\mathbf{z}}_{1:k-1}) = \sum_{\mathbf{x}_{k-1}} p(\mathbf{x}_k, \mathbf{x}_{k-1}|\hat{\mathbf{z}}_{1:k-1})$$

$$= \sum_{\mathbf{x}_{k-1}} p(\mathbf{x}_k|\mathbf{x}_{k-1}) \, p(\mathbf{x}_{k-1}|\hat{\mathbf{z}}_{1:k-1}) \tag{4}$$

where, $p(\mathbf{x}_k|\mathbf{x}_{k-1}, \hat{\mathbf{z}}_{1:k}) = p(\mathbf{x}_k|\mathbf{x}_{k-1})$ describes a 1st order *Markov* process.

(b) Update step: At time t_k, use the measurement $\hat{\mathbf{z}}_k$ to *update* the prior via

$$p(\mathbf{x}_k|\hat{\mathbf{z}}_{1:k}) = \frac{p(\mathbf{x}_k, \hat{\mathbf{z}}_k, \hat{\mathbf{z}}_{1:k-1})}{p(\hat{\mathbf{z}}_k, \hat{\mathbf{z}}_{1:k-1})}$$

$$= \frac{p(\hat{\mathbf{z}}_k|\mathbf{x}_k, \hat{\mathbf{z}}_{1:k-1}) p(\mathbf{x}_k|\hat{\mathbf{z}}_{1:k-1})}{p(\hat{\mathbf{z}}_k|\hat{\mathbf{z}}_{1:k-1})}, \tag{5}$$

where the normalizing constant is given by

$$p(\hat{\mathbf{z}}_k|\hat{\mathbf{z}}_{1:k-1}) = \sum_{\mathbf{x}_k} p(\hat{\mathbf{z}}_k|\mathbf{x}_k, \hat{\mathbf{z}}_{1:k-1}) p(\mathbf{x}_k|\hat{\mathbf{z}}_{1:k-1}), \tag{6}$$

with

$$p(\hat{\mathbf{z}}_k|\mathbf{x}_k, \hat{\mathbf{z}}_{1:k-1}) = \sum_{\mathbf{z}_k} p(\hat{\mathbf{z}}_k, \mathbf{z}_k|\mathbf{x}_k, \hat{\mathbf{z}}_{1:k-1})$$

$$= \sum_{\mathbf{z}_k} p(\hat{\mathbf{z}}_k|\mathbf{z}_k) p(\mathbf{z}_k|\mathbf{x}_k) \tag{7}$$

where $p(\hat{\mathbf{z}}_k|\mathbf{z}_k)$ denotes the non-ideal sensor characteristics; precisely, how the sensor maps $\mathbf{z}_k$ to $\hat{\mathbf{z}}_k$. From a practical stand point, one could relate this to sensor reliability characteristics (see Example 1 for an illustration).

Example 1. Consider a 3-state dynamic system described by state- and measurement-models of the form

$$p(\mathbf{x_k}|\mathbf{x}_{k-1}) = \begin{vmatrix} \alpha & \frac{1-\alpha}{2} & \frac{1-\alpha}{2} \\ \frac{1-\alpha}{2} & \alpha & \frac{1-\alpha}{2} \\ \frac{1-\alpha}{2} & \frac{1-\alpha}{2} & \alpha \end{vmatrix} ; \quad p(\mathbf{z_k}|\mathbf{x}_k) = \begin{vmatrix} \beta & \frac{1-\beta}{2} & \frac{1-\beta}{2} \\ \frac{1-\beta}{2} & \beta & \frac{1-\beta}{2} \\ \frac{1-\beta}{2} & \frac{1-\beta}{2} & \beta \end{vmatrix} ,$$

where the parameters $\alpha, \beta \in \Re$ satisfy $1/3 \leq \alpha, \beta \leq 1$ (note that $1/3$ generate a uniform distribution). When sensors are ideal (or assumed to be ideal), one directly observes the noisy measurement $\mathbf{z}_k$, which is used for state updating.

Suppose we can only obtain $\hat{\mathbf{z}}_\mathbf{k}$ via some non-ideal sensor, which now introduce epistemic uncertainty into the measurement process. For analysis, let us use a probabilistic mapping $p(\hat{\mathbf{z}}_k|\mathbf{z}_k)$ to map a 'true' observation $\mathbf{z}_k$ to a noisy or erroneous measurement $\hat{\mathbf{z}}_k$, where $p(\hat{\mathbf{z}}_k|\mathbf{z}_k)$ is given by

$$p(\hat{\mathbf{z}}_k|\mathbf{z}_k) = \begin{vmatrix} \gamma & \frac{1-\gamma}{2} & \frac{1-\gamma}{2} \\ \frac{1-\gamma}{2} & \gamma & \frac{1-\gamma}{2} \\ \frac{1-\gamma}{2} & \frac{1-\gamma}{2} & \gamma \end{vmatrix},$$

4 Belief Theoretic Approach to Integrity Preserving Update

4.1 Integrity of Existing Evidence

Preserving the integrity of existing body of knowledge requires one to compare the likelihood of the occurrence of current measurements given the current state of the system. While the prediction step takes this into account to a certain degree, it is also important to understand the system level requirements for enabling such tasks (Fig. 1).

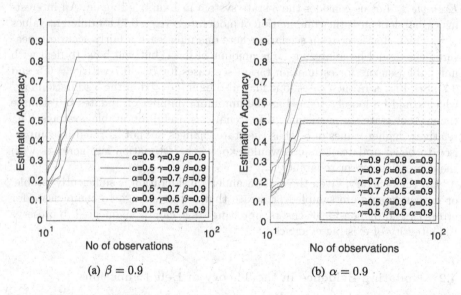

(a) $\beta = 0.9$ (b) $\alpha = 0.9$

Fig. 1. The relationship of estimation accuracy versus sensor reliability, where subfigure (a) and subfigure (b) show the behavior for $\beta = 0.9$ and $\alpha = 0.9$, respectively. Here, a hidden Markov model with state transition pmf $p(\mathbf{x}_k|\mathbf{x}_{k-1})$ and emission pmfs $p(\mathbf{z}_k|\mathbf{x}_k)$ are used to generate state and observation sequences of length $N = 100$ given by $\mathcal{X} \equiv \{\mathbf{x}_k \in \{1,2,3\} \mid k = 1,\ldots,N\}$ and $\mathcal{Z} \equiv \{\mathbf{z}_k \in \{1,2,3\} \mid k = 1,\ldots,N\}$, respectively. We then utilize $\mathcal{Z}$ and $p(\hat{\mathbf{z}}_k|\mathbf{z}_k)$ to generate non-ideal observation sequence $\hat{\mathcal{Z}} \equiv \{\hat{\mathbf{z}}_k \in \{1,2,3\} \mid k = 1,\ldots,N\}$. Also, the estimation error is the averaged mean squared error given by $\frac{1}{N}\sum_k \|\mathbf{x}_k - \hat{\mathbf{x}}_k\|$, where the experiment was repeated for 1000 times.

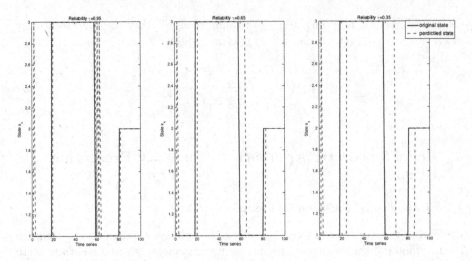

Fig. 2. The relationship of 'estimation lag' and sensor reliability γ, illustrating the potential for using unreliable sensors in rather stable systems.

Example 2. Let us consider the 3-state system in Example 1 again. An interesting case to look at is the combination of moderate β (e.g., 0.7) for different values of γ, which characterizes a scenario where one may learn a fairly accurate measurement model by analyzing large amount of data, but will have to deal with unreliable sensors for estimation tasks (see cases for $\beta = 0.7$ with $\gamma = 0.5$ and 0.7). See Fig. 2. In such cases, one may also be interested in the 'estimation lag,' which could be loosely defined as the minimum number of updates to estimate the current state. In particular, this scenario is useful for 'stable' systems (i.e., relatively higher values of α, thus the state changes are not as rapid in comparison to belief updates). As one would expect, the estimation lag increases with the decreasing sensor reliability.

On the contrary, given the system under consideration is sufficiently 'stable' or measurements are sampled at a rate that is fast enough to compensate for errors caused by non-ideal sensors, updating stage can be augmented to preserve the integrity of existing evidence.

4.2 Updating Evidence in the Theory of Belief Functions

Updating evidence or revision of belief refers to the process of updating a BoE $\mathcal{E}_i[k]$ with evidence received from the BoEs $\mathcal{E}_j[k]$, $j = \{1, \ldots, n\} \setminus i$, to arrive at $\mathcal{E}_i[k+1]$. As in probability theory, *conditioning* is the primary tool for evidence updating [21] in belief theory. The *Fagin-Halpern (FH) conditional,* one of the many conditionals available, offers a unique probabilistic interpretation and a natural transition to the Bayesian conditional notion [22].

Theorem 1 (FH Conditionals [22]). *Given a BoE* $\mathcal{E} = \{\Theta, \mathfrak{F}, m\}$, *the conditional belief* $\mathrm{Bl}(B|A) : 2^{\Theta} \mapsto [0, 1]$ *and the conditional plausibility* $\mathrm{Pl}(B|A)$:

$2^{\Theta} \mapsto [0,1]$ *of an arbitrary* $B \subseteq \Theta$ *given the conditioning event* A *s.t.* $\mathrm{Bl}(A) > 0$ *are*

$$\mathrm{Bl}(B|A) = \frac{\mathrm{Bl}(A \cap B)}{\mathrm{Bl}(A \cap B) + \mathrm{Pl}(A \cap \overline{B})}; \qquad \mathrm{Pl}(B|A) = \frac{\mathrm{Pl}(A \cap B)}{\mathrm{Pl}(A \cap B) + \mathrm{Bl}(A \cap \overline{B})},$$

respectively.

In terms of assigning support to a probabilistic event, the FH conditional belief and plausibility correspond to the inner and outer measures of a non-measurable event [22]. Moreover, the extensive study undertaken in [23] identifies various elegant properties of the FH conditionals including their equivalence to other popular notions of DS theoretic conditionals (such as those in [24, 25]) under the unifying umbrella of the *Choquet integral*. Therefore, FH conditionals perhaps provide the best avenue to handle epistemic uncertainties introduced by non-ideal sensors within a recursive bayesian filtering setup.

4.3   Conditions for Preserving Existing Body of Evidence

Let us now look at conditions that can be set to preserve the integrity of existing evidence in a recursive bayesian filtering setting. In particular, we are interested in deriving conditions under which the integrity of current state estimates are preserved by potentially erroneous measurements received from non-ideal sensors. He we assume that the system under consideration is either stable or measurements are sampled at a fast enough rate to skip several update steps.

Problem Statement. Suppose the non-ideal sensor reports $\hat{\mathbf{z}}_k$ instead of reporting $\mathbf{z}_k$ for system state $\mathbf{x}_k$, where $\mathbf{z}_k$ is now not observable. Let us assume that the reliability γ of the non-ideal sensor is given (or estimated outside of this problem). Let $p(\mathbf{x}_0|\hat{\mathbf{z}}_0) \equiv p(\mathbf{x}_0)$ denote the initial pdf. Given $p(\mathbf{x}_{k-1}|\hat{\mathbf{z}}_{1:k-1})$, we are interested in recursively computing $p(\mathbf{x}_k|\hat{\mathbf{z}}_{1:k})$ as measurement $\hat{\mathbf{z}}_k$ become available at time t_k. Also, assume the belief and plausibility counterparts of $p(\mathbf{x}_{k-1}|\hat{\mathbf{z}}_{1:k-1})$ as given by $\mathrm{Bl}(\mathbf{x}_{k-1}|\hat{\mathbf{z}}_{1:k-1})$ and $\mathrm{Pl}(\mathbf{x}_{k-1}|\hat{\mathbf{z}}_{1:k-1})$ are also maintained, where $\mathrm{Bl}(\mathbf{x}_{k-1}|\hat{\mathbf{z}}_{1:k-1}) \leq p(\mathbf{x}_{k-1}|\hat{\mathbf{z}}_{1:k-1}) \leq \mathrm{Pl}(\mathbf{x}_{k-1}|\hat{\mathbf{z}}_{1:k-1})$.

State Estimation. Given $p(\mathbf{x}_{k-1}|\hat{\mathbf{z}}_{1:k-1})$,
    (a) Prediction step: obtain the prior pdf of state at time t_k via

$$p(\mathbf{x}_k|\hat{\mathbf{z}}_{1:k-1}) = \sum_{\mathbf{x}_{k-1}} p(\mathbf{x}_k|\mathbf{x}_{k-1}) \, p(\mathbf{x}_{k-1}|\hat{\mathbf{z}}_{1:k-1}) \tag{8}$$

where, the system model $p(\mathbf{x}_k|\mathbf{x}_{k-1})$ is utilized to generate the predicted state. Similarly, use the system model $\mathrm{Bl}(\mathbf{x}_k|\mathbf{x}_{k-1}) = p(\mathbf{x}_k|\mathbf{x}_{k-1})$ to generate the belief theoretic counterparts of predicted state given by $\mathrm{Bl}(\mathbf{x}_k|\hat{\mathbf{z}}_{1:k-1})$ and $\mathrm{Pl}(\mathbf{x}_k|\hat{\mathbf{z}}_{1:k-1})$. Trivially, we will have $\mathrm{Bl}(\mathbf{x}_k|\hat{\mathbf{z}}_{1:k-1}) \leq p(\mathbf{x}_k|\hat{\mathbf{z}}_{1:k}) \leq \mathrm{Pl}(\mathbf{x}_k|\hat{\mathbf{z}}_{1:k-1})$.

(b) Update step: The update step now must be carried out in such a manner to preserve the integrity of current estimates from potentially erroneous measurement $\hat{\mathbf{z}}_k$. The conditional approach to DS theoretic evidence updating, which espouses these FH conditional notions [26–29], perhaps provide an ideal solution for the task at hand.

Definition 2 (Conditional Update Equation (CUE)). *The CUE that updates* $\mathcal{E}_1[k]$ *with the evidence in* $\mathcal{E}_2[k]$ *is*

$$Bl_1(B)[k+1] = \alpha_1[k]\,Bl_1(B)[k] + \sum_{A \in \mathfrak{F}_2[k]} \beta_2(A)[k]\,Bl_2(B|A)[k], \ \forall k \geq 0,$$

where $\alpha_1[k], \beta_2(\bullet)[k] \in \Re^+$ *satisfy,* $\alpha_1[k] + \sum_{A \in \mathfrak{F}_2[k]} \beta_2(A)[k] = 1$

and the conditional belief $Bl(B|A)$ is given by the Fagin-Halpern conditional $Bl(B|A) = Bl(A \cap B)/[Bl(A \cap B) + Pl(A \cap \overline{B})]$ [22] (please refer to [26–29] for guidelines on selection of parameters $\alpha[k]$ and $\beta[k]$).

In order to preserve the integrity of exiting evidence, we will enforce that

$$Bl(\mathbf{x}_k|\hat{\mathbf{z}}_{1:k-1}) \leq Bl(\mathbf{x}_k|\hat{\mathbf{z}}_{1:k}) \leq Pl(\mathbf{x}_k|\hat{\mathbf{z}}_{1:k-1}) \tag{9}$$

must be satisfied by the update step. If this condition is satisfied, then choose an appropriate conversion to generate the probabilistic counterpart $p(\mathbf{x}_k|\hat{\mathbf{z}}_{1:k})$ of $Bl(\mathbf{x}_k|\hat{\mathbf{z}}_{1:k})$. Otherwise, set $p(\mathbf{x}_k|\hat{\mathbf{z}}_{1:k}) = p(\mathbf{x}_{k-1}|\hat{\mathbf{z}}_{1:k})$ and discard measurement $\hat{\mathbf{z}}_k$.

5 Conclusion

Recursive bayesian filtering methods provide a well-established mechanism for 'tracking' the behavior of a dynamic system via a sequence of noisy measurements. However, little attention has been given to the case, where the sensors utilized are 'non-ideal' that introduce epistemic uncertainties into the measurement process. By utilizing a tandem approach, we present an on-going effort on utilizing belief theoretic notions in the update stages of bayesian recursive tracking application, thus allowing one to conveniently and accurately model such epistemic uncertainties that are originated by the use of non-ideal sensors. Furthermore, an approach for state update while preserving the integrity of existing evidence is presented.

References

1. Shafer, G.: A Mathematical Theory of Evidence. Princeton University Press, Princeton (1976)
2. Yager, R.R., Fedrizzi, M., Kacprzyk, J.: Advances in the Dempster-Shafer Theory of Evidence. Wiley, New York (1994)
3. Blackman, S., Popoli, R.: Design and Analysis of Modern Tracking Systems. Artech House, Norwood (1999)

4. Parsons, S.: Current approaches to handling imperfect information in data and knowledge bases. IEEE Trans. Knowl. Data Eng. **8**(3), 353–372 (1996)
5. Boston, J.R.: A signal detection system based on Demspter-Shafer theory and comparison to fuzzy detection. IEEE Trans. Syst. Man Cybern. **30**(1), 45–51 (2000)
6. Altincay, H., Demirekler, M.: Speaker identification by combining multiple classifiers using Dempster-Shafer theory of evidence. Speech Commun. **41**(4), 531–547 (2003)
7. Chen, T.M., Venkataramanan, V.: Demspter-Shafer theory for intrusion detection in ad hoc networks. IEEE Internet Comput. **9**(6), 35–41 (2005)
8. Dewasurendra, D.A., Bauer, P.H., Premaratne, K.: Evidence filtering. IEEE Trans. Signal Process. **55**(12), 5796–5805 (2007)
9. Bogler, P.L.: Shafer-Demspter reasoning with applications to multisensor target identification systems. IEEE Trans. Syst. Man Cybern. **17**(6), 968–977 (1987)
10. Leung, H., Wu, J.: Bayesian and Dempster-Shafer target identification for radar surveillance. IEEE Trans. Aerosp. Electron. Syst. **36**(2), 432–447 (2000)
11. Delmotte, F., Smets, P.: Target identification based on the transferable belief model interpretation of Dempster-Shafer model. IEEE Trans. Syst. Man Cybern. Part A: Syst. Hum. **34**(4), 457–471 (2004)
12. Le Hegarat-Mascle, S., Bloch, I., Vidal-Madjar, D.: Application of Dempster-Shafer evidence theory to unsupervised classification in multisource remote sensing. IEEE Trans. Geosci. Remote Sens. **35**(4), 1018–1031 (1997)
13. Anand, S.S., Bell, D.A., Hughes, J.G.: EDM: a general framework for data mining based on evidence theory. Data Knowl. Eng. **18**, 189–223 (1996)
14. Cai, D., McTear, M.F., McClean, S.I.: Knowledge discovery in distributed databases using evidence theory. Int. J. Intell. Syst. **15**(8), 745–761 (2000)
15. Elouedi, Z., Mellouli, K., Smets, P.: Belief decision trees: theoretical foundations. Int. J. Approx. Reason. **28**(2/3), 91–124 (2001)
16. Altincay, H.: A Dempster-Shafer theoretic framework for boosting based ensemble design. Pattern Anal. Appl. J. **8**(3), 287–302 (2005)
17. Hewawasam, K.K.R.G.K., Premaratne, K., Shyu, M.-L.: Rule mining and classification in a situation assessment application: a belief theoretic approach for handling data imperfections. IEEE Trans. Syst. Man Cybernet. Part B: Cybernet. **37**(6), 1446–1459 (2007)
18. Hewawasam, R., Premaratne, K.: Dependency based reasoning in a Dempster-Shafer theoretic framework. In: Proceedings of the International Conference on Information Fusion (FUSION), Quebec, Canada, pp. 1–8, July 2007
19. Arulampalam, M.S., Maskell, S., Gordon, N., Clapp, T.: A tutorial on particle filters for online nonlinear/non-gaussian Bayesian tracking. IEEE Trans. Signal Process. **50**(2), 174–188 (2002)
20. Sinopoli, B., Schenato, L., Franceschetti, M., Poolla, K., Jordan, M.I., Sastry, S.S.: Kalman filtering with intermittent observations. IEEE Trans. Autom. Control **49**(9), 1453–1464 (2004)
21. Chrisman, L.: Incremental conditioning of lower and upper probabilities. Int. J. Approx. Reason. **13**(1), 1–25 (1995)
22. Fagin, R., Halpern, J.Y.: A new approach to updating beliefs. In: Bonissone, P.P., Henrion, M., Kanal, L.N., Lemmer, J.F. (eds.) Proceedings of the Conference on Uncertainty in Artificial Intelligence (UAI), pp. 347–374. Elsevier Science, New York (1991)
23. Denneberg, D.: Conditioning (updating) non-additive measures. Ann. Oper. Res. **52**(1), 21–42 (1994)

24. Walley, P.: Statistical Reasoning with Imprecise Probabilities. Chapman and Hall, London (1991)
25. Jaffray, J.Y.: Bayesian updating and belief functions. IEEE Trans. Syst. Man Cybern. **22**(5), 1144–1152 (1992)
26. Kulasekere, E.C., Premaratne, K., Dewasurendra, D.A., Shyu, M.-L., Bauer, P.H.: Conditioning and updating evidence. Int. J. Approx. Reason. **36**(1), 75–108 (2004)
27. Premaratne, K., Dewasurendra, D.A., Bauer, P.H.: Evidence combination in an environment with heterogeneous sources. IEEE Transa. Syst. Man Cybern. Part A: Syst. Hum. **37**(3), 298–309 (2007)
28. Premaratne, K., Murthi, M.N., Zhang, J., Scheutz, M., Bauer, P.H.: A Dempster-Shafer theoretic conditional approach to evidence updating for fusion of hard and soft data. In: Proceedings of the International Conference on Information Fusion (FUSION), Seattle, WA, pp. 2122–2129, July 2009
29. Wickramarathne, T.L., Premaratne, K., Murthi, M.N., Scheutz, M.: A Dempster-Shafer theoretic evidence updating strategy for non-identical frames of discernment. In: Proceedings of the Workshop on the Theory of Belief Functions (BELIEF), Brest, France, April 2010

An Evidential RANSAC Algorithm
and Its Application to GNSS Positioning

Salim Zair[✉], Sylvie Le Hégarat-Mascle, and Emmanuel Seignez

SATIE, Université Paris-Sud, ENS Cachan, CNRS, Université Paris-Saclay,
91405 Orsay, France
{salim.zair,sylvie.le-hegarat,emmanuel.seignez}@u-psud.fr

Abstract. The RANSAC (random sampling consensus) approach was
proposed for robust estimation in presence of outliers, that are detected
as inconsistent with the solution. In this paper, we adapt its principle to
derive an algorithm detecting inconsistent sources based on their modelling in evidential framework. We compare two (in)consistency criteria:
the classic empty set mass and Pichon's consistency measure that was
recently proposed. The proposed approach is applied to positioning from
Global Navigation Satellite Systems (GNSS), specifically in constrained
environments, i.e. in the presence of Non Line Of Sight and multipath
receptions. Results are compared with former approaches either in belief
functions framework or using interval analysis, stating the interest of the
proposed algorithm.

Keywords: Outlier detection · Belief function theory · Consistency
measure · Global navigation satellite systems

1 Introduction

Positioning is required in many applications involving autonomous navigation.
Among Global Navigation Satellite Systems (GNSS), the Global Positioning
System (GPS) is the most popular one, widely used for outdoor localization.
However, localization is still an issue in constrained environments such as urban
canyons because of the presence of multipath signals and Non-Line-Of-Sight
(NLOS) receptions. These phenomena induce an overestimation of the distance
between satellite and receiver called *pseudo-range* (PR), and then, degrade the
precision of the positioning. Several strategies have been proposed to detect some
erroneous measurements (called outliers) or/and to improve the positioning accuracy. One of them is to combine GNSS data with embedded sensors (e.g., cam-
era, inertial measurement unit) and/or geographical informations (e.g., digital
maps). Focusing on localization using only-GPS data, the proposed approaches
can be divided into two main categories: (i) methods that aim at enhancing
GNSS accuracy by filtering, estimating or correcting the PR errors or multipath
biases (e.g. [5]) and (ii) methods that consist in detecting and discarding the erroneous PR from the localization process. The statistical tests such as used in the

© Springer International Publishing Switzerland 2016
J. Vejnarová and V. Kratochvíl (Eds.): BELIEF 2016, LNAI 9861, pp. 241–250, 2016.
DOI: 10.1007/978-3-319-45559-4_25

Receiver Autonomous Integrity Monitoring (RAIM) [2] and the interval analysis belongs to this second category just as the method we propose. The RAIM method allows us to detect at most one outlier per epoch (i.e., time sample) that may be insufficient for urban areas. Then, some probabilistic approaches have been proposed to deal with several simultaneous outliers, e.g. coupling failure detection and exclusion with RAIM or adapting the classic RANSAC (RANdom SAmple Consensus) algorithm [4]. Zair et al. [10] proposes a very robust free-parameter approach based on an a-contrario modeling and a Number of False Alarms (NFA) criterion. However, if the uncertainty is modelled in a rather fine and sophisticated way using probabilist approaches, the imprecision is not distinguished from uncertainty. Then, besides statistical approaches, some methods specifically focus on the modelling of the imprecision of the sensors. In particular, Interval Analysis (IA), that takes into account the imprecision of all the sources, was applied to indoor localization and to outdoor GNSS localization. In IA, the q-relaxation technique was proposed to deal with outliers by removing until q sources out of the N initial sources, in order to get a non-empty solution. Recently, [7] presented the idea of relaxing sources in belief function combination generalizing the IA q-relaxation technique. Assuming that only r sources have to be considered out of the N available sources, we denote by H_r^N this hypothesis about the number of reliable sources. Then, for any N-tuple $\boldsymbol{A}$ of hypotheses A_i: $\forall i \in [1, N], A_i \in 2^\Omega$, $\boldsymbol{A} = \{A_1, A_2, \ldots, A_N\}$, $\Gamma_r(\boldsymbol{A})$ represents this metaknowledge:

$$\Gamma_r(\boldsymbol{A}) = \bigcup_{\mathcal{A} \subseteq \{A_1, \cdots, A_N\}, |\mathcal{A}| = r} (\cap_{A_i \in \mathcal{A}} A_i), \tag{1}$$

where r is the parameter representing the assumed number of reliable sources.

Then, the mass value of an hypothesis B is the sum, over $\Gamma_r(\boldsymbol{A})$ corresponding to B, of the products of masses of elements of $\boldsymbol{A}$:

$$m[H_r^N](B) = \sum_{\substack{\boldsymbol{A} \subseteq \Omega^N; \\ \Gamma_r(\boldsymbol{A}) = B}} \left[\prod_{i=1}^N m_i^\Omega(A_i) \right], \tag{2}$$

where m_i^Ω denotes the mass function. Besides generalizing the classic combination rules [7], e.g. conjunctive rule ($r = N$) and disjunction rule ($r = 1$), the approach is similar to the q-relaxation technique in IA when the knowledge is categorical (one focal element).

In this paper, we propose an approach inspired from RANSAC algorithm. It allows us to detect iteratively the outliers and, based on an evidential consistency measure (either the opposite of the classical Belief Function Theory (BFT) conflict measure, namely the empty set mass, or the maximum of the contour function as proposed by [3]) to partition the dataset between two subsets respectively containing the inliers and the outliers.

In our application, the discernment frame is the set of possible discrete localizations, in East and North coordinates. Depending on the a priori hypothesis about whole research area and discretization step, the cardinality of such 2D discernment frame may be very large. For instance, considering an area of 100 m by 100 m with $1\,m^2$ resolution, $|\Omega| = 10000$, which is huge comparing to classical applications of BFT. This issue may be handled representing the focal elements by subsets of 2D boxes and taking advantage of their low number for easy manipulation [1,8]. While remaining tractable thanks to the redefinition of the basic set operators (intersection, union), such a representation is finer than processing independently 1D intervals as in [6].

2 Proposed Approach

RANSAC algorithm is based on two ideas. The first one is to avoid the whole exploration of the solution space. For this the solutions to test are computed according to a given process (that generally corresponds to only considering exact solutions for a subset of measurements). In this work, we follow this idea of a 'guided' exploration of the space solution. However, the way to explore it differs from those used in classic RANSAC: it is based on addition/removal of a data measurement (i.e. an information piece) in/from the current set of measurements (information pieces) considered as inliers (i.e. truthful).

The second idea is to keep the solution that is the most 'consensual', i.e. that induces the highest number of inliers defined as measurements presenting a noise level lower than a given threshold (that is a parameter of the method). Following this idea that is also those of the q-relaxation (since a criterion maximizing the number of inliers boils down to a criterion minimizing the number of outliers), after exploring partially the solution space, we keep the solution corresponding to the highest number of inliers given a threshold applied on the chosen measure of consistency or inconsistency.

In the following, the proposed algorithm is called 'Evidential-RANSAC' (EV-RANSAC) since instead of handling data or measurements, it handles bbas.

2.1 Evidential RANSAC Algorithm

The measure of inconsistency or conflict is still an issue (e.g., [9]) since it may have different origins: the conjunctive combination of an important number of sources, a too high confidence in a source possibly noised, etc. Algorithm 1 presents the evidential RANSAC in the case where the conflict $m(\emptyset)$ is used as inconsistency measure. It is straightforward to change the considered measure of consistency or inconsistency. For instance, we also run it using the contour function as consistency measure.

As said, the basic idea is to displace in the solution space according some moves. These latter are defined through a graph $\mathcal{G}$: Considering N sources, $\mathcal{G}$ nodes are the 2^N subsets of sources and two nodes are connected by an edge (or arc) if the two subsets of sources (represented by the two considered nodes) only differ by one source. Practically, the nodes are denoted by binary words representing the subsets of sources (e.g., for $N = 4$, any word of 4 bits, with 1-source

---

Algorithm 1. EV-RANSAC algorithm having as inputs: bba set $\mathcal{M}$, discernment frame Ω, conflict threshold κ_{th}, maximum number of iterations l_{max}; and as output the set of sources labelled as inlier $\mathcal{I}_S$.

---

1   $N \leftarrow |\mathcal{M}|$; $l \leftarrow 1$;

2   Create graph $\mathcal{G}$ having 2^N nodes (coded by binary words) and edges between nodes at a Hamming distance equal to 1;

3   Initialize $\mathcal{G}$ nodes (conflict and 'father') values to -1;

4   **for** $j \leftarrow 1$ **to** $\frac{N \times (N-1)}{2}$ **do**

5      $b \leftarrow$ binary code of the jth 2-source node;

6   Set i_1 and i_2 equal to the indices of the sources in b subset (e.g., $\{i_1, i_2\} \leftarrow \{n \,|\, b\&(1 << n) = 1\}$);

7      $\kappa_b \leftarrow \bigcirc_{i \in \{i_1, i_2\}} m_i(\emptyset)$;

8   **end**

9   Starting node $b_0 \leftarrow \arg\min_{b, |b|=2} \kappa_b$;

10   Set κ_{b_0} to b_0 node conflict value;

11   Call function RecursiveEvRANSAC($\mathcal{G}, \mathcal{M}, \Omega, \kappa_{th}, b_0, l, l_{max}$);

12   $\kappa_{\hat{b}} = +\infty$; $n \leftarrow N$;

13   **while** $\kappa_{\hat{b}} > \kappa_{th}$ *and* $n > 0$ **do**

14   **for** $j \leftarrow 1$ **to** $\binom{n}{N}$ **do**

15          $b \leftarrow$ binary code of the jth n-source node; $\kappa_b \leftarrow$ conflict value of b;

16   **If** $\kappa_b \in [0, \kappa_{\hat{b}})$ **then** $\kappa_{\hat{b}} \leftarrow \kappa_b$; $\hat{b} \leftarrow b$;

17   **end**

18   **if** $\kappa_{\hat{b}} \geq \kappa_{th}$ **then** $n \leftarrow n - 1$;

19   **end**

20   Set in $\mathcal{I}_S$ the indices of the sources in $\hat{b}$ (e.g., $\mathcal{I}_S \leftarrow \{n \,\big|\, \hat{b}\&(1 << n) = 1\}$);

---

nodes $\in \{0001, 0010, 0100, 1000\}$, 2-source nodes $\in \{0011, 0101, 0110, 1001, 1010, 1100\}$, etc.). Then, nodes are four neighbours: 0000, 0011, 0101 and 1001). Finally, for any binary word b, $|b|$ denotes its number of bits equal to 1 that corresponds to the cardinality of the subset of sources represented by b node. $\mathcal{G}$ nodes also contain two values: the conflict value induced by the combination of the node sources and the previous node on the path (called 'father'). These values are filled during the exploration but, since the exploration will be only partial, some of these values will never be computed.

Having defined the graph $\mathcal{G}$, the proposed algorithm explores it according to a path (ordered succession of $\mathcal{G}$ nodes linked by edges) that starts from the two-source node presenting the lowest conflict value. This choice is a compromise between complexity and distinction between nodes in terms of conflict value. Indeed, on the one hand, for 1-source nodes, every conflict values are equal (to 0) and, even for 2-source nodes, null conflict value can be reached by several nodes. On the other hand, considering k-source nodes, the number of source combinations, to test in order to choose the initial node, is $\binom{k}{N}$, that increases exponentially for k lower than $\frac{N}{2}$. Then, we prefer a low complexity and if several

Algorithm 2. Function `RecursiveEvRANSAC` having as parameters: source subset graph $\mathcal{G}$, bba set $\mathcal{M}$, discernment frame Ω, κ_{th} conflict threshold, current node b, current iteration l, maximum number of iterations l_{max}

---

1 Set $N \leftarrow |\mathcal{M}|$ and initialize $\kappa_{min} \leftarrow \kappa_{th}$ and $\hat{b} \leftarrow \emptyset$;
2 **for** $j \leftarrow 1$ **to** N **do**
3   **if** $j \notin b$ **then**
4          $b' \leftarrow b \cup j$; $\kappa_{b'} \leftarrow \bigcirc_{i \in b'} m_i(\emptyset)$;
5   **if** $\kappa_{b'} < \kappa_{min}$ **then** $\kappa_{min} \leftarrow \kappa_{b'}$; $\hat{b} \leftarrow b'$;
6   **end**
7 **end**
8 **if** $l < l_{max}$ and $\left|\hat{b}\right| < N$ **then**
9   **while** $\hat{b} = \emptyset$ and $|b| > 0$ **do**
10         $\kappa_b \leftarrow$ conflict value of b; $\hat{b} \leftarrow \arg\min_{b', |b'|=|b|, \kappa_b' > \kappa_b} \kappa_b'$;
11         $b \leftarrow$ its 'father' node;
12   **end**
13   `RecursiveEvRANSAC`$\left(\mathcal{G}, \mathcal{M}, \Omega, \kappa_{th}, \hat{b}, l+1, l_{max}\right)$;
14 **end**

---

nodes reach the lowest conflict value, we select randomly one of them. At the end, i.e. after exploration, we select, as best solution, the one having the highest cardinality provided that conflict value be lower than conflict threshold. In case of several solutions (having same cardinality), we keep the one with the lowest conflict value.

Algorithm 1 presents the proposed EV-RANSAC. The input data are the N bbas (gathered in $\mathcal{M} = \{m_i, i \in \{1, \ldots, N\}\}$) and their discernment frame Ω, the *a priori* threshold on conflict κ_{max} and the maximum number of iterations l_{max}. The output is the set of inlier sources.

Algorithm 1 involves a recursive function used to browse through the graph $\mathcal{G}$. It is described in Algorithm 2 using the following notations. As previously b denotes a node $\mathcal{G}$ representing the subset of sources having as indices the position of 1-bit in b. Then, for any source having index $j \in \{1, \ldots, N\}$, $j \in b$ ($j \notin b$, resp.) means that j source belongs (does not belongs, resp.) to b subset of sources, $j \cup b$ means that j source has been added to b subset of sources. Note that all these operations or tests are very simply achieved by bitwise operators.

The recursion is stopped at the end of a maximal number of iterations ($l_{max} << 2^N - \binom{1}{N} - \binom{2}{N}$) or because a solution involving all sources has been found. From the current node, it adds a new source (the one minimizing the conflict) provided that the conflict remains below the conflict threshold. Otherwise, it searches the node having same cardinality (of source subset) n and next increasing conflict value (smallest value among the greatest values than current node one). In terms of graph, this boils down to come back to the 'father' node (cardinality $n-1$) and then search among its neighbours of cardinality n (whose conflict value has already been computed when processing the father node). If

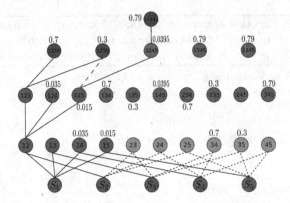

Fig. 1. Illustration of EV-RANSAC algorithm with 5 sources among which 1 is faulty; one level of the graph corresponds to a given cardinality of source combination (level $n \leftrightarrow n$-sources), with the involved sources indices denoted inside the nodes, and conflict values indicated by real numbers beside the nodes except when it is null (for information, conflict values of unexplored nodes are also indicated in grey).

such a node does not exist (all 'brother' nodes have been tested), the next node is searched among the 'brothers' of the 'father' and so on.

To illustrate the algorithm, Fig. 1 shows an example with 5 sources among which 1 is erroneous. The discernment frame is $\Omega = \{\theta_1, \theta_2, \theta_3\}$. According to Algorithm 1, we compute the conflict associated to every pair of sources (first level of combination on the graph), only considering (for this example) the combinations involving source S_1. On Fig. 1, conflict is null for combination between S_1 and S_2 and for combination between S_1 and S_3; We randomly select combination $S_{1\cap2}$ and pursue our graph exploration from this node. Minimum (i.e. null here) conflict is achieved for combination $S_{1\cap2\cap3}$. Pursuing graph exploration from $S_{1\cap2\cap3}$, we found conflict values greater that the considered conflict threshold $\kappa_{th} = 0.2$, so that the exploration returns to the father node $S_{1\cap2}$ to pursue the exploration from $S_{1\cap2\cap5}$ (second less conflicting node from $S_{1\cap2}$). The conflict value found for $S_{1\cap2\cap4\cap5}$ is lower than κ_{th} and indeed it is the solution in terms of consistent data set. At the end, 10 nodes instead of 25 have been tested.

2.2 Toy Example

To illustrate the interest of the evidential RANSAC, we consider the classical toy example of the estimation of straight line from several points including inliers and outliers.

Specifically, Fig. 2a show 10 points randomly drawn: 8 of them only presenting noise around the ground truth straight line (slope 1 and offset 0) whereas two of them are outliers. Several efficient approaches have been proposed for this problem: either from statistical estimation (e.g., M-estimators, classic RANSAC) or from pattern recognition (e.g., Hough's transform). Here, our purpose is to

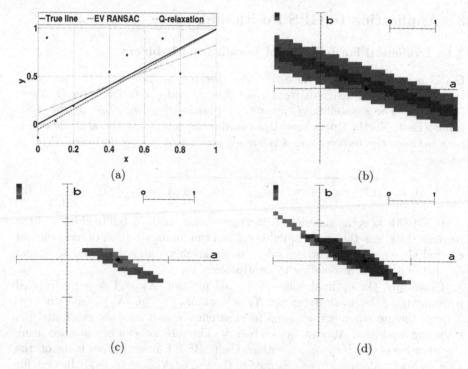

Fig. 2. Comparison between EV-RANSAC and evidential q-relaxation in the case of the toy example (straight line $y = ax + b$) with 10 points and 2 outliers: (a) dataset; (b) 4th point bba focal elements in the space parameter axis (a, b); solution provided (c) by EV-RANSAC, (d) by evidential q-relaxation. (Color figure online)

illustrate the kind of results provided by evidential RANSAC and its ability to perform robust estimation. Since two parameters (slope a and offset b of the straight line) should be estimated the chosen discernment frame is a discretized 2D compact bounded such that $a \in [-1, 3]$ and the bias $b \in [-2, 2]$ (then, for a discretization step equal to 0.1, $|\Omega| = 40 \times 40$). The sources are the 2D points (inliers and outliers). Each of them generates a bba having two 2D consonant focal elements (as further in the actual localization application) such that $A_1 \subseteq A_2$, $m(A_1) = 0.49$ and $m(A_2) = 0.51$. For straight line estimation, the 2D focal elements generated by point (x_0, y_0) have the shape of strips around line segment $b = y_0 - a \times x_0, (a, b) \in [-1, 3] \times [-2, 2]$. Figure 2b shows an example of bba generated by a point, with two focal elements: A_1 (blue strip) having width equal to 0.1 and A_2 (red strip) having width equal to 0.3.

Figure 2a allows us to compare the results obtained by conjunctive combination of the bbas selected as inliers either by EV-RANSAC, $m_{\mathcal{I}_s}$, or by evidential q-relaxation [7], m_{q-r}. Figure 2c (resp. 2d) shows the focal elements of $m_{\mathcal{I}_s}$ (resp. m_{q-r}) with false colours representing their ordering by size from the largest (red) to the smallest (blue). We note that, in this example, our result is much more specific than the evidential q-relaxation one, while also being more accurate.

3   Application to GPS Positioning

3.1   Evidential Formulation of Localization Problem

GNSS positioning consists in estimating receiver position from the measured travel time of GNSS signals from a satellite S_i and the GNSS receiver $\boldsymbol{X_r} = (e_r, n_r, u_r)$. For a satellite S_i located at position $(e_{S_i}, n_{S_i}, u_{S_i})$ in the ENU frame (East, North, Up) where 'Up' coordinates represents the altitude difference between the receiver and a reference position, the 'pseudo-range' (PR) ρ_i writes:

$$\rho_i = \sqrt{\left(e_r - e_{S_i}\right)^2 + \left(n_r - n_{S_i}\right)^2 + \left(u_r - u_{S_i}\right)^2} + c\delta_t + \epsilon_{ae} + \epsilon_{mp}. \tag{3}$$

In Eq. (3), δ_t is the time bias (difference) between the satellite clock and the receiver clock, c is the speed of light, ϵ_{ae} is a random realization of independent centred Gaussian noise corresponding to atmospheric and electronic noise and ϵ_{mp} is the noise corresponding to multipaths.

Classically, the optimal value of the 3D position $\boldsymbol{X_r}$ and δ_t are estimated by minimizing the quadratic error: $\hat{\boldsymbol{X}}_{\boldsymbol{r}} = \arg\min_{\boldsymbol{X_r}} \sum_i \left[\tilde{\rho}_i\left(\boldsymbol{X_r}\right) - \rho_i\right]^2$ where ρ_i denotes the measurement acquired from satellite i, and $\tilde{\rho}_i$ is the estimated PR assuming a position $\boldsymbol{X_r}$ and a clock bias δ_t. The solution can be obtained using the iterative Gauss-Newton algorithm. Using BFT framework, we focus on the East en North coordinates represented in the vector $\boldsymbol{X_{bba}} = (e_r, n_r)$. Indeed, for land receivers, the altitude (Up coordinate) can be obtained from $\boldsymbol{X_{bba}}$ using a Digital Elevation Model and the clock bias is derived using a Kalman filter and assuming it follows a linear model with constant drift. Then, the estimation of the PR is:

$$\tilde{\rho}_i\left(\boldsymbol{X_{bba}}\right) = \sqrt{\left(e_r - e_{S_i}\right)^2 + \left(n_r - n_{S_{i,t}}\right)^2} + \alpha_i + \beta, \tag{4}$$

where α_i is the square of the difference between Up coordinates of satellite S_i and receiver and β is the estimated clock bias multiplied by speed of light. Like in the toy example, the discernment frame Ω is bounded, here to (w, h), and discretized, here with same discretization R along the East and North coordinates, so that $|\Omega| = \frac{w \times h}{R^2}$.

Bbas derived from PR measurements are consonant with only two focal elements, A_1 and A_2, that are defined according to PR model described by Eq. (3): A_1 contains the imprecision due to atmospheric and electronic noise where A_2 includes multipath signals.

3.2   Results on Experimental Data

Experimental data (PR measurements) have been acquired with a Ublox GPS receiver EVK-5T having a factory parameter precision equal to 5 m and frequency acquisition of 1 Hz. The experiment was performed in an urban canyon (La Défense, Paris, France) in static conditions. The receiver was surrounded by high buildings, so that the probability of multipaths signal and NLOS receptions is high. The GPS receiver remains static during 40 min acquiring signals from four to seven satellites. The estimation of the receiver location is performed independently at each epoch so that each time sample is an independent test sample to compute performance statistics.

Our approach is compared with the method proposed by Pichon et al. [7] and Interval Analysis (IA) also using q-relaxation. In Algorithm 1, parameter $\kappa_{th} = 0.2$ and $l_{max} = min\left(3N, N + 2^{N-3}\right)$. Besides, having determined the subset of inlier bbas, these latter are combined conjunctively to obtain the bba on which the location will be estimated. In [7], the used threshold deals with consistency measure ϕ_{min}. We take $\phi_{min} = 0.8$. Finally, for the IA q-relaxation, the number of relaxed constraints is the minimum such that there is a solution $(\neq \emptyset)$. Note also that for this latter approach there is only one 'focal element' that is taken equal to the larger one when considering evidential approaches.

Finally, by interpreting the pignistic function of the final bba as the probability distribution function (pdf) of receiver location values, two kinds of errors can be computed. The first one allows us to evaluate if the location estimation is biased. It writes as the statistical expectation, being given the pdf, of the errors:

$$E_1 = \sum_{i=1}^{|\Omega|} \epsilon(H_i) BetP(H_i),$$ where $\epsilon(H_i)$ is the difference between the centroid of the singleton 2D hypothesis H_i and the ground truth. The second error measure allows us to evaluate the imprecision of the solution (since errors do not compensate). It writes as the expectation of the L_1 error: $E_2 = \sum_{i=1}^{|\Omega|} |\epsilon(H_i)| BetP(H_i)$.

Table 1 shows the achieved errors for different localization methods (first column) and for different widths of focal elements A_1 and A_2. It allows us to evaluate the robustness of the approaches to this parameter that can generally only empirically be derived. Table 1 presents the p-values corresponding to the 68 and 95 percentiles ($1 \times \sigma$ and $2 \times \sigma$ cut of the normal distribution). We note that the proposed approach has better performance according to E_2 measure

Table 1. Statistical comparison varying the widths of focal element(s).

Method	Focal element width	E_1 (m)		E_2 (m)	
		68 %	95 %	68 %	95 %
EvRansac	$(4, 20)$	10.72	20.81	15.43	23.45
	$(6, 15)$	10.07	**16.54**	**12.36**	**17.84**
	$(6, 20)$	9.51	17.74	13.36	20.25
Pichon and al.	$(4, 20)$	10.92	31.63	23.90	49.49
	$(6, 15)$	**8.31**	29.22	15.92	40.46
	$(6, 20)$	8.63	17.95	19.10	32.38
IA q-relaxation	(12)	10.63	17.71	15.99	20.36
	(15)	11.18	18.31	14.35	20.24
	(20)	11.86	23.57	18.32	25.59

and according to the 95 percentiles of E_1 measure. Indeed, using conjunctive combination of the inlier bbas, the result is much more committed than with q-relaxation (either evidential or interval analysis), like in the case of the toy example. We also note that best results correspond to assumed noise levels equal to 6 m and 15 m that are rather classic values used in GPS localization processes.

4   Conclusion

In this work, we propose an adaptation of the RANSAC principle to select inlier sources in an evidential framework. Accordingly, several solutions are tested so that the one selected is the most 'consensual', i.e. compatible with the highest number of observations viewed as information sources. This approach is compared to the classic q-relaxation and its evidential version that both search the solution that removes the smallest number of sources. Applying these algorithms to the processing of GNSS pseudo-range measurements, we observe that evidential RANSAC provides a more accurate localization.

References

1. André, C., Le Hégarat-Mascle, S., Reynaud, R.: Evidential framework for data fusion in a multi-sensor surveillance system. Eng. Appl. Artif. Intell. **43**, 166–180 (2015)
2. Brown, R.G.: A baseline GPS RAIM scheme and a note on the equivalence of three RAIM methods. Navigation **39**(3), 301–316 (1992)
3. Destercke, S., Burger, T.: Toward an axiomatic definition of conflict between belief functions. IEEE Trans. Cybern. **43**(2), 585–596 (2013)
4. Fischler, M.A., Bolles, R.C.: Random sample consensus: a paradigm for model fitting with applications to image analysis and automated cartography. Commun. ACM **24**(6), 381–395 (1981)
5. Giremus, A., Tourneret, J.-Y., Calmettes, V.: A particle filtering approach for joint detection/estimation of multipath effects on GPS measurements. IEEE Trans. Signal Process. **55**(4), 1275–1285 (2007)
6. Nassreddine, G., Abdallah, F., Denoeux, T.: State estimation using interval analysis, belief function theory: application to dynamic vehicle localization. IEEE Trans. Syst. Man Cybern. Part B **40**(5), 1205–1218 (2010)
7. Pichon, F., Destercke, S., Burger, T.: A consistency-specificity trade-off to select source behavior in information fusion. IEEE Trans. Cybern. **45**(4), 598–609 (2015)
8. Rekik, W., Le Hégarat-Mascle, S., Reynaud, R., Kallel, A., Hamida, A.B.: Dynamic estimation of the discernment frame in belief function theory: application to object detection. Inf. Sci. **306**, 132–149 (2015)
9. Roquel, A., Le Hégarat-Mascle, S., Bloch, I., Vincke, B.: Decomposition of conflict as a distribution on hypotheses in the framework on belief functions. Int. J. Approx. Reason. **55**(5), 1129–1146 (2014)
10. Zair, S., Le Hégarat-Mascle, S., Seignez, E.: A-contrario modeling for robust localization using raw GNSS data. IEEE Trans. Intell. Transp. Syst. **17**(5), 1354–1367 (2016)

Author Index

Printed in the United States
By Bookmasters